Congressional Elections

CONGRESSIONAL ELECTIONS

Campaigning at Home
and in Washington

Sixth Edition

Paul S. Herrnson
UNIVERSITY OF MARYLAND

Los Angeles | London | New Delhi
Singapore | Washington DC

Los Angeles | London | New Delhi
Singapore | Washington DC

FOR INFORMATION:

CQ Press
An Imprint of SAGE Publications, Inc.
2455 Teller Road
Thousand Oaks, California 91320
E-mail: order@sagepub.com

SAGE Publications Ltd.
1 Oliver's Yard
55 City Road
London, EC1Y 1SP
United Kingdom

SAGE Publications India Pvt. Ltd.
B 1/I 1 Mohan Cooperative Industrial Area
Mathura Road, New Delhi 110 044
India

SAGE Publications Asia-Pacific Pte. Ltd.
33 Pekin Street #02-01
Far East Square
Singapore 048763

Acquisitions Editor: Charisse Kiino
Production Editor: Belinda Josey
Copy Editor: Talia Greenberg
Typesetter: C&M Digitals (P) Ltd.
Proofreader: Talia Greenberg
Indexer: Joan Shapiro
Cover Designer: Mike Pottman, M Design & Print
Marketing Manager: Jonathan Mason

Printed in the United States of America

Library of Congress Cataloging-in-Publication Data

Herrnson, Paul S.

Congressional elections: campaigning at home and in Washington/Paul S. Herrnson. — 6th ed.

p. cm.
Includes bibliographical references and index.

ISBN 978-0-87289-965-0 (pbk.: alk. paper)

1. United States. Congress—Elections. 2. Political campaigns—United States. 3. Campaign management—United States. I. Title.

JK1976.H47 2011
324.973′0931—dc23   2011038821

This book is printed on acid-free paper.

11 12 13 14 15 10 9 8 7 6 5 4 3 2 1

In Memory of
Harry Perlman

Contents

Tables and Figures

Tables

Figures

Preface

The 2010 congressional elections showcased many exciting developments in campaign politics. Large numbers of House and Senate campaigns, party committees, and interest groups made extensive use of Facebook, YouTube, Twitter, and other social media for the first time. Use of the Internet became even more prevalent, as virtually every organization participating in the election launched a website. In the realm of party strategy, the Republican Party sought to capitalize on a national political environment that favored its candidates by distributing contributions, campaign assistance, and independent expenditures to broaden the field of competition rather than following the conventional strategy of focusing resources on a few contests. In the areas of interest group politics and campaign finance, federal court rulings handed down during the election cycle led to the formation of super PACs and unleashed a torrent of outside spending by groups that previously had been barred from participating in federal elections. In matters related to grassroots politics, members of the conservative Tea Party movement mobilized enough like-minded voters to successfully challenge several establishment Republican politicians in congressional primaries and to help its champions defeat many Democratic incumbents in the general election. Finally, Republican candidates won a sufficient number of Democratic-held seats to take control of the House and significantly diminish the size of the Democratic majority in the Senate.

Each congressional election cycle unveils continuities and changes in the way congressional campaigns are conducted, and the 2010 cycle was no different. Writing this new edition of *Congressional Elections* gave me the opportunity not only to analyze in depth these campaigns and election outcomes but also to gauge the far-reaching changes that have taken place in recent years. It has been my challenge in this edition to show how changes in congressional campaigns and the context in which they are waged help to shape an enduring but imperfect election system.

Among the most important changes is the growth of outside campaigns. These party- and interest group-sponsored campaigns consist of massive efforts in election agenda setting, television and radio advertising, direct mail and phone banks, and grassroots mobilization, some of which are financed with soft-money. Their importance in competitive House and Senate races cannot be overstated.

The increasing complexity of interest group participation constitutes a related area of transformation. Groups have created a veritable alphabet soup of legal entities for the purpose of carrying out political activities designed to influence elections. Political action committees (PACs), 527 committees, 501(c) organizations, super PACs—defined by different provisions of federal law—offer different organizational advantages, such as the ability to contribute directly to congressional campaigns, to collect tax-deductible donations, to claim tax-exempt status, or to raise and spend soft-money. As a result of a string of federal court rulings most notably *Citizens United v. Federal Election Commission*, corporations, unions, and other groups are now free to spend treasury funds to make independent expenditures expressly advocating the election—or, more often, defeat—of candidates or finance organizations that will do this for them. These rulings emboldened many groups to more fully participate in the 2010 election, resulting in interest groups setting a new record for outside spending.

The coming of age of Internet campaigning and social media built on relatively recent trends. By 2010 almost all major-party congressional candidates used the Internet to raise money, introduce themselves to voters, communicate their messages, and recruit and organize volunteers. Some campaign websites featured online chat rooms that supporters could use to voice their opinions, plan "meet-ups," and encourage the "viral" campaigning first introduced by Democratic National Committee chair Howard Dean during his 2004 presidential nomination campaign. Podcasting, tweeting, and other communications innovations enabled candidates and others to fire barrages of messages to voters at low cost.

A final development I discuss in this edition involves the evisceration of the Bipartisan Campaign Reform Act of 2002, which was designed to close some major loopholes in the campaign finance system. Its ban on party soft-money, restrictions on issue advocacy advertising, and increased contribution limits promised to have a major impact on the ways in which campaigns were financed and waged. Although the law had profound effects on some aspects of campaign finance, it did not signal the death knell of political parties, nor did it result in interest groups dominating congressional campaigns, as some had predicted. Rather, campaigns remain candidate-centered, and incumbents' advantages in fundraising persist. This is likely to remain the case even though the U.S. Supreme Court overturned some aspects of the law concerned with interest group soft-money, electioneering communications, and independent expenditures.

My focus on these developments characterizes this revision, but the sixth edition of *Congressional Elections* remains a comprehensive text about congressional elections and their implications for Congress and, more generally, for American government. Most congressional elections are contests between candidates who have vastly unequal chances of victory. Incumbents generally win, not only because of their own efforts but also because of the catch-22 situation in which many challengers find themselves. Without name recognition, challengers have trouble raising funds; without funds, they cannot enhance their name recognition or attract enough support to run a competitive race. This conundrum hints at a fundamental truth of congressional elections: candidates wage two campaigns—one for votes and another for money and other resources. The former takes place in the candidate's district or state. The latter is conducted primarily in Washington, D.C.,—the location of many political consultants, PACs, interest groups, and the parties' national, senatorial, and congressional campaign committees. The timing of the two campaigns overlaps considerably, but candidates and their organizations must conceptualize them as separate and plot a different strategy for each.

Although congressional election campaigns are the main focus of this book, voters, candidates, party committees, and interest groups receive considerable attention. The influence of these individuals and groups on election outcomes also receives substantial coverage. I conclude that the norms and expectations associated with congressional campaigns affect who runs, the kinds of organizations the candidates assemble, how much money they raise, the types of party and interest group support they attract, the strategies and communications techniques they use, and, ultimately, whether they win or lose. Incumbents are the major beneficiaries of the congressional election system, but the system constrains their reelection campaigns, as it does the efforts of challengers and candidates for open-seats.

The need to campaign for votes and resources affects how members of Congress carry out their legislative responsibilities and the types of reforms they are willing to consider. These observations may seem intuitive, but they are rarely discussed in studies of voting behavior and are usually overlooked in research that focuses on the role of money in politics. Given their importance,

it is unfortunate that congressional campaigns have not received more attention in the scholarly literature.

Throughout this book, I systematically analyze empirical evidence collected
from candidates, consultants, parties, and interest groups that have participated in congressional elections since the early 1990s. The analysis in this
edition is based primarily on interviews with and questionnaires from hundreds of House and Senate candidates and other political insiders who participated in the elections. It also relies on campaign finance data furnished by
the Federal Election Commission and the Center for Responsive Politics, as
well as public opinion data collected from a variety of surveys. Memoranda
and interviews provided by campaign organizations, party committees, PACs,
and other interest groups further contributed to the study. Generalizations
derived from the analysis are supported with concrete—and, I hope, lively—
case studies of individual campaigns.

The analysis also draws insights from my own participation in congressional
campaigns and from the questionnaires and interviews provided by the more
than 1,300 candidates and campaign aides who have contributed information
and data for past editions. I hope the evidence presented convinces readers that
the campaigns candidates wage at home for votes, and in Washington for
money and campaign assistance, significantly affect the outcomes of congressional elections. My analysis of these sources also leads to the conclusion that
the activities of party committees, interest groups, campaign volunteers, and
journalists are important as well.

This book gives students of politics a powerful tool to help them think
about campaigns, elections, and their own political involvement. Professors
using the book as a classroom text may be interested in reviewing the
questionnaires I used to collect information from congressional campaigns. Students in my seminars found them valuable in guiding their
field research on campaigns. The questionnaires, my syllabus, class assignments, and other course materials, links to Internet resources, and meth-
odological background information are all available at http://college
.cqpress.com/sites/partiesandelectionsir/. Adopters can register and download these materials.

ACKNOWLEDGMENTS

The publication of *Congressional Elections* would not have been possible without
the cooperation of many individuals and institutions. I am indebted to the hundreds of people who consented to be interviewed, completed questionnaires, or

shared election targeting lists and other campaign materials with me. Their participation in this project was essential to its success.

The Center for American Politics and Citizenship at the University of Maryland provided a stimulating and productive environment in which to work. Virtually every member of the Center's staff participated in some aspect of the project. The data collection, data entry, statistical analysis, and case study research proceeded smoothly because of all of their efforts, particularly those of James Curry, Jeffrey Taylor, and Mike Charlebois. Bob Biersack, Paul Clark, and Jeff Chumley of the Federal Election Commission and Douglas Weber of the Center for Responsive Politics provided insights into the campaign finance data provided by their organizations. Chris Bailey, William Bianco, Bob Biersack, Anthony Corrado, James Gimpel, John Green, Thomas Kazee, Jonathan Krasno, Rogan Kersh, Sandy Maisel, Kelly Patterson, Stephen Salmore, Frank Sorauf, James Thurber, Eric Uslaner, and Clyde Wilcox made helpful comments on earlier editions of the book. David Damore, University of Nevada–Las Vegas; Patrick Fisher, Seton Hall University; Brad Gomez, Florida State University; Steven Greene, North Carolina State University; Laurie Rhodebeck, University of Louisville; and William Wallis, California State University, Northridge made valuable suggestions for this edition, as did Bob Biersack and former Federal Election Commission Chairman Michael Toner. At CQ Press Charisse Kiino and Nancy Loh played vital roles in preparing the manuscript, as did Belinda Josey and Talia Greenberg. I am especially pleased to put into writing my gratitude to my wife Golda and son Geoffrey for their love and support.

Finally, a few words are in order about the person to whom this book is dedicated. My uncle, Harry Perlman, did not live to see the completion of this book, but his contributions to it were critical. The construction jobs he gave me were the most important form of financial aid I received while pursuing my college education. His ideas about politics and philosophy helped me to appreciate the virtues of democratic elections and to recognize the inferiority of other means of conferring political power. His unwavering belief that people can be taught to value what is good about their political system and to recognize its shortcomings was a source of inspiration that helped me complete the first edition of this book, and it continues to inspire me today.

Introduction

Elections are the centerpiece of democracy. They are the means Americans use to choose their political leaders, and they give those who have been elected the authority to rule. Elections also furnish the American people with a vehicle for expressing their views about the directions they think this rule ought to take. In theory, elections are the principal mechanism for ensuring "government of the people, by the people, for the people."[1]

An examination of the different aspects of the electoral process provides insights into the operations of the U.S. political system. Separate balloting for congressional, state, and local candidates results in legislators who represent parochial interests, sometimes to the detriment of the formation of national policy. Private financing of congressional campaigns, which is consistent with Americans' belief in capitalism, favors incumbents and increases the political access of wealthy and well-organized segments of society. Participatory primaries and caucuses, which require congressional aspirants to assemble an organization in order to campaign for the nomination, make it necessary for candidates to rely on political consultants rather than on party committees for assistance in winning their party's nomination and the general election. These factors encourage congressional candidates and members of Congress to act more independently of party leaders than do their counterparts in other democracies.

Congressional elections are affected by perceptions of the performance of government. Americans' satisfaction with the state of the economy, the nation's foreign policy and security, and their own standard of living provides a backdrop for elections and a means for assessing whether presidents, individual representatives, and Congress as an institution have performed their jobs adequately. Issues related to the internal operations of Congress—such as the perquisites enjoyed by members—can affect congressional elections. Conversely, congressional elections can greatly affect the internal operations of Congress, the performance of government, and the direction of domestic and foreign policy. Major political reforms and policy reversals generally follow elections in which substantial congressional turnover has occurred.

One of the major themes developed in this book is that campaigns matter a great deal to the outcome of congressional elections. National conditions are significant, but their impact on elections is secondary to the decisions and actions of candidates, campaign organizations, party committees, organized interests, and other individuals and groups. After all, the choices of these individuals and groups determine whether a race against an incumbent or for an open seat is contested, the quality of the candidates who enter the fray, the level of funding and organizational resources they collect, the strategy and tactics they employ, and the level of outside help they receive. This comes as no surprise to those who toil in campaigns, but it is in direct contrast to what many scholars would argue.

To win a congressional election, or even to be remotely competitive, candidates must compete in two campaigns: one for votes and one for resources. The campaign for votes is the campaign that generally comes to mind when people think about congressional elections. It requires a candidate to assemble an organization and to use that organization to target key groups of voters, select a message they will find compelling, communicate that message, and convince supporters to go to the polls on Election Day.

The other campaign, which is based largely in Washington, D.C., requires candidates to convince the party operatives, interest group officials, political consultants, and journalists who play leading roles in the nation's political community that their races will be competitive and worthy of support. Gaining the backing of these various individuals is a critical step in attracting the money and campaign services that are available in the nation's capital and in other wealthy urban centers. These resources enable the candidate to run a credible campaign back home. Without them, most congressional candidates would lose their bids for election.

In this book I present a systematic assessment of congressional election campaigns that draws on information from a wide variety of sources. Background information on the roughly 24,000 major-party contestants who ran between 1978 and 2010 furnished insights into the types of individuals who try to win a seat in Congress and the conditions under which they run. Personal interviews and survey data provided by roughly 9,000 candidates and campaign aides who were involved in the House or Senate elections held between 1992 and 2010 permitted analysis of the organization, strategies, tactics, issues, and communications techniques used in congressional campaigns. They also provided insights into the roles of political parties, political action committees (PACs), and other groups in those contests.

Case studies of campaigns conducted during the 2010 elections are interwoven throughout the book to illustrate with concrete examples the generalizations drawn from the larger sample. These include some typical elections, such as Democratic representative Jerrold Nadler's 50-point victory over Republican Susan Kone in New York's 8th congressional district and Republican open-seat candidate Robert Dold's win over Dan Seals in Illinois' GOP-held 8th district. They also include a few unusual contests, such as Republican challenger Steve Southerland's victory over seven-term Democratic representative Allen Boyd in Florida's 2nd district. The Senate contest in Nevada is included because the incumbent Democratic majority leader, Harry Reid, was reelected despite his low standing in the polls, his aggressive efforts to enact unpopular elements of President Barack Obama's policy agenda, and a statewide economic decline that ranked among the worst in the nation. The latter three contests highlight the importance of money, organization, and strategy in congressional elections. They also are noteworthy because political parties and many interest groups made considerable efforts in them.

Some races are included because they illustrate the role of scandal or negative campaigning. Fourteen-term incumbent Alan Mollohan, Democrat of West Virginia, lost his primary election contest to state senator Mike Oliverio, largely as a result of scandal. Mudslinging and personal attacks by the candidates, parties, and interest groups were a prominent feature in the donnybrook that was the open-seat Senate race in Kentucky, where a negative TV ad by Democratic attorney general Jack Conway is believed to have cost him the election against the Tea Party movement favorite, Republican Rand Paul. Other elections, such as the Senate contest in Delaware, demonstrate the limits of party influence in candidate recruitment and the impact organizational disarray can have on a campaign.

Most of the discussion focuses on House candidates and campaigns because they are easier to generalize about than Senate contests. Differences in the sizes, populations, and political traditions of the fifty states and the fact that only about one-third of all Senate seats are filled in a given election year make campaigns for the upper chamber more difficult to discuss in general terms. Larger, more diverse Senate constituencies also make Senate elections less predictable than House contests. Nevertheless, insights can be gained into campaigns for the upper chamber by contrasting them with those waged for the House.

Interviews with party officials, conducted over the course of the 1992 through 2010 elections, provide insights into the strategies used by the Democratic and Republican national, congressional, and senatorial campaign committees. Similar information provided by a representative group of interest group leaders is used to learn about the strategies that PACs use to guide their contributions and the strategies behind their endorsements, mass media advertisements, and grassroots mobilization efforts. Campaign contribution and spending data furnished by the Federal Election Commission and the Center for Responsive Politics are used to examine the role of money in politics. Newspaper coverage, media releases, websites, and advertising materials disseminated by candidates, parties, interest groups, and others furnish examples of the communications that campaigns disseminate. Public opinion surveys provide insights into voters' priorities and the roles of issues. Surveys of individual campaign contributors furnish similar insights into their opinions and motives. Collectively, these sources of information, along with scholarly accounts published in the political science literature and insights drawn from my own participation in congressional and campaign politics, result in a comprehensive portrayal of contemporary congressional election campaigns.

In the first five chapters I examine the strategic context in which congressional election campaigns are waged and the major actors who participate in those contests. Chapter 1 provides an overview of the institutions, laws, party rules, and customs that constitute the framework for congressional elections. The framework has a significant impact on who decides to run for Congress; the resources that candidates, parties, and interest groups bring to bear on the campaign; the strategies they use; and who ultimately wins a seat in Congress. The chapter also focuses on the setting for the congressional elections held since the 1990s, with special emphasis on 2010.

Chapter 2 contains a discussion of candidates and nominations. I examine the influence of incumbency, redistricting, national conditions, and the personal and career situations of potential candidates on the decision to run for Congress. I also assess the separate contributions that the decision to run, the nomination process, and the general election make to producing a Congress that is overwhelmingly white, male, middle-aged, and drawn from the legal, business, and public service professions.

The organizations that congressional candidates assemble to wage their election campaigns are the subject of Chapter 3. Salaried staff and political consultants form the core of most competitive candidates' campaign teams. These professionals play a critical role in formulating strategy, gauging public opinion, fundraising, designing communications, and mobilizing voters.

Political parties and interest groups—the major organizations that help finance elections and provide candidates with important campaign resources—are the subjects of the next two chapters. Chapter 4 includes an analysis of the goals, decision-making processes, and election activities of party committees. In it I discuss the contributions and other forms of campaign assistance parties give directly to candidates, as well as the independent media campaigns and coordinated grassroots campaigns they carry out to influence elections. Chapter 5 concentrates on the goals, strategies, and election efforts of PACs and other interest group organizations. Among the innovations covered are business- and union-sponsored electioneering ads and the increased campaign activity of groups that enjoy tax-exempt status that resulted from a string of Federal Election Commission (FEC) decisions and court rulings, culminating with the Supreme Court's ruling in *Citizens United v. FEC*.[2] In this case, the Court set out to decide whether a partisan documentary (*Hillary: The Movie*) financed by corporate money was prohibited under federal law. In a sweeping and highly controversial decision, the Court overturned decades of election law prohibiting corporations, unions, and other groups from spending general treasury funds in federal elections.[3] It changed the balance of spending, and perhaps the outcome, in many close elections.

Chapter 6 examines the fundraising process from the candidate's point of view. The campaign for resources requires a candidate to formulate strategies for raising money from individuals and groups in the candidate's own state, in Washington, D.C., and in the nation's other major political and economic centers. It is clear from Chapters 4, 5, and 6 that Washington-based elites have a disproportionate effect on the conduct of congressional elections.

In Chapters 7 through 9, I concentrate on the campaign for votes. A discussion of voters, campaign targeting, issues, and other elements of strategy makes up Chapter 7. Campaign communications, including television, radio, the Internet, direct mail, social media, and field work, are the focus of Chapter 8. The subject of winners and losers is taken up in Chapter 9, in which I analyze what does and does not work in congressional campaigns.

In Chapter 10, I address the effects of elections on the activities of individual legislators and on Congress as an institution, including the collective impact that individual elections have on the policy-making process and substantive policy outcomes. Finally, Chapter 11 examines the highly charged topic of campaign reform. In it, I review the near-collapse of the legal framework that has governed elections since 1976, recommend specific reforms, and discuss the obstacles to their passage and implementation.

CHAPTER ONE

The Strategic Context

Congressional elections, and elections in the United States in general, are centered more on the candidates than are elections in other modern industrialized democracies. Why is this the case, and how does it affect the conduct of congressional elections? In this chapter I discuss the candidate-centered U.S. election system and explain how the Constitution, election laws, and the political parties form the system's institutional framework. I explain how the nation's political culture and recent developments in technology have helped this system flourish.

Other important topics I cover involve the political setting. The political setting in a given election year has a substantial influence on electoral competition and turnover in Congress. It includes some predictable factors, such as the decennial redrawing of House districts; some highly likely occurrences, such as the wide-scale reelection of incumbents; and transient, less predictable phenomena, such as congressional scandals, acts of nature or terrorism, and major economic upheavals. The setting in a given election year or district affects the expectations and behavior of potential congressional candidates; the individuals who actually run for Congress; the political parties, interest groups, and others that help finance their campaigns; and, of course, voters.

THE CANDIDATE-CENTERED CAMPAIGN

Candidates, not political parties, are the major focus of congressional campaigns, and candidates, not parties, bear the ultimate responsibility for election outcomes. These characteristics of congressional elections are striking when viewed from a comparative perspective. In most democracies, political parties are the principal contestants in elections, and campaigns almost always focus on national issues, ideology, and party programs and accomplishments. In the United States, parties do not run congressional campaigns, and only rarely do they become the major focus of elections. Instead, candidates run their own campaigns, and parties and interest groups contribute money or election services to some of them. Parties and groups also may advertise or mobilize voters on behalf of candidates. A comparison of the terminology commonly used to describe elections in the United States with that used in Great Britain more than hints at the differences. In the United States, candidates are said to *run* for Congress, and they do so with or without party help. In Britain, by contrast, candidates are said to *stand* for election to Parliament, and their party runs most of the campaign. The difference in terminology only slightly oversimplifies reality.

Unlike candidates for national legislatures in most other democracies, U.S. congressional candidates are self-selected rather than recruited by party organizations. Candidates must earn the right to run under their party's label by winning a participatory primary, caucus, or convention, or by scaring off all opposition. Only after they have secured their party's nomination are major-party candidates ensured a place on the general election ballot. Until then few candidates receive significant assistance from party committees, although some may get help from party members in Congress and groups allied with the candidate's party. Independent and minor-party candidates can get on the ballot in other ways, usually by paying a registration fee or collecting several thousand signatures from district residents.

In most other countries, the nomination process begins with a small group of party activists pursuing the nomination by means of a "closed" process that allows only formal, dues-paying party members to select the candidate.[1] Whereas the American system amplifies the input of primary voters, and in a few states caucus or convention participants, these other systems respond more to the input of party members and place more emphasis on peer review.

The need to win a party nomination forces congressional candidates to assemble their own campaign organizations, formulate their own election strategies, and conduct their own campaigns. The images and issues they convey to voters in trying to win the nomination carry over to the general election. The efforts of individual candidates and their campaign organizations typically have a larger impact on election outcomes than do the activities of party organizations and other groups.

The candidate-centered nature of congressional elections has evolved in recent years as political parties and interest groups, including many based in Washington, D.C., have used independent media campaigns and coordinated grassroots campaigns, involving sophisticated voter targeting and outreach efforts to communicate with and mobilize voters in competitive races. However, the basic structure of the system remains intact. That structure has a major impact on virtually every aspect of campaigning, including who decides to run, the types of election strategies candidates employ, and the resources available to them. It affects the decisions and activities of party organizations, interest groups and the political action committees (PACs) and other entities they use to influence elections, and the journalists who cover campaign politics. It also has a major influence on how citizens make their voting decisions and on the activities that successful candidates carry out once they are elected to Congress. Finally, the candidate-centered nature of the congressional election system affects the election reforms that those in power are willing to consider.

THE INSTITUTIONAL FRAMEWORK

In designing a government to prevent the majority from depriving the minority of its rights, the framers of the Constitution created a system of checks and balances to prevent any one official or element of society from amassing too much power. Three key features of the framers' blueprint have profoundly influenced congressional elections: the separation of powers, bicameralism, and federalism. These aspects of the Constitution require that candidates for the House of Representatives, Senate, and presidency be chosen by different methods and constituencies. House members were, and continue to be, elected directly by the people. Senators were originally chosen by their state legislatures but have been selected in statewide elections since the passage of the Seventeenth Amendment in 1913. Presidents have always been selected by the Electoral College. The means for filling state and local offices were omitted from the Constitution, but candidates for these positions were, and continue to be, elected independently of members of Congress.

Holding elections for individual offices separates the political fortunes of members of Congress from one another and from other officials. A candidate for the House can win during an election year in which his or her party suffers a landslide defeat in the race for the presidency; experiences severe losses in the House or Senate; or finds itself surrendering its hold over neighboring congressional districts, the state legislature, the governor's mansion, and various local offices. The system encourages House, Senate, state, and local candidates to communicate issues and themes that they perceive to be popular in their districts, even when those messages differ from those advocated by their party's leader. The system does little to encourage teamwork in campaigning or governance. In 2006 a considerable number of Republican candidates distanced themselves from the Republican president, George W. Bush, whose job approval ratings had reached historic lows. Several publicly opposed the president's proposals to privatize part of the Social Security system, allow illegal immigrants to get temporary work permits, and ban funding for stem cell research. Four years later, it was President Barack Obama's turn to witness some of his party's congressional candidates exhibit the same behavior on the campaign trail. Low approval scores and a failing economy encouraged these candidates to criticize the president's economic stimulus package, the Troubled Asset Relief Program (often referred to as "TARP"), health care reform program, and air pollution control program (cap-and-trade), and to generally disassociate themselves from him and other Democratic Party leaders. Such opposition would be considered unacceptable under a parliamentary system of government, with its party-focused elections, but it is entirely consistent with the expectations of the Constitution's framers. As James Madison wrote in *Federalist* no. 46,

> A local spirit will infallibly prevail . . . in the members of Congress. . . . Measures will too often be decided according to their probable effect, not on the national prosperity and happiness, but on the prejudices, interests, and pursuits of the governments and people of the individual States.

When congressional candidates differ from their party's presidential nominee or national platform on major issues, they seek political cover not only from the Constitution but also from state party platforms, local election manifestos, or fellow party members who have taken similar positions.

Of course, congressional candidates usually adopt issue positions held by other party candidates for the House, Senate, or presidency. In 1932 most Democrats embraced Franklin D. Roosevelt's call for an activist government to battle the Great Depression. In 2006 Democratic candidates also were presented with strong incentives to campaign on national issues. Many Democrats made the Iraq War, the failure of President George W. Bush's administration to respond effectively to the aftermath of Hurricane Katrina, rising energy prices, and a range of scandals involving Republican members of Congress the subjects of their campaigns. In 2008 Democrats added the economic meltdown to their lists of issues. Republican politicians responded to national conditions in both of these election years by trying to focus voters' attention on local issues. By the 2010 election season, the shoe was on the other foot. Public anger over rising unemployment, lost retirement savings, and falling home values associated with the economic recession; widespread frustration over corporate bailouts and a new health care program that did not address their immediate concerns; declining job approval ratings for President Obama and Congress; and historically low levels of trust in the federal government gave Republican congressional candidates strong motivations to highlight national issues and encouraged their Democratic opponents to campaign on local issues and their records of performance.

Federal and state laws further contribute to the candidate-centered nature of congressional elections. Originally, federal law regulated few aspects of congressional elections, designating only the number of representatives a state was entitled to elect. States held congressional elections at different times, used different methods of election, and set different qualifications for voters. Some states used multimember at-large districts, a practice that awarded each party a share of congressional seats proportional to its share of the statewide popular vote; others elected their House members in odd-numbered years, which minimized the ability of presidential candidates to pull House candidates of their own party into office on their coattails. The financing of congressional campaigns also went virtually unregulated for most of the nation's history.

Over the years, Congress and the states passed legislation governing the election of House members that further reinforced the candidate-centered nature of congressional elections at the expense of parties. The creation of geographically defined, single-member, winner-take-all congressional districts was particularly important in this regard. These districts, which were mandated by the Apportionment Act of 1842, encouraged individual candidates to build locally based coalitions. Such districts gave no rewards to candidates who came in second, even if their party performed well throughout the state or in neighboring districts.[2] Thus, candidates in the same party had little incentive to work together or to run a party-focused campaign. Under the multimember district or general ticket systems that existed in some states prior to the act—and that continue to be used in most European nations—members of parties that finish lower than first place may receive seats in the legislature. Candidates have strong incentives to run cooperative, party-focused campaigns under these systems because their electoral fortunes are bound together.

The timing of congressional elections also helps to produce a candidate-centered system. Because the dates are fixed, with House elections scheduled biennially and roughly one-third of the Senate up for election every two years, many elections are held when there is no burning issue on the national agenda. If an election cycle occurs when there are few salient national issues to capture the voters' attention, House and Senate candidates base their campaigns on local issues or on their personal qualifications for holding office. If an election cycle is nationalized on one or more salient policy concerns, virtually all candidates address those issues, but the outcomes of most congressional elections still revolve around the qualifications of the candidates and other local factors.

In contrast, systems that do not have fixed election dates, including most of those in Western Europe, tend to hold elections that are more national in focus and centered on political parties. The rules regulating national elections in those systems require that elections be held within a set time frame, but the exact date is left open. Elections may be called by the party in power at a time of relative prosperity, when it is confident that it can maintain or enlarge its parliamentary majority. Elections also may be called when a critical problem divides the nation and the party in power is forced to call a snap election because its members in parliament are unable to agree on a policy for dealing with the crisis. Compared to congressional elections, which are often referenda on the performance of individual officeholders and their abilities to meet local concerns, these elections focus almost exclusively on national conditions and the performance of the party in power.

Because the boundaries of congressional districts rarely match those of statewide or local offices, and because terms for the House, the Senate, and many state and local offices differ from one another, a party's candidates often lack incentives to work together. House candidates consider the performance of their party's candidates statewide or in neighboring districts to be a secondary concern, just as the election of House candidates is usually not of primary importance to candidates for state or local office. In some realms of campaigning, such as fundraising, recruiting volunteers, and attracting news coverage, members of the same party compete for limited resources. Differences in election boundaries and timing also encourage a sense of parochialism in party officials similar to that of their candidates. Cooperation among party organizations can be achieved only by persuading local, state, and national party leaders that it is in their mutual best interest. Cooperation is often heightened during presidential election years, when the presidential contest dominates the political agenda and boosts voter turnout. Elections that precede or follow the census also are characterized by increased cooperation because politicians at many levels of government focus on the imminent redrawing of election districts or on preserving or wresting control of new districts or those that have been significantly altered.

Although the seeds for candidate-centered congressional election campaigns were sown by the Constitution and election laws, not until the middle of the twentieth century did the candidate-centered system firmly take root. Prior to the emergence of this system, during a period often called the "golden age" of political parties, party organizations played a major role in most election campaigns, including many campaigns for Congress. Local party organizations, often referred to as "old-fashioned political machines," had control over the nomination process, possessed a near-monopoly over the resources needed to organize the electorate, and provided the symbolic cues that informed the electoral decisions of most voters. The key to their success was their ability to command the loyalties of large numbers of individuals, many of whom were able to persuade friends and neighbors to support their party's candidates. Not until the demise of the old-fashioned machine and the emergence of new campaign technology did the modern, candidate-centered system finally blossom.[3]

Reforms intended to weaken political machines played a major role in the development of the candidate-centered system. One such reform was the Australian ballot, adopted by roughly three-quarters of the states between 1888 and 1896.[4] This government-printed ballot listed every candidate for each office and enabled individuals to cast their votes in secret, away from the prying eyes of party officials. The Australian ballot replaced a system of voting in which each party supplied supporters with its own easily identifiable ballot that included only the names of the party's candidates. By ensuring secrecy and simplifying split-ticket voting, the Australian ballot made it easy for citizens to focus on candidates rather than parties when voting. This type of ballot remains in use today.

State-regulated primary nominating contests, which were widely adopted during the Progressive movement of the early 1900s, deprived party leaders of the power to handpick congressional nominees and gave that power to voters who participated in their party's nominating election.[5] The merit-based civil service system, another progressive reform, deprived the parties of patronage. No longer able to distribute government jobs or contracts, the parties had difficulty maintaining large corps of campaign workers.[6] Issues, friendships, the excitement of politics, and other noneconomic incentives could motivate small numbers of people to become active in party politics, but they could not motivate enough people to support a party-focused system of congressional elections.

Congressional candidates also lacked the patronage or government contracts needed to attract large numbers of volunteer workers or to persuade other candidates to help them with their campaigns. By the mid-twentieth century the "isolation" of congressional candidates was so complete that a major report on the state of political parties characterized congressional candidates as the "orphans of the political system." The report, published by the American Political Science Association's Committee on Political Parties, went on to point out that congressional candidates "had no truly adequate party mechanism available for the conduct of their campaigns . . . enjoy[ed] remarkably little national or local support, [and] have mostly been left to cope with the political hazards of their occupation on their own."[7]

Voter registration drives, get-out-the-vote efforts, and redistricting were about the only areas of election politics in which there was extensive cooperation among groups of candidates and party committees. But even here the integration of different party committees and candidate organizations—and especially those involved in congressional elections—was and continues to be short of that exhibited in other democracies.

The Bipartisan Campaign Reform Act of 2002 (BCRA), the Federal Election Campaign Acts that preceded it, and the regulatory rulings and court verdicts that have shaped federal campaign finance law have further reinforced the pattern of candidate-centered congressional elections. Federal law places strict limits on the amounts of money party committees can contribute to or spend in coordination with their congressional candidates' campaigns (see Tables 1-1 and 1-2). It does allow parties to make unlimited independent expenditures *expressly* advocating the election or defeat of a candidate, but these must be made without the knowledge or consent of the candidate or anyone involved with the candidate's campaign, including consultants or party staff who are directly assisting the candidate. Further provisions of the law that limit the parties' involvement in congressional elections place ceilings on contributions from individuals to national party committees and an outright ban on parties accepting contributions from the general treasuries of corporations, unions, and trade associations.[8] Moreover, the law provides no subsidies for party research or other activities, including generic, party-focused campaign efforts. The two exceptions to this rule are a federal subsidy to help finance presidential nominating conventions and eligibility for discount bulk postage—a subsidy available to all nonprofit organizations. The law requires that virtually all of a party's financial transactions be reported to the Federal Election Commission (FEC), which publishes campaign finance data and oversees the administration of the law.[9]

The law's provisions for political parties stand in marked contrast to the treatment given to parties in other democracies. Most of these countries provide subsidies to parties for campaign and interelection activities. The United States is the only democracy in which parties are not given free television or radio time.[10] The support that other democracies give to parties is consistent with the central role they play in elections, government, and society, just as the lack of assistance afforded to American parties is consistent with the candidate-centered system that has developed in the United States.

Lacking independent sources of revenue, local party organizations have a moderate role in the modern, cash-based system of congressional campaign politics. The national and state party committees that survived the reform

TABLE 1-1

Federal Contribution Limits to Congressional Candidates, Political Parties, and PACs

Contributors	House candidates	Senate candidates	National party committees	State and local party committees	PACs
Individuals	*$2,000 per election	*$2,000 per election	*$25,000 per year	$10,000 per year	$5,000 per year
National party committees	$15,000 per election	*$35,000 per election	Unlimited transfers to other party committees	Unlimited transfers to other party committees	$5,000 per year
State, district, and local party committees (combined limit)	$5,000 per election	$5,000 per election	Unlimited transfers to other party committees	Unlimited transfers to other party committees	$5,000 per year
PACs	$5,000 per election	$5,000 per election	$15,000 per year	$5,000 per year	$5,000 per year
Super PACs	Prohibited	Prohibited	Prohibited	Prohibited	Prohibited
Corporations, trade associations, and labor unions	Prohibited	Prohibited	Prohibited	Prohibited	Prohibited
527 committees	Prohibited	Prohibited	Prohibited	Prohibited	Prohibited
501(c)(4), 501(c)(5), 501(c)(6) and other social welfare organizations	Prohibited	Prohibited	Prohibited	Prohibited	Prohibited

Source: Adapted from Federal Election Commission, *Contribution Limits for 2009–2010*, www.fec.gov/info/contriblimits0910.pdf.

Notes: Contribution limits denoted by "*" are adjusted for inflation. In 2010 individuals could give $2,400 each to House and Senate candidates in each phase of the election (primary, general, and runoff). The biennial limits for individual contributions, originally set at $95,000 ($37,500 to all federal candidates and $57,500 to all party committees and PACs), were adjusted to $115,500 ($45,600 and $69,900) in 2010. The limits for parties' national, congressional, and senatorial campaign committees are considered separate committees when making contributions to House candidates, so they can each contribute up to $5,000, for a total of $15,000.

TABLE 1-2
Federal Spending Limits in Congressional Elections

	Coordinated expenditures on behalf of candidates		Other expenditures		
	House candidates	Senate candidates	Independent expenditures	Electioneering communications	Levin funds
Individuals	Considered a contribution	Considered a contribution	Unlimited	Unlimited	Whatever state law permits, up to $10,000
National party committees	*$10,000	*$20,000 or $.02 times a state's voting age population, whichever is greater	Unlimited	Unlimited	Prohibited
State party committees	*$10,000	*$20,000 or $.02 times a state's voting age population, whichever is greater	Unlimited	Unlimited	Prohibited
PACs	Considered a contribution	Considered a contribution	Unlimited	Unlimited	Whatever state law permits, up to $10,000
Super PACs	Prohibited	Prohibited	Unlimited	Unlimited	Whatever state law permits, up to $10,000

(Table continues)

TABLE 1-2 (continued)
Federal Spending Limits in Congressional Elections

	Coordinated expenditures on behalf of candidates		Other expenditures		
	House candidates	Senate candidates	Independent expenditures	Electioneering communications	Levin funds
Corporations, trade associations, and labor unions	Prohibited	Prohibited	Unlimited	Unlimited	Whatever state law permits, up to $10,000
527 committees	Prohibited	Prohibited	Unlimited	Unlimited	Whatever state law permits, up to $10,000
501(c)(4), 501(c)(5), 501(c)(6), and other social welfare organizations	Prohibited	Prohibited	Unlimited	Unlimited	$10,000 if permitted by state law

Source: Adapted from Federal Election Commission, *2010 Coordinated Party Expenditure Limits,* www.fec.gov/info/charts_441ad_2010.shtml.

Notes: The limits for party coordinated expenditures in House and Senate elections (denoted by "*") are indexed for inflation. The limit for House elections in 2010 was $43,500 each for all national party committees and for state party committees, except for states with only one representative, in which case the limit was $87,000. The limit for Senate elections in 2010 ranged from $87,000 for all national party committees for the smallest states to $2,395,400 for the largest state (California). State party committees can provide additional funds, up to the same limit imposed on the national committees.

movements and changes in federal election laws lack sufficient funds or staff to dominate campaign politics. They also understand that few, if any, candidates desire this. For the most part, party leaders believe that a party should bolster its candidates' campaigns, not replace them with a campaign of its own.[11]

The availability of campaign support from interest groups also has limited the electoral influence of American political parties relative to their counterparts in other democracies and has helped to foster candidate-centered congressional elections. Interest groups can influence elections, and politics in general, using a variety of legal structures, each of which provides specific political and financial advantages. For more than three decades, interest groups have used federally registered PACs, numbering more than 5,400 in 2010, to distribute billions of dollars in contributions and independent expenditures in congressional elections. In the 1990s, the weakening of the regulations governing campaign finance enabled some groups to use 527 committees and 501(c) organizations (named after their sections in the Internal Revenue Code) that were not registered with the FEC to try to influence federal elections. Since then some 501(c) groups, whose tax classification states they exist for charitable, educational, or other social welfare purposes, and some 527 committees, which the tax code defines as existing for the purpose of influencing elections, spent billions of dollars in "soft-money." Soft-money consists of unregulated funds that flow outside of the federal campaign finance system— including millions of dollars raised from the general treasuries of corporations, unions, and other groups—and are used to finance independent media campaigns and coordinated grassroots campaigns intended to affect federal elections. "Hard-money," by contrast, includes all funds raised within that framework. These funds originate as donations by individuals to candidates, party committees, or PACs and are subject to a variety of contribution and expenditure limits and public disclosure requirements.

In January 2010 the Supreme Court ruled in *Citizens United v. FEC* that corporations, unions, and other groups can spend funds from their treasuries to make independent expenditures to expressly advocate the election or defeat of a federal candidate. A later ruling by the U.S. Court of Appeals for the District of Columbia in *Speechnow.org v. FEC* held that these groups also can form super PACs (sometimes referred to as "independent expenditure-only committees") for this purpose.[12] Although these rulings were handed down well after the midpoint of the 2010 election cycle, they enabled corporations, unions, and other groups, and the super PACs they sponsored to make more than $131 million in independent expenditures during the 2010 congressional elections.

Just as the weakening of federal regulations governing campaign finance enabled interest groups to enhance existing entities and create new ones to influence elections, political conditions encouraged them to do so. The polarization of the political parties, the substantial differences in their policy agendas, and the slim margins determining party control in both houses of Congress raised the stakes for groups affected by the federal government. Given that the turnover of just a few House or Senate seats could greatly influence policies dealing with taxation, regulation, or the distribution of federal funds, many wealthy (and some other) interests were primed to respond to the opportunities created by the new regulatory situation. They used a variety of individual and interlocking organizations to ratchet up their campaign spending and increase their political clout. As a result, interest groups are estimated to have spent an unprecedented $690 million during the 2010 congressional elections.[13] Some of this spending took the form of cash contributions and campaign services delivered to candidates; contributions and transfers to party committees and other election-oriented groups; television, direct mail, radio, Internet, social media, and other communications designed to persuade or mobilize voters; polling and other political research; and the employment of campaign consultants and other staff. The sheer numbers of interest group organizations and the amounts they spend on congressional elections amply demonstrate that candidates can and do turn to sources besides party organizations for support.

The evolution of campaign finance law has created an environment that includes huge numbers of organizational and individual donors, but it has not fully ushered political parties to the periphery of congressional campaigns. Rather, party committees based in Washington, D.C., have adapted to the contemporary national economy of campaign finance. The individuals, PACs, and other organizations that are suppliers of campaign funds in this economy are primarily located in and around Washington, New York City, Los Angeles, and the nation's other wealthy population centers. The funds' recipients are candidates contesting House and Senate seats located across the country. They include both powerful incumbents and the relatively small group of non-incumbents who are involved in close races in a typical election season. As will be discussed in Chapter 4, the parties have responded to the nationalization of the campaign finance system by becoming the major brokers or mediators between the financiers of congressional elections and the candidates who compete in them. In some cases, the relationship between party committees and the individuals and groups that spend money on elections is so strong that it is appropriate to consider these donors party allies.[14]

POLITICAL CULTURE

Historically, U.S. political culture has supported a system of candidate-centered congressional elections in many ways, but its major influence stems from its lack of foundation for a party-focused alternative. Americans have traditionally held a jaundiced view of political parties. *Federalist* no. 10 and President George Washington's farewell address are evidence that the framers of the Constitution and the first president thought a multitude of overlapping, wide-ranging interests were preferable to class-based divisions represented by ideological parties. The founders designed the political system to encourage pragmatism and compromise in politics and thus to mitigate the harmful effects of factions. Although neither the pluralist system championed by the framers nor the nonpartisan system advocated by Washington have been fully realized, both visions of democracy have found expression in candidate-centered campaigns.

Congressional elections test candidates' abilities to build coalitions of voters and elites from diverse individuals. The multiplicity of overlapping interests, lack of a feudal legacy, and relatively fluid social and economic structure in the United States discourage the formation of class-based parties like those that have developed in most other democracies.[15] The consensus among Americans for liberty, equality, and property rights and their near-universal support of the political system further undermine the development of parties aimed at promoting major political, social, or economic change.[16]

Americans' traditional ambivalence about political parties has found expression during reform periods. The Populist movement of the 1890s, the Progressive movement that came shortly after it, and the rise of the New Left in the 1960s all resulted in political change that weakened the parties. Reformers at the turn of the twentieth century championed the Australian ballot, the direct primary, and civil service laws for the explicit purpose of taking power away from party bosses.[17] Similarly, the reform movement that took hold of the Democratic Party during the 1960s and 1970s opened party conventions, meetings, and leadership positions to the increased participation of previously underrepresented groups. The reforms, many of which were adopted by Republican as well as Democratic state party organizations, made both parties more permeable and responsive to pressures from grassroots activists. They weakened what little influence party leaders had over awarding nominations, thereby giving candidates, their supporters, and issue activists more influence over party affairs.[18] The Tea Party movement's defeat of several Republican establishment candidates in 2010, including three incumbent senators, showcases the impact that local grassroots activists can have on nomination politics.

Post–World War II social and cultural transformations undermined the parties even further. Declining immigration and increased geographic mobility eroded the working-class ethnic neighborhoods that were an important source of party loyalists. Increased educational levels encouraged citizens to rely more on their own judgment and less on party cues in political matters. The development of the mass media gave voters less biased sources of information than the partisan press. The rise of interest groups, including PACs and other forms of functional and ideological representation, created new arenas for political participation and new sources of political cues.[19] The aging of the parties, generational replacement, and the emergence of new issues that cut across existing fault lines led to the decline of party affiliation among voters and to more issue-oriented voting.[20] These developments encouraged voters to rely less on local party officials and opinion leaders for political information. Cultural transformations created a void in electoral politics that individual candidates and their organizations eventually filled.

Voters' attitudes toward the parties reflect the nation's historical experience. Survey research shows that most citizens believe that parties "do more to confuse the issues than to provide a clear choice on the issues" and "create conflict where none exists." Half of the population believes that parties make the political system less efficient and that "it would be better if, in all elections, we put no party labels on the ballot."[21]

Negative attitudes toward the parties are often learned at an early age. Many schoolchildren are routinely instructed to "vote for the best candidate, not the party." This lesson appears to stay with some of them into adulthood. Typically, less than 10 percent of all registered voters maintain that the candidate's political party is the biggest factor in their vote decision. Candidates and issues rank higher.[22]

Although American history and culture extol the virtues of political independence and candidate-oriented voting, the electoral behavior of citizens reveals an element of partisanship in congressional elections. In 2010 about 63 percent of all voters were willing to state that they identified with either the Democratic or the Republican Party, which is comparable to the preceding two decades. About three-fourths of all self-identified independents indicate they lean toward a major party, holding attitudes and exhibiting political behaviors similar to those of self-identified partisans. Although few registered voters are willing to state that they cast their votes chiefly on a partisan basis, 90 percent of them cast their congressional ballots along party lines in 2010.[23] Such high levels of partisan voting are common in modern American politics, and party identification is among the best predictors of voting behavior in congressional elections. The fact that 76 percent of the voting population perceives, retains, and responds to political information in a partisan manner means that elections are not entirely candidate centered.[24] Yet the degree of partisanship that exists in the contemporary United States is still not strong enough to encourage a return to straight-ticket voting or foster the development of a party-focused election system.

CAMPAIGN TECHNOLOGY

Political campaigns are designed to communicate ideas and images that will motivate voters to cast their ballots for particular candidates. Some voters are well informed; have strong opinions about candidates, issues, and parties; and will vote without ever coming into contact with a political campaign. Others will never bother to vote, regardless of politicians' efforts. Many voters need to be introduced to the candidates and made aware of the issues to become excited enough to vote in a congressional election. The communication of information is central to democratic elections, and those who are able to control the flow of information have enormous power. Candidates, campaign organizations, parties, and other groups use a variety of technologies to affect the flow of campaign information and win votes.

Person-to-person contact is one of the oldest and most effective approaches to winning votes. Nothing was or is more effective than a candidate, or a candidate's supporters, directly asking citizens for their votes. During the golden age of parties, local party volunteers assessed the needs of voters in their neighborhoods and delivered the message that, if elected, their party's candidates would help voters improve their situations.[25] Once these organizations lost their control over the flow of political information they became less important, and candidate-assembled campaign organizations became more relevant players in elections.

The dawning of the television age and the development of modern campaign technology helped solidify the system of candidate-centered congressional elections.[26] Television and radio studios, printing presses, public opinion polls, personal computers, and sophisticated targeting techniques are well suited to candidate-centered campaign organizations because they, and the services of the political consultants who know how to use them, are readily available for hire. Congressional candidates can assemble organizations that meet their specific needs without having to turn to party organizations for assistance, although many candidates request their party's help.

Technology has encouraged a major change in the focus of most congressional election campaigns. It has enabled campaigns to communicate more information about candidates' personalities, issue positions, and qualifications for office. As a result, little campaign activity is now devoted to party-based appeals. Radio and television were especially important in bringing about this change because they are effective at conveying images and less useful for providing information about abstract concepts, such as partisan ideologies. The Internet reinforces the focus on candidate-centered appeals. Internet websites enable candidates to post as many pictures, streaming video or radio ads, or other information as they wish. Websites enable voters to access this information whenever they want and make it easy for voters to contact the campaign. Social media, including Twitter, YouTube, and Facebook, also enable campaigns and voters to disseminate information about candidates and issues. They are routinely used by campaigns and their supporters to provide voters who may never have heard of a candidate with some campaign information and to encourage voters to visit that candidate's website.[27] Some sites also enable voters who support the same candidate to directly contact each other. Because these media allow for direct candidate-to-voter, voter-to-candidate, and voter-to-voter communication, their overall effect, like that of the electronic mass media more generally, is to direct attention away from parties and toward candidates.

The increased focus on candidate imagery that is associated with contemporary campaigns encourages candidates to hire professionals to help them convey their political personas to voters. These include communications directors, press secretaries, pollsters, and issue and opposition researchers; mass media, direct mail, and social media experts; and website designers. Local party activists became less important in congressional elections as the importance of political consultants grew and the contributions of semiskilled and unskilled volunteers diminished. Skyrocketing campaign costs; the emergence of a national economy of campaign finance; and the rise of a cadre of fundraising specialists with the skills, contacts, and technology to raise money from individuals and PACs further increased the candidate-centered character of election campaigns because they provided politicians with the means for raising the contributions needed to purchase the services of political consultants.

Changes in technology transformed most congressional campaigns from labor-intensive grassroots undertakings, at which local party committees excelled, to money-driven, political marketing efforts requiring the services of skilled experts. Most local party committees were unable to adapt to the new style of campaign politics.[28] Initially, party committees in Washington, D.C., and in many states also were unprepared to play a significant role in congressional elections. However, the parties' national, congressional, and senatorial campaign committees and many state party organizations proved more adept at making the transition to the new-style politics. They began to play meaningful roles in congressional election campaigns during the late 1970s and early 1980s, and continue to do so in the twenty-first century.[29]

THE POLITICAL SETTING

Candidates, campaign managers, party officials, interest group leaders, and others who are active in congressional elections consider more than the institutional framework, the culturally and historically conditioned expectations of voters, and the available technology when planning and executing electoral strategies. Individuals connected to the campaign also assess the political atmosphere, including the circumstances in their district, their state, and the nation as a whole. At the local level, important considerations include the party affiliation and intentions of the incumbent or other potential candidates and the partisan history of the seat. Relevant national-level factors include whether it is a presidential or midterm election year, the state of the economy, the president's popularity, international affairs, and the public's current attitudes toward the federal government.

Of course, one's perspective on the limits and possibilities associated with the political environment depends largely on one's vantage point. Although they talk about the competition and are, indeed, wary of it, congressional incumbents, particularly House members, operate in a political context that works largely to their benefit. As explained in later chapters, incumbents enjoy significant levels of name recognition and voter support, are able to assemble superior campaign organizations, and can draw on their experience in office to speak knowledgeably about issues and claim credit for the federally financed programs and improvements in their state or district. Incumbents also tend to get favorable treatment from the media. Moreover, most can rely on loyal followers from previous campaigns for continued backing: supporters at home tend to vote repeatedly for incumbents, and supporters in Washington and the nation's other wealthy cities routinely provide incumbents with campaign contributions.

Things look different from the typical challenger's vantage point. Most challengers, particularly those with some political experience, recognize that most of the cards are stacked against an individual who sets out to defeat an incumbent. Little in the setting in which most congressional campaigns take place favors the challenger. Most challengers lack the public visibility, money, and political experience to wage a strong campaign. Moreover, because those who work in and help finance campaigns recognize the strong odds against challengers, they usually see little benefit in helping them. As a result, high incumbent success rates have become a self-fulfilling prophecy. House incumbents enjoyed an overall reelection rate of better than 90 percent between 1950 and 2008; Senate reelection rates averaged more than 80 percent. Even during the "wave" elections of 1994 and 2006, more than 90 percent of all

House members and 85 percent of all senators who sought to remain in office were able to do so. Similarly, the 2010 congressional elections, which broke a record set in 1938 for the net increase in House seats for a single party and witnessed the defeat of fifty-eight sitting House members, resulted in a reelection rate of about 85 percent. The reelection rate for senators that year was 84 percent. Given their limited prospects for success in contesting a congressional seat, before running for office most experienced politicians wait until an incumbent retires, runs for another office, or dies. Indeed, substantial numbers of incumbents, especially in the House, are reelected without opposition or with weak opposition at best.

Most elections for open seats are highly competitive. They attract extremely qualified candidates who put together strong campaign organizations, raise huge amounts of money, and mount lively campaigns. Even House candidates of one party campaigning for seats that have been held by the other party for decades can often attract substantial resources, media attention, and votes. In more than just a few instances, they go on to win.

Many explanations exist for the relative lack of competition in House elections. Some districts are so dominated by one party that few individuals of the other party are willing to commit their time, energy, or money to running for office. One-party dominance is often the result of the "sorting out" of the population into like-minded communities, as conservatives choose to live in neighborhoods largely populated by others who share their lifestyles and values, and liberals settle in areas with other liberals.[30] The tradition of one-party dominance is so strong in some congressional districts that virtually all the talented, politically ambitious individuals living in the area join the dominant party. When an incumbent in these districts faces a strong challenge, it usually takes place in the primary, and the winner is all but guaranteed success in the general election.

Uncompetitive House districts also may result from a highly political redistricting process. In states where one party controls both the governorship and the state legislature, partisan gerrymandering is often used to maximize the number of House seats the dominant party can win. In states where each party controls at least some portion of the state government, compromises are frequently made to design districts that protect congressional incumbents. Party officials and political consultants armed with computers, election histories, and demographic statistics can "pack" and "crack" voting blocs in order to promote either of these goals.[31] The result is that large numbers of congressional districts are designed to be uncompetitive. The post-redistricting election held in California in 2002 exemplifies this. Only three of the state's fifty-three House elections were decided by a margin of less than 20 points.[32]

The relatively few states that use nonpartisan commissions for redistricting tend to produce more competitive House races because the commissions generally place less emphasis on partisanship and incumbency. In contrast to the situation in California, four of Iowa's five House seats were decided by less than 15 points in 2002.

Elections that immediately follow redistricting traditionally have been marked by a temporary increase in competition. The creation of many new House seats and the redrawing of others typically results in increased numbers of incumbent defeats in both the primaries and the general election. The pitting of incumbents against each other almost always accounts for some of these losses, as does the fact that the prospect of newly drawn seats often encourages a surge in congressional retirements and more candidates than usual to challenge sitting House members. As a result, the decennial reapportionment and redistricting of House seats has historically produced a ten-year, five-election cycle of political competition. However, as will be noted later, the 2002 elections proved to be an exception to this rule.

Another cyclical element of the national political setting that can influence congressional elections is the presence or absence of a presidential race. Presidential elections have higher levels of voter turnout than do midterm elections, and they have the potential for coattail effects. A presidential candidate's popularity can become infectious and lead to increased support for the party's congressional contestants. A party that enjoys much success in electing congressional candidates during a presidential election year is, of course, likely to lose some of those seats in the midterm election that follows, especially when their party also controls both chambers of Congress.[33] An unpopular president can further drag down a party's congressional contestants.[34] Presidential election politics had a strong impact on the election of 1932, in which the Democrats gained ninety seats in the House and thirteen seats in the Senate. The Democratic congressional landslide was a sign of widespread support for the Democratic presidential candidate, Franklin D. Roosevelt, as well as a repudiation of the incumbent president, Herbert Hoover, and his policies for dealing with the Great Depression. Presidential coattail effects have declined since the 1930s, and Bill Clinton's and George W. Bush's presidential elections were conspicuous for their lack of them.[35] Of course, one cannot expect a presidential candidate's coattails to be long when the victory comes in at less than 50 percent of the popular vote, as was the case with Clinton in 1992 and 1996 and Bush in 2000. Barack Obama's decisive victory in 2008 had a somewhat larger impact, increasing the number of Democrats in the House by twenty-one and in the Senate by eight.

Congressional candidates who belong to the same party as an unpopular president also run the risk of being blamed for the failures of their party's chief executive during midterm elections. Unable to vote against the president in a midterm election, voters who are unhappy with the president's performance or the state of the nation under his leadership may cast their vote against a congressional candidate who belongs to his party.[36] The president's party has historically lost congressional seats in midterm elections when economic trends are unfavorable, although the relationship between economic performance and congressional turnover has weakened in recent years.[37] The Republicans' forty-nine-seat House and four-seat Senate losses in 1974 are an example of a midterm election that was, in many ways, a referendum on a president. To a significant extent these losses grew out of voters' disgust with the roles of President Richard Nixon and members of his administration in the break-in at Democratic Party headquarters at the Watergate Hotel during the 1972 presidential campaign and the decision of his successor, President Gerald Ford, to pardon Nixon.[38] Another example is the Democrats' loss of fifty-two seats in the House and eight seats in the Senate in 1994, which was caused largely by voter animosity toward Clinton, dissatisfaction with his party's failure to enact health care reform or a middle-class tax cut, and the Republicans' successful portrayal of the White House and the Democratic-controlled Congress as corrupt and out of step with the views of most voters. The 2006 and 2010 midterm elections are more recent examples of how voter discontent with presidential leadership, the performance of the federal government, and the state of the nation laid the groundwork for a president's party to lose substantial numbers of seats in the House and Senate. However, some of the blame for those outcomes also lay at the feet of Congress, which was controlled by the party of the president in both years.

The economy, foreign affairs, homeland security, civil rights, and other national issues can affect congressional elections. The economic recession was a major factor in Republican losses in 2008 and Democratic defeats two years later. The civil rights revolution, the women's movement, the emergence of the hippie counterculture, and the protests they spawned influenced voting in congressional and other elections during the 1960s and 1970s.[39] The Vietnam War contributed to the Democrats' congressional losses in 1972, and the wars on terrorism and in Afghanistan may have cost Democrats seats in 2002 and 2004. The war in Iraq and the poor federal government response to Hurricane Katrina certainly contributed to the losses of some Republicans in 2006 and 2008. Political scandal, and the widespread distrust of government that usually follows, can lead to the defeat of politicians accused of committing ethical transgressions. Individual members of Congress who are not directly impli-cated in scandal can also suffer at the polls, as the 1974, 1994, 2006, and other recent elections demonstrate. As a general rule, Americans tend to be less con-cerned with "guns" than with "butter," so international events generally have less effect on elections than domestic conditions.

Recent congressional election cycles can be divided into two types. The first, sometimes referred to as a "status quo" or "normal" election, is characterized by contests that focus primarily on the abilities, experiences, and public service records of the candidates and issues of primary concern to local voters. Because of the many advantages they enjoy over challengers, an overwhelming number of incumbents who seek reelection in status quo election cycles win.

The second type of election cycle, often referred to as a "nationalized" or "wave" election, is one in which national political, economic, or social forces create an electoral environment that strongly favors one party—usually the party out of power—and results in a significant change in the partisan com-position of Congress and other elective institutions. An election that is nation-alized in one party's favor provides that party and its candidates with many benefits. It encourages greater enthusiasm and participation by the party's contributors, activists, and electoral base, thereby increasing the support the party and its candidates are able to attract. It also increases the level of support congressional and other candidates receive from the independent or "swing" voters whose backing is often the key to victory in marginal districts.

The ability to campaign on the same, or very similar, issues is a major stra-tegic advantage that congressional and other candidates who belong to the favored party enjoy in a nationalized election. When the issues that dominate the national political agenda are the same as the major concerns of local voters, candidates who address those concerns benefit from the fact that their political party and the interest groups and political commentators allied with it are dis-seminating the same message. Consistency in political communications helps candidates break through the cacophony of voices heard in competitive con-gressional elections and is especially beneficial to challengers, who are typically at a major disadvantage in getting their message heard by voters. Nationalized elections result in virtually all of the favored party's incumbents successfully defending their seats, an unusually large number of its challengers getting elected, and the success of most of its open-seat candidates.

The desire of incumbents to protect their congressional careers from the uncertainties of both status quo and nationalized elections has changed Congress in ways that tend to discourage electoral competition and help insu-late incumbents against political tides. Congress has adapted to the career aspirations of its members by providing them with resources they can use to increase their odds of reelection. Free mailings, unlimited long-distance telephone calls, e-mail, websites, district offices, and subsidized travel help members gain visibility among their constituents. Federal pork-barrel projects also help incumbents win the support of voters.[40] Congressional aides help members write speeches, respond to constituent mail, resolve problems that constituents have with executive branch agencies, and follow the comings and goings in their bosses' districts.[41] Congressional hearings provide incumbents with forums in which to address issues of concern to their constituents and attract media coverage. These perquisites of office give incumbents enormous advantages over challengers. They also discourage experienced politicians who could put forth a competitive challenge from taking on an entrenched incumbent.

The dynamics of campaign finance have similar effects. Incumbents have huge fundraising advantages over challengers, especially among PACs and wealthy individual donors. They capitalize on this by hosting and attending fundraising events and meeting with and calling donors in their districts, in Washington, and in other wealthy urban areas. Devoting so much time to soliciting contributions is part of a reelection strategy that involves building up a large war chest to discourage potential challengers. With the exception of millionaires and celebrities, challengers who decide to contest a race against a member of the House or Senate usually find they are unable to raise the funds needed to mount a viable campaign.

Because the cards tend to be stacked so heavily in favor of congressional incumbents, most electoral competition takes place in open seats. Open-seat contests draw a larger-than-usual number of primary contestants. They also attract significantly more money and election assistance from party committees, individuals, PACs, and other groups than challenger campaigns. Special elections, which are called when a seat becomes vacant because of an incumbent's resignation or death, are open-seat contests that tend to be particularly competitive and unpredictable. They bring out even larger numbers of primary contenders than normal open-seat elections, especially when the seat that has become vacant was formerly held by a longtime incumbent.

RECENT CONGRESSIONAL ELECTIONS

The political settings that have shaped the opportunities presented to politicians, parties, interest groups, and ultimately voters since the early 1990s have some important similarities. Many recent elections took place during a period of divided control, which made it difficult to credit or blame only one party for the government's performance or the nation's affairs. Most of the elections held in the last few decades took place under the shadow of a weak economy and were haunted by the specter of huge budget deficits, which thrust concerns about jobs, housing, and the country's economic future onto the political agenda.

Civil rights and racial and gender discrimination were issues in several campaigns during this period as a result of the highly publicized studies of the unequal salaries and advancement prospects for women and African Americans. Women's issues were highlighted prior to the 2010 elections after President Obama signed the Lilly Ledbetter Fair Pay Act to allow individuals who experienced gender, racial, or other identity-based discrimination in the workplace to sue for back pay and when provisions concerning publicly subsidized abortions threatened to derail the Democrats' health care reform legislation. Gay rights found its place on the agenda as federal courts overturned the military's "don't ask, don't tell" policy regarding homosexuals serving in the armed forces, and Obama signed an executive order requiring all hospitals that receive Medicare and Medicaid payments (virtually all hospitals in the United States) to grant same-sex couples the same visitation, consultation, and proxy rights as heterosexual couples.

Another arena in which civil rights became entangled with the politics of congressional elections was redistricting. In 1986 the Supreme Court ruled that any gerrymandering of a congressional district that purposely diluted minority strength was illegal under the 1982 Voting Rights Act.[42] Most states interpreted the ruling cautiously, redrawing many districts afterward with the explicit purpose of giving one or more minority group members better-than-even chances of being elected to the House. However, redistricting did not proceed without contention. Dozens of lawsuits were filed over the redrawing of House districts before the 1992 and 2002 elections, and more lawsuits should be anticipated prior to the 2012 elections.

Dissatisfaction with the political establishment in Washington also occupied a prominent position on the political agenda at the onset of the twenty-first century. Problems associated with the economy, immigration, the environment, rising health care and energy costs, the performance of the nation's schools, and a myriad of other seemingly intractable issues resulted in voter frustration with national politicians. Much of this hostility was directed toward Congress, and many incumbents responded with the time-tested strategy of running for reelection by campaigning against Congress itself.[43]

Political scandal and the anti-Washington mood gave open-seat and challenger candidates for Congress many powerful issues to use in campaigns during the elections held in the early 1990s through 2010. Support for the national legislature plummeted prior to the 1994 elections, when an unprecedented three-fourths of all Americans disapproved of Congress's performance—a record that was virtually matched during the 2006, 2008, and 2010 election seasons.[44] Not surprisingly, members of the congressional majority pay a higher price for public disapproval of Congress than those in the minority, especially when a member of their party also occupies the White House.[45]

The first of several recent nationalized elections was held in 1994. National conditions were ripe for the Republicans to pick up a significant number of congressional seats. Public hostility toward the Democratic Party–controlled executive and legislative branches of the national government, and Clinton in particular, energized Republicans and demoralized Democrats. Under Newt Gingrich's leadership, the Republicans capitalized on these circumstances by running an anti-Washington campaign that drew on the *Contract with America*.[46] The result was that many incumbent Democrats were defeated, and the GOP won control of both chambers of Congress for the first time in forty-two years.

The 1996, 1998, and 2000 contests were status quo elections that were promising for incumbents of both parties. Most Americans benefited from a strong economy marked by rising incomes, low inflation, a high employment rate, and a booming stock market.[47] This environment favored neither party. Rather, it benefited incumbents in general, few of whom were defeated.

At its outset, the stage was set for the 2002 election to resemble a typical status quo election. The political environment appeared to favor incumbents across the board. In the House this outlook was, in part, the result of an exceptional round of redistricting that bucked previous precedents by increasing the number of secure, incumbent-held seats and reducing the number of competitive contests. One reason for this result was an increase in the number of divided state governments, which gave Democrats and Republicans in many states the ability to influence the redrawing of congressional districts. Another was improved technology that enabled district mapmakers to estimate with tremendous precision the numbers of Democratic, Republican, and independent voters. Still another was that House incumbents, who were unusually risk averse, enlisted their allies to carve out extremely safe seats for themselves instead of sacrificing a little political security to improve the chances of increasing their party's House membership. Moreover, public approval of Congress was relatively high, which had the potential to advantage incumbents in both the House and the Senate.

The attacks of September 11, 2001, nationalized the political agenda in ways that benefited the Republican Party in the 2002 election. National security and the war on terrorism, which previously had barely registered among the public, rose to prominence in national opinion polls. The president's approval ratings skyrocketed, as has historically occurred when the United States has become involved in an international crisis. President George W. Bush, drawing on his increased popularity and role as commander in chief, sought to capitalize on the situation in 2002 by helping Republican congressional candidates raise money and making public appearances on their behalf.[48] Most Democrats responded by running on local issues and claiming that they, too, were tough on defense. The result was that the GOP bucked the historical trend of losing seats in a midterm election and enjoyed a net gain of eight House and two Senate seats.

The 2004 election was a typical status quo election. Although issues pertaining to national security, the war in Iraq, and foreign policy more generally were important, local factors were more significant than in the previous election. Few incumbents of either party were defeated. The Republicans gained a mere three seats in the House and four seats in the Senate.

The 2006 election took place in a national political environment that favored the Democrats. Growing numbers of military fatalities and the limited military and political progress made in Iraq and Afghanistan were sources of voter dissatisfaction. The inadequacy of the federal government's response to Hurricane Katrina, its failure to enact an immigration policy, an unpopular GOP-sponsored prescription drug reform, and the economic insecurities felt by many voters further contributed to voter discontent. Corruption scandals involving convicted lobbyist Jack Abramoff, Republican House majority leader Tom DeLay of Texas, and other GOP lawmakers enraged many voters. A scandal involving sexually suggestive e-mails and instant messages that Rep. Mark Foley, R-Fla., sent to some former House pages, and Republican leaders' failure to properly report them, added to the GOP's woes. Moreover, President Bush was the subject of widespread dissatisfaction. The Republicans responded to these conditions by campaigning on their congressional records and local concerns. The Democrats, on the other hand, offered voters a national message based on an appeal for change. First, they sought to hold the Republicans accountable for the Middle East wars, their incompetence in handling the Katrina crisis, and for corruption in Washington. Second, they focused on health care reform, energy independence, improved jobs and wages, and other domestic issues popular with middle- and working-class Americans. Third, the Democrats used their Red to Blue Program to take the unusual step of committing party resources to expand the field of competition. Their efforts were highly successful. In 2006 the Democratic Party enjoyed a net gain of thirty-one seats in the House and six seats in the Senate and won control of both chambers.[49]

The political environment in 2008 bore many similarities to that of two years earlier. In addition to the issues that influenced voting decisions in 2006, Republicans had to contend with a massive economic downturn. Moreover, the campaign of their presidential nominee, Sen. John McCain of Arizona, had a hard time finding its footing, and the Democrats' nominee, Sen. Barack Obama of Illinois, ran what most commentators regarded as an inspired campaign. Democratic congressional candidates capitalized on the national environment by campaigning, once again, on the theme of change; their Republican counterparts tried to focus constituents on more parochial concerns. On Election Day the Democrats were set to increase their numbers by twenty-one seats in the House and eight seats in the Senate.

Economic unrest and voter discontent with the federal government resulted in the 2010 election becoming the third nationalized election in a row. When asked, "What made the biggest difference in how you voted for Congress in your district?" 39 percent answered, "The direction of the nation as a whole," and another 17 percent cited a specific national issue. Only 36 percent zeroed in on the candidates or local or state issues—the factors that dominate most status quo elections (see Figure 1-1). The 2010 election was similar to and different from the election of 1994. The similarities included the following: the political environment for both contests was shaped by deep voter discontent with the state of the nation and a Democratic Party that controlled both the White House and Congress; the Democrats were unable to allay many voters' major concerns, enacted some unpopular policies, and failed to offer a positive message to counter the largely negative one proffered by Republicans; the GOP published *A Pledge to America*, a campaign manifesto similar to the *Contract with America* it offered sixteen years earlier; and both elections were characterized by a political protest movement. Among the differences are that in 2010 the Democrats had controlled Congress for only two terms, as opposed to forty-two in 1994; both parties were held in extremely low regard, whereas most voter disgust was with the Democrats in 1994; the economy overwhelmed all other public concerns in 2010, whereas scandals and charges of government corruption were prominent in 1994; and the Tea Party movement in 2010 was less centrally coordinated than the protest movement that began with the presidential candidacy of H. Ross Perot and helped fuel the turnover in the 1994 elections.

The Tea Party movement had a substantial role in the 2010 elections. Evolving from hundreds of small groups and rallies organized by local conservative activists to a national movement loosely coordinated by some prominent Republican politicians and consultants, the Tea Party tapped into a vein of anger against the federal government. Primarily united by their opposition

FIGURE 1-1

Factors That Influenced How Individuals Voted in the 2010 House Elections

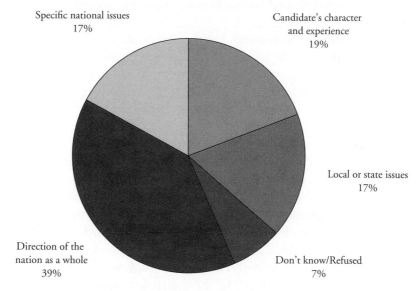

Specific national issues
17%

Candidate's character
and experience
19%

Local or state issues
17%

Direction of the
nation as a whole
39%

Don't know/Refused
7%

Source: Kaiser Family Foundation Health Tracking Poll (conducted November 3–6, 2010).

to the status quo, these Republican-leaning voters also favored cutting the size of the federal government, reducing government spending, lowering taxes, and strictly adhering to the U.S. Constitution.[50] The grassroots efforts of local Tea Party members, and the campaign expenditures made by national groups in support of them, contributed to the defeat of large numbers of members of Congress. Tea Party–backed candidates defeated three Republican incumbents in House and Senate nominating contests and ninety-seven Democratic incumbents in the general election. Tea Party loyalists claim credit for enabling the GOP to win control of the House. Some critics, on the other hand, argue the Tea Party cost the Republicans the opportunity to win a Senate majority.

The 2010 elections, like several other recent contests, demonstrated that despite the inherent advantages of incumbency, the political setting in a given year can pose obstacles for some lawmakers and result in significant numbers losing their seats. Nineteen House incumbents lost their primaries in 1992, a post–World War II record, and thirty-four lost in the general election two years later—the most since the post-Watergate housecleaning of 1974 (see Table 1-3). The 1994, 1996, 2006, and 2008 elections also

TABLE 1-3

Number of Unchallenged and Defeated House Incumbents, 1986–2010

	1986	1988	1990	1992	1994	1996	1998	2000	2002	2004	2006	2008	2010
Incumbents unchallenged by major-party opposition in general election	71	81	76	25	54	20	94	63	78	64	55	64	27
Incumbents defeated													
In primary	3	1	1	19	4	2	1	3	8	2	2	3	4
In general election	6	6	15	24	34	20	6	6	8	7	20	19	54

Sources: Compiled from various editions of *CQ Weekly* and *Congressional Roll Call* (Washington, D.C.: CQ Press). The primary and general results are from Norman J. Ornstein, Thomas E. Mann, and Michael J. Malbin, *Vital Statistics on Congress: 2001–2002* (Washington, D.C.: AEI Press, 2002), 69, and author's data.

Notes: The 1992, 2002, and 2004 figures include incumbent-versus-incumbent races. Also, Henry Bonilla, R-Texas, was defeated in a runoff in 2006 and is included among incumbents defeated in the general elections. Shelley Sekula-Gibbs, R-Texas, who ran as a write-in candidate for the seat of Tom DeLay, is included in the incumbent category because she replaced DeLay after his resignation.

witnessed moderate to high levels of incumbent losses. In 2010 there was a huge uptick in incumbent losses, with four House members losing their primaries and fifty-four—all but two Democrats—losing in the general election.

The increased competition in 2010 is also evident when candidates are divided into categories on the basis of the closeness of their elections. During that election, 38 percent of the House candidates in major-party contested races ran in competitive districts, compared with 22 percent in 2004. This group is composed of the 17 percent of the candidates classified as "incumbents in jeopardy" on the basis of their having lost the general election or having won by a margin of 20 percent or less of the two-party vote; the 17 percent of the candidates who opposed them—labeled "hopeful challengers"; and the 4 percent of the candidates—classified as open-seat "prospects"—who ran in contests decided by 20 percent or less of the two-party vote (see Table 1-4). The remainder of the candidates, who were involved in uncompetitive races, are referred to as incumbent "shoo-ins," "long-shot" challengers, and "mismatched" open-seat candidates.[51]

Similarly, the mood surrounding the 2010 elections led to heightened competition in the Senate. Sens. Robert Bennett, R-Utah, and Lisa Murkowski, R-Alaska, were both defeated for renomination by conservative Tea Party–backed candidates, although Murkowski was able to reclaim her seat by waging

TABLE 1-4

Competition in House Elections, 1986–2010

	1986	1988	1990	1992	1994	1996	1998	2000	2002	2004	2006	2008	2010
Incumbents													
In jeopardy	9%	8%	15%	14%	17%	15%	14%	11%	8%	9%	14%	14%	17%
Shoo-ins	35	39	32	25	27	29	31	35	35	37	32	32	28
Challengers													
Hopefuls	9	8	15	14	17	15	14	11	8	9	14	14	17
Long shots	35	39	32	25	27	29	31	35	35	37	32	32	28
Open-seat candidates													
Prospects	7	5	5	13	9	8	7	6	8	4	5	6	4
Mismatched	4	3	1	9	5	4	3	3	5	4	4	3	6
N	*720*	*712*	*696*	*794*	*766*	*812*	*680*	*746*	*694*	*732*	*754*	*758*	*812*

Source: Compiled from Federal Election Commission data.

Notes: Figures are for major-party candidates in contested general elections, excluding incumbent-versus-incumbent races (which occasionally follow redistricting), runoff elections, and contests won by independents. Incumbents in jeopardy are defined as those who lost or who won by 20 percent or less of the two-party vote. Shoo-ins are incumbents who won by more than 20 percent of the two-party vote. Hopeful challengers are those who won or who lost by 20 percent or less of the two-party vote. Long-shot challengers are those who lost by more than 20 percent of the two-party vote. Open-seat prospects are those whose election was decided by 20 percent or less of the two-party vote. Mismatched open-seat candidates are those whose election was decided by more than 20 percent of the two-party vote. Some columns do not add to 100 percent because of rounding.

a successful write-in campaign against GOP nominee Joe Miller.[52] Sen. Arlen Specter of Pennsylvania, who had served in the Senate as a Republican for twenty-eight years and switched parties in April 2009 in order to avoid a likely loss in an upcoming GOP primary, was defeated in the Democratic primary by Rep. Joseph Sestak. Two other incumbents, both Democrats, lost in the general election (see Table 1-5). When the classification scheme used for House candidates is applied to the Senate (see Table 1-6), it becomes clear that the number of competitive contests has increased since 2004. Collectively, the results for 2010 provide further evidence that the political setting in a given election year has an impact on incumbents' prospects for reelection.

This overview of House and Senate elections demonstrates that substantial numbers of incumbents have faced significant opposition in recent years. It may be that in place of presidential coattails, members of the House and Senate now have to deal with a new era of electoral volatility that is both a cause and effect of the close competition over control of both chambers of

TABLE 1-5

Number of Unchallenged and Defeated Senate Incumbents, 1986–2010

	1986	1988	1990	1992	1994	1996	1998	2000	2002	2004	2006	2008	2010
Incumbents unchallenged by major-party opposition in general election	0	0	5	1	0	0	0	1	4	0	1	1	1
Incumbents defeated													
In primary	0	0	0	1	0	1	0	0	1	0	1	0	3
In general election	7	4	1	4	2	1	3	6	3	1	6	4	2

Sources: Compiled from various editions of *CQ Weekly* and *Congressional Roll Call* (Washington, D.C.: CQ Press). The primary and general results are from Norman J. Ornstein, Thomas E. Mann, and Michael J. Malbin, *Vital Statistics on Congress: 2001-2002* (Washington, D.C.: AEI Press, 2002), 70, and author's data.

Note: Sen. Joseph I. Leiberman, I Conn., was defeated in the 2006 Democratic primary in Connecticut and then won the general election as an independent candidate. Sen. Lisa Murkowski was defeated in the 2010 Republican primary in Alaska and then won the general election as a write-in candidate. They are included among the primary candidates but excluded from the general election data because they were not listed as major-party candidates on the general election ballot.

Congress. Regardless of whether legislators now face stronger challenges in nominating contests, in the general election, or in neither contest, as one member of Congress explained, "One can't be overconfident these days; I'm running scared. So are most of my colleagues."

The competitiveness of congressional elections influences the number of new faces in Congress. As a group, those serving in Congress are more diverse than those who served a decade ago. The House opened its first session of the 112th Congress with twelve more women, four more African Americans, and ten more Hispanics than had served in the 107th Congress. Change generally comes more slowly to the upper chamber. Seventeen female senators serve in the 112th Congress, three more than had served in the 107th. The Senate currently has no African Americans and only two Hispanics.

Despite this increased diversity, the vast majority of newcomers had at least one thing in common with one another and with their more senior colleagues: they came to Congress with significant political experience under their belts. Sixty of the ninety-four freshmen House members in the 112th Congress had previously held another public office; nine had served as party officials, worked as political aides or consultants, or run for Congress at least once

TABLE 1-6

Competition in Senate Elections, 1986–2010

	1986	1988	1990	1992	1994	1996	1998	2000	2002	2004	2006	2008	2010
Incumbents													
In jeopardy	20%	17%	20%	22%	23%	21%	15%	17%	18%	12%	22%	19%	13%
Shoo-ins	20	24	25	16	14	9	28	26	20	27	23	24	17
Challengers													
Hopefuls	20	17	20	22	23	21	15	17	18	12	22	19	13
Long shots	20	24	25	16	14	9	28	26	20	27	23	24	17
Open-seat candidates													
Prospects	12	12	3	21	14	35	9	15	24	22	7	6	25
Mismatched	6	6	7	3	11	6	6	0	0	0	3	9	17
N	*68*	*66*	*60*	*68*	*70*	*68*	*68*	*66*	*60*	*64*	*60*	*68*	*72*

Source: Compiled from Federal Election Commission data.

Notes: Figures are for major-party candidates in contested general elections. Incumbents in jeopardy are defined as those who lost or who won by 20 percent or less of the two-party vote. Shoo-ins are incumbents who won by more than 20 percent of the two-party vote. Hopeful challengers are those who won or who lost by 20 percent or less of the two-party vote. Long-shot challengers are those who lost by more than 20 percent of the two-party vote. Open-seat prospects are those whose election was decided by 20 percent or less of the two-party vote. Mismatched open-seat candidates are those whose election was decided by more than 20 percent of the two-party vote. Some columns do not add to 100 percent because of rounding.

before getting elected; and an unusually large group of twenty-six were political amateurs. Of the fifteen candidates sworn into the Senate for the first time in 2010, only Ron Johnson, R-Wis., had neither elective nor significant unelected political experience.[53]

SUMMARY

The Constitution, election laws, campaign finance regulations, and participatory nominations provide the institutional foundations for the candidate-centered congressional election system. The United States' history and individualistic political culture, which inform Americans' traditional ambivalence toward political parties, shore up that system. Candidates who can afford to hire political consultants to learn about and contact voters have benefited from technological advancements, which have allowed the system to assume its contemporary pro-incumbent, professionally oriented, money-fueled form.

How campaigns are conducted in the future will be influenced by changes currently under way in the strategic environment in which congressional seats are contested. Recent changes in campaign finance regulations, for example, especially those concerning soft-money expenditures on independent media campaigns and coordinated grassroots campaigns, will affect the abilities of candidates, political parties, and interest groups to influence the tenor and outcomes of congressional elections.

CHAPTER TWO

Candidates and Nominations

Can I win? Is this the right time for me to run? Who is my competition likely to be? These are the types of questions that go through the minds of prospective candidates. During the golden age of political parties, party bosses helped individuals decide whether to run for Congress. In many places the bosses' control over the party apparatus was so complete that, when in agreement, they could guarantee the nomination to the person they wanted to run. Moreover, receiving the nomination usually was tantamount to winning the election because strong political machines typically were located in one-party areas.[1]

After the golden age, party leaders had less control over the nomination process and less ability to ensure that the individuals they recruited would, in fact, win the nomination or the general election. Political parties are no longer the primary recruiters of congressional candidates. Party leaders encourage some individuals to run for office and discourage others, but local and national party committees serve more as vehicles that self-recruited candidates use to advance their careers than as gatekeepers that can make or break those careers. Party recruitment has been largely replaced by a process referred to as "candidate emergence."[2]

In this chapter I examine who decides to run for Congress, how potential candidates reach their decisions, and the influence of different individuals and groups on these decisions. I also examine the impact of candidate emergence and political experience on an individual's prospects of winning the nomination and the general election, and the implications of these contests on the representativeness of the national legislature.

STRATEGIC AMBITION

The Constitution, state laws, and the political parties pose few formal barriers to running for Congress, enabling virtually anyone to become a candidate. Members of the House are required to be at least twenty-five years of age, to have been U.S. citizens for at least seven years, and to reside in the state they represent. The requirements for the Senate are only slightly more stringent. In addition to having a state residence, senators must be at least thirty years old and have been U.S. citizens for nine or more years. Some states bar prison inmates, convicted felons, or individuals who have been declared insane from running for office, and most states require candidates to pay a small filing fee or to collect anywhere from a few hundred to several thousand signatures before having their names placed on the ballot. As is typical for election to public offices in many democracies, a dearth of formal requirements allows almost anyone to run for Congress. More than 1,600 people typically declare themselves candidates in most election years.

Although the formal requirements are minimal, other factors related to the candidate-centered nature of the election system favor individuals with certain personal characteristics. Strategic ambition—the combination of a desire to get elected, a realistic understanding of what it takes to win, and an ability to assess the opportunities presented by a given political context—is one such characteristic that distinguishes most successful candidates for Congress from the general public. Most successful candidates are self-starters because the electoral system lacks a tightly controlled party-recruitment process or a well-defined career path to the national legislature. Because the system is candidate centered, the desire, skills, and resources that candidates bring to the electoral arena are the most important criteria separating serious candidates from those who have little chance of getting elected. Ambitious candidates— sometimes referred to as "strategic," "rational," or "quality" candidates—are political entrepreneurs who make rational calculations about when to run. Rather than plunge right in, they assess the political context in which they would have to wage a campaign, consider the effects that a bid for office could have on their professional career and family, and carefully weigh their prospects for success.[3]

Strategic politicians examine many institutional, structural, and subjective factors when considering a bid for Congress.[4] The institutional factors include filing deadlines, campaign finance laws, nomination processes that allow or prohibit pre-primary endorsements, and other election statutes and party rules.

The structural factors include the social, economic, and partisan composition of the district; its geographic compactness; the media markets that serve it; the degree of overlap between the district and lower-level electoral constituencies; and the possibilities for election to some alternative office. One structural factor that greatly affects the strategic calculations of nonincumbents and is prone to fluctuate more often than others is whether an incumbent plans to run for reelection.

Potential candidates also assess the political climate when deciding whether to run. Strategic politicians focus mainly on local circumstances, particularly whether a seat will be vacant or whether the results of the previous election suggest that an incumbent is vulnerable.[5] National forces, such as a public mood that favors Democrats or Republicans or challengers or incumbents, are usually of secondary importance. The convergence of local and national forces can have a strong impact on the decisions of potential candidates. The widespread hostility the public directed at Congress and its members had a major influence on who ran in the 1994, 2006, 2008, and 2010 primaries and general elections. These forces motivated many would-be House members to believe that a seat in Congress was within their reach. In 1998, 2000, 2002, and 2004 national conditions and the public's positive feelings toward incumbents had the opposite effect.

Incumbents

For House incumbents the decision to run for reelection is usually an easy one. Congress offers its members many reasons to want to stay, including the ability to affect issues they care about, a challenging work environment, political power, and public recognition. It is also an ideal platform for pursuing a governorship, cabinet post, or even a seat in the Oval Office. Name recognition and the advantages inherent in incumbency—such as paid staff and the franking privilege (which have an estimated worth of between $2 million and $3 million per member per term)—are two factors that discourage strong opposition.[6] Furthermore, House members recognize that the "home styles" they use to present themselves to constituents create bonds of trust that have important electoral implications.[7]

Incumbents undertake a number of additional preelection activities to build support and ward off opposition. Most raise large war chests early in the election cycle to intimidate potential opponents.[8] Many keep a skeletal campaign organization intact between elections and use it to send their supporters campaign newsletters and other political communications. Some even shower their constituents with greeting cards, flowers, and other gifts.[9] Incumbents' activities in office and preelection efforts, as well as the fact that they have been elected to Congress at least once before, make most incumbents fairly certain that they will be reelected.

In some circumstances, however, incumbents recognize that it may be more difficult than usual to hold on to their seats. Redistricting, for example, can change the partisan composition of a House member's district, or it can force two incumbents to compete for one seat.[10] A highly publicized ethical transgression usually weakens an incumbent's reelection prospects. A weak economy, an unpopular president, a poor presidential candidate of the same party, or a wave of antigovernment hostility also can undermine legislators who represent marginal districts. These factors can influence incumbents' expectations about the quality of the opposition they are likely to face, the kinds of reelection campaigns they will need to wage, the toll those campaigns could take on them and their families, and their desire to stay in Congress.

When the demands of campaigning outweigh the benefits of getting reelected, strategic incumbents retire. Elections that immediately follow redistricting are often preceded by a jump in the number of incumbents who retire, as was the case in 1952, 1972, 1982, and 1992 (see Figure 2-1). The number of retirees jumped slightly in 2002 relative to the previous two elections, but fewer House members retired that year in comparison with most previous post-redistricting elections. This is most likely because of the pro-incumbent orientation of the redistricting that preceded the 2002 elections.

Elections held during periods of voter frustration, congressional scandal, or incivility within Congress itself also are preceded by high numbers of retirements.[11] A combination of redistricting, anti-incumbent sentiment, and a decline in comity in the House led 15 percent of all House members to retire in 1992—a post–World War II record. Whereas the numerous hard-fought elections that took place in 1994 inspired many congressional retirements in 1996, the number of members deciding not to run for reelection declined between 1998 and 2008. The relatively high appraisals of Congress that preceded some of those elections helped reduce the number of retirements. The efforts of party leaders, who wanted to minimize the number of open seats they had to defend so they could compete more effectively for control of the chamber, also helped to avert many retirements in those years. Similar efforts, mainly on the part of Democratic and Republican leaders, helped to minimize the number of retirements in 2010.[12]

Elections that occur following upheaval within Congress itself also are marked by large numbers of congressional retirements. The political reforms passed during the mid-1970s, which redistributed power from conservative senior House members to more liberal junior members, encouraged many senior

FIGURE 2-1

Number of Retirements by House Incumbents, 1950–2010

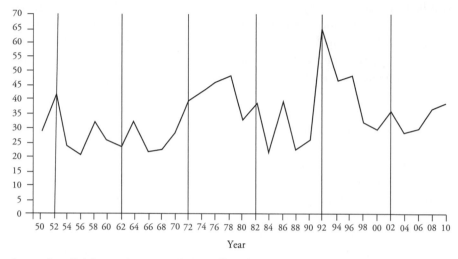

Sources: Compiled from various issues of *CQ Weekly* and *Congressional Roll Call* (Washington, D.C.: CQ Press), and Norman J. Ornstein, Thomas E. Mann, and Michael J. Malbin, *Vital Statistics on Congress, 2001–2002* (Washington, D.C.: AEI Press, 2002), 71.

members to retire from the House.[13] The Republican takeover of the House in 1994 encouraged large numbers of Democrats, and some Republicans, to retire. The Democrats' reclaiming control of the House in 2006 led to substantially more Republican than Democratic retirements prior to the 2008 election. The expansion of the Democrats' House majority following the 2008 election had a similar effect on retirements prior to the 2010 contest. For some Republicans, retirement was preferable to waging a reelection campaign that, if successful, could result in their continuing to suffer the powerlessness associated with being in the minority. For Democrats who were unpopular with their colleagues, leaving the House was preferable to enduring the indignity of being passed over for a committee chairmanship or some other leadership post.

The individuals most likely to retire from Congress are senior members who decide they would rather enjoy the fruits of old age than gear up for a tough reelection campaign; members who are implicated in some type of scandal; or members who have lost influence, anticipate losing it, or tire of having little in the first place.[14] The retirements that took place before the

2010 elections occurred for the usual reasons. Rep. Bart Stupak, D-Mich., chose to retire from an eighteen-year career in Congress after many of his constituents complained that his switch in position on health care reform was a flip-flop on a lifelong stance against abortion and he became a top target for defeat by Republicans and members of the Tea Party movement.[15] Rep. John Shadegg, R-Ariz., chose to end his six-year career in Congress after first losing the race for minority leader to current House Speaker John Boehner of Ohio, and next being defeated in the contest for minority whip by then-Rep. Roy Blunt of Missouri.

Scandal certainly cut short the careers of at least a few who left the House prior to the 2010 elections. Eric Massa, D-N.Y., resigned in March 2009, citing a health scare, but the ongoing House Ethics Committee investigation into allegations of sexual harassment of a male staffer undoubtedly contributed to his decision. Similarly, Rep. Mark Souder, R-Ind., an outspoken social conservative, decided to leave the House after it was revealed that he was having an extramarital affair with an aide in his district office. Rep. Nathan Deal, R-Ga., resigned in an effort to stop an Ethics Committee investigation of a conflict of interest between Deal's congressional duties and his ownership of an automobile salvage business.

At least some legislators give some thought to influencing future politics in their districts as they consider retirement. Rep. John Linder, R-Ga., for example, endorsed his former chief of staff Rob Woodall's bid to replace him in 2010.[16] Six years earlier, Rep. William Lipinski, D-Ill., announced his retirement from the House after easily winning renomination, laying the groundwork for his son Dan to replace him on the ballot. Lipinski Sr.'s attempt at legacy politics is not unusual; retiring members often try to create or continue family dynasties in Congress.[17]

Nonincumbents

More individuals with previous experience in elective office run for the House in election cycles that follow redistricting than in other years (see Figure 2-2).[18] Many of these candidates anticipate the opportunities that arise from the creation of new districts, the redrawing of old ones, or the retirements that often accompany elections after redistricting. The "pulling effects" of redistricting at the congressional level are sometimes accompanied by the "pushing effects" of the redistricting of state legislatures, county councils, and other offices. Term limits for state legislators, which were on the books in fifteen states in 2010, can have

FIGURE 2-2

Number of House Primary Candidates by Political Experience, 1978–2010

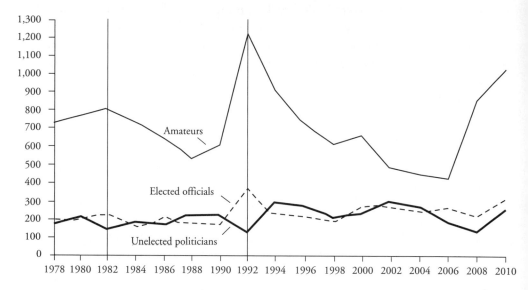

Sources: Compiled from candidates' websites and other public sources.

Note: Includes nonincumbent candidates for major-party nominations only.

the same impact.[19] The combined effects of redistricting, term limits, and other aspects of the political environment encouraged almost 300 major-party candidates who had experience holding an elective office to run in 2002. Roughly 250 individuals threw their hats into the ring in each of the four elections cycles that ensued, including in the 2010 cycle, at least in part due to their reading of the political conditions they would encounter.

Candidates who have significant campaign and political experience but who have never held elective office also respond to the opportunities that emerge in specific election years. These "unelected politicians" comprise legislative and executive branch aides, political appointees, state and local party officials, political consultants, and individuals who previously ran for Congress. Most of these politicians think strategically. Prior to deciding to run, they monitor voter sentiment, assess the willingness of political activists and contributors to support their campaigns, and keep close tabs on who is likely to oppose them for the nomination or in the general election.

Unelected politicians differ somewhat from elected officials and former officeholders in their perceptions of what constitutes a good time to run because elected officials weigh heavily in the strategic calculations of the unelected politicians. Unelected politicians appreciate that most elected officials possess more name recognition and fundraising advantages than they do. Unelected politicians typically balk at the opportunity to contest a primary against an elected official, even when other circumstances appear favorable. However, if a candidate with elective experience does not come forward, individuals with other significant forms of political experience will usually run. Relatively few unelected politicians viewed the 1982 and 1992 post-redistricting election cycle as promising for their causes. The pro-incumbent political environment discouraged unelected politicians from running. However, in 2002 and 2004 similar numbers of unelected politicians ran as did politicians with office-holding experience. In 2006 and 2008 the numbers of unelected politicians dropped off slightly, only to rebound to 307 in 2010.

Political amateurs are an extremely diverse group, and it is difficult to generalize about their political decision making. Only a small subgroup of amateurs, referred to as "ambitious amateurs," behave strategically, responding to the same opportunities and incentives that influence the decisions of more experienced politicians. Most amateurs do not spend much time assessing these factors. "Policy amateurs," comprising another subgroup, are driven by issues, whereas "experience-seeking amateurs" or "hopeless amateurs" run out of a sense of civic duty or for the thrill of running itself.[20] Republican challenger Susan Kone, who in 2010 ran against nine-term representative Jerrold Nadler in New York, exemplifies an experience-seeking challenger. Motivated by her discontent with "politics as usual" in Washington, D.C., disagreements with the incumbent over the issues, and disapproval of his treatment of constituents who opposed building a mosque near the site of the World Trade Center (located in the district), she also felt that no one should be elected to Congress without opposition. If elected, Kone, a self-styled "citizen statesman," planned to suspend her law practice, spend a few years in Congress trying to put the federal government on a better course, and then return to the private sector.[21]

The large number of amateurs who ran in the 1992 elections set a modern record, one not even approached until 2010. Some of the candidates who ran in recent election cycles were ambitious amateurs who, after weighing the costs of campaigning and the probability of winning, declared their candidacies. Many policy-oriented and experience-seeking amateurs also ran in these years. The 1992 and 1994 elections occured in political landscapes that were ideal for running issue-oriented or anti-incumbency campaigns. Calls for change and relentless government-bashing in the media provided reform-minded amateurs from both parties, but especially Republicans, with ready-made platforms. Those leaning toward the GOP ran in large numbers in both cycles, in large part as a response to the Democrats' longtime dominance of Congress. The political setting in 2010 was alluring to GOP amateurs of all types because of a groundswell of energy from the Tea Party movement and the public hostility toward the Democratic Party as a result of its control of the White House and both chambers of Congress during a period of sharp economic decline.

What appears to be a year of opportunity for strategic politicians of one party is often viewed as a bad year by their counterparts in the other party. Democrats with experience holding lower office considered 1986 to be a good year to run for the House; Republicans with similar levels of experience did not (see Figure 2-3). Elected officials of both parties were less enthusiastic about running in 1988, but GOP officeholders were more enthusiastic about running in 1990. The 1992 election was somewhat unusual in that strategic politicians from both parties judged the effects of redistricting, a weak economy, congressional scandal, and voter antipathy to hold tremendous possibilities.

The Republican takeover of Congress had a significant effect on candidate emergence in the 1996 elections. The number of Republican candidates with elective or significant nonelective experience decreased slightly after 1994 because many individuals in the GOP's candidate pool undoubtedly believed that their party had captured virtually every vulnerable Democrat-held seat in the tidal wave of that year. Demoralized by their party's low standing in the polls, President Bill Clinton's unpopularity, the House Republicans' initial legislative success, and the risk of political defeat, many Democratic elected officials also opted not to run in 1996, even against some vulnerable GOP freshmen. Democratic unelected politicians filled the void in some of these districts; political amateurs did likewise in others.

Riding the wave of President George W. Bush's popularity and widespread support for the Iraq War and the war on terrorism, more Republican than Democratic elected officials and unelected politicians ran for the House in 2004. This pattern reversed in 2006 as the president's poll numbers declined, support for continuation of the conflict in the Middle East waned, political scandals dominated the headlines, and the performance of the Republican-controlled federal government was heavily criticized. In 2008 the political environment did little to encourage the candidacies of Republicans with political experience, and the Democratic Party's success in the previous election reduced the number of opportunities for politically experienced Democrats to win a seat in the chamber.

The 2010 elections, however, provided Republicans with many opportunities. The outcomes of the previous two elections resulted in many first- and

FIGURE 2-3

House Primary Candidacies of Politicians by Party and Experience, 1978–2010

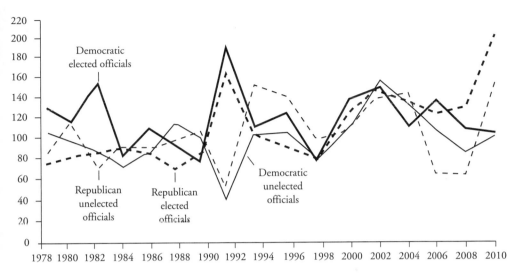

Sources: Compiled from various issues of *CQ Weekly,* candidates' websites, and other public sources.

Note: Includes candidates for major-party nominations only.

second-term Democrats occupying Republican-leaning seats. In addition to the vulnerabilities of these individual legislators, the nation's high jobless rate and overall economic difficulties combined with voters' antigovernment mood to create a positive environment for the GOP. As a result there was a substantial upsurge in the candidacies of Republicans who had office-holding and other significant political experience. Republican House candidates with relevant political experience outnumbered their Democratic counterparts by 75 percent.

Typically, most of the best-qualified office seekers wait until a seat opens, through either the retirement or the death of the incumbent, before throwing their hats into the ring.[22] Once a seat becomes vacant it acts like a magnet, drawing the attention and candidacies of many individuals. Usually several strategic politicians will express interest in an open seat. Open-seat races, defined as contests in which there is no incumbent at the beginning of the election season, accounted for roughly 10 percent of the 2010 House elections.[23] More than one-third of the elected officials of both parties who ran for the House that year competed in open-seat races (see Table 2-1). Substantially fewer numbers of unelected politicians and political amateurs

TABLE 2-1

Effect of Seat Status on Nonincumbent Candidates for House Nominations in 2010

	Democrats			Republicans		
	Elected	Unelected	Amateur	Elected	Unelected	Amateur
Open seat	37%	17%	19%	35%	15%	14%
Democratic incumbents seeking reelection	36	29	34	52	75	72
Republican incumbents seeking reelection	28	54	48	13	10	14
N	*104*	*100*	*263*	*203*	*155*	*768*

Source: Compiled from candidates' websites and other public sources.

Note: Some columns do not add to 100 percent because of rounding.

did likewise. Many undoubtedly were scared off by the candidacies of top-tier local officeholders.

   Incumbency usually discourages competition in primary elections, especially within the incumbent's party. In 2010, however, 36 percent of the Democratic elected officials who ran for the House were willing to challenge one of their party's incumbents for the nomination. Another 28 percent were willing to run in an incumbent-opposing primary—that is, in a primary that had the potential to earn them the right to oppose a Republican incumbent. It is not surprising that fewer Republican politicians were willing to attempt political fratricide. Voters are less likely to direct their anger at incumbents of the out-party during troubled times. Thus, GOP lawmakers did not appear as vulnerable as their Democratic counterparts. The result was that only 13 percent of the Republican-elected officials who ran for the House in 2010 challenged a GOP lawmaker in the primary and 52 percent ran in incumbent-opposing primaries to challenge a sitting House Democrat.

   The candidacies of unelected politicians and amateur candidates contrast with those of elected officials: unelected politicians are more likely to view as an opportunity a seat held by an incumbent of the opposing party, and amateurs are just about as likely as unelected politicians to run in these same contests. Compared with elected officials, these other candidates have fewer political costs to weigh when considering whether to enter a congressional primary. Prospective candidates who do not hold an elective office do not have to give up a current office to run for Congress, as do most officeholders whose positions are coterminous with congressional elections.[24] They also do not have to be as concerned about the effect a defeat could have on an established political career.

Others Involved in the Decision to Run

The drive to hold elective office may be rooted in an individual's personality and tempered by the larger political environment, but potential candidates rarely reach a decision about running for Congress without touching base with a variety of people.[25] Nearly all candidates single out their family and friends as being highly influential in their decision to enter a race.[26] Many young, talented, experienced, and well-connected local politicians who wanted a seat in Congress have remarked, only half in jest, that family members would probably shoot them if they decided to run. Family concerns, financial considerations, and career aspirations have kept many ambitious and highly regarded community leaders from running for Congress.

Political parties, labor unions, other organized groups, and political activists and consultants also can affect a prospective candidate's decision, but they have much less impact than the people directly involved in an individual's daily life. Potential candidates usually discuss their plans with these groups only after mulling over the idea of running with family members and friends. Sometimes would-be candidates approach local party leaders; fellow party members in the House or the Senate; or officials from their party's state, national, congressional, or senatorial campaign committees to learn about the kinds of assistance that would be available should they decide to run. On other occasions the party initiates the contact, seeking to nurture the interest of good prospects.

Barred from simply handing out the nomination, party leaders can influence a prospective candidate's decision to run in a variety of ways. They can help size up the potential competition and try to encourage some and discourage others from contesting the nomination.[27] In some states party leaders can help a candidate secure a pre-primary endorsement, but this does not guarantee nomination.

Members of Congress and the staffs of the Democratic and Republican congressional and senatorial campaign committees often encourage prospective candidates to run. Armed with favorable polling figures and the promise of party assistance in the general election, they search out local talent. Party leaders crisscross the country looking to sound out the best possible candidates for competitive districts. Sometimes they have a profile in mind, such as a candidate who can afford to self-finance most of an election campaign. Beginning in 2006, both parties sought out war veterans to run for Congress. These candidates enjoyed considerable success: almost three-fourths won their party's nomination in 2006, and about two out of five were victorious in 2008 and 2010.

Once the parties have identified promising individuals, they take steps to entice them to run. This can be a major challenge in districts or states in which a congressional seat is occupied by a member of the opposing party and may not look winnable at first glance, as appeared to be the case with many seats that the Republicans ultimately won in 2010. To help convince individuals to contest those seats, party leaders invite them to meet with members of Congress and other leaders in Washington, and to attend campaign seminars. They also give them lists of PACs and political consultants who possess some of the resources and skills needed to conduct a congressional campaign.[28] Some potential candidates are promised fundraising and campaign assistance by members of Congress and other politicians. Presidents, vice presidents, cabinet officials, high-ranking White House aides, or individuals who have previously held those posts also are often asked to try to entice prospective candidates to enter the race. In 2010 President Obama and Vice President Joe Biden participated in recruiting potential Democratic candidates. For the GOP, Republican National Committee Chair Michael Steele, former Alaska governor Sarah Palin, and some leaders from George W. Bush's administration were heavily involved in candidate recruitment. GOP primary activity was somewhat unusual in that some favorites of the Republican establishment faced strong opposition from outsider candidates associated with the Tea Party movement, including a few challenges that were successful.

When more than one candidate runs for a nomination, national party committees usually remain neutral unless a primary challenger seriously threatens an incumbent. On rare occasions, however, the parties' congressional and senatorial campaign committees will provide their preferred candidate with assistance in winning the primary. In addition, incumbent members of Congress are free to support primary candidates of their choosing. Many do because they consider a pre-primary contribution an opportunity to help elect a candidate who has a strong chance of winning, who shares their policy stances, or who is likely to support their own advancement up the ranks of the congressional leadership.

Party recruitment is especially important and difficult when local or national forces favor the opposing party. Just as a strong economy or popular president can encourage members of the president's party to run, it can discourage members of the opposition party from declaring their candidacies, most notably when an incumbent of the opposing party is seeking to remain in the seat. Sometimes the promise of party support can encourage a wavering politician to run under what, at the outset, appear to be less than optimal conditions.

Recruiting candidates to run for traditionally uncompetitive seats is not a major priority, but party committees work to prevent those seats from going uncontested. According to staffers from both parties' congressional and senatorial campaign committees, convincing candidates to run for these seats is an important part of building for the future. These efforts can expand the farm team from which candidates emerge and strengthen state and local party committees by giving them a campaign on which to focus. They also help prepare a party for opportunities that might arise when an incumbent retires, House districts are redrawn, or a scandal or some other event changes the partisan dynamics in the district.

Following their aggressive recruitment and success in Republican-occupied seats in the 2006 and 2008 elections and the anti-establishment mood taking hold of the nation, House Democrats recognized that they would have relatively few opportunities to recruit Democrats to contest traditionally GOP-held districts in 2010. However, an example of such a district was the Illinois 10th seat, which had been occupied by Republicans since 1980 and became open when the incumbent, Mark Kirk, decided to run for the Senate. The Democratic Congressional Campaign Committee (DCCC) provided encouragement and some support to Dan Seals and Julie Hamos, both of whom contested the Democratic primary in that district.[29]

The Republicans, sensing that the 2010 political environment would work to their advantage, pursued a recruitment strategy that aimed to broaden the field of competition. In addition to focusing on Republican-leaning seats that they had lost in the previous two elections, the National Republican Congressional Committee (NRCC) was also active in districts that were long considered Democratic strongholds. Finding candidates to run against very senior Democratic incumbents posed challenges, but the NRCC succeeded in recruiting strong candidates to run against Ike Skelton of Missouri, Jim Oberstar of Minnesota, Simon Ortiz of Texas, and many others who were elected as far back as the 1970s. Their efforts met with much success, as the GOP defeated several "old bulls," "wave babies" who were elected in 2006 and 2008, and incumbents whose seniority ranked in between.[30]

Labor unions, PACs, and other organized groups typically play limited roles in candidate recruitment compared to parties. A few labor PACs and some trade association committees, such as the Committee on Political Education (COPE) of the American Federation of Labor–Congress of Industrial Organizations (AFL-CIO) and the American Medical Association's AMPAC, take polls to encourage experienced politicians to run.[31] Others, such as the National Federation of Independent Business's PAC, sponsor campaign training seminars to encourage individuals who support the group's position to run for the House. Some ideological PACs, such as pro-abortion rights EMILY's List and Women's Campaign Fund, search out members of specific demographic groups and offer them financial and organizational support.[32] Labor unions focus most of their candidate-recruitment efforts, and campaign activities in general, on Democrats. Ideological groups are among the most aggressive in searching out candidates, and many offer primary assistance to those who share their views. Few corporate PACs become involved in recruiting candidates because they fear offending incumbents.

Political movements also can influence who enters the candidate pool. During the 2010 election, Tea Party activists motivated some individuals to run for Congress and offered encouragement, volunteer support, and modest contributions to their champions. Later in the election season, nationally affiliated organizations, such as the Tea Party Express, Tea Party Patriots, and FreedomWorks (led by former House Republican majority leader Dick Armey), offered endorsements, substantial financial support, and strategic assistance. The same is true of national leaders, such as Palin, and Republican senator Jim DeMint, R-S.C. However, it is important to note that few candidates received much in the way of formal Tea Party endorsements or campaign assistance until after they had won the Republican nomination.

Finally, political consultants can become involved in a potential candidate's decision. In addition to taking polls and participating in candidate-training seminars, consultants can use their knowledge of a state or district to assist a would-be candidate in assessing political conditions and sizing up the potential competition. Politicians who have had long-term relationships with consultants usually seek their advice before running for Congress.

PASSING THE PRIMARY TEST

There are two ways to win a major-party nomination for Congress: in an uncontested nominating race or by defeating an opponent. It is not unusual for incumbents to receive their party's nomination without a challenge. Even in the 1992 elections, which were marked by a record number of nonincumbent candidacies, 52 percent of all representatives and 42 percent of all senators who sought reelection were awarded their party's nomination without having to defeat an opponent. In 2010 about 56 percent of all representatives and 12 percent of all senators seeking reelection faced no primary opponent.

Incumbent Victories in Uncontested Primaries

Victories by default occur mainly when an incumbent is perceived to be invulnerable. The same advantages of incumbency and preelection activities that make incumbents confident of reelection make them seem invincible to those contemplating a primary challenge. Good constituent relations, policy representation, and other job-related activities are sources of incumbent strength. A hefty campaign account is another.

The loyalties of political activists and organized groups also discourage party members from challenging their representatives for the nomination. While in office, members of Congress work to advance the interests of those who supported their previous election, and in return they routinely receive the support of these individuals and groups. With this support comes the promise of endorsements, campaign contributions, volunteer campaign workers, and votes. Would-be primary challengers recognize that the groups whose backing they would need to win the nomination are often among the incumbent's staunchest supporters.[33]

Freshmen, sophomores, and other junior incumbents rarely have the same kind of clout in Washington or as broad a base of support as senior legislators, but because these members tend to devote a great deal of time to expanding their bases of support, they too typically discourage inside challenges.[34] Members lacking in seniority also may receive special attention from national, state, and local party organizations. Both the DCCC and the NRCC hold seminars immediately after each election to instruct these legislators on how to use franked mail, town meetings, and the local press to build voter support. Prior to the start of the campaign season, these party committees advise junior members on how to defend their congressional roll-call votes, raise money, and discourage opposition.

State party leaders also give junior members of Congress advice and assistance. During the redistricting process, many of these legislators receive what is perhaps the most important form of help state party leaders can bestow: a supportive district. Party leaders in state houses add areas with high concentrations of party identifiers who are predisposed to support the candidate. As a result, these candidates usually face little or no primary opposition and weak opposition in the general election. Indeed, almost immediately after the 2010 elections, Republican operatives began planning to use the redistricting process to protect newly elected GOP House members and senior Republicans in marginal seats, as well as reduce the reelection prospects of incumbent Democrats.

Considerations of teamwork rarely protect House members who are vulnerable because of scandal or party switching. These incumbents face stronger challenges from within their own party than do others. Experienced politicians often are willing to take on an incumbent whose reputation is tainted by scandal.

Contested Primaries with an Incumbent

When incumbents do face challenges for their party's nomination, they almost always win. Of the 175 House members who were challenged for their party's nomination in 2010, only four lost: Parker Griffith, R-Ala., who was elected to Congress in 2008 as a Democrat and switched parties a year later, was defeated by Madison County commissioner and longtime Republican Mo Brooks; Alan Mollohan, D-W.Va., who was under investigation for allegedly using his office to benefit family members and campaign contributors, was defeated by state senator Mike Oliverio; Carolyn Cheeks Kilpatrick, D-Mich., who was defeated by state senator Hansen Clarke in a campaign that was dominated by questions about her son, Kwame Kilpatrick, the former mayor of Detroit who went to prison over numerous corruption charges; and Bob Inglis, R-S.C., who was defeated by the Tea Party–backed candidate, solicitor Trey Gowdyn, in a primary run-off election after being portrayed as out of touch with the district.

What kinds of challengers succeed in knocking off an incumbent for the nomination? The answer is candidates who have had significant political experience. Only 18 percent of the Democratic and 18 percent of the Republican challengers who sought to defeat an incumbent in a 2010 House primary had been elected to lower-level office. Yet, these elected officials accounted for all of the four primary challengers who managed to wrest a party nomination away from an incumbent that year (see Table 2-2). This is typical, although unelected politicians also are occasionally successful. Experienced candidates occasionally succeed where others almost always fail because they are able to take advantage of previous contacts to gain the support of the political and financial elites who contribute to or volunteer in political campaigns. Elected officials can make the case that they have

TABLE 2-2
Political Experience and Major-Party Nominations for the House in 2010

	Challenges to incumbent		Contests to challenge an incumbent		Open seats	
	Demo-crat	Repub-lican	Demo-crat	Repub-lican	Demo-crat	Repub-lican
Level of experience						
Elected	18%	18%	14%	13%	39%	33%
Unelected	19	10	26	15	16	12
Amateur	62	72	60	72	45	55
N	*125*	*139*	*199*	*750*	*136*	*225*
Primary winners						
Elected	100%	100%	16%	24%	43%	56%
Unelected	0	0	27	14	23	14
Amateur	0	0	57	62	34	31
N	*2*	*2*	*114*	*208*	*35*	*36*
Primary success rates						
Elected	9%	8%	65%	51%	28%	27%
Unelected	0	0	59	26	37	19
Amateur	0	0	54	24	19	9

Source: Compiled from candidates' websites and other public sources.

Note: Figures are for nonincumbents only. Some columns do not add to 100 percent because of rounding.

represented some of the voters in the district and know what it takes to get elected. Some of these candidates consciously use a lower-level office as a stepping-stone to Congress.[35]

Oliverio's victory over Mollohan in West Virginia's 1st district primary highlights some of the factors that are usually present when a challenger defeats an incumbent in a nomination contest. Mollohan was first elected to Congress in 1982 to take the seat his father had held for sixteen years. He won a close reelection contest in 1984, but since then had faced little opposition in either a primary or general election. He won all of his bids for reelection with more than 60 percent of the vote. Indeed, he was reelected five times with no Republican opposition and faced a primary challenger only twice prior to 2010. He was a powerful figure on Capitol Hill, serving as the chair of the Commerce, Justice, Science, and Related Agencies Subcommittee of the House Appropriations Committee. Like others on the Appropriations Committee, he used his position to help his constituents. Between 1995 and 2006 he funneled $480 million in earmarks to his district.[36]

Mollohan's fourteen-term congressional career began to unravel in April 2006 when the Justice Department opened an investigation into his finances following a complaint by the conservative National Legal and Policy Center. Although dogged by the investigation, Mollohan was able to win reelection by substantial margins in the next two elections. He had weak Republican opposition in 2006 and none in 2008, in part because of the strong political environment favoring Democrats in those election cycles.[37]

In 2010 Oliverio, who had served in the West Virginia State Senate for sixteen years, provided Mollohan with his toughest primary challenge. Sensing the anti-Washington, conservative tide, Oliverio ran as a Washington outsider and to the right of Mollohan. He attacked the incumbent for not vigorously opposing cap-and-trade legislation, which had the potential to endanger the state's mining industry, and for supporting federal funding for abortions by voting for health care reform. These accusations were highly effective, if not entirely accurate—Mollohan did vote against cap-and-trade, had received the endorsement of the United Mineworkers PAC, and voted for the health care reform bill only after President Obama agreed to pass an executive order against using federal funds for abortions. Oliverio avoided raising questions about Mollohan's ethics problems, leaving that issue to be raised by the media. The challenger received favorable news coverage and won the endorsement of the Ogden Newspaper Group, which owns eight large newspapers in the district. On primary day, he defeated Mollohan with 56 percent of the vote.[38]

Oliverio's success can be attributed to a number of factors. He had a strong message and campaigned on issues that resonated with voters in the district. His campaign was well-organized, funded adequately, and received positive media coverage. He also ran in a political environment that favored change and against an opponent implicated in a scandal that was, to many voters, the embodiment of what was wrong in the nation's capital. As is often the case when a member of Congress loses a nomination contest, the challenger had significant political experience and adequate campaign resources, and the incumbent was accused of a serious ethical lapse.

Open Primaries

In opposing-incumbent primaries, contestants seek the nomination of one party when an incumbent of the opposing party has decided to seek reelection.

Another type of open nomination, called an open-seat primary, occurs in districts in which no incumbent is seeking reelection. Both types of primaries attract more candidates than do contests in which a nonincumbent must defeat an incumbent to win the nomination, but opposing-incumbent primaries are usually the less hotly contested of the two.

In opposing-incumbent primaries, political experience is usually a determining factor. Elected officials and unelected politicians do well in such primaries. In 2010 elected officials made up 14 percent of the Democratic candidates and 16 percent of the winners in these races. They enjoyed a nomination rate of 65 percent. Among the Republicans, they comprised 13 percent of the candidates and 24 percent of the winners, and had a success rate of 51 percent. Unelected politicians also did well in opposing-incumbent primaries in 2010. Among the Democrats, they included slightly more than one-fourth of both the candidates and winners, and they enjoyed a success rate of almost 60 percent. In the case of the Republicans, smaller numbers of unelected politicians ran in or won opposing-incumbent primaries, and those candidates had a substantially lower success rate. Political amateurs typically outnumber politically experienced candidates, and as a consequence they win more primaries. The contests in the 2010 election cycle were no exception. They also were typical in that the amateurs enjoyed lower success rates than the candidates who had more political experience.

Open-seat primaries are the most competitive of all nominating contests. They typically attract many highly qualified candidates, especially individuals who have experience holding elective office. Politically experienced candidates make up the largest share of primary winners and have the highest success rates. The 2010 elections were typical in that the success rates of political amateurs were substantially lower.

The Democratic and Republican primaries in Illinois' 10th district, like most open-seat primaries, were hard-fought contests. The seat became open when the Republican incumbent, Mark Kirk, decided to run for the Senate seat that was vacated when Barack Obama was elected president and thereafter held by Sen. Roland Burris, who, among much controversy concerning his Senate appointment, chose not to run for reelection. Numerous individuals contemplated running for the seat, and twelve declared their candidacies.

Five Democrats originally sought the House seat, including Dan Seals, who had lost to Kirk by 5-point margins in both 2006 and 2008, and Julie Hamos, Elliot Richardson, Michael Bond, and Milton Sumption. Four had considerable political experience. In addition to running for Congress twice, Seals had been an aide to Sen. Joseph Lieberman, D-Conn., and had worked in the U.S. Department of Commerce; Hamos had served ten years in the

Illinois General Assembly; Bond was a state senator; and Sumption worked as a legislative assistant for former Senate majority leader Tom Daschle, D-S.D. Richardson was the only political amateur. Bond and Sumption dropped out early in the race, due in part to a lack of funds, and it soon evolved into a hard-fought contest between Seals and Hamos. Each had good name recognition—Seals from his previous bids for the seat and Hamos from her state legislative career. Each was able to raise about $500,000 to contest the primary. Hamos received many endorsements from Illinois politicians, which would have been of major benefit in most years but were of limited help in the anti–political establishment 2010 election environment. Hamos suffered from some significant weaknesses. She had been running for state attorney general prior to declaring for the House, and she moved into the congressional district after declaring her candidacy for that office. Both of these facts raised some questions among Democratic primary voters about her political ambitions. Finally, the Seals campaign hammered her for being a political insider—ironically, that accusation would be levied against him in the general election. The primary was a nail-biter. Seals won with 48 percent of the vote and defeated Hamos by fewer than 1,000 votes. Richardson ran a distant third.[39]

Seven contestants lined up to contest the Republican primary, including five who had at least some political experience: Elizabeth Coulson had served seven terms in the Illinois legislature; Robert Dold had worked as an investigative counsel for the U.S. House Government Reform and Oversight Committee; William Cadigan had worked for former 10th district representative John Porter; Dick Green had been chair of the New Tier Republican Organization; and Patricia Bird had previously run for mayor of a city in the district. The race also featured two candidates who had no political experience: pediatrician Arie Friedman and retired electrical engineer Paul Hamann. Cadigan and Bird pulled out of the contest early, citing fundraising shortfalls, and the race quickly boiled down to a two-person contest between Dold and Coulson. Both candidates were strong fundraisers: each raised more than $500,000 to contest the primary. However, Dold enjoyed some significant advantages, including the support of the Tea Party movement and the fact that Coulson's thirteen years in state government, normally an asset, became a liability in an election environment focused on change. Dold won the nomination with 38 percent of the vote, followed by Coulson, who garnered 34 percent.

These contests support some generalizations about primaries for open seats. First, they attract relatively large numbers of candidates, including candidates with relevant political experience. Second, they are expensive. Third, with no incumbent in the race, they can be strongly influenced by the political environment. And finally, the lack of an incumbent increases potential for the influence of activist groups, such as the Tea Party movement.

A Note on the Tea Party

Although the Tea Party movement motivated many individuals to run for Congress and many of its candidates were victorious in the general election, it is virtually impossible to gauge the movement's impact on primary election outcomes in 2010.[40] Despite the fact that some candidates for a GOP nomination claimed Tea Party affiliations, it is important to recognize that Tea Party groups are on record as having made fewer than thirty pre-primary endorsements. This is in part because the movement did not have much of a presence until relatively late in the nomination season. In addition, most nascent locally based movements often lack the leadership and procedures to endorse candidates, which allows activists and candidates who self-associate with groups such as the Tea Party to give and claim various indications of group support; however, this falls far short of a formal endorsement. When many individuals and candidates involved in a nomination contest publicize that they have bestowed or received the backing of a group associated with a movement like the Tea Party, it presents a muddled picture to primary voters and is of limited usefulness.

NOMINATIONS, ELECTIONS, AND REPRESENTATION

The electoral process—which transforms private citizen to candidate to major-party nominee to House member—greatly influences the makeup of the national legislature. Those parts of the process leading up to the general election, especially the decision to run, play an important role in producing a Congress that is not demographically representative of the U.S. population. The willingness of women and minorities to run for Congress during the past few decades and of voters to support them has helped make the national legislature somewhat more representative in regard to gender and race. Still, in many respects, Congress does not mirror U.S. society.

Occupation

Occupation has a tremendous effect on the pool of House candidates and on their prospects for success. Individuals (many of whom have legal training) who claim law, politics, or public service as their professions are only about 2

TABLE 2-3

Occupational Representativeness of 2010 House Candidates and Members of the 112th Congress

	General population	Nomination candidates	General election candidates	House members
Agriculture or blue-collar workers	23%	2%	2%	2%
Business or banking	10	36	34	30
Clergy or social work	1	3	2	1
Education	4	7	7	7
Entertainer, actor, writer, or artist	1	2	2	1
Law	1	15	22	26
Politics or public service	1	9	15	21
Medicine	5	6	5	6
Military	—	4	2	1
Other white-collar prefessionals	19	6	4	3
Outside workforce	35	1	1	—
Unidentified, not politics	—	9	3	—
N	224.9 million	2,157	840	435

Sources: General population figures are from U.S. Department of Commerce, Bureau of the Census, *Statistical Abstract of the United States* (Washington, D.C.: U.S. Government Printing Office, 2010); candidate data were compiled from candidates' websites and other public sources.

Notes: Figures include major-party House candidates and House members only. The Census Bureau calculates occupation figures for individuals aged sixteen and older. — = less than 0.5 percent. Some columns do not add to 100 percent because of rounding.

percent of the working population, but in the 2010 elections they made up almost 24 percent of all nomination candidates and 37 percent of all general election candidates. In the 112th Congress they comprised 47 percent of all House members (see Table 2-3). The analytical, verbal, and organizational skills required to succeed in the legal profession or in public service help these individuals undertake a successful bid for Congress. The high salaries that members of these professions earn give them the wherewithal to take a leave of absence from work so that they can campaign full time. These highly paid professionals also can afford to make the initial investment needed to get a campaign off the ground. Moreover, their professions place many attorneys and public servants, particularly those who already hold office, in places where they can rub elbows with political activists and contributors whose support can be crucial to winning a House primary or general election.

Business professionals and bankers, comprising 10 percent of the population, are not as overrepresented among general election candidates or House members as are public servants and lawyers, but they also are very successful in getting elected. Many possess money, skills, and contacts that are useful in politics. Educators (particularly college professors) and other white-collar professionals also enjoy a modicum of success in congressional elections. Of these, educators are the most successful group of candidates. They rarely possess the wealth of lawyers and business professionals, but educators frequently have the verbal, analytical, and organizational skills needed to get elected. Although both parties have taken to recruiting veterans in recent years and ninety-two House members serving in the 112th Congress, including twenty-five freshman, have done some form of military service, typically very few members of Congress are drawn from the ranks of the career military.[41]

Just as some professions are overrepresented in Congress, others are underrepresented. Disproportionately few persons employed in agriculture or blue-collar professions either run for Congress or are elected. Even fewer students, homemakers, and others who are considered outside the workforce attempt to win a congressional seat.

Closely related to the issue of occupation is wealth. Personal wealth is a significant advantage in an election system that places a premium on a candidate's ability to spend money. Between 6 and 7 percent of House members have assets worth in excess of $5 million; the percentage of the general population who enjoy a similar level of wealth is much lower.[42]

Gender

The 2010 elections represent a small setback for women. Although record numbers ran for the House, only seventy-two were elected, and the number of women sworn into Congress actually declined for the first time since 1979. Women constitute only 17 percent of the House in the 112th Congress.

The major reason for the underrepresentation of women in the legislative branch is that fewer women than men run for Congress (see Figure 2-4). Only 14 percent of all contestants for major-party nominations in 2010 were female. Women are underrepresented among congressional candidates for many reasons. Active campaigning demands greater time and flexibility than most people, particularly women, can afford. Women continue to assume primary parenting responsibilities in most families, a role that is difficult to

FIGURE 2-4

Gender Representativeness of 2010 House Candidates and Members of the 112th Congress

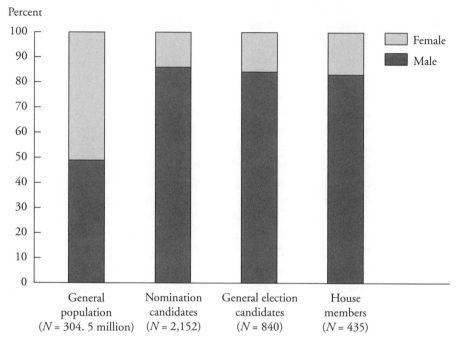

Sources: General population figures are from U.S. Department of Commerce, Bureau of the Census, and *Statistical Abstract of the United States* (Washington, D.C.: U.S. Government Printing Office, 2010); candidate data were compiled from candidates' websites and other public sources.

Note: Figures include major-party House candidates and House members only.

combine with long hours of campaigning. Only since the 1980s have significant numbers of women entered the legal and business professions, which often serve as training grounds for elected officials and political activists. Despite making significant gains over the last few decades, women also continue to be underrepresented in state legislatures and the other elective offices that commonly serve as stepping-stones to Congress. Moreover, women who occupy positions in society from which congressional candidates usually emerge are less likely than similarly situated men to believe they possess the qualifications, skills, or traits needed to campaign for or hold public office.[43]

Nevertheless, once women decide to run, gender does not undermine their election prospects.[44] Indeed, although they typically face more competition in congressional primaries, women are at least as likely as men to advance from primary candidate to nominee to House member.[45] As more women occupy

FIGURE 2-5

Age Representativeness of 2010 House Candidates and Members
of the 112th Congress

Percent

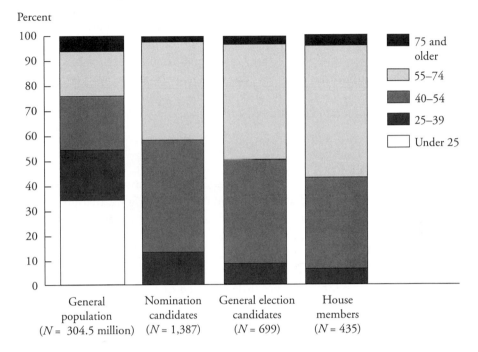

Sources: General population figures are from U.S. Department of Commerce, Bureau of the Census, and *Statistical Abstract of the United States* (Washington, D.C.: U.S. Government Printing Office, 2010); candidate data were compiled from candidates' websites and other public sources.

Note: Figures include major-party House candidates and House members only.

lower-level offices or hold positions in the professions from which congressional candidates usually emerge, one can expect that the number of women who consider a bid for Congress, run, and get elected will increase.[46]

Age

Congressional candidates also are somewhat older than the general population, and this is due only partly to the age requirements imposed by the Constitution. The typical candidate for nomination is almost three times as likely to be forty to fifty-four years of age as twenty-five to thirty-nine (see Figure 2-5). Moreover, successful nomination candidates tend to be slightly older than those whom they defeat. There is a strong selection bias in favor of those who are fifty-five and older that continues into the general election; as a result, Congress is made up largely of persons who are middle-aged or older.

The underrepresentation of young people is due to an electoral process that enables older individuals to benefit from their greater life experience. People who have reached middle age typically have greater financial resources, more political experience, and a wider network of political and professional associates to help them with their campaigns. Moreover, a formidable group of people who are forty to seventy-four years old—current representatives—also benefit from considerable incumbency advantages.

Religion

Religion has an impact on candidate emergence, sometimes providing politicians with a policy concern, such as abortion or human rights, that gives them the motivation to run. Jews, mainline Protestants, and other Christians are overrepresented in the candidate pool (see Figure 2-6). Those belonging to other religions—including Buddhists and Muslims—and individuals who profess to have no religious affiliation are underrepresented. Yet, once individuals enter the pool, religion has little effect on how they do.

Individuals who claim no religious identification make up the most underrepresented "belief" group in Congress for a few reasons. People who do not participate in church activities typically have fewer political and civic skills compared with those who do, which may discourage them from running for Congress.[47] Atheists and agnostics also may believe that it would be impossible for them to get elected given the large role that organized religion plays in politics in many parts of the country. As a result, they have little presence in politics or national government.

Race and Ethnicity

Race and ethnicity, like gender and religion, have a greater effect on candidate emergence than on electoral success.[48] Whites are heavily overrepresented in the pool of nomination candidates, whereas persons of other races are underrepresented (see Figure 2-7). This situation reflects the disproportionately small numbers of minorities who have entered the legal or business professions or who occupy state or local offices.

Once minority politicians declare their candidacies, they have fairly good odds of winning their party's nomination and getting elected. The recent

FIGURE 2-6

Religious Representativeness of 2010 House Candidates and Members
of the 112th Congress

Percent

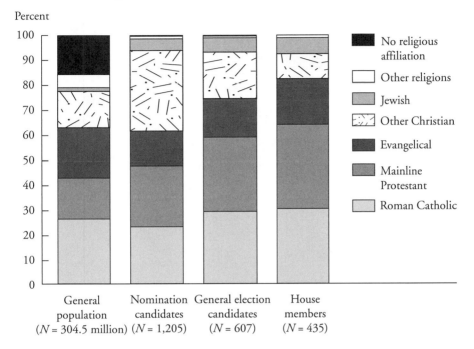

Legend:
- No religious affiliation
- Other religions
- Jewish
- Other Christian
- Evangelical
- Mainline Protestant
- Roman Catholic

General population (*N* = 304.5 million) Nomination candidates (*N* = 1,205) General election candidates (*N* = 607) House members (*N* = 435)

Sources: General population figures are compiled from Barry A. Kosmin and Ariela Keysar, *American Religious Identification Survey,* Program on Public Values, Trinity College, March 2009; candidate data were compiled from candidates' websites and other public sources.

Note: Figures include major-party House candidates and House members only.

successes of minority House candidates are largely due to redistricting processes intended to promote minority representation.[49] A few House members,
such as Tim Scott, R-S.C., and Allen West, R-Fla., both elected with the support of the Tea Party in 2010, won seats that were not specifically carved to
promote minority representation in Congress. Still, most minority candidates
are elected in districts that have large numbers of voters belonging to their
racial or ethnic group, and once they win these seats they tend to hold onto
them. Only two such incumbents were defeated in 2010: Reps. Solomon
Ortiz, D-Texas, and Carolyn Cheeks Kilpatrick, D-Mich.[50] The success of the
minority members of Congress can be attributed to their ability to build mul-
tiracial coalitions and the advantages that incumbency confers on them.[51]

FIGURE 2-7

Racial and Ethnic Representativeness of 2010 House Candidates and
Members of the 112th Congress

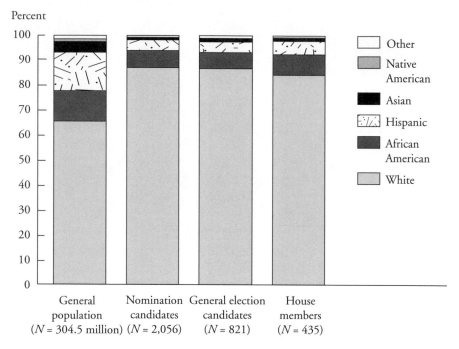

Sources: General population figures are from U.S. Department of Commerce, Bureau of the Census, and
Statistical Abstract of the United States (Washington, D.C.: U.S. Government Printing Office, 2010); candidate data were compiled from candidates' websites and other public sources.

Note: Figures include major-party House candidates and House members only.

Party Differences

Public servants and members of the legal profession make up a large portion
of each party's candidate pool, but more Republican candidates come from the
business world and more Democratic candidates are lawyers and public servants (see Table 2-4). The GOP's overrepresentation of business professionals
continues through virtually each stage of the election, as does the Democrats'
overrepresentation of lawyers and career politicians. Attorneys and career public servants from both parties do well in elections, but they are more strongly
represented in the Democratic than the Republican Party. Business executives,
in contrast, have a bigger presence in the ranks of Republican legislators. Even

TABLE 2-4

Major-Party Nomination and General Election Candidates in 2010 and House Members of the 112th Congress

	Nomination candidates		General election candidates		House members	
	Dem	Rep	Dem	Rep	Dem	Rep
Occupation						
Agriculture or blue collar worker	2%	2%	3%	1%	2%	2%
Business or banking	25	42	24	44	18	40
Clergy or social work	4	2	4	1	2	0
Education	11	5	11	4	10	5
Entertainer, actor, writer, or artist	3	2	2	2	1	1
Law	19%	13%	24%	19%	31%	23%
Medicine	5	6	3	7	3	8
Military	2	5	2	3	0	3
Other white-collar professionals	5	6	5	3	3	3
Outside workforce	2	1	1	1	1	0
Politics or public service	14	7	20	11	29	15
Unidentified, not politics	9	10	3	3	1	0
N	*763*	*1,395*	*405*	*421*	*193*	*242*
Gender						
Male	79%	89%	77%	90%	75%	90%
Female	21	11	23	10	25	10
N	*760*	*1,392*	*407*	*421*	*193*	*242*
Age						
25–39	11%	15%	8%	9%	5%	7%
40–54	37	50	34	50	26	46
55–74	50	34	55	38	64	44
75 and over	3	1	3	3	6	3
N	*537*	*850*	*354*	*345*	*193*	*242*
Religion						
Catholic	28%	21%	32%	26%	37%	26%
Protestant	26	24	27	33	25	41
Evangelical	12	15	12	18	16	20
Jewish	10	2	11	1	14	—

(Table continues)

TABLE 2-4   *(continued)*

	Nomination candidates		General election candidates		House members	
	Dem	Rep	Dem	Rep	Dem	Rep
Other Christian	21%	39%	16%	21%	6%	13%
Other	2	1	2	—	2	—
No affiliation	1	—	—	—	—	—
N	*419*	*786*	*304*	*332*	*193*	*242*
Race and Ethnicity						
White	76%	93%	80%	93%	69%	96%
African American	14	3	10	3	18	1
Hispanic	7	3	6	3	8	3
Other	2	2	4	1	5	—
N	*723*	*1,329*	*402*	*419*	*193*	*242*

Sources: Compiled from candidates' websites and other public sources.

Notes: Figures are for major-party House candidates and House members only. — = less than 0.5 percent. Some columns do not add to 100 percent because of rounding.

though Republicans have historically been viewed as the defenders of the rich, members of both parties are found among Congress's wealthiest legislators.[52]

Despite a record number of women contesting GOP House primaries in 2010, typically more women run as Democrats than as Republicans. This gender gap reflects the greater number of women who identify with the Democratic Party and that party's greater acceptance of female candidates. Democratic women also are more successful in winning the nomination and getting elected to the House than are their GOP counterparts.

Democratic primary candidates tend to be somewhat older than their Republican counterparts, reflecting the different orientations of the individuals in the parties' candidate pools. Democratic primary candidates are more likely to come from the ranks of politicians and to consider a congressional election as a somewhat risky opportunity to take a step up the career ladder. Members of the Republican candidate pool are more apt to have careers in the private sector. Many run for Congress before they have taken major strides in their profession, recognizing that if they wait too long, they may have advanced too far professionally to want to sacrifice a career in order to run. The initial age difference between Democratic and Republican candidates lays the foundation for an uneven trend toward a Congress dominated by members of both parties who are middle-aged or older.

The parties also draw candidates from different racial and ethnic groups. Republican primary contestants, nominees, and House members are overwhelmingly white, while their Democratic counterparts include substantially more African Americans and Hispanics. The Democratic Party also attracts and elects candidates who have a somewhat wider array of religious backgrounds than the GOP. Reflecting each party's electoral base, the Democratic Caucus has more Catholics and Jews and the Republican Conference has greater numbers of mainstream and evangelical Protestants and other Christians.

THE SENATE

The Senate historically has been less demographically representative than the House. The election of more women and minorities during the past few decades has resulted in a slow move toward more accurately mirroring the U.S. population. However, descriptions of the Senate as a bastion for white, wealthy, middle-aged, professional men are very close to the mark.

Part of the reason why the Senate has been slower to change than the House is that Senate terms are six years, and only one-third of the upper chamber is up for election at a time. Other reasons have to do with the heightened demands of Senate campaigns. As statewide races, Senate primary and general election campaigns require larger amounts of money, more extensive organization, and more complex strategies than do House campaigns. Successful Senate candidates generally possess more skill, political connections, and campaign experience than do their House counterparts. The fact that so many members of the Senate had extensive political experience prior to their election suggests that the dearth of women and minorities in lower-level offices may help to explain why the upper chamber is changing more slowly than the lower. To gain seats in the Senate, traditionally underrepresented groups have had to place their members in positions that serve as stepping-stones to that body. As more women, African Americans, and members of other underrepresented groups are elected or appointed to local, state, and federal offices, their numbers in the Senate will probably increase.

Nevertheless, a single election can have a great effect on the Senate's makeup. After the polls closed in 1992, the number of women was set to increase from two to six, including the Senate's first African American woman, Illinois Democrat Carol Moseley-Braun. In addition, the Senate prepared to swear in its first Native American, Coloradan Ben Nighthorse Campbell. Few ensuing elections had as big an impact on the demographic makeup of the

Senate. Indeed, its diversity has increased at a slow pace. Following the 2010 election, there were seventeen women, two Hispanics, two Asian Pacific Americans, and no African Americans.

Even though traditionally underrepresented groups have increased their numbers in the Senate, this does not mean that the upper chamber has become a place of employment for individuals with a diverse array of backgrounds. Thirty-nine of the senators in the 112th Congress were drawn from the legal profession, including several who also worked in other fields. About a dozen or so had careers in public service. Nineteen had worked in business or banking. Nine had been involved in education. Four had been journalists and another three had practiced medicine. One—Sen. Al Franken, D-Minn.—had been a comedian. The average age for a senator was sixty-two when the 112th Congress was sworn in.[53]

Most senators had significant political experience prior to getting elected, often having held more than one elective office. Forty-nine of the senators in the 112th Congress had previously served in the U.S. House of Representatives, nine had been governors of their states, ten had held some other elected state-wide office, and nineteen had been elected to a state legislature or local office.[54] Nine senators, including four freshmen, had not previously held elective office, but it is important to note that three of the freshmen—Kelly Ayotte, R-N.H., Michael Lee, R-Utah, and Rand Paul, R-Ky.— had significant political experience and exposure to elective politics: Ayotte served as the attorney general of New Hampshire; Lee as U.S. solicitor general in the Reagan administration; and Paul, the son of Texas House member and 2008 and 2012 candidate for the Republican presidential nomination Ron Paul, was founder and chair of the anti-tax organization Kentucky Taxpayers United.

Although senators are more likely than representatives to have to defend their nominations, Senate primaries tend to be less competitive than those for the House. Between 1982 and 2008, only four senators were defeated in their bids for renomination.[55] In 2010 three incumbent senators went down in defeat, a recent record. However, one—Lisa Murkowski of Alaska—was able to resurrect her Senate career by mounting a victorious write-in campaign in the general election.

The relative ease with which members of the Senate usually retain their party's nomination can be attributed to a number of factors besides the tremendous demands that Senate primary contests make on challengers. For one thing, senators and Senate candidates are highly strategic. Like their counterparts in the House, members of the Senate use their office to help their state receive its share of federal projects, to garner positive coverage in the press, and to build support among voters. Senators, like representatives, also build huge campaign treasuries to discourage potential opponents. In addition, most members of the Senate are shrewd enough to recognize when it is time to step down. In 2010, twelve senators opted for voluntary retirement from politics. This unusually large number of retirees included four who were appointed rather than elected, four who were over the age of sixty-seven, two who were involved in ethical controversies, and one who ran for governor. The retirees of 2010 amply demonstrate that the effects of scandal, aging, infirmity, declining public support, and strategic ambition on Senate turnover tend to be felt more through members' retirements than primary defeats. Another important explanation for the fact that senators are rarely defeated for their party's nomination is that the most qualified opponent a senator is likely to face is another strategic politician. Whether a current House member or another elected official, few of these individuals are willing to risk their current positions by picking a primary fight. Most prefer to wait until a seat becomes open.

When an incumbent does announce an upcoming retirement, or a member of the opposite party appears vulnerable, political parties and interest groups help to shape the field of Senate candidates by encouraging potential candidates to declare their candidacies. These organizations promise the same types of support, under the same kinds of circumstances, to potential Senate candidates as they offer to House candidates. In 2010, for example, the National Republican Senatorial Committee (NRSC) played a significant role in encouraging the Senate candidacies of Rep. Mike Castle of Delaware, Lieutenant Governor Jane Norton of Colorado, and business executive Carly Fiorina of California, and the Democratic Senatorial Campaign Committee (DSCC) helped recruit Missouri secretary of state Robin Carnahan and New Hampshire representative Paul Hodes.[56] The DSCC also sought to get Delaware attorney general Beau Biden, son of Vice President Biden, to commit to a race for the Senate. However, the younger Biden declined. Perhaps he anticipated he would be unable to defeat Castle, who two years earlier was reelected to Delaware's at-large House with more than 61 percent of the vote.

Traditionally, party organizations have not become involved in contested Senate primaries, even though they may promise a candidate from hundreds of thousands to millions of dollars in campaign support upon winning the nomination. The major exception to this rule is when an incumbent faces a difficult challenge. Under this circumstance, the DSCC and NRSC, like their House counterparts, support the incumbent. Both committees were very active in the nomination contests that resulted in defeated incumbents and a few others. Senators, on the other hand, are free to become involved in primaries, and many do. Sometimes this leads to conflict within a party. During the 2010 nomination season, there were some high-profile instances when

Republican Senate leaders backed relatively moderate so-called "establishment" candidates, and Sen. Jim DeMint, R-S.C., and other conservative GOP members supported candidates backed by the Tea Party. Regardless of the outcomes of divisive nomination contests, the parties' senatorial campaign committees seek to unite the party behind the victor and provide campaign support in the general election.

Whether successful or not in specific cases, the senatorial campaign committees are singled out by candidates as the most influential organizations involved in the candidate recruitment process. They are not as important as family and friends, issues, or a desire to improve government or become a national leader, but they are more influential in the decisions of candidates than are other political organizations.[57] In this sense, candidate emergence in Senate elections is similar to that in the House.

SUMMARY

Virtually anyone can run for Congress because there are few legal requirements for serving, and neither party committees nor interest groups have the power to simply hand out a congressional nomination. Strategic politicians, mainly individuals who have held office or have some other significant nonelective experience, carefully assess political conditions before deciding to run. Most incumbents—who are the most strategic of all politicians—choose to run again, but personal considerations, a loss of political clout in Congress, redistricting, scandal, or a wave of voter hostility toward the federal government or their party can encourage incumbents to retire. These factors also have an impact on the candidacy decisions of strategic nonincumbents, but the opening of a congressional seat is even more important than other political conditions in spurring on their candidacies. Amateur politicians tend to be less discriminating and are less likely to win their party's nomination.

Candidate emergence, nomination, and election processes have a major impact on who serves in Congress. Most members of the contemporary House and Senate are white, middle- or upper-class males. Most are middle-aged or older and belong to a mainstream religion. The vast majority also had significant political experience prior to getting elected. Overall, the number of national legislators who belong to underrepresented groups has increased in recent years, but change comes slowly to Congress, especially in the Senate.

CHAPTER THREE

The Anatomy of a Campaign

What types of organizations do candidates assemble to run for Congress? How do they budget their resources? This chapter addresses these two questions. During the parties' golden age, the answers were simple: most House and Senate candidates relied on state and local party committees to campaign for them, and the parties decided how much to spend on different election activities. An individual candidate's "organization" was often little more than a loyal following within the party. But by the mid-1950s, few congressional candidates could count on party organizations to obtain their nominations and wage their campaigns. Senate campaigns became significantly more professional during the 1950s and 1960s; House campaigns followed suit during the 1970s.[1] The decline of the political machine and the legal and systemic changes that fostered that decline led to the development of the modern campaign organization.[2]

Most contemporary congressional campaigns are conducted by specialized, professional organizations. Few campaign organizations are fully self-sufficient. Most employ paid staff and volunteers to carry out some of the tasks associated with running for Congress and hire political consultants to perform skilled campaign activities such as taking polls and producing campaign ads. But consultants do more than carry out isolated campaign tasks. Political consulting has become a profession, replete with its own standards, trade association, newsletters, and magazine. Consultants help budding politicians learn what to expect and what will be expected of them during the campaign. Consultants' opinions of what is strategically and tactically advisable and ethical have a major impact on candidate conduct.[3] In this chapter I describe campaign organizations, focusing on the political consultants and other personnel who work in them and on how campaigns spend their money.[4]

CAMPAIGN ORGANIZATIONS

Candidates need to achieve several interrelated objectives to compete successfully in an election, including raising money, formulating a strategy, and communicating with and mobilizing voters. Specialized skills and training are required to meet many of these objectives. Senate campaigns, which are larger and must typically reach out to more voters, employ more paid staff and consultants than do their House counterparts.

The biggest factor in House campaigns is incumbency. Assembling a campaign organization is an easy task for incumbents. Most reassemble the personnel who worked on their previous campaign. A substantial number of incumbents keep elements of their organizations intact between elections. Some of these consist only of a part-time political aide or fundraiser. Others are quite substantial, possessing the characteristics of a permanent business. They own a building and have a large professional staff; a fundraising apparatus; an investment portfolio; a campaign car; an entertainment budget; and a team of lawyers, accountants, and consultants on retainer. House incumbents typically spend hundreds of thousands of dollars on organizational maintenance during the two years leading up to an election. Some members of Congress put together "Cadillac" campaigns. The 2010 campaign of nine-term representative Jerrold Nadler, D-N.Y., who has won with at least 75 percent of the vote in every one of his elections including 2010, was a top-of-the-line luxury model. Nadler spent approximately $1.5 million, including roughly 60 percent allocated to administration and fundraising and another 17 percent given away to candidates, party committees, and other groups. Two-term House member Michele Bachmann, R-Minn., whose political aspirations extend beyond the House (she announced her presidential candidacy in June 2011), fielded a campaign that could be likened to a NASCAR vehicle. She spent more than $11.6 million on reelection, including $1.6 million on staff, rent, office equipment, and other administrative costs, and another $3.7 million on fundraising.[5]

Few House challengers or open-seat candidates possess even a temporary organization capable of contesting a congressional election until just before their declaration of candidacy. Nonincumbents who have held an elective post usually have advantages when assembling a campaign organization. Some have steering committees, "Friends of Candidate *X*" clubs, or working relationships with political consultants from previous elections. Candidates who have never held an elective office but have been active in politics usually have advantages over political amateurs when building an organization. Previous political involvement gives party committee chairs, political aides, individuals who have previously run for office, and other unelected politicians some knowledge of how to wage a campaign and ties to others who can help them. The organizational advantages that incumbents possess over challengers are usually greater than the advantages that unelected politicians have over political amateurs.[6]

Almost nine out of ten House members' campaign organizations are managed by a paid staffer or some combination of a paid staffer and outside consultant (see Table 3-1). Often the campaign manager is the administrative assistant or chief of staff in the House member's congressional office. Administrative assistants and other congressional staffers routinely take leaves of absence from their jobs to work for their boss's reelection, sometimes as volunteers because they consider the bonuses or high salaries they receive as congressional aides to be compensation enough. Shoo-in incumbents (those who were reelected by more than 20 percent of the two-party vote) are just about as likely as incumbents in jeopardy (those who lost or won by less than 20 percent of the two-party vote) to hire a paid staffer to handle day-to-day management and a general consultant to assist with campaign strategy. Most hopeful challengers (those who eventually won or lost by 20 points or less) have professionally managed campaigns, but only 37 percent of all long-shot challengers (those who eventually lost by more than 20 percent of the vote) have campaigns managed by a paid staffer or general consultant. Many of these campaigns rely on volunteer managers, but some have no managers at all, and the candidates run their own campaigns.

Open-seat campaigns are similar to those waged by incumbents. All but 12 percent of the open-seat prospects (whose races were eventually decided by margins of 20 percent or less) rely on a paid staffer or general consultant to manage their campaigns. Many open-seat candidates who are considered mismatched (whose election was decided by more than 20 percent of the vote) also have professional managers, but a substantial portion of them rely on the candidate or volunteers for campaign management. Few campaigns are managed by personnel provided by a political party or interest group, regardless of their competitiveness.

Professional staffs carry out press relations in most campaigns. More than 85 percent of all incumbents in close races rely on a paid staffer, frequently a congressional press secretary who is on a leave of absence, to handle their relations with the media. A small number of incumbents also hire campaign consultants to issue press releases and handle calls from journalists. Challengers and open-seat candidates in close races are just as likely as incumbents to rely on paid staff to handle media relations. A somewhat larger number hire political consultants for this purpose. Slightly fewer open-seat candidates in one-sided contests rely on paid staff. Only 42 percent of all challengers in uncompetitive races are able to turn to campaign professionals to help them work the press, relying on volunteers and their own efforts instead.

TABLE 3-1

Staffing Activities in House Elections

	All	Incumbents		Challengers		Open-seat candidates	
		In jeopardy	Shoo-ins	Hope-fuls	Long shots	Pros-pects	Mis-matched
Campaign management							
Paid staff	62%	79%	82%	81%	35%	77%	65%
Consultant	6	4	6	12	2	11	12
Party/interest groups	2	—	1	—	3	—	—
Volunteer	9	3	4	3	17	3	6
Candidate	22	10	10	12	41	6	18
Not used	4	3	5	—	6	3	—
Press relations							
Paid staff	66%	86%	84%	84%	37%	89%	71%
Consultant	5	—	5	12	5	3	12
Party/interest groups	1	—	—	—	1	3	—
Volunteer	10	3	4	3	20	3	—
Candidate	19	10	7	3	38	3	18
Not used	4	—	4	—	7	—	—
Issue and opposition research							
Paid staff	40%	38%	57%	62%	28%	23%	35%
Consultant	21	38	21	22	8	43	35
Party/interest groups	10	17	4	16	6	29	12
Volunteer	11	—	2	3	22	6	12
Candidate	14	3	1	3	29	3	24
Not used	10	7	17	—	12	3	—
Fundraising							
Paid staff	52%	83%	75%	59%	25%	63%	53%
Consultant	14	14	20	16	6	23	24
Party/interest groups	5	—	4	6	3	14	6
Volunteer	9	3	5	6	15	3	6
Candidate	28	7	10	25	50	11	24
Not used	4	—	—	—	10	—	—
Polling							
Paid staff	7%	3%	10%	3%	6%	14%	6%
Consultant	49	86	56	81	17	74	71
Party/interest groups	6	7	5	3	6	9	6
Volunteer	4	—	1	—	6	6	—
Candidate	4	—	3	3	6	—	—
Not used	32	3	26	12	58	—	18

(Table continues)

TABLE 3-1 *(continued)*

	All	Incumbents		Challengers		Open-seat candidates	
		In jeopardy	Shoo-ins	Hope-fuls	Long shots	Pros-pects	Mis-matched
Media advertising							
Paid staff	27%	17%	40%	28%	22%	17%	41%
Consultant	46	72	51	69	20	80	53
Party/interest groups	3	3	—	6	4	3	—
Volunteer	6	—	2	3	11	3	6
Candidate	15	7	5	—	35	—	—
Not used	9	—	10	9	13	—	6
Direct mail							
Paid staff	27%	31%	41%	31%	16%	23%	24%
Consultant	34	52	42	44	10	60	65
Party/interest groups	6	—	2	12	6	11	12
Volunteer	12	7	6	12	20	6	—
Candidate	7	3	4	—	15	3	—
Not used	21	10	14	9	39	3	—
Internet website							
Paid staff	41%	69%	41%	59%	27%	46%	41%
Consultant	17	21	21	22	7	29	35
Party/interest groups	6	3	4	12	6	6	6
Volunteer	18	—	14	6	30	20	6
Candidate	10	—	1	3	24	—	6
Not used	10	7	22	—	7	3	6
Mass phone calls							
Paid staff	15%	10%	21%	16%	13%	11%	6%
Consultant	25	31	25	34	11	46	59
Party/interest groups	12	14	7	9	11	23	18
Volunteer	24	24	21	28	23	34	18
Candidate	3	—	1	3	6	3	—
Not used	29	24	34	9	43	3	—
Get-out-the-vote							
Paid staff	30%	38%	31%	50%	14%	54%	47%
Consultant	4	—	9	6	2	6	6
Party/interest groups	33	28	30	28	34	46	29
Volunteer	31	28	29	22	37	23	35
Candidate	6	3	4	—	10	3	6
Not used	11	3	10	3	19	6	6

(Table continues)

TABLE 3-1   *(continued)*

	All	Incumbents		Challengers		Open-seat candidates	
		In jeopardy	Shoo-ins	Hope-fuls	Long shots	Pros-pects	Mis-matched
Legal advice							
Paid staff	15%	10%	15%	19%	11%	23%	18%
Consultant	20	21	27	19	11	26	29
Party/interest groups	13	24	9	34	4	26	6
Volunteer	13	14	10	9	15	11	18
Candidate	9	—	3	9	17	—	6
Not used	35	35	38	19	42	14	41
Accounting							
Paid staff	51%	62%	64%	56%	31%	71%	59%
Consultant	11	14	17	12	6	14	12
Party/interest groups	3	10	1	12	—	6	—
Volunteer	19	7	12	16	30	9	18
Candidate	10	—	2	—	24	3	—
Not used	7	7	5	3	11	—	12
Average number of activities performed by paid staff or consultants	6.7	8.8	8.4	8.8	3.6	9	8.6

Source: "2002 Congressional Campaign Study," Center for American Politics and Citizenship, University of Maryland.

Notes: Figures are for general election candidates in major-party contested races, excluding those in incumbent-versus-incumbent races. The categories are the same as those in Table 1-4. Figures for interest groups include labor unions.— = less than 0.5 percent. Some columns do not add to 100 percent because some activities were performed by more than one person or because of rounding. $N = 316$.

Issue and opposition research is often carried out by a combination of professional staff, outside consultants, party committees, interest groups, and volunteers. Incumbents, challengers, and open-seat candidates in one-sided races are more likely to rely on volunteers or the candidate to conduct research (or not even bother with it) than are candidates in close races. Some shoo-in incumbents turn to memos that congressional staff write about the major issues facing the nation and the district. These memos are usually drafted to help House members represent their constituents, but the political payoffs from them are significant. Most long-shot challengers, who could benefit from the research, are unable to afford it.

Although most incumbents in jeopardy, hopeful challengers, and open-seat prospects depend on paid professionals for research, some also benefit from research packages assembled by party organizations and a few interest groups. From the mid-1980s through 2006 the National Republican Congressional Committee (NRCC) furnished more candidates with opposition and issue research than the Democratic Congressional Campaign Committee (DCCC) did.[7] However, the Democrats have since reached parity. Some labor unions, trade associations, advocacy groups, and other organizations also provide candidates with campaign research.

Fundraising is a campaign activity that requires skill and connections with individuals and groups that are able and willing to make political contributions. Some campaigns use a mix of a paid campaign staffer, a professional finance director, and volunteers to raise money. Incumbent campaigns rely heavily on paid staff and professional consultants, regardless of the competitiveness of their races. Some keep fundraising experts, including those who specialize in direct mail or in organizing fundraising events, on the payroll to collect contributions between elections. Apparently a few reduce the costs of keeping their fundraising operations in place by putting fundraising experts on the payrolls of their PACs or charitable foundations.[8] Direct mail is typically used to collect modest contributions, and fundraising events are known for raking in sums of all sizes, including large contributions from individuals and PACs.[9] Fewer nonincumbents, particularly those anticipating one-sided contests, hire professional staff and consultants to help with fundraising. Their campaigns depend more heavily on the candidate, volunteers, party committees, and interest groups to raise money.

Polling, mass media advertising, and direct mail are three specialized aspects of campaigning that are handled primarily by political consultants hired on a contractual basis. Most candidates running for marginal seats hire an outside consultant to conduct polls. Substantial numbers of incumbents who are shoo-ins and mismatched open-seat candidates do not feel the need to take polls. But a much greater number of challengers in lopsided races, who could benefit from accurate public opinion information, do not take them either. Most long-shot challengers opt not to conduct surveys, to save money for other campaign activities. Consultants typically consider this an ill-advised approach to campaigning. In the words of one pollster, "It's like flying without the benefit of radar."

Incumbents are the most likely to have professionally produced campaign communications. The vast majority of incumbents hire a media consultant or use some combination of media consultant and campaign aide to produce television and radio commercials. Most challengers and open-seat candidates in closely contested races also hire professional media consultants. Challengers in one-sided contests, who face the biggest hurdles in developing name recognition among voters and conveying a message, are by far the least likely to employ the services of a media consultant.

Similarly, relatively few long-shot challengers hire professional staff or consultants for direct mail, one of the most effective means House campaigns can use to reach voters. Indeed, 39 percent said that they do not use direct mail at all. The vast majority of competitive challengers, open-seat candidates, and incumbents, by contrast, rely mainly on a combination of paid staff and consultants to write their direct-mail copy and compile address lists.

Although the Internet is a fairly new weapon in campaign arsenals, it can serve a number of purposes, including providing campaigns with an inexpensive and reliable means to communicate with and organize voters, raise money, disseminate press releases, and showcase streaming video and audio ads. Websites also furnish voters and journalists with a place to turn for unmediated information about a candidate's professional qualifications, personal achievements, and issue positions.[10] Virtually all general election candidates create websites. Most employ professional staff or consultants to develop and maintain them. Many also use social media. The exception is long-shot challengers, who rely more heavily on volunteers or themselves to create and maintain their Internet presence.[11]

Mass telephone calls can be made live at phone banks or can be automated and prerecorded. Although such calls are not used as routinely as mass media advertising or direct mail, roughly 70 percent of all House campaigns use telephone calls to identify and mobilize supporters. Most of the campaigns that use mass telephone calls rely on a combination of consultants and volunteers, although some candidates turn to paid campaign aides, parties, or interest groups for help with writing their scripts and making calls.

Field work involves voter identification, registration, literature drops, and get-out-the-vote (GOTV) drives. Campaign staff, parties, interest groups, and volunteers figure prominently in the GOTV activities of virtually all campaigns. Incumbents depend almost as much on these sources of help as do challenger and open-seat candidates. Where these campaigns differ is that incumbents rely somewhat less on paid staff for field work than do open-seat candidates and competitive challengers. Democratic House candidates also receive significantly more help with mobilizing voters from unions, reflecting their party's historical ties with the labor movement.

Because of the intricacies of campaign finance laws, the rules governing the use of mass media, and requirements for getting on the ballot, almost two-thirds of all House candidates need legal expertise at some point in the campaign.

House campaigns call on paid staff, volunteers, lawyers they keep on retainer, or they get legal assistance from one of the high-powered attorneys employed by a party committee or an interest group. As is the case with most other aspects of campaigning, challengers running in lopsided races are the most likely to rely on volunteers or the candidate, or to forgo the use of legal counsel.

Finally, accounting has become an important aspect of contemporary cash-driven congressional election campaigns. Most candidates hire staff with accounting skills to file their Federal Election Commission (FEC) reports and oversee the books. Fewer long-shot challenger campaigns have a salaried employee or professional consultant in charge of accounting. As is the case in some other areas of electioneering, these campaigns often turn to volunteers or the candidate to perform this function.

The overall professionalism of contemporary House campaigns is apparent from the fact that the typical House campaign uses paid staff or political consultants to carry out roughly seven of the preceding twelve activities (see the bottom of Table 3-1); this is three times the number of activities conducted by campaign professionals in a typical 1984 House race. Average incumbents in jeopardy, hopeful challengers, and open-seat prospects use skilled professionals to carry out nine of these activities. Incumbents and open-seat candidates in uncompetitive elections also assemble very professional campaigns. Only challengers in one-sided contests are substantially less reliant on professional help. Nonincumbents who are officeholders and unelected politicians assemble campaign organizations that are more professional than those of political amateurs.[12]

The organization Representative Nadler assembled to conduct his 2010 reelection campaign in New York's 8th congressional district is typical of those put together by most shoo-in incumbents. Given his eighteen-year dominance of the district, lack of primary opposition, and perception that he would face weak opposition in the general election, it is not surprising that Nadler mounted a low-key campaign. He relied on Gilliard Blanning Wysocki & Associates, Inc., a general consulting firm based in Sacramento, California, to provide strategic advice, media advertising, and assistance with fundraising. The Hammond Group, specializing in PAC fundraising and located in Alexandria, Virginia, organized the campaign's Washington-area fundraising events. Light Graphics of Sacramento designed his website, and the KAL Group was responsible for accounting.[13] The campaign also was assisted by numerous volunteers, including many who had worked on Nadler's previous campaigns. Volunteers helped to staff the office, organize events, stuff envelopes, make telephone calls, and do other activities associated with grassroots politicking and field work. Had Nadler perceived the race to be more competitive, he probably would have put together a larger team and campaigned more aggressively.

The campaign team Susan Kone put together to challenge Nadler was underfunded and understaffed, as is typical of most campaigns waged by long-shot challengers. Kone—who runs her own law firm—relied on a grassroots organization, comprising family members, friends, college students, Republican activists, and other members of her community. Although the campaign had no paid staffers, about sixty volunteers participated on a regular basis. They helped collect the 2,000 signatures needed to place Kone's name on the ballot and organized fundraisers and outreach events. They also accompanied her to subway stations, community meetings, and other places where New Yorkers gather. The campaign did not employ the services of a professional manager, strategy firm, pollster, voter contact firm, or most of the other the types of consultants that usually advise campaigns. However, Kone was able to employ Political Media Inc. of Washington, D.C., to design her website and a videographer to record the streaming video it featured. She also received some professional assistance with honing her communications skills. By fielding an amateur campaign organization and hiring the services of few consultants, she was able to minimize her overhead and marshal her scarce resources to communicate to voters.[14]

The 2010 campaign waged in Florida's 2nd district by Republican challenger Steve Southerland contrasts sharply with those of Nadler and Kone, but it is typical of the campaigns of hopeful challengers. Southerland entered the race with limited political experience, but working in his family's fifty-five-year-old funeral home business and his leadership of the Bay County Chamber of Commerce and several other local organizations helped him form relationships with activists and voters across the district. Southerland assembled a campaign organization that was both homegrown and professional. Located in a vacated family home, the campaign employed eleven paid staffers. The campaign manager was Jonathan Hayes, a Florida Republican Party state committee member who had previously run for office in the district. He was assisted by finance director Jennifer Bowman and three regional district directors—all from Florida. The Kozlow Group of Ashburn, Virginia, provided strategic consulting services, including help with message development and media relations. The Revolution Agency, a prominent Washington, D.C.–based media firm, was responsible for the campaign's broadcast and cable television ads, radio spots, and much of its written materials. National Research of New Jersey did the campaign's polling, and the Oorbeek Group of Maryland provided fundraising assistance. Teletarget of Nashville, Tennessee, made the voter identification and robo-calls used to identify and turn out Southerland supporters. Washington-based experts provided legal and FEC compliance services. The campaign was assisted by an army of volunteers drawn from the ranks of family and friends, Republican activists, local business leaders, and college students. They helped the campaign indentify Southerland supporters, contact vote-by-mail applicants, and carry out other grassroots efforts.[15]

Southerland also drew assistance from party organizations and interest groups. After the NRCC named him a member of its Young Guns Program, comprising its top-tier nonincumbent candidates, it began providing his campaign with issue and opposition research, fundraising assistance, and strategic advice. The NRCC's regional political director, press secretary, finance director, and opposition researcher were involved in developing a campaign plan and budget, and in providing strategic and tactical advice. The Bay County Republicans, a variety of other state and local Republican committees, some Tea Party–affiliated groups, as well as numerous other local organizations contributed to the roughly 100 volunteers per week who showed up at Southerland campaign headquarters.

Allen Boyd, the Democratic incumbent in the 2nd district, approached the 2010 election with an expensive and highly professional organization that was fairly typical for an incumbent in jeopardy. Knowing he would be involved in both a tough primary fight and a close general election battle—he won the former by 2,423 votes and lost the latter by more than 31,000 votes—Boyd assembled a campaign team that drew from top-flight Democratic consulting firms from across the country. Main Street Communications handled his television ads, Sutter's Mill provided additional media consulting, Cooper and Secrest did his polling, Winning Connections provided phone services, and Halloran Development assisted with fundraising—all are firms located in the Washington, D.C., area. Liberty Concepts of Allston, Massachusetts, designed and maintained the campaign's website; Stanford Research of Austin, Texas, provided issue and opposition research; and the Baughman Company of San Francisco was responsible for direct mail. One unusual feature of the Boyd campaign was its lack of reliance on local talent. Among the few Floridians providing high-level services was fundraising expert Matthew Gotha. The DCCC provided Boyd with strategic and tactical advice but no financial assistance because the candidate had a large war chest and tremendous personal wealth he could have drawn from to finance his reelection campaign. Although Boyd drew support from the ranks of local Democratic activists, in contrast to Southerland's heavily grassroots effort, Boyd did not make heavy use of volunteers.

The campaigns by Democrat Dan Seals and Republican Robert Dold in Illinois' 10th congressional district are representative of those undertaken by most open-seat prospects. Both campaigns employed a full coterie of professional staff, political consultants, and volunteers. Each was led by a manager who had extensive political experience and strong party ties. Seals's campaign manager in the general election was David Mason, who had successfully managed a number of elections at the federal, state, and local levels across the country. Dold's campaign manager, Kelley Folino, a veteran of Lake County politics, had served as the event director of the Lake County Young Republicans. Each campaign hired some of the top general consultants, pollsters, media consultants, direct-mail experts, and fundraisers available from around the country. To this core of professional political operatives, each campaign added a substantial army of volunteers who assisted with organizing events, staffing the office, carrying out literature drops, reaching out to voters via telephone calls and door-to-door visits, and various other grassroots campaign activities.[16]

Both the Seals and Dold campaigns also received substantial party and interest group assistance, which is typical of a campaign that appears on the national radar for competitive elections. The DCCC provided the Seals campaign with strategic and tactical advice, opposition research, and fundraising assistance—as it did with other candidates in its Red to Blue Program, which focused on electing the party's most competitive nonincumbents. The DCCC, the Democratic National Committee, and the Illinois Democratic State Central Committee also put together a coordinated grassroots campaign effort under the guise of the Illinois Victory Committee, which worked to register, persuade, and mobilize pro-Democratic voters. Several labor unions provided volunteers; hosted fundraising events; and organized voter identification, education, and mobilization programs. Dold, a Young Gun, benefited from similar forms of assistance from the NRCC. In addition, the Republican National Committee used its data files to develop a list of voters for microtargeting and took the lead in running the campaign's voter mobilization effort. State and local Republican party committees, the U.S. Chamber of Commerce, several of its local affiliates, and other business groups also provided assistance to Dold.

Although the above campaigns varied in their degrees of professionalism and the levels of party and interest group support they received, they were similar in that they were smooth-running operations that worked to advance their candidate's cause. Not all campaigns work that way. Campaigns that place both professional consultants and activists drawn from political movements into prominent positions are often fraught with tension. On the one hand, the professionals try to use their expertise to chart and follow a path to victory. On the other, the activists focus heavily on promoting the values and principles that brought them to the campaign in the first place—sometimes to the detriment of the candidate's electoral prospects. Some of the campaigns of Tea Party candidates suffered from these tensions, as illustrated by the campaign Senate challenger Sharron Angle, R-Nev., waged against Senate majority leader Harry Reid. After drawing on Tea Party support to defeat an establishment candidate in the Republican primary, Angle had trouble integrating strategy, fundraising, and communications experts sent by the National Republican Senatorial Committee (NRSC) into her existing organization. Not surprisingly, the staffers and volunteers who were critical to Angle's primary victory resented the professionals, considering them arrogant and untrustworthy; the national operatives brought in to help with the general election were equally disparaging, nicknaming the original campaign team "The Island of Misfit Toys." Angle exacerbated these tensions by failing to establish a clear chain of command within the organization and by following her own instincts rather than seeking her strategists' advice. As a result, the campaign has been described as spending as much time maintaining the peace as in trying to defeat Reid.[17]

CAMPAIGN BUDGETS

The professionalism of contemporary congressional campaigns influences how they budget their money. House candidates spend 56 percent of their campaign funds on communicating with voters and 40 percent on fundraising, staff salaries, travel, and other miscellaneous expenses (see Figure 3-1). Polling and other research account for about 4 percent of campaign costs. The substantial amounts budgeted for electronic media demonstrate the important role played by modern communications techniques in most House campaigns and their rising costs. The typical House campaign spent approximately 22 percent of its budget on television and 12 percent on radio. The next-largest expenses are for direct mail and campaign literature, each of which accounted for 8 percent of total costs. The remaining 5 percent was spent largely on voter registration and GOTV drives, newspaper ads, and Internet websites, as well as billboards, yard signs, and other campaign paraphernalia.

One of the most interesting facts about congressional elections is how little different types of candidates vary in their approaches to budgeting. One of the largest differences is that nonincumbents commit about 65 percent of their budgets to campaign communications, whereas incumbents apportion only 48 percent. The nonincumbents compensate by scrimping on overhead, especially fundraising and the salaries and fees that incumbents incur when conducting various campaign-related activities between elections. Candidates in contests decided by 20 percent or less of the two-party vote dedicate about half of their budgets to television and radio, more than twice the amount allocated by candidates in one-sided races. The amounts that Democratic and

FIGURE 3-1
Budget of a Typical House Campaign

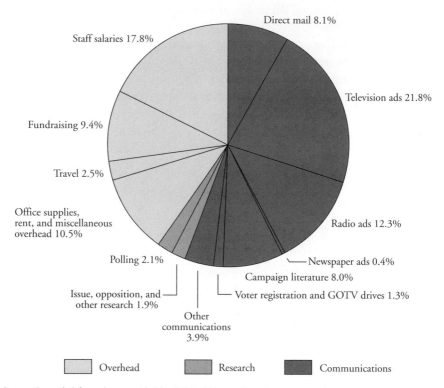

Source: Compiled from data provided by Political Money Line (www.tray.com).

Notes: Staff salaries include some miscellaneous consulting fees. Figures are for major-party candidates in contested general elections. $N = 694$.

Republican House candidates budget for various campaign activities are virtually the same.

The Boyd, Southerland, Nadler, and Kone campaigns illustrate how incumbency, competitiveness, finances, and media markets can influence certain aspects of spending. The Boyd campaign allocated almost $2.6 million (about 71 percent of its budget) for television and radio ads, compared with the $639,000 (50 percent) spent by the victorious Southerland campaign. The Nadler and Kone campaigns invested no money in broadcast TV because of the inefficiency of advertising in the extremely high-priced New York media market, which covers a huge metropolitan area; the one-sided nature of the race; and, in Kone's case, a very small campaign budget.

The overall similarity in campaign budgets is remarkable given the different sums that incumbent, open-seat, and challenger campaigns spend. The widespread availability of campaign technology; the tremendous growth of the political consulting industry; and the extensive dissemination of information through the American Association of Political Consultants, *Campaigns & Elections* magazine, and campaign seminars sponsored by nonpartisan organizations, political parties, and interest groups have fostered a set of shared expectations about how a campaign should spend its funds. These expectations are reinforced when campaign personnel negotiate their fees and draw up budgets, when political consulting firms set their rates, and when party officials and PAC managers scrutinize campaign budgets before making contributions.

SENATE CAMPAIGNS

Senate campaigns are more expensive, are run by more professional organizations, and attract more party and interest group attention than do House campaigns. Because most campaigns for the upper chamber need to reach out to more voters and senators run only once every six years, candidates for the Senate typically raise and spend more money.[18] They also rely primarily on paid staffs and nationally known political consultants to develop their strategies and carry out their bids to remain in office. Most Senate incumbents keep a substantial organization intact between elections, often spending millions of dollars on overhead and fundraising. As is the case with sitting House members, senators typically assemble campaign organizations that are more professional than those of their opponents.

Senate campaigns often have combinations of individuals sharing responsibilities for various aspects of the campaign. Virtually every campaign assigns a paid aide to work with a mass media advertising firm to develop the candidate's communications. Opposition research is typically conducted by a campaign aide, often in conjunction with a private consultant or party official. Campaign staff, consultants, volunteers, party committees, and interest group representatives make substantial contributions to Senate candidates' fundraising efforts. Most Senate campaigns also hire one or more field managers to participate in coordinated grassroots campaigns that draw on the resources of national, state, and local party committees to register and mobilize supporters. Democratic Senate candidates also coordinate their field work with labor unions, and most Senate candidates of both parties rely on volunteers to help with their voter registration and GOTV efforts.

The major difference in spending between Senate and House contests is the allocation of media expenditures. Senate campaigns spend about one-third of their money on television advertising, as opposed to the one-fifth spent by House campaigns. Senate campaigns also allocate smaller portions of their budgets to radio advertising, campaign literature, newspaper ads, billboards, and yard signs than do House contestants. The differences in communications expenditures reflect both the greater practicality and the necessity of using television advertising in statewide races.

SUMMARY

Contemporary congressional elections are waged primarily by candidate-centered organizations that draw on the expertise of political consultants for polling, mass media advertising, and other specialized functions. Few candidates depend on parties and interest groups to carry out many campaign activities; the important exception is voter mobilization. Incumbents and open-seat candidates in competitive races wage the most professional campaigns; challengers in lopsided contests rely the most on amateur organizations. Despite these variations in organizations and tremendous disparities in funding, campaigns are more alike than different in how they budget their resources. The match between district boundaries and media markets and the preferences of individual candidates and their campaign aides affect campaigns' budgetary allocations more than incumbency, party affiliations, or the closeness of the race.

CHAPTER FOUR

The Parties Campaign

Political parties in the United States have one overriding goal: to elect their candidates to public office. Policy goals are secondary to winning control of the government. The parties' influence has waxed and waned as the result of legal, demographic, and technological changes in U.S. society and reforms instituted by the parties themselves. During the golden age of political parties, local party organizations dominated elections in many parts of the country. They picked the candidates, gauged public opinion, raised money, disseminated campaign communications, and mobilized voters, most of whom had strong partisan allegiances. "The parties were, in short, the medium through which the campaign was waged."[1]

By the 1950s most state and local party organizations had been ushered to the periphery of the candidate-centered system. Party organizations at the national level had yet to develop into repositories of money and campaign services for congressional candidates. Most contenders for the House and Senate were largely self-recruited and relied on campaign organizations that they themselves had assembled to wage their bids for office. Professional consultants helped fill the void left by deteriorating party organizations by providing campaign fundraising, communications, polling, and management services to clients willing to pay for them.[2]

During the late 1970s and early 1980s, first Republican and then Democratic national party organizations in Washington, D.C., began to adapt to the contemporary candidate-centered system. This system emphasizes campaign activities requiring technical expertise, in-depth research, and money. Many candidates, especially nonincumbents running for the House, lack the funds or professional know-how needed to conduct a modern congressional campaign. Candidates' needs created the opportunity for party organizations to assume a more important role in congressional elections.[3] The national parties responded to these needs, not by doing away with the candidate-centered election system but by assuming a more important role in it.[4]

In the late 1990s the national parties expanded their activities to include issue advocacy advertisements financed with soft-money. Both major parties, and numerous interest groups, began conducting "outside" campaigns comprising millions of dollars of spending on television, radio, direct mail, mass telephone calls, social media, and other communications and voter mobilization efforts. Following enactment of the Bipartisan Campaign Reform Act of 2002 (BCRA), with its ban on national party soft-money, the parties adapted by raising more hard-money and pumping it into competitive elections using independent expenditures. Party leaders in and out of government, including former party committee chairs and advisers, also helped the parties adapt by strengthening their alliances with existing interest groups or forming new ones. These efforts more firmly placed each party's national organization at the center of a vast network of interest groups, political consultants, media elites, think tank researchers, and individual donors who participate in elections and the policy-making process.[5] By tailoring their efforts to meet the circumstances in which contemporary congressional elections are fought, the parties have greatly increased their influence in those contests, thereby assuming an even greater role in the candidate-centered system.

In this chapter I discuss the roles of party organizations in congressional elections, including their influence on the agendas around which campaigns are fought, the types of assistance they give to House and Senate candidates, the strategies that inform their giving, how they select candidates for support, and the effects of their assistance on candidates' campaigns. Special attention is given to four Hill committees in recognition of their impact on congressional elections.

NATIONAL AGENDA SETTING

Contemporary House elections are usually fought on local issues, Senate elections address statewide concerns, and campaigns for both chambers focus on the qualifications of the candidates. The factors that contribute to the candidate-centered nature of congressional elections, discussed in Chapter 1, are primarily responsible for this situation. During periods of divided government, it is especially difficult for one party to claim credit or cast blame for the state of national affairs. However, this does not prevent Democratic or Republican leaders from working to steer the agenda toward issues that voters associate positively with their party or negatively with the opposition.[6] Since the early 1980s, Democratic and Republican congressional leaders have produced lengthy issues handbooks, white papers, and "talking points" for congressional candidates that discuss national issues and explain how to use rhetoric and statistics compiled in Washington to address local concerns.[7] Many candidates find these materials useful, but the materials are not intended to produce nationalized campaigns and do not do so.

However, congressional elections are not always dominated by local issues. In 1932 the Great Depression dominated the national political agenda and the outcomes of many House and Senate races. In 1974 Democrats nationalized the elections on the issues of Watergate, the Nixon administration's ethical lapses, and reform. During the 1994 elections House Republicans focused on the ethical and policy failures of the Clinton administration and congressional Democrats and Newt Gingrich's *Contract with America*.[8] During the two elections following the terrorist attacks of September 11, 2001, President George W. Bush and other GOP leaders crisscrossed the country to benefit from voters' concerns about national security and make the case that congressional Republicans were better able than Democrats to protect the United States from foreign attacks.[9] Ironically, during the 2006 election it was the Democrats who benefited from policies put in place following the terrorist attacks. Many voters who were unhappy with the conduct of the wars in Afghanistan and Iraq, government corruption, rising health care costs, and President Bush's job performance expressed their displeasure by voting against congressional Republicans.[10] In addition to these issues, the Democrats sought to nationalize the 2008 elections on the economic recession. As luck would have it, that same economic meltdown provided the foundation for the Republicans to nationalize the political agenda during the 2010 midterm election.

Political parties and candidates must respond to and attempt to influence the political agenda in order to maximize their opportunities to gain power. Because the Democrats were in control of the federal government following the 2008 election and voters were deeply disgruntled about the national economic conditions, the Republicans had a prime opportunity to make the 2010 election a referendum on the nation's economic recovery under Democratic leadership. Republican members of Congress capitalized on the political environment by opposing virtually every Democratic legislative proposal.[11] Their success can be measured by the fact that almost every major bill in the 111th Congress passed with no Republican votes, including bills that sought to improve the economy.

In an attempt to expand the impact of the wave of voter discontent they saw forming, the Republicans' congressional, senatorial, and national committees formulated an aggressive plan to make 80 percent of their communications attacks on the Democrats and the federal government; they used the remaining 20 percent to portray the GOP in a positive light. In the spring of 2010 the National Republican Congressional Committee's (NRCC) media campaign raised the question "Where are the jobs?" and framed the economic stimulus package, the Troubled Asset Relief Program (TARP), health care reform, and other high-profile, recently enacted, Democratic-backed legislation as job killers that hurt the economy. Because of President Barack Obama's relatively high spring approval rating (about 50 percent), they decided to make two other prominent Democrats "poster children" in many of their attacks.[12] House Speaker Nancy Pelosi, D-Calif., was selected because of her highly visible role in passing health care reform and other high-profile Democratic legislation, her reputation as a staunch liberal, and her high national visibility. Moreover, NRCC polling showed that she had name recognition among almost 90 percent of all voters in swing districts, and most held negative views of her. Senate majority leader Harry Reid also was selected because of his highly visible role in passing the Democratic policy agenda. The fact that he was locked in a tight reelection campaign of his own added to the value of using Reid as a vehicle to attack other candidates. The Republicans' early and continued success of blaming the Democrats for the nation's economic pain led them to use this message through the remainder of the election.[13]

The Democrats, by contrast, entered the 2010 election season knowing it would be a referendum on the stalled economic recovery and voter disapproval of some of their high-profile policy initiatives. As is almost always the case when a party controls the White House, the president took the lead in their agenda-setting efforts. The message provided by the White House and at the core of the Democratic Party's communications was that voters should support "a Democratic candidate who had done everything possible to get us out of the mess versus a Republican candidate whose party caused the mess and protected special interests."[14] Besides placing blame on the Republicans at the national level, this message sought to use Democratic incumbents' prior voting records and constituent services as a bulkhead against the tidal wave that was forming.

Even though both parties spent millions of dollars airing television commercials, issuing media releases, posting information on their websites, and using Twitter and other social media to contact voters, the GOP was the overwhelming beneficiary of the 2010 political agenda. When asked, "What one factor mattered most to you in deciding how you voted in the congressional election?" and "What would you say was the second most important factor to your vote?", voters volunteered three types of answers: specific

FIGURE 4-1

Most Important Issues in Congressional Voting Decisions in 2010

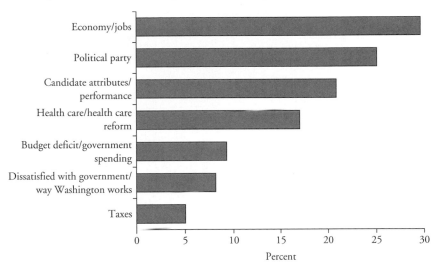

Source: Kaiser Family Foundation Health Tracking Poll (conducted November 3–6, 2010).

Note: Respondents mentioned up to two issues.

substantive issues, party-based considerations, and candidate assessments.[15] Leading with 29 percent of the voters' responses was the economy or jobs (see Figure 4-1). The next most important influences were party- and candidate-based factors. These were followed by health care–related concerns. The budget deficit and government spending, general dissatisfaction with government and politics in Washington, and taxes were substantially less important voting issues.

Republican congressional candidates clearly benefited from the political agenda. Of the 29 percent of all voters stating that the economy or jobs was their first or second most important voting concern, 34 percent voted for a Republican congressional candidate and only 24 percent voted for a Democrat (see Figure 4-2). This gave the Republicans a 10-point advantage on the issue. The Democrats enjoyed significant, but lesser, advantages among voters who reported that party- and candidate-based matters were central to their vote. However, Democratic candidates were penalized by voters on every other issue. Health care reform and concerns about the spending habits and overall performance of the federal government were particularly harmful to the Democrats' cause.

FIGURE 4-2

Partisan Issue Advantages in Congressional Voting Decisions in 2010

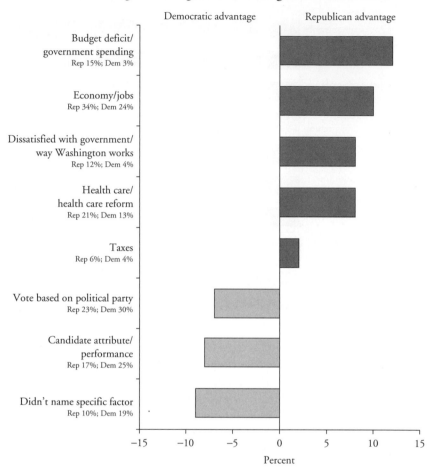

Source: Kaiser Family Foundation Health Tracking Poll (conducted November 3–6, 2010).

Note: Respondents mentioned up to two issues.

THE NATIONAL, CONGRESSIONAL, AND SENATORIAL CAMPAIGN COMMITTEES

Party organizations in the nation's capital have developed into major sources of campaign money, services, and advice for congressional candidates. The Democratic National Committee (DNC) and the Republican National Committee (RNC) focus most of their efforts on presidential elections but also become involved in some gubernatorial and state house elections and in a small number of mayoral elections. They also seek to influence the national political agenda and strengthen state and local party organizations. The national committees' involvement in House and Senate elections tends to be relatively limited. It includes conducting some candidate training seminars; furnishing candidates with party platforms, campaign manifestos, and generic talking points; and coordinating with congressional, senatorial, state, and local party campaign committees to mobilize partisan voters. Congressional candidates in search of money, election services, or assistance in running campaigns rarely turn to their national committee for help. Any assistance the national committee offers is usually channeled through a congressional or senatorial campaign committee or distributed in coordination with one of these organizations.[16]

The parties' congressional and senatorial campaign committees, sometimes referred to as the "Hill committees," have developed into major support centers for House and Senate candidates.[17] The congressional campaign committees focus their efforts on House races, and the senatorial campaign committees focus on Senate contests. Three of the four Hill committees set post-BCRA fundraising records for midterm elections in 2010; only the NRCC fell short of previous fundraising levels. The Democratic Congressional Campaign Committee (DCCC) raised $163.9 million, about $30 million more than the NRCC. The Democratic Senatorial Campaign Committee (DSCC) raised $129.5 million, roughly $15 million more than the National Republican Senatorial Committee (NRSC). The DNC and Democratic state and local party committees also set records for midterm elections in 2010. All told, Democratic Party organizations outraised their Republican opponents by $51.4 million—a reversal of the pattern that existed in every election in the past three decades.[18]

The Democrats' congressional majorities, Barack Obama's occupancy of the White House, and the close competition for control over the House and Senate helped that party rake in record funds in 2010. President Obama's fundraising efforts and the donor base he built during his 2008 presidential campaign were especially important in this regard. Undeniably out of favor with most Republican and many independent voters, Obama capitalized on his popularity among members of his party's donor pool by traveling around the country to raise hundreds of millions of dollars for Democratic candidates and party committees. The Republicans, on the other hand, suffered from their position as the out-party and from some highly publicized fundraising scandals.

The chairs, vice chairs, and members of the Hill committees are members of Congress who are selected by their colleagues in the House or Senate. For the most part the members of each committee act like a board of directors, setting priorities and giving the committee staff the support it needs to participate in campaigns. In one area, however, members play an essential role:

fundraising. Congressional and senatorial campaign committee chairs, vice chairs, and other party leaders always have raised money from individuals and interest groups, but in recent years they have tapped into a another source—their colleagues in the House and Senate.

Party leaders in the House have established dues for their incumbent colleagues. These vary by seniority, leadership position, and reelection prospects. For example, during the 2010 election cycle, the dues levels for House Democrats were $800,000 for the top leaders; $500,000 for the chairs of Appropriations, Ways and Means, and other exclusive committees; $300,000 for DCCC vice chairs and the House's chief deputy whips; $250,000 for committee chairs and exclusive subcommittee chairs; $200,000 for members on exclusive committees; $150,000 for subcommittee chairs on nonexclusive committees; and $125,000 for junior lawmakers. Exceptions are made for incumbents in jeopardy, who are not required to pay dues.[19] The Republicans had a similar series of rates and exemptions. Of course, some House members of both parties fell short, while others went beyond expectations. Leading for the House Democrats were then-Speaker Nancy Pelosi and Majority Leader Steny Hoyer, D-Md., who each gave at least $1.7 million to the DCCC. Pelosi and DCCC chair Chris Van Hollen, D-Md., also are credited with contributing or raising $43 million and $20 million, respectively, for Democratic candidates in close contests and the DCCC itself.[20] The top donors among House Republicans were then–Minority Leader John Boehner, R-Ohio, and Rep. Cliff Stearns, R-Fla., who contributed $3.7 million and $840,000 to the NRCC. Boehner is also credited with raising tens of millions of dollars for the NRCC and effectively putting the squeeze on GOP House members. Seeking to spur more member participation, he took out a check made out to the NRCC for $1 million at a meeting of the Republican Conference and vowed not to deposit it unless his colleagues contributed $3 million, an amount they readily exceeded.[21] The final tallies for the contributions members transferred from their election committees and leadership PACs were $30.8 million to the DCCC and $28.7 million to the NRCC.

Democratic and Republican Senate leaders also expect their members, particularly those not up for reelection, to contribute to their party's senatorial campaign committee. However, unlike their counterparts in the House, neither the DSCC nor the NRSC have formal dues levels, reflecting the nature of the smaller and more informal upper chamber. During the 2010 election season Senate Democrats transferred $10.3 million from their election committees and leadership PACs to the DSCC, and Senate Republicans transferred $4.5 million to the NRSC and GOP candidates. The top donors to these committees were Charles Schumer, D-N.Y., who contributed $3 million, and Tom Coburn, R-Okla., who transferred $1.2 million.

Member contributions to party committees are a first step in the massive redistributions of money from the powerful politicians who can raise it to the candidates who need it. They demonstrate that Hill committee leaders can get locally elected legislators to look beyond their own campaigns to consider their party's national goals. A sense of enlightened self-interest, particularly as it relates to control of the House and Senate, encourages members to raise money for national, state, and local party organizations. Once involving only a few party leaders and senior members, in 2010 this redistribution of wealth involved hundreds of lawmakers and candidates, including some first-term legislators who aspire to leadership posts. The Democrats traditionally have contributed substantially more to party committees than the Republicans—a pattern that continued during the 2010 elections.

Regardless of partisan affiliation or ideological leanings, the politicians who contribute to their party's campaign committees share an understanding that such contributions are an effective way to build political alliances that can be used to advance their careers and legislative goals. Pelosi's contributions to the DCCC, Democratic candidates, and other party causes helped her get elected Speaker after her party won control of the House in 2006. Boehner's support for the NRCC was instrumental in his being elected House Republican leader in 2006 and Speaker in 2011. Similarly, Schumer's chairmanship of the DSCC during the 2006 and 2008 elections facilitated his becoming the third-ranking Democrat in the Senate, and Kentucky senator Mitch McConnell's two terms as NRSC chair put him on a path to election as Senate Republican leader.

Some members of Congress provide fundraising assistance to party campaign committees in addition to any direct contributions they make. One popular method is to create "joint fundraising committees," which enable party committees and candidates to jointly raise money through political events. Joint fundraising committees usually first distribute the legal maximum amount an individual or PAC can contribute to participating candidates, then distribute the remainder to one or more party committees. This enables their sponsors to raise large contributions from individuals who, although they are in their party's donor network, may have had little or no prior contact with the party's national apparatus or may have been unfamiliar with the participating candidates.[22]

The parties' congressional and senatorial campaign committees are composed of many highly skilled political professionals in addition to members of Congress. During the 2010 elections the DCCC and the NRCC each employed about eighty full-time staff, and the two senatorial campaign committees each employed about sixty. The staffs conduct the committees' daily operations, influence the formulation of party strategies, and play a major role in their implementation. The staffs are divided along functional lines; different divisions are responsible for administration, fundraising, research, communications, and campaign activities. Staffers working in these divisions draw expertise from the constellation of consultants who serve their party's candidates, including many individuals who formerly worked for a party committee or an allied interest group. Pollsters, media experts, and other campaign professionals also are hired to provide Hill committees and selected candidates with campaign services.[23]

In addition, because federal law requires that independent expenditures be made without the knowledge or consent of the candidate, campaign aides, and others involved in a particular campaign, and because party staff routinely communicate with the campaigns of their candidates in close races, the party committees set up separate organizations, located on other premises, for the purposes of making independent expenditures. These so-called independent expenditure groups, routinely referred to as "IE groups," are prohibited from receiving any information from their parent party committee other than communications about the funds the party is transferring to their bank accounts. They also are prohibited from providing their parent committee with information about their electioneering efforts. Regular party staff remark that they usually learn about their IE group's specific undertakings after they have occurred, through mass media coverage or from information the parties make publicly available. However, because of the revolving doors of employment among political operatives, regular party staffs have a good idea of the strategies and tactics preferred by colleagues and consultants who work for their party's IE group, allied interest groups, or candidates' campaign organizations. Others who belong to a party's network of campaign experts also have more than an inkling of what to expect from that party's IE group. As is explained later, because party IE groups signal their strategies, tactics, and even the timing and content of specific ads, others rarely experience any major surprises.

As major centers of political expertise and campaign support, the Hill committees are expensive to operate. They typically spend between 45 percent and 55 percent of their budgets on voter lists, computers, salaries, consulting fees, fundraising, loan repayments, and other overhead. The GOP committees have traditionally invested more than their Democratic rivals in maintaining and updating their Washington operations, but both parties have made major strides in improving their databases, targeting capabilities, and physical infrastructures in recent years.

STRATEGY, DECISION MAKING, AND TARGETING

The Hill committees have a common overriding goal of maximizing the number of seats their parties hold in Congress.[24] They become heavily involved in some elections, giving selected candidates large contributions and making substantial expenditures on their behalf, including on independent media advertising and voter mobilization efforts. They also give these candidates strategic, research, technical, and transactional assistance. The latter form of help enables candidates to raise the money and other resources needed to conduct a congressional campaign. Finally, the Hill committees participate with the national committees and state and local party organizations in coordinated grassroots campaign activities designed to help elect candidates to Congress and other offices.

The campaign committees try to focus most of their efforts on competitive House and Senate contests. Protecting incumbents in jeopardy is a major priority. Pressures from nervous incumbents can skew the distribution of committee resources from competitive challenger and open-seat candidates toward members of Congress who hold safe seats. The funds available to a committee also affect the way it distributes its resources. Other institutional forces that influence committee decision making are the aspirations of its chair and other members. The two individuals who had the most significant roles in modernizing the NRCC and DCCC, former representatives Guy Vander Jagt and Tony Coelho, sought to use their chairmanships as vehicles for advancement in the ranks of the House leadership.[25] The same is true of most of their successors, including DCCC chair Van Hollen, whom House Democrats elected to be their top-ranking member of the House Budget Committee after the 2010 elections, and NRCC chair Pete Sessions of Texas, who was chosen vice chair of the House Rules Committee after 2010. Similarly, Senate Democrats selected DSCC chair Robert Menendez of New Jersey to chair the Western Hemisphere, Peace Corps, and Narcotics Affairs Subcommittee of the Foreign Relations Committee, and Senate Republicans rewarded NRSC chair John Cornyn of Texas with a coveted seat on the Armed Services Committee.

National political and economic conditions are additional factors that influence which candidates get campaign resources. When the president is popular or the economy is strong, the campaign committees of the president's party usually invest more resources in challenger and open-seat races. Conversely, the out-party committees use more of their resources to support incumbents. When national conditions do not favor the president's party, the patterns are reversed: the in-party committees take a defensive posture that favors incumbents, and the out-party committees go on the offensive, using more of their resources to help nonincumbents.[26] The unpredictable nature of national political conditions and economic trends and of events that take place in states and congressional districts means that committee decision making and targeting are necessarily imperfect. As a result, some safe incumbents and uncompetitive nonincumbents inevitably receive committee assistance, whereas some competitive nonincumbents get little or no help.

The conditions surrounding the elections held in recent decades have made strategic decision making and targeting difficult, especially for the two House campaign committees.[27] Redistricting, always fraught with ambiguities, became more complicated by issues involving race, which led to some districts being challenged in the courts and redrawn. Reconfigured districts or newly created seats are only two of several factors that complicate the committees' tasks. The president's popularity often shifts up and down, making it difficult for the committees to decide whether to pursue an offensive or a defensive strategy. Scandals and voter frustration with Congress result in some incumbents unexpectedly finding themselves in jeopardy and their challenger opponents receiving an unanticipated boost. The late retirements of some House members and the primary defeats of others further complicate the committees' efforts.

Because of the uncertainty surrounding post-redistricting elections, in the early 1990s the NRCC and DCCC drew up huge "watch" lists of so-called "opportunity," or competitive, races. During the 1992 elections, each committee's watch list initially included approximately 300 elections. The committees shortened the lists over the course of the campaign season, but going into the last week of the election each list still had more than 150 opportunity races—more than three times the number included at that point in the 1990 election. During the elections held between 1994 and 2000, the committees initially focused on about 150 seats before they pared down their lists to about 75 priority races midway in the campaign season and further reduced them later.[28] As discussed in Chapter 1, 2002 was very different from previous election years in that the redistricting had reduced the number of marginal House seats. This had a major impact on party strategy in House elections, as the DCCC and NRCC initially concentrated on about 90 races each before honing in on around 45 competitive contests midway through the election season and about 20 during the last two weeks or so.[29] Among the lingering effects of redistricting was that the 2004 elections also were characterized by a concentration of competition in only a very few districts. Prior to the 2006 elections the Democrats recognized that to have any chance at all of retaking the House, they would need to expand the number of competitive districts beyond the small number that had been in play in the previous two elections. This was the major objective of the House Democrats' Red to Blue Program, which helped them net a total of 55 seats in the 2006 and 2008 elections. With the Democrats in control of both chambers of Congress in 2010, it was the GOP's turn to attempt to expand the field of competition in their party's favor. House Republicans used their Young Guns Program to accomplish this objective and enjoy a record-breaking net gain of 63 seats.

Individual candidates are selected for placement on the committees' watch lists according to several criteria. The competitiveness of the district and incumbency are the first two considerations. Candidates running in districts that were decided by close margins in the most recent election or who are competing for open seats are likely to be placed on a committee's watch list. The strength of the candidate is another consideration in the case of non-incumbents. The campaigns of those who have had political experience and local or national celebrity status are likely to be monitored. Challengers and open-seat contestants who demonstrate an ability to mount a viable campaign also are likely to receive support.

A variety of idiosyncratic factors also come into play when the committees select the candidates who will be given the most support initially. An incumbent who is accused of committing an ethical transgression, perceived to be out of touch with people in the district, in poor health, or in trouble for some other reason is a likely candidate for extra help. These difficulties often provoke a response by the other party's campaign committee, resulting in the incumbent's opponent also benefiting from extra party money and campaign services. Although party leaders work aggressively to recruit women and minorities to run for Congress, neither party uses gender or race as a criterion for determining who gets campaign assistance, nor is ideology used to select candidates for support. Candidates are assisted only to the degree that their races are expected to be competitive. Van Hollen, cochair of the Democrats' Red to Blue Program in 2006 and DCCC chair in the 110th and 111th Congresses, explains, "We have a big-tent approach, not an ideological purity test. We have two questions: does the candidate want to help build our majority in Congress? . . . And, can he or she win?"[30]

The committees' initial lists of competitive elections are revised throughout the election season. Regional coordinators who monitor congressional races in designated parts of the country advise their colleagues in Washington about the latest developments in individual elections. As a result, some candidates lose priority or are cut off from party help, and others gain more committee attention and support.

Because of the uncertainty surrounding recent congressional elections, the Democratic and Republican congressional and senatorial campaign committees distribute their resources incrementally. Rather than drop a large quantity of money or extensive election services in a candidate's lap early in the campaign season, the committees distribute assistance piecemeal in response to the candidate's ability to meet a series of discrete fundraising, organizational, and publicity goals. Incumbents in tough reelection campaigns in need of support from the DCCC's Frontline Program, the NRCC's Patriot Program, or some other incumbent retention program must sign a contract stating that they understand that party assistance will only be forthcoming if they meet the goals that are set for them. Similarly, nonincumbents who would like help from the DCCC's Red to Blue Program or the NRCC's Young Guns Program also must meet a set of requirements. Both the Red to Blue and Young Guns programs confer tiered levels of recognition on candidates, depending on the candidate's ability to raise money, demonstrate a level of visibility, field a professional campaign organization, and outline a viable campaign plan. The Young Guns Program, for example, has three tiers of support: candidates who raise between $100,000 and $200,000, attract some press coverage, and have assembled the basic nuts-and-bolts of a campaign are listed as "On the Radar"; those who raise between $300,000 and $400,000 and build the basic infrastructure of a campaign organization are identified as "Contenders"; and those who raise more than $400,000, assemble a good campaign organization and consulting team, write a comprehensive campaign plan, and can demonstrate with polling a path to victory are featured as "Young Guns." Republicans who achieve Young Gun status and Democrats who are featured as Red to Blue candidates (the DCCC's top ranking) benefit from party contributions, expenditures, extensive fundraising assistance, and other campaign services.

By design the Red to Blue, Young Guns, Frontline, and Patriot programs are intended to help party decision makers minimize the resources they waste and maximize the resources candidates gather from others. Candidates who continue to meet program goals continue to benefit from party assistance; those who do not find themselves cut off. The programs' "carrot and stick" approach is additionally cost-effective in that it motivates candidates to conduct many of the campaign activities needed to win on their own, thereby reducing the resources their party needs to invest to keep their races competitive. Another benefit, especially important to Red to Blue and Young Gun candidates, is that the programs help them attract money, volunteers, and media attention unavailable to other candidates. Finally, because these programs conserve resources, they enable the congressional campaign committees to assist more candidates. Thus, a party that is advantaged by the national political environment can use its savings to spread the field of competition, and a party that faces a hostile environment can use its reserves to assist incumbents and others who unexpectedly face diminishing prospects for success. In 2010 the NRCC increased the number of districts they targeted, from seventy in February 2009 to more than one hundred on Election Day, which helped them claim a historic victory.[31] The DCCC, by contrast, shifted more than $10 million from the candidates who were targeted early in the election cycle to support twenty-six incumbents, preventing the loss of an estimated fifteen to twenty seats.[32]

CAMPAIGN CONTRIBUTIONS AND COORDINATED EXPENDITURES

Party contributions to congressional candidates are restricted by federal law. The national and congressional party campaign committees are permitted to give a total of $15,000 to each House candidate during each stage of the election process (primary, runoff, and general election), and state party committees can give $5,000 (see Chapter 1, Table 1-1).[33] The parties' national and senatorial campaign committees are allowed to give a combined total of $35,000 in an election cycle to a candidate for the Senate. State committees can contribute an additional $5,000 to Senate candidates.

Parties also can spend larger sums in direct coordination with a candidate's campaign. Referred to as "coordinated expenditures," they typically are campaign services that a Hill committee or some other party organization gives to a candidate or purchases from a political consultant on the candidate's behalf. Coordinated expenditures often take the form of polls, TV commercials, radio ads, fundraising events, direct-mail solicitations, issue research, or voter targeting assistance. They differ from campaign contributions in that the party and the candidate share control of them, giving the party the ability to influence some aspects of how the campaign is run. Originally set at $10,000 for all national party organizations, the limits for coordinated expenditures on behalf of House candidates are adjusted for inflation and reached $43,500 in 2010.[34] The limits for national party coordinated expenditures in Senate elections vary by state population and are indexed to inflation. In 2010 they ranged from $87,000 per committee in the smallest states to $2,395,400 in California.

State party committees are authorized to spend the same amounts in coordinated expenditures in House and Senate races as are the parties' national organizations. When a state party lacks resources to participate in a contest its party's congressional or senatorial campaign committee deems important, the state and national party organizations form "agency agreements" that transfer the state party's quota for coordinated expenditures to the national party.[35] Such agreements enable the parties to concentrate funds raised from across the

TABLE 4-1

Party Contributions and Coordinated Expenditures in the 2010
Congressional Elections

	House		Senate	
	Contributions	Coordinated expenditures	Contributions	Coordinated expenditures
Democratic				
DNC	$25,000	$698	$0	$191,699
DCCC	34,745	3,733,499	0	0
DSCC	0	0	578,800	10,514,678
State and local	341,983	3,870,080	122,712	4,527,337
Total Democratic	$401,728	$7,604,278	$701,512	$15,233,714
Republican				
RNC	$36,500	$1,012,398	$21,300	$19,361
NRCC	581,811	6,102,623	0	0
NRSC	0	0	1,046,100	17,256,638
State and local	343,360	1,564,537	31,947	1,014,993
Total Republican	$961,671	$8,679,559	$1,099,347	$18,290,992

Source: Compiled from Federal Election Commission data.

Note: Figures include party spending in all congressional elections, including primaries, runoffs, and uncontested races.

nation into competitive House and Senate races. Agency agreements are among the methods Washington-based party organizations use to coordinate national spending strategies in congressional elections.

From the mid-1970s through the early 1990s, most party activity in congressional elections took the form of cash contributions or coordinated expenditures. The 1996 contests were the first in which the parties were permitted to make independent expenditures with hard-money and issue advocacy ads with soft-money. Most of the national party spending that ensued involved issue advocacy ads because soft-money was easier to collect than hard-money. Following the BCRA's prohibition against national party soft-money, the parties committed more resources to contributions, coordinated expenditures, and independent expenditures. The Democrats distributed roughly $401,000 in contributions and more than $7.6 million in coordinated expenditures in the 2010 House races; the Republicans distributed roughly $962,000 and $8.7 million in these contests (see Table 4-1). Both parties distributed even more financial assistance in the 2010 Senate contests.

Coordinated expenditures are an important aspect of party activity in congressional elections. In addition to enabling party committees to influence the conduct of individual campaigns by infusing them with large amounts of resources, coordinated expenditures enable the parties to take advantage of economies of scale when purchasing and distributing campaign services. Because the parties purchase the services of political consultants in large quantities, they pay below-market rates; this enables them to provide candidates with services whose true market value exceeds the law's coordinated expenditure limits.

The four Hill committees determine the parties' congressional campaign spending strategies and are an important source of party funds spent in congressional elections. Some funds are distributed directly to candidates; others are first transferred to state or other party committees and then given to candidates. The Hill committees also guide the flow of most of the contributions of many other party organizations. Finally, the Hill committees deliver most of the parties' campaign services.

Party committees distribute most of their campaign support to candidates in close elections (see Table 4-2). The Republicans' allocation patterns for House candidates in 2010 indicate the party went on the offensive. The party directed 92 percent of its contributions to challengers and open-seat candidates—primarily Young Guns. The Republicans committed their remaining funds to incumbents, mostly in support of members of the Patriot Program and a few others who were in jeopardy. The minority party usually takes a more aggressive posture than does the majority party, especially in a midterm election year in which a member of the opposing party occupies the White House. The 2010 elections were clearly no exception. The NRCC responded to low approval ratings of a Democratic president, a Democratic-controlled Congress, and a political landscape that was hostile to Democratic candidates with a strategy designed to pick up some Democratic-held seats.

Republican Party contributions and coordinated expenditures were extremely well targeted in 2010. The party delivered 80 percent of these resources to hopeful challengers, 8 percent to open-seat prospects, and 5 percent of its funds to incumbents in jeopardy. The party's ability to distribute 93 percent of its funds to candidates in elections decided by 20 or fewer percentage points was a substantial improvement over some years, including 2004 when it distributed only 77 percent of its funds to candidates in close races, and 1992 when only 53 percent of its funds found their way into campaigns of similarly classified candidates.[36] The 2010 elections were remarkable for the Republicans' aggressive support of competitive nonincumbents.

In contrast to the Republicans' strategy, the plan adopted by the Democratic Party in the 2010 House elections was extremely defensive. The economy,

TABLE 4-2

Allocation of Party Contributions and Coordinated Expenditures in the 2010 Congressional Elections

	House		Senate	
	Democrats	Republicans	Democrats	Republicans
Incumbents				
In jeopardy	78%	5%	51%	3%
Shoo-ins	3	3	2	2
Challengers				
Hopefuls	4	80	1	39
Long shots	3	1	4	1
Open-seat candidates				
Prospects	9	8	39	39
Mismatched	2	3	4	16
Total	$7,655,103	$9,156,450	$14,633,466	$18,804,384

Source: Compiled from Federal Election Commission data.

Notes: Figures include contributions and coordinated expenditures by all party committees to major-party general election candidates in contested races. Columns do not add to 100 percent because of rounding. The categories of candidates are the same as those in Table 1–4. N = 812 for the House; N = 72 for the Senate.

joblessness rates, the housing crisis, and public dissatisfaction with the federal government encouraged the DCCC to focus on protecting members of its Frontline Program and other endangered incumbents. Indeed, the DCCC's allocation of contributions and coordinated expenditures was almost the mirror image of the Republicans' allocation: the GOP spent four-fifths of its funds on hopeful challengers and one-twentieth on incumbents in jeopardy, the Democrats distributed 78 percent of their resources to incumbents locked in close races and a mere 4 percent on hopeful challengers trying to defeat Republican incumbents. Only in House races featuring open-seat prospects did the two parties spend similar portions of their funds. The Democratic Party organizations distributed their resources about as effectively as did the Republicans, as both parties delivered more than 90 percent of their funds to House candidates in competitive contests in 2010.

It is relatively easy for the parties to target their money in Senate elections. DSCC and NRSC officials typically have to assess their candidates' prospects in only thirty-three or thirty-four races per election season, and those races take place within borders that do not shift every ten years because of redistricting.

Polling data also are available for all of the races. As a result, virtually all the parties' funds are usually spent on close elections. The 2010 general elections were fairly typical, but overall party spending in the election cycle was influenced to some degree by an unusually large number of hotly contested primaries and volatile political environments in some states. The Republicans, who were overwhelmingly favored by the national environment, distributed 95 percent of their funds to nonincumbents. The Democrats, on the other hand, disbursed 53 percent of their funds to incumbent senators seeking reelection. As was the case in the House elections, the Republicans were in an aggressive posture and the Democrats in a defensive one. One crucial difference in the spending patterns of the two parties is that the Republicans spent substantially more in elections for mismatched open seats. This was mainly a response to the party's concern with retaining GOP-held seats in Alaska and Florida, where the Republican nominees had to defeat both a Democrat and a Republican whom they had defeated in the primary in order to win the general election.

In addition to distributing campaign contributions and coordinated expenditures directly to candidates, the Hill committees encourage the flow of "party-connected" contributions from incumbents' leadership PACs and reelection committees to candidates in hotly contested elections. Leadership PACs have been involved in congressional elections since Rep. Henry Waxman, D-Calif., founded the first one in 1978, but they were few in number and distributed relatively little money before the late 1980s.[37] Their numbers had grown to 392 by 2010, when they distributed $38 million in contributions to congressional candidates. Although leadership PACs are technically political action committees, not party organizations, and contributions from one candidate to another are not the same as those from a party committee, the candidates who make these contributions share several of the party's objectives. Many also rely on party cues when making them. Their ties to the congressional parties, their reliance on them for information, and the fact that, with the rarest exceptions, all of their contributions flow to members of their party warrant the labeling of these contributions as party connected.[38]

During the 2010 elections, former and current members of Congress—mostly incumbents seeking reelection—and a small number of other prominent politicians contributed almost $50.7 million from their campaign accounts or leadership PACs to 846 primary and general election candidates (see Table 4-3). Republican politicians redistributed substantially more funds in the form of party-connected contributions to House and Senate candidates than did their Democratic opponents. Members of

TABLE 4-3

Party-Connected Contributions in the 2010 Congressional Elections

	House		Senate	
	Democrats	Republicans	Democrats	Republicans
Leadership PAC contributions	$12,264,485	$13,077,785	$5,353,935	$6,370,481
Candidate contributions	6,777,564	3,925,124	252,282	208,644
Contributions from retirees and members not up for reelection	969,822	690,755	404,793	395,211
Total	$20,011,871	$17,693,664	$6,011,010	$6,974,336

Source: Compiled from Federal Election Commission data.

Note: Figures include party spending in all congressional elections, including primaries, runoffs, and uncontested races.

the GOP strongly preferred to make donations directly to each other, while Democratic politicians were more likely to make their donations to party committees, allowing the party an intermediary role in redistributing the wealth. The biggest contributors to other candidates were party leaders. Rep. Eric Cantor of Virginia, the Republicans' whip, and Democratic House majority leader Steny Hoyer of Maryland led their respective parties, contributing almost $1.8 million and $1.6 million from their leadership PACs and campaign committees. Another fifteen party leaders and policy entrepreneurs in the House and Senate redistributed more than $500,000 each to House and Senate candidates. Republican presidential hopeful and former Massachusetts governor Mitt Romney and former Alaska governor Sarah Palin contributed $794,000 and $460,000, respectively. Each clearly recognized the benefits of using political contributions to build the alliances needed to run for president.

Party-connected contributions were distributed strategically, the vast majority to candidates in competitive contests in order to help the party maximize the seats under its control (see Table 4-4). The major difference between party-connected contributions and money contributed by formal party organizations is that the distribution of party-connected funds is somewhat more favorable to incumbents, including those who are shoo-ins for reelection. This difference exists because the contributors of party-connected funds are concerned with more than seat maximization. Some want to support candidates

TABLE 4-4
Distribution of Party-Connected Contributions in the 2010 Congressional Elections

	House		Senate	
	Democrats	Republicans	Democrats	Republicans
Incumbents				
In jeopardy	82%	12%	39%	9%
Shoo-ins	4	12	11	21
Challengers				
Hopefuls	4	56	1	19
Long shots	1	1	5	1
Open-seat candidates				
Prospects	8	11	31	36
Mismatched	2	8	13	14
Total	$19,655,837	$16,367,176	$5,594,010	$5,939,888

Source: Compiled from Federal Election Commission data.

Notes: Figures are for contributions from leadership PACs, candidates, retired members, and members of Congress not up for reelection in 2010 to general election candidates in major-party contested races. Some columns do not add to 100 percent because of rounding. N = 812 for the House; N = 72 for the Senate.

who share their ideological and policy perspectives. Many also want to do favors for congressional colleagues on which they can later collect, which obviously includes those who occupy safe seats. Party-connected contributions, like politicians' donations to party committees, demonstrate that parties have become important vehicles for redistributing resources among congressional candidates.

CAMPAIGN SERVICES

The parties' congressional and senatorial campaign committees provide selected candidates with assistance in specialized campaign activities such as management, gauging public opinion, issue and opposition research, and communications.[39] They also provide transactional assistance, acting as brokers between candidates and the interest groups, individual contributors, political consultants, and powerful incumbents who possess some of the money, political contacts, and campaign expertise that candidates need. The DCCC and NRCC typically become closely involved in the campaigns of candidates on their watch lists and have little involvement in others. The DSCC and NRSC focus most of their attention on Senate candidates in competitive contests, but with so few elections to monitor, they are better able to structure their relationships in response to the specific needs of individual candidates. As former DSCC political director Andrew Grossman explains,

> We love all of our campaigns as much as they need to be loved. Some campaigns need a huge amount of help; some need little help, but help of a specific kind. Some campaigns build relationships around one party service; some campaigns build relationships around several services. Our help is customer based.[40]

Although it is difficult to estimate precisely the value of Hill committee assistance, candidates in close races often receive campaign services that would cost hundreds of thousands of dollars if purchased from a professional political consultant.

Campaign Management

Candidates and their campaign organizations can get help from their Hill committees with hiring and training campaign staff, making strategic and tactical decisions, and other management-related activities. The committees maintain directories of campaign managers, fundraising specialists, media experts, pollsters, voting list vendors, and other political consultants. Candidates can use these for free when purchasing campaign services. Committee officials sometimes recommend that candidates, particularly nonincumbents in targeted races, hire from a list of "trusted" consultants, many of whom have worked for the party or an interest group that routinely supports the party. In some cases, hiring from a Hill committee's list of recommended consultants is a requirement for receiving other forms of party assistance. Sometimes a staff change or replacement of a consultant is stipulated. Political operative Guy Cecil, who has held several senior posts at the DSCC, recounts that his committee has taken things a step further and requires that a campaign's manager, communications director, finance director, and research director meet with DSCC approval before it will provide campaign assistance.[41]

The Hill committees' field representatives and political staffs in Washington also serve as important sources of strategic advice. In most close races, party aides or consultants the parties hire are assigned to work with individual campaigns. Because they have established "war rooms" to monitor elections nationwide and can draw on experiences from previous elections, the Hill committees are among the few organizations that have the information, knowledge, and institutional memory to advise candidates and their managers on how to deal with some of the dilemmas they encounter. The congressional and senatorial campaign committees' political staffs are usually most heavily involved in the planning and tactical decision making of open-seat and challenger candidates. In addition, they provide a great deal of advice to first-term members and other legislators in close races. National party strategic advice is usually appreciated, but some candidates and campaign aides have complained that Hill committee staff can be heavy-handed or fail to understand the politics of their state or district.

The six Washington party organizations also introduce candidates—both incumbents and challengers—and their aides to the latest campaign techniques. At committee headquarters the DCCC and NRCC hold seminars for incumbents that cover topics such as staying in touch with constituents, getting the most political mileage out of franked mail, defending unpopular votes, and effectively utilizing the latest campaign technologies. These seminars are especially important for incumbents who find themselves facing a strong challenge for the first time in many years. The national committees host seminars for challengers and open-seat candidates and political activists around the country. These seminars focus on more basic subjects, such as giving the stump speech, fundraising, and building coalitions. Even long-term members of the House and Senate find the seminars beneficial as reminders of what they ought to be doing. Such reminders are particularly important to endangered incumbents who wish to remain enrolled in the House Democrats' Frontline Program or the House Republicans' Patriot Program. Nevertheless, Hill committee assistance is generally more important to hopeful challengers and open-seat prospects than to incumbents in jeopardy, reflecting the fact that incumbents' electoral difficulties are rarely the result of inexperience or a lack of knowledge about how to campaign.

National party organizations provide an array of opportunities for candidates and activists to develop campaign skills. In 2010 both the DNC and the RNC hosted campaign training seminars across the nation for political candidates and activists. The DCCC held fifteen training sessions for candidates and campaign aides at its Washington headquarters.[42] These featured presentations by DCCC directors and deputy directors on how to outline a campaign budget and develop finance, field, and media plans. The NRCC held two three-day training seminars in Washington to advise challengers, open-seat candidates, campaign aides, and even a few spouses on how to run for Congress. Both parties typically provide their top-tier candidates with extra opportunities to develop their campaign skills. For example, in 2010 more than 100 Young Guns received training on media appearances and fundraising and were invited to a reception attended by Republican House leaders and members of the PAC community. Senatorial committee training sessions are more individualized. Party staffers meet one on one with nonincumbent candidates in Washington and visit their campaign headquarters to help develop budget, fundraising, and communication plans. Both parties seek to help candidates staff their campaign properly so they can do the bulk of the work on their own and call on their party for assistance when needed.

Gauging Public Opinion

The national party committees possess expertise in assessing public opinion, and many candidates find the party's assistance in this area significant. The DNC and RNC disseminate the findings of nationwide polls via newsletters, memoranda, faxes, Internet postings, and e-mails to members of Congress, party activists, and congressional and other candidates. The parties' congressional and senatorial campaign committees commission hundreds of district and statewide polls and targeting studies in a given election season. Early in the campaign cycle they use recruitment surveys to show potential candidates the possibilities of waging competitive races as well as benchmark polls to inform declared candidates of their levels of support and of public opinion on the major issues. They use tracking polls to assist a small group of candidates who are running neck and neck with their opponents at the end of the campaign season. Some of these surveys are paid for entirely by a Hill committee and reported to the Federal Election Commission as in-kind contributions or coordinated expenditures. Most are jointly financed by a committee and the candidates who receive them.

Parties have significant advantages over individual candidates when it comes to commissioning polls. Parties are able to purchase them at discount rates because they contract for so many of them. Parties also can use their extensive connections with polling firms to arrange to piggyback questions on polls taken for other clients. All six Washington party organizations commission polls to research issues they expect to influence the national agenda or public opinion in particular elections. In 2010 both parties spent millions of dollars on gauging public opinion through benchmark, trend, and tracking surveys. The NRCC, for example, spent about $1.5 million in connection with close House races.[43] The NRSC took more than seventy-five polls, the vast majority of which were taken for nonincumbents.[44] Although exact figures are not available for the DCCC or DSCC, these committees took surveys in most of the same races. Officials from all six national party organizations emphasize that polling is essential to waging an effective campaign.

Selected candidates also receive detailed targeting studies from party committees. Some studies are based on microtargeting, taken from the field of marketing research and pioneered in politics by the RNC. Microtargeting involves using voter files that overlay previous election results with individuals' voter turnout histories, contact information, and detailed demographic and consumer information that is correlated with political preferences. Other candidates receive targeting studies that are based on small geographic units rather than individual voters. These combine precinct-level demographic data with previous election results and current polling figures. Both types of studies are useful in guiding direct-mail programs, media purchases, voter mobilization drives, and other campaign efforts.

Issue and Opposition Research

During the 1980s party organizations in Washington became major centers for political research. The DNC and RNC extended their research activities in several directions, most of which were and continue to be focused on matters of concern to party members nationally, rather than the comings and goings of individual congressional districts. The national committees routinely send materials on salient national issues to candidates for Congress, governorships, and state legislatures; to allied consultants and interest groups; and to activists at all levels. This research includes statistics, tables, and charts drawn from major newspapers, the Associated Press wire service, the LexisNexis computerized political database, national public opinion polls, government publications, and a variety of Internet sources. It weaves factual information into partisan themes and powerful anecdotes to underscore major campaign issues. Some receive this information through the U.S. mail, but most get it by way of "blast" faxes and e-mails, tweets, and website postings that the committees transmit daily to hundreds of thousands during the campaign season. Many journalists and political commentators also are sent issue research—albeit with a partisan spin—by the national committees.

The congressional and senatorial campaign committees also disseminate massive amounts of issue-related materials by e-mail, Internet postings, and faxes to candidates, party activists, and partisan political consultants. During the past few Congresses, both parties' House and Senate leaderships distributed talking points and other memoranda designed to help candidates develop issue positions, write speeches, and prepare for debates. Most of this information also was available online. In keeping with the overall national political agenda in 2010, the Republicans' research focused on jobs and the economy and ways to blame the Democrats for the nation's economic woes. The Democrats' research, on the other hand, sought to help their candidates blame the economic mess on the Republicans.

More important than this generic research are the more detailed materials that the Hill committees distribute to individual candidates. Each committee routinely distributes information on the substance and political implications of congressional roll-call votes. Many nonincumbents, who are unable to turn to congressional aides, the Library of Congress, or Washington-based interest groups for information on important issues, use this information to develop policy positions. Challengers also use it to plan attacks on incumbents.

The two House campaign committees assemble highly detailed issue research packages for virtually all of their candidates involved in competitive races. These packages present hard facts about issues that are important to local voters and talking points that help candidates discuss these issues in a thematic and interesting manner. The committees also provide information pinpointing vulnerabilities in an opponent's issue positions, roll-call votes, and professional and personal lives. A fairly new aspect of their research concerns the use of satellite technology, websites, and social media to monitor opponents' campaigns. These technologies enable the committees to identify almost immediately the attacks opponents use against their candidates. They greatly accelerate a campaign's ability to prepare a response.

During the 2010 elections the NRCC spent approximately $2 million to produce individualized research packages for 151 candidates, including 11 incumbents, 118 challengers, and 22 running for open seats. Each package presented detailed information on the Democratic opponent's vulnerabilities, including congressional roll-call votes and speeches on the economic stimulus package, health care reform, and other issues that were part of the GOP's national message.[45] The DCCC prepared individualized research packages on Republican candidates' vulnerabilities for 92 Democrats contesting targeted House races.[46] Both the NRSC and the DSCC also went to great efforts to ensure that their priority candidates had all of the policy and opposition research they needed. Research may not be as visible as televised campaign communications or as easy to objectively measure as campaign contributions and expenditures, but party leaders and staff emphasize its importance. As former NRSC executive director Mark Stephens maintains, "All campaigning starts with research, whether it is concerned with fundraising, television, radio, direct mail, speeches, or press conferences."[47]

The parties also assist candidates with "tracking" their opponents. This refers to assigning a videographer to record an opponent's activities, with the goal of causing or catching a misstatement or some other negative moment that can be used to embarrass that candidate. In 2010 a tracker assigned by the NRCC captured Democratic House incumbent Bob Etheridge of North Carolina knocking down a camera held by a student who aggressively questioned him about his ties to President Obama's political agenda.[48] The video, made available to the media and others, resulted in a major setback for Etheridge's campaign and contributed to his defeat.

Campaign Communications

The Hill committees assist selected candidates with campaign communications. During the 1980s and 1990s the Hill committees owned television and radio production facilities, and they furnished large numbers of candidates with creative, technical, and editorial assistance in producing campaign ads. By 1998, technological advancements made it possible for candidates and media consultants to gain access to high-quality, inexpensive recording and editing equipment without visiting their party's Washington headquarters or renting an editing suite. As a result, very few contemporary candidates use party media production facilities. Some incumbents and a few others use these facilities' satellite capabilities to appear "live" on television news shows, at fundraisers, or at events in their districts. The facilities are occasionally used by party staff to produce low-budget streaming video communications that are disseminated on the Internet.

Although they no longer produce candidates' mass media ads, the Hill committees continue to play an important role in the communications of candidates in competitive contests. They advise candidates on the issues, themes, and messages that could attract voters in their districts and assist with hiring media strategists, often influencing their choice of consultants. They also comment on drafts of television, radio, telephone, direct-mail, and e-mail scripts before they are disseminated to voters. In 2010 the NRCC and NRSC staffs advised Republican candidates to use the party's "80 percent negative/20 percent positive" media strategy and link their campaign's message to the party's national message by addressing local concerns that exemplified the issues raised in national party communications.[49] Their Democratic counterparts, on the other hand, advised their candidates to localize their campaigns as much as possible and focus on the flaws of their opponents. The use of e-mail attachments and secure websites enables committee aides to provide timely information and feedback on campaign messages and strategy to candidates and their consultants.

The Hill committees also take on supporting roles in other aspects of campaign communications by doing work that candidates' campaign committees cannot. They help the candidates attract media coverage from the national and local media, often by planting stories with journalists. They release negative information about the opposing party's candidates. And, as is discussed later, their independent media campaigns can have a major impact on the tenor of a congressional race. The effects of party communications extend beyond the communications themselves. When party organizations spin the news, place streaming video and other information on Internet "microsites" dedicated to individual races, or make media buys for TV ads, they signal to others the races they consider important, the content of the ads they plan to disseminate, and even the timing of those advertisements. This signaling gives their interest group allies an opportunity to use their own resources to supplement a party's efforts, thereby increasing the volume of the party's message and the number of locations in which it is heard. It also provides media outlets with content for their news stories. Senatorial and congressional campaign committee research and communication efforts have clearly contributed to the nationalization of American politics.

Fundraising

In addition to providing contributions, coordinated expenditures, and campaign services directly to candidates and steering party-connected contributions to them, the Hill committees help candidates in competitive contests raise money from individuals and PACs. To this end, the committees give the candidates strategic advice and fundraising assistance, and they disseminate information about these candidates to their top donors. They also furnish PACs and individual donors with other forms of information they can use when formulating their contribution and spending strategies and selecting individual candidates for support.

All six national party organizations give candidates tips on how to organize fundraising committees and events. The Hill committees even furnish some candidates with contributor lists, with the proviso that the candidates surrender their own lists to the committee after the election. The committees have conference rooms and dozens of telephone suites that incumbents can use to meet with donors or make fundraising calls when in Washington; these are important because it is illegal to solicit contributions in the Capitol and other federal office buildings. The parties also host high-dollar events in Washington or make arrangements for party leaders to attend events held around the country, either in person or via satellite uplink. The Speaker of the House and other congressional leaders can draw lobbyists, PAC managers, and other big contributors to even the most obscure candidate's fundraising event. Of course, nothing can draw a crowd of big contributors like an appearance by the president, and in 2010 President Obama, First Lady Michelle Obama, and members of the cabinet and the White House staff actively participated in campaign fundraising.

The Hill committees also steer large contributions from wealthy individuals, PACs, or members of Congress to needy candidates. It is illegal for the parties to earmark checks they receive from individuals or PACs for specific candidates, but committee members and staff can suggest to contributors that they contribute to one of the candidates on the committee's watch list. Sometimes they reinforce this message by sending out fundraising letters or e-mails on behalf of a candidate, sponsoring events that list congressional leaders as hosts, or organizing joint fundraising events. Major components of the DCCC's Red to Blue Program and the NRCC's Young Guns Program involve bringing promising nonincumbent candidates and powerful members of Congress together with deep-pocketed party supporters at hundreds of events in Washington, D.C., and across the nation. These introductions enable candidates to raise contributions from donors who otherwise may not have even heard of them. The programs enable some little-known challengers and open-seat candidates to exploit a part of their party's donor pool that otherwise would be inaccessible to them.

The Hill committees give candidates the knowledge and tools they need to obtain money from PACs. The committees help candidates design "PAC kits" they can use to introduce themselves to members of the PAC community.[50] They also distribute lists of PACs that include the name of a contact person at each PAC and indicate how much cash the PAC has on hand, so that candidates will neither waste their time soliciting committees that have no money nor take no for an answer when a PAC manager claims poverty but still has funds. Candidates are coached on how to fill out the questionnaires that some PACs use to guide their contributions and how to build coalitions of local PAC contributors so that they can raise money from national PACs.

The committees also help candidates raise money from PACs and wealthy individuals by manipulating the informational environment in which donors make their contribution decisions. The committees' PAC directors work to channel the flow of PAC money toward their party's most competitive congressional contenders and away from their opponents. This is an especially difficult task to perform for House challengers and open-seat candidates, and even for some junior House members, because they are largely unknown to the PAC community.

Several methods are used to circulate information about House and Senate elections to PACs and other potential contributors. Party contributions, expenditures, lists of priority candidates, and press briefings draw the attention of PACs and wealthy individual contributors. Party website postings have a similar effect and make it convenient to give a contribution. Party-sponsored "meet and greets" in Washington and elsewhere give candidates, especially targeted nonincumbents, an opportunity to ask PAC managers and lobbyists for donations. Every week during the peak election season, campaign updates are e-mailed or faxed to about 1,000 of the largest PACs to inform them of priority candidates' electoral prospects, financial needs, poll results, endorsements, campaign highlights, and revelations about problems experienced by their opponents. Streams of communications also are sent to the editors of the *Cook Political Report,* the *Rothenberg Political Report, Politico,* and other online newsletters that handicap congressional races. A favorable write-up in one of these can help a nonincumbent raise more money.

The Hill committees' PAC directors and party leaders spend a tremendous amount of time making telephone calls on behalf of their most competitive and financially needy candidates. Some of these calls are made to PAC managers who are recognized leaders of PAC networks. The DCCC and DSCC, for example, work closely with the National Committee for an Effective Congress (NCEC) and the American Federation of Labor–Congress of Industrial Organizations' Committee on Political Education (AFL-CIO COPE); their GOP counterparts work closely with the Business-Industry Political Action Committee. The committees encourage these "lead" PACs to endorse the party's top contestants and to communicate their support to other PACs and to individuals in their donor networks.

One of the more controversial practices is to use the political clout of party leaders to leverage contributions. Hill committee staffs organize functions and clubs that promise PAC managers, lobbyists, and others access to congressional leaders in return for large contributions to the committees and needy candidates. The former Republican majority leader, Tom DeLay, for example, greeted lobbyists with a list that categorized the 400 largest PACs as "friendly" or "unfriendly," depending on the proportion of their contributions that went to Republicans, in order to hammer home the message that groups that wanted access to GOP leaders would be expected to give most of their contributions to Republican candidates and party committees in the future.[51] One can anticipate that regardless of which party is in control of the House or Senate, its leaders will use similar tactics to increase their party's share of PAC contributions.

The Hill committees also use "buddy systems" to match financially needy but promising nonincumbents and freshmen with committee chairs and other powerful incumbents for fundraising purposes. These senior incumbents offer their partners contributions, provide advice on campaign-related topics, and use their influence to persuade PAC managers and individuals who have made large contributions to their campaigns to contribute to their "buddy." The buddy system's impact on fundraising is hard to estimate, but during the 2010 elections congressional party leaders, committee chairs, and ranking members raised tens of millions of dollars for candidates in spirited races. As suggested by the number of incumbents who contributed to other candidates, many members of Congress were involved in redistributing the wealth in 2010.

The Hill committees' relationships with members of Congress, PACs, and individuals who make large contributions have resulted in the parties becoming important brokers between candidates and contributors. These relationships are based largely on exchanges of information that enable the Hill committees and members of their donor pools to advance their mutual and individual interests, as well as those of candidates involved in close elections. Party communications to PACs and wealthy individual donors are somewhat controversial because even though they help the fundraising prospects of some candidates, they inevitably harm those of others. Candidates who receive their Hill committee's endorsement derive significant fundraising advantages from such communications, but challengers and open-seat candidates who do not are usually unable to collect significant funds. Some groups and individuals who routinely make large contributions justify refusing a contribution request because a nonincumbent was not included on a Hill committee's priority list. Hill committee fundraising efforts can create both winners and losers in the campaign for resources. Thus, they have a major impact on congressional elections.

OUTSIDE CAMPAIGNS

Party campaigning extends beyond money and campaign services contributed directly to candidates and party assistance in helping candidates collect resources from others. Parties also use coordinated grassroots and independent media campaigns involving pollsters, targeting experts, issue and opposition researchers, communications consultants, and other strategists to influence congressional elections. These efforts are often referred to as "outside campaigns" because they are waged primarily by organizations outside a candidate's own campaign apparatus.

Coordinated Grassroots Campaigns

National party organizations in Washington, D.C., are central to the financing and planning of coordinated grassroots campaigns that rely heavily on the participation of state and local party committees. Numerous party-connected groups sponsored by current and former members of Congress and allied interest groups also participate in party grassroots efforts. Some make financial contributions; others furnish voter lists or other targeting information. Still others provide volunteers. Labor unions have a long history of participating in Democratic Party grassroots campaigns. The Tea Party movement was an important source of volunteers for Republican grassroots efforts in 2010. Ideological groups on the left and right routinely participate in party grassroots campaign activities.

Party grassroots campaigns entail traditional voter mobilization efforts enhanced by innovations in data collection, statistical analysis, and communications technologies. Important elements of the coordinated campaign involve voter registration, targeting, and turnout efforts. These activities are especially important during midterm congressional elections because, absent the excitement of a presidential contest, many voters who have low or medium levels of political engagement need extra encouragement to show up at the polls.

Beginning in the 1960s first the RNC and then the DNC assisted state party organizations with voter registration, voter list development, targeting, get-out-the-vote (GOTV) drives, and other campaign efforts designed to benefit their party's entire ticket. The Republicans' coordinated grassroots campaign, called the Victory Program, is largely funded and directed by the RNC. It has three parts: a targeting component that uses its Voter Vault data files, microtargeting techniques, and lists of volunteers to help Republican state parties identify, educate, and target likely Republican voters; an infrastructure component to help state and local parties set up local Victory Committees that provide the office space, computers, telephone banks, maps, voter lists, and the other resources needed to implement voter registration and turnout drives; and a voter mobilization program called the 72-Hour Program. Modeled after the marketing operation created by the Amway homecare products company, the 72-Hour Program uses paid organizers to recruit and train volunteers who, in turn, recruit and train other volunteers in order to build a multilayered grassroots organization. Individuals at the top layers of the organization coordinate those in lower layers who are primarily responsible for registering voters; assisting with absentee ballot applications; knocking on doors; making telephone calls; sending out U.S. mail, e-mails, and tweets; arranging rides; and other personalized forms of neighborhood-oriented direct voter contacts. The program's reliance on targeted grassroots activities is so reminiscent of party campaigning at the dawn of the twentieth century that party officials have referred to it as a "back to the future approach."[52]

The Democrats did not begin to develop their own microtargeting operation or assemble their Data Mart voter file until after the 2004 election. However, since then they have made tremendous strides in assembling voter databases and targeting methods. Democratic coordinated grassroots campaigns are less centralized than the Republicans' efforts. They rely on some outside organizations, such as the NCEC and Catalist, for targeting assistance. Democrats' grassroots efforts typically involve national, senatorial, congressional, state, and local party campaign committees; aides and volunteers who work in presidential, statewide, and local campaigns; and coalitions of labor unions and other interest group organizations. The degree of participation by a campaign, party committee, or interest group depends, to a large extent, on how much of their jurisdiction overlaps with that covered by the coordinated campaign.

In recent years both parties and their candidates have had to adjust their grassroots campaigns in response to election reforms. By 2010 thirty-two states provided some form of early voting and thirty states permitted "no excuse" absentee voting. A conservative estimate is that 30 percent of all voters used one of their forms of "convenience voting" that year.[53] This has changed the nature and timing of voter mobilization efforts in a number of ways. First, in addition to registering potential supporters, grassroots volunteers encourage as many voters as possible to vote absentee. Second, GOTV drives now begin about a month earlier because campaign volunteers contact voters as soon as local boards of elections put absentee ballots in the mail and a few days before early voting begins. Third, GOTV efforts have become more reliant on the services of experts who can update voter files to account for absentee and early voters. Finally, convenience voting saves money and volunteer resources because campaigns can eliminate the names of individuals who cast their ballots prior to Election Day from their contact list. An added benefit of convenience voting is what some campaign professionals refer to as "vote banking." That is, by securing votes early, they prevent a late-breaking scandal or potentially harmful event from costing their candidates votes.

The 2010 elections were unusual in that the RNC had a significantly reduced role in its party's Victory Program. Plagued by scandals, a huge debt, and headed by a chair who was not an effective fundraiser, the committee transferred only $21.4 million to Republican state and local parties to help underwrite their Victory Committees (compared to $37.5 million during the 2006 midterm election). Moreover, it decided to all but abandon voter mobilization efforts to support Republican Senate candidates in favor of focusing its limited resources on House candidates in competitive races. The NRCC and NRSC compensated for the national committee's shortfall by transferring

$3.5 million and $3 million (substantial increases from $474,000 and $300,000 in 2006). As a result, there was "a presence" of a Victory Program in forty-five states, and Victory Committees were organized in about 100 House districts. Led by 350 paid organizers assisted by 25 RNC political field staff, 20 contractors, and 50,000 volunteers, the GOP's Victory Program contacted loyal Republicans, Republican-leaning independents, and Republican-leaning disgruntled Democrats to urge them to vote early, absentee, or on Election Day. As impressive as these figures appear, it is important to recognize that for the first time in decades, entire states and parts of states received little or no RNC support, leaving candidate campaigns, the NRSC, other Republican Party committees, and interest groups to organize and finance the ground game in Senate elections.[54]

Reflecting its more decentralized administration, the Democrats' coordinated grassroots campaign was financed by a variety of organizations. DNC, DCCC, and DSCC transfers of $32 million, $17.6 million, and $10.5 million paid for most of it. Like the GOP, the Democrats established field offices across the nation. Most were in areas hosting competitive House, Senate, or gubernatorial races and staffed by regional field organizers, consultants, party activists, and tens of thousands of volunteers. Together they worked to register and mobilize Democratic and Democratic-leaning voters. As was the case for the Republicans, each Democratic Party committee pursued its own priorities while participating in a cooperative effort. For example, the DCCC used its voter contact program to place an unprecedented 4.9 million personal GOTV phone calls and 2.2 million volunteer recruitment calls, and knock on 1.8 million doors in seventy-five of its targeted districts in 2010.[55] Designed to benefit Democratic House contestants, these efforts also benefited other Democratic candidates running in these areas.

One major difference between the parties' grassroots campaign efforts concerns the types of voters they targeted. Given the greater enthusiasm of Republican voters going into the 2010 election and the unpopularity of the Democratic-controlled federal government, the GOP was able to focus beyond active members of its base and target nonhabitual voters (who generally do not turn out in midterm elections), as well as individuals who do not consistently vote Republican. The Democrats, on the other hand, had to expend substantial resources to mobilize their base.

Independent Media Campaigns

The political parties' independent media campaigns involve independent expenditures that expressly exhort voters to vote for or against a candidate or call for a candidate's election or defeat. They are conducted almost exclusively in targeted races, and they are generally more negative and hard hitting than candidate communications. The parties were first allowed to make these in 1996 after the Supreme Court's ruling in *Colorado Republican Federal Campaign Committee v. FEC.*[56] As noted above, independent expenditures must be made with federally regulated funds and without the knowledge or consent of the candidate or anyone involved in the candidate's campaign. They usually take the form of television ads, radio ads, direct mail, or mass telephone calls. Sometimes these communications are posted on websites or distributed using social media.

Unlike candidate ads, party independent expenditures that appear on television or radio do not qualify for lowest unit rate charges. This, and the cost of establishing a separate IE group to research and produce the ads, makes them very expensive. Given that control over the House and Senate was at stake in 2010 and the BCRA prohibits parties from financing issue advocacy ads with soft-money, it is not surprising that the parties made substantial independent expenditures. Party committees—mainly the four Hill committees—spent about $185 million in independent expenditures in connection with House and Senate elections (see Figure 4-3). The vast majority of this money was used to finance television ads that were largely negative in tone. One explanation for this is that many political operatives believe that it is easier to tear down an opponent than build up their own candidate. Indeed, academic studies have shown that negative campaign ads are more likely than positive ads to be remembered and to motivate voters to go to the polls.[57] Negative ads tend to be especially harmful to nonincumbents who are not as well known to voters as current officeholders.[58] A second explanation is that it makes more sense strategically for parties to do most of the dirty work associated with attack politics so that their candidates can take the high road and air mainly positive ads. This de facto division of labor enables candidates to claim truthfully they had nothing to do with a negative ad or the IE group responsible for it, and it is beyond their power to have the ad pulled from the airwaves. Some candidates go a step further and publicly denounce the offending ad.

Almost all of the parties' independent media spending takes place in competitive elections. In 2010 the Democrats spent about $65.3 million to influence the outcomes of 133 House elections (see Table 4-5). Seventy-seven percent of these funds were devoted to helping Democratic incumbents in jeopardy defend their seats, 2 percent were used to assist hopeful challengers, and the remaining 21 percent were devoted to the causes of open-seat prospects. The Republicans made almost $46.1 million in

FIGURE 4-3

Party Independent Expenditures in the 2010 Elections

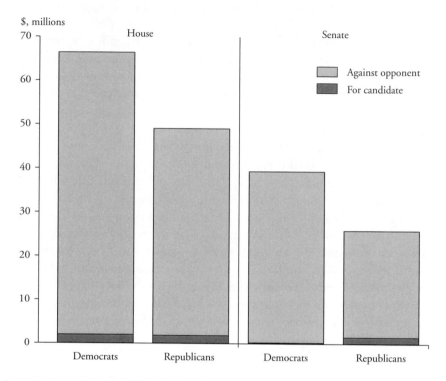

Source: Compiled from Federal Election Commission data.

independent expenditures to influence seventy House contests. Their spending patterns roughly mirrored the Democrats', with a mere 1 percent used to defend incumbents, 83 percent to support the efforts of challengers, and the remainder devoted to open seats. Most party independent expenditures in Senate elections focused on the same ten races. The distribution of these ads demonstrates that the Democrats were primarily concerned with protecting incumbents, the Republicans were heavily focused on defeating them, and both parties perceived substantial opportunities for picking up open seats.

Because of the Democrats' control of the federal government and voter dissatisfaction with it and the overall state of the nation, the tenor of the parties' independent expenditure ads was very different. Most of the GOP's

TABLE 4-5

Distribution of Party Independent Expenditures in the 2010
Congressional Elections

	House		Senate	
	Democrats	Republicans	Democrats	Republicans
Incumbents				
In jeopardy	77%	1%	35%	—
Shoo-ins	—	—	—	—
Challengers				
Hopefuls	2	83	—	48
Long shots	—	—	—	—
Open-seat candidates				
Prospects	21	14	64	50
Mismatched	—	2	1	2
Total	$65,322,998	$46,060,133	$39,362,293	$25,866,594

Source: Compiled from Federal Election Commission data.

Notes: Figures in cells include all independent expenditures designed to help a candidate (i.e., those for the candidate and against the opponent). The categories of candidates are the same as those in Table 1-4. N = 812 for the House; N = 72 for the Senate.

emphasized national themes. They blamed Democrats for the state of the economy; criticized their support for health care reform, environmental regulations, and other bills they labeled as "job-killing"; or tied them to unpopular Democratic leaders and the federal government. The Democrats' independent expenditure ads were more locally oriented, concentrating mainly on the weaknesses of specific Republican candidates. Overall, the allocation of party independent expenditures and the messages conveyed in them are consistent with the distribution of party contributions, coordinated expenditures, campaign services, and national agenda-setting efforts. The major differences between the parties' independent expenditures and other activities are that the independent expenditures were concentrated in fewer races and were more negative.

Beyond their direct effects on individual races, party independent expenditures (and other activities) have the indirect effect of encouraging a party's interest group and other allies to pour their resources into the party's targeted races. This is in part due to the relationships among members of the PAC and political consulting communities who belong to a party's network and because of the signaling by party IE groups. For example, party IE groups signal to others the content of televised party independent expenditure ads as well as where and when they will be aired, enabling interest groups to consider party priorities and messages when formulating their own advertising strategies. When allied groups complement or supplement a party's independent advertising in a House or Senate race, it frees the party to devote its resources to some other contest. During the 2010 elections, all four Hill committees redeployed some of their independent expenditures when allied groups began heavily advertising in targeted contests. In a few cases, some interest groups broadcast TV spots featuring a nearly identical message a party had been signaling it would use, enabling the party to spend its money elsewhere.[59]

Party outside advertising is predominantly negative, and thus it has become highly controversial. One of the most notorious and effective independent television ads to air in recent years was run in 2006 by the RNC against Democrat Harold Ford Jr., an African American member of the House who was in Tennessee's open-seat Senate contest. The ad opened with a woman remarking, "Harold Ford looks nice"; then it moved on to another woman who commented that "terrorists need their privacy" and a middle-aged man who stated, "When I die Harold Ford will let me pay taxes again." Several other individuals, apparently representing various other elements of society, made other outrageous and hilarious statements. The ad closed with a scantily clad white woman saying, "Harold, call me."[60] The ad's use of humor and innuendo made it entertaining and memorable, and it had the effect of generating a great deal of free coverage in the media, which multiplied its effect. Its attacks on ethical issues were potent because Ford was running a campaign highlighting his values, and he was using television ads recorded in a church. Its closing scene probably evoked some racial prejudices that are still quite potent in parts of Tennessee. Although not the sole cause of the outcome, the ad undoubtedly contributed to Ford's defeat.

Not all party independent expenditures are as effective as the anti-Ford ad, and some can do more harm than good. The prohibitions against coordination between the party IE group making the ads, the candidate whose election the ads are intended to influence, and other party organizations supporting the candidate can result in ads that may backfire. First, some ads can take a candidate off message and have an adverse affect on targeted voters. Second, voters sometimes blame a candidate for a party attack ad that offends local sensibilities, even though the candidate had nothing to do with the ad and could do nothing about it. The last few election cycles offer numerous examples of candidates disavowing party independent expenditure ads, including several candidates who attribute their loss to them.

THE IMPACT OF PARTY CAMPAIGNING

How valuable do House and Senate candidates find the campaign services they receive from party organizations? When asked to rate the importance of campaign assistance from local, state, and national party organizations and union, business, and advocacy groups and PACs in aspects of campaigning requiring professional expertise or in-depth research, candidates and campaign aides involved in House elections rank their party's Hill committee highly. Campaigners gave top evaluations to the Hill committees for campaign management, information about voters, issue and opposition research, mass media advertising, and development of the candidate's public image. Interest groups received somewhat higher evaluations for assistance in fundraising.[61]

Recall that congressional campaign committee assistance is generally targeted to a small number of close contests. For example, about one-half of all Republican House candidates in elections decided by 20 percent or less of the vote, as well as 28 percent of their Democratic counterparts, rated their party's congressional campaign committee as moderately, very, or extremely helpful in campaign management (see Table 4-6).[62] More than half of each party's candidates in competitive races considered the fundraising and mass communications assistance they received from their party's congressional campaign committee to have been at least moderately important. Competitive Republicans gave even more favorable evaluations to Hill committee assistance in campaign management, public opinion assessment, and issue and opposition research than did their Democratic counterparts. With the exception of fundraising, for which more incumbents in jeopardy reported receiving the most congressional campaign committee assistance, open-seat prospects provided the most positive evaluations of Hill committee campaign services. In sum, the evaluations of House campaigners indicate the Hill committees are important campaign service providers, and most congressional campaign committee help is given to candidates in close races, consistent with the parties' goal of winning as many seats in Congress as possible.

Local party committees received the strongest evaluations for assistance with registering voters, GOTV drives, and providing campaign volunteers. Roughly half of all campaigners assessed their local party's contributions to have been moderately, very, or extremely important. State party committees were rated next highest for voter mobilization activities. Republicans reported their party's state committee played a substantial role in providing campaign workers. Many Democrats were somewhat less impressed with their state party's performance in this regard; most maintained that labor unions provided them with more volunteer campaign workers. These evaluations demonstrate the vibrancy of

TABLE 4-6

House Campaigners' Appraisals of the Assistance Provided by the Congressional Campaign Committees

	DCCC						NRCC					
	Incumbents		Challengers		Open-seat candidates		Incumbents		Challengers		Open-seat candidates	
	In jeopardy	Shoo-ins	Hopefuls	Long shots	Prospects	Mis-matched	In jeopardy	Shoo-ins	Hopefuls	Long shots	Prospects	Mis-matched
Campaign management	12%	9%	33%	3%	37%	13%	42%	3%	47%	9%	60%	10%
Fundraising	53	30	46	9	53	25	67	8	47	7	57	20
Media advertising	47	16	50	2	67	13	58	19	53	15	63	20
Information about voters	31	42	53	13	74	25	64	29	47	18	75	20
Issue and opposition research	25	15	57	9	53	38	46	14	71	30	80	40
Voter mobilization	18	18	43	6	21	13	25	9	25	9	47	10
Volunteer workers	—	2	36	3	42	25	42	—	12	—	40	10

Source: "2002 Congressional Campaign Study," Center for American Politics and Citizenship, University of Maryland.

Notes: Figures represent the percentage of House campaigners who evaluated their congressional campaign committee as moderately, very, or extremely helpful in each campaign activity. Figures are for general election candidates in major-party contested races, excluding those in incumbent-versus-incumbent races. — = less than 0.5 percent. N = 314.

state and local parties in some parts of the country. They also show the limited visibility of the congressional, senatorial, and national committees' involvement in grassroots campaigning, which frequently amounts to providing leadership and funding rather than directly recruiting armies of volunteers.

The 2010 race in Florida's 2nd congressional district between the incumbent Allen Boyd and the challenger Steve Southerland is an example of a race in which both parties became heavily involved.[63] Because of Boyd's large war chest (he began the election cycle with almost $1.2 million) and fundraising prowess, the DCCC provided him with no contributions and made only $19,480 in coordinated expenditures on his behalf. Democratic members of Congress, retirees, and other federal politicians contributed an additional $247,000 from their campaign accounts and leadership PACs. Total party and party-connected contributions accounted for almost 14 percent of the resources under Boyd's control. The DCCC also provided the campaign with briefings, research, and fundraising assistance. DCCC regional director B. J. Neidhardt provided strategic advice throughout the race.

The Democrats' coordinated grassroots campaign, led by the Florida Democratic State Central Committee, organized foot canvasses, telephone banks, and other direct voter contact activities to mobilize its base and Democratic-leaning voters on behalf of Boyd and the party's other candidates. Special efforts were made to turn out Hispanic voters and secure the votes of supporters who requested absentee ballots. These efforts were important because midterm elections normally generate low voter turnout, and the political climate did much to whip up enthusiasm among Republican supporters and little to stimulate turnout among Democrats. The grassroots campaign was financed in part by the $3.7 million that the DNC and DCCC transferred to the Florida State Central Committee.

The Democrats also executed a significant independent media campaign. The DCCC spent almost $347,000 in independent expenditures attacking Southerland. Much of these funds were spent on two television ads. The first focused on a comment Southerland made during the Republican primary in support of repealing the Seventeenth Amendment, which instituted the direct election of senators. The second ad fixed on Southerland's support for the flat tax and desire to cut Social Security. According to Neidhardt, the ads were designed to make the challenger so unacceptable to voters who were unhappy with Boyd that they would support one of the minor-party candidates in the race and thus divide the anti-Boyd vote.

The Republican Party also committed significant resources to the campaign. It provided Southerland with $6,950 in contributions and $85,000 in coordinated expenditures. Republican members of Congress and other federal politicians contributed an additional $120,000 from their campaign committees and leadership PACs. Party and party-connected dollars accounted for more than 16 percent of Southerland's resources. As a Young Gun, Southerland received extensive strategic and tactical advice, a poll, an opposition research package, and substantial fundraising assistance.

As is typical in close contests, the RNC's Victory Program in Florida took primary responsibility for the coordinated grassroots campaign, including voter identification, targeting, and mobilization. It worked with the GOP's state central committee, the Bay County Republicans, local chapters of the Young Republicans and College Republicans, and other local party organizations to turn out pro-Republican early, absentee, and Election Day voters. National Rifle Association members, military veterans, and pro-life, evangelical, and other social conservatives were targeted for door-to-door visits and telephone calls. In support of these efforts, the RNC and NRCC transferred $1 million to the Florida GOP.

The Republican Party's independent media campaign was better funded than the Democrats'. The NRCC spent almost $700,000 attacking Boyd for supporting health care reform, cutting more than $500 billion from Medicare, and costing his constituents their jobs by helping to shut down a local loan processing facility. By localizing national issues, the GOP sought to link the incumbent to the national wave of voter dissatisfaction with the federal government.

Most Senate candidates and campaign aides give evaluations of Hill committee assistance that are as favorable as those given by House candidates. The senatorial campaign committees are ranked above any other group in every area of campaigning, except providing information about voters, mobilizing voters, and recruiting volunteers. State and local party organizations and interest groups were ranked higher for these activities.[64]

Senate candidates in battleground races receive more campaign resources from their party than from any other group. The contest in Nevada between Democratic Senate majority leader Harry Reid and the Republican challenger, Tea Party favorite and former state representative Sharron Angle, demonstrates how important party activity can be in an election for the upper chamber. The race was a nail-biter until the very end. Nevada is a swing state that has recently elected Democrats and Republicans to the Senate, the House, and the governor's office. The setting for the 2010 Senate election was particularly perilous for Reid. As a result of the economic meltdown, Nevada led the nation in unemployment, bankruptcy, and home foreclosure rates. The personal incomes of Nevadans tumbled more quickly than those of citizens in any other state. And, as noted above, Reid was instrumental in enacting policies the Republicans claimed were responsible for these outcomes. The election turned out to be the most expensive in the state's history and the second most costly in the nation. Not surprisingly, both parties focused heavily on the contest.

Reid benefited from a broad range of Democratic Party efforts. Party luminaries President Obama, former president Bill Clinton (each of whom visited twice), Vice President Joe Biden, and First Lady Michelle Obama made campaign visits to mobilize Democratic donors, campaign activists, and voters. Democratic Party committees made $42,000 in contributions and $143,000 in coordinated expenditures in the race. Democratic senators and other politicians contributed $505,000 from their campaign committees and almost $343,000 from their leadership PACs. Because of his difficult race and position as their party's Senate leader, any requests Reid made for information, advice, or other assistance were made a top priority by the DSCC.

Reid also received help in the form of a massive Democratic Party coordinated grassroots campaign effort. The DSCC transferred more than $1.8 million to Democratic Party committees in the state, which was accompanied by another $381,000 in transfers from the DNC and DCCC. These funds were used for voter identification, targeting, registration, and GOTV programs. The DSCC also mounted a formidable independent media campaign on Reid's behalf, spending almost $2 million calling for Angle's defeat. Most of these expenditures painted Angle as unfit to represent Nevada voters. They pointed to Angle's proposals to phase out Social Security and Medicare and her unwillingness to tackle unemployment. The most powerful ads made use of the challenger's remarks, including one ad that quoted Angle as stating, "It's not a senator's job to create jobs," and "The unemployed are spoiled."[65]

Like the Democrats, the Republicans also were very active in the race. Angle benefited from campaign visits made by the 2008 Republican presidential candidate, Sen. John McCain, his former running mate Sarah Palin, and former Republican House Speaker Newt Gingrich, among others. The GOP contributed $42,600 directly to the Angle campaign and carried out $292,000 in coordinated expenditures on her behalf. Republican members of Congress contributed roughly $270,000 to the Angle campaign, most of it from their leadership PACs. The NRSC's political division provided Angle with extensive strategic advice, issue and opposition research, and fundraising assistance. NRSC efforts were critical to helping Angle raise an impressive $28.2 million—an amount that is all the more impressive because of the fact that it exceeded Reid's total by $3.4 million. In addition, the NRSC helped Angle shape and disseminate her message.

The Republican Party also conducted an impressive coordinated grassroots campaign on her behalf. Led by the NRSC, GOP committees in Washington transferred more than $847,000 to Republican Victory Committees in Nevada.

These funds were used to create a cooperative field effort involving the NRSC, NRCC, Nevada Republican State Central Committee, local Republican Party organizations, and Tea Party groups committed to mobilizing Republicans and other voters inclined to support Angle, GOP gubernatorial candidate Brian Sandoval, and Republican candidates for the House and other offices. The GOP also spent $1.36 million in independent expenditures demanding Reid's ouster. Most of the messages blamed Reid for the nation's deficit, the recession, and the economic hardships felt by Nevadans in particular. One particularly hard-hitting TV ad argued that these downward economic trends took place "under his watch" and asserted that "while Harry lives in the Ritz-Carlton, thousands are losing their homes." It concludes that "the nation needs a new direction; Nevada needs jobs; say no to Harry Reid."[66]

It is impossible to identify with certainty what determined the outcomes of many elections. Nevertheless, party help can be crucial. It certainly was important in Nevada's 2010 Senate contest and Florida's 2nd district House race. Combined, party organizations and party-connected committees spent $7 million, almost 10 percent of the total expenditures in the former election, and almost $2.1 million, or 26 percent, in the latter.[67] In addition to these funds, the parties provided extensive campaign services. Had the Democratic Party failed to participate in the Nevada contest, it is likely that Reid would not have emerged victorious; had the Republican Party been absent, it is likely that Angle would have lost by a larger margin. Similarly, Southerland's victory over Boyd may not have occurred in the absence of Republican Party involvement, and Boyd's defeat may have been more convincing had the Democratic Party abstained from the race.

Despite all of the money, campaign services, and strategic advice party committees can provide a campaign, it would be wrong to assume that relations between campaign organizations and party committees are always harmonious or productive. As noted in Chapter 3, campaigns that are dominated by local politicos and activists sometimes resent the advice of Washington-based party operatives and out-of-town consultants, especially when the locals have been inspired to join the campaign by a popular political uprising, such as the Tea Party movement. Candidate-party relations also can become tense when a congressional or senatorial campaign committee makes the replacement of a campaign aide by one of its preferred consultants a precondition for the receipt of party funding and campaign services. Bitter feelings almost always persist when a candidate loses and sometimes continue even when the candidate wins.

SUMMARY

Political parties, particularly the congressional and senatorial campaign committees, play important supporting roles in contemporary congressional elections. Their agenda-setting efforts encourage voters to focus on issues that work to the advantage of their candidates. Their contributions, coordinated expenditures, and campaign services strengthen the campaigns of the select group of candidates who receive them. Their transactional assistance helps these candidates attract funding and other campaign resources from influential politicians, PACs, other politically active groups, and individual contributors. Their independent media campaigns can amplify a candidate's message or put an opponent on the defensive. The coordinated grassroots campaigns the Hill committees carry out in partnership with their party's national, state, and local party committees help mobilize voters in support of their candidates.

Republican Party organizations historically have been wealthier than their Democratic counterparts, and GOP party committees, particularly at the national level, have traditionally assumed a greater role than Democratic Party organizations in congressional elections. The Democrats closed that wealth gap considerably in 2006, and in 2008 they outfundraised and outspent the GOP for the first time in modern history. Aided by President Obama's occupancy of the White House and their congressional majorities, in 2010 the Democrats again raised more than the Republicans. This put them in a position to deliver substantially more support to congressional candidates than did the Republicans. Having lost control of the House after the 2010 election, whether the Democrats will maintain these advantages in upcoming election cycles remains an open question.

CHAPTER FIVE

The Interests Campaign

Organized interests, pejoratively referred to as "special interests," have always been involved in American elections. During the earliest days of the Republic, leaders of agricultural and commercial groups influenced who was on the ballot, the coverage they received in the press, and the voting patterns that determined election outcomes. As the electorate grew and parties and candidates began to spend more money to reach voters, steel magnates, railroad barons, and other captains of industry increased their roles in political campaigns. Labor unions counterorganized with workers and dollars. Religious and ethnic groups also influenced elections, but their financial and organizational efforts paled next to those of business and labor.

Interest groups continue to flourish and several developments have affected their roles in congressional elections. The growth in the number of organizations that located to or hired representatives in Washington, D.C., resulted in the formation of a community of lobbyists that was, and continues to be, attuned to the rhythms of legislative and campaign politics. The association of interest groups with money, power, and corruption led to efforts to limit their influence in federal elections or, at the very least, to promote a modicum of political accountability through the disclosure of the financing of their election activities. The enactment of the Federal Election Campaign Act of 1974 (FECA) was such an effort. It resulted in virtually all of the interest group spending in federal elections being channeled through political action committees (PACs). PACs were, and continue to be, required to raise their money through relatively modest contributions and report their financial activities to the Federal Election Commission (FEC). These requirements made it easy for voters, the media, and government watchdog groups to monitor interest group activity in congressional elections. They also made it possible for candidates, consultants, political parties, and others to keep track of the fundraising and expenditures of their interest group allies and opponents. Federal court decisions, FEC rulings, the exploitation of legal loopholes, and the enactment of the Bipartisan Campaign Reform Act of 2002 (BCRA) enabled some groups to augment their federal PAC activities using funds from their general treasuries and associated nonprofit organizations. Many channel this activity through some other organization that has a patriotic or innocuous-sounding name. As a result, interest group participation in contemporary congressional elections is much more complex and considerably less transparent than when it principally involved PACs.

This chapter covers the growth and development of the PAC community and the roles of PACs and other interest group entities in congressional elections. I analyze the motives that inform PAC strategies, the methods traditional PACs use to select candidates for support, and the distribution of PAC contributions. I also discuss the coordinated grassroots and independent media campaigns waged by PACs and other interest group entities.

ORGANIZING FOR ELECTORAL INFLUENCE

Once defined by the letters *P, A, C,* a veritable alphabet soup of interest group entities currently participates in congressional elections. In addition to traditional PACs, these include 527 committees, 501(c) organizations, and super PACs (sometimes referred to as independent expenditure–only committees). Corporations, labor unions, trade associations, and other incorporated organizations also are free to spend general treasury funds to try to influence elections, provided they do so independently of candidates. Although the nuances associated with each form of organization are indistinguishable to the voters who are the groups' ultimate targets, different legal entities offer their sponsors different financial and strategic advantages.[1]

Political Action Committees

A PAC is an organization that collects funds that are voluntarily donated by individuals and redistributes those funds to federal candidates with the goal of influencing election outcomes, the formation of public policy, or both.[2] Some PACs also contribute to political parties or make independent expenditures that *expressly* call for the election or defeat of federal candidates. Most PACs have a sponsoring organization, such as a corporation, labor union, trade association, or other group. However, for "nonconnected" PACs, the PAC itself is the organizing group.

Federal campaign finance reform set the scene for the PAC explosion of the mid-1970s. One of the goals of reform was to dilute the influence of moneyed interests on federal elections. As noted in Chapter 1, federal law bars corporations, labor unions, trade associations, cooperatives, and other groups from giving contributions directly from their general treasuries to federal candidates, party committees, and PACs. The law also limits the amount an individual can contribute to a single PAC and the amount a PAC can contribute to a federal candidate. These and other aspects of the law encourage congressional candidates to solicit donations from a broad array of interests and individuals.

The law also encouraged many interest groups to establish PACs. Although neither the BCRA nor its forerunner, the FECA, mentions the term *political action committee,* both laws allow for "a multicandidate committee" that raises money from at least fifty donors and spends it on at least five candidates for federal office to contribute a maximum of $5,000 per candidate at each stage of the election.[3] The relatively low ceilings that federal campaign finance statutes established for individual contributions to candidates and the $5,000-per-year limit it set for individual contributions to any one PAC have the combined effect of making PAC contributions a popular vehicle among wealthy individuals who wish to influence congressional elections and public policy.

In November 1975, in an advisory opinion written for Sun Oil Company, the FEC counseled the company that it could pay the overhead and solicitation costs of its PAC, thereby freeing the PAC to spend on federal elections all the funds it collected from donors. The Sun PAC decision clarified a gray area in the law and in the process made PACs an attractive vehicle for collecting and disbursing funds. The advisory ruling contributed to an explosion in the number of PACs that lasted from the mid-1970s to the mid-1980s.

The Supreme Court's ruling in *Buckley v. Valeo* allowed PACs to make unlimited independent expenditures in federal elections (made without the knowledge or consent of a candidate, the candidate's campaign organization, or others advising the campaign).[4] Both the FEC advisory opinion and the Supreme Court decision created new opportunities for organized groups to participate in politics. The advisory opinion was especially important, encouraging a wide range of political leaders, business entrepreneurs, and others to form new PACs.

The major advantage that PACs currently offer over other organizational entities that participate in elections is that a PAC can directly contribute cash or in-kind services to a candidate. With the exception of independent expenditures, PACs also can coordinate their efforts with candidates or party committees. The major disadvantage associated with PACs concerns the limits on the sources and amounts of the contributions they can accept. Another disadvantage that

FIGURE 5-1

Growth in the Number of Registered PACs, 1974–2010

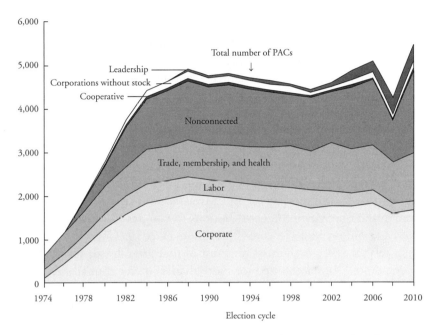

Sources: Compiled from Federal Election Commission and Center for Responsive Politics data.

Note: Leadership PACs are classified separately from nonconnected PACs.

applies to nonconnected PACs is that they must finance their own fundraising and organizational maintenance out of the donations they collect. The sponsoring organizations of other PACs can cover these costs out of the group's general treasury.

Between 1974 and the 2010 elections, the PAC community grew from more than 600 to 5,431 committees (see Figure 5-1). Most of the growth occurred in the business sector, with corporate PACs growing in number from 89 in 1974 to 1,809 in 2006 before declining to 1,592 in 2010. Labor unions, many of which already had PACs in 1974, created the fewest new PACs, increasing the number from 201 to 315 in 2006 and then retrenching to 295 in 2010. The centralization of the labor movement into a relatively small number of unions greatly limited the growth of labor PACs. The slight decline in the number of labor PACs is emblematic of the consolidations of some unions and the difficult times organized labor has weathered in recent decades.

In addition, three new species of PAC—the nonconnected PAC (mostly ideological and issue-oriented groups) and PACs whose sponsors are either cooperatives or corporations without stock—emerged on the scene in 1977. The nonconnected PACs are the most important of these. By 2010 their number had grown to 1,923; in contrast, the combined total for the two other types of PAC had reached only 143.[5]

Leadership PACs, covered in Chapter 4, are the most recently formed type of PAC. Sponsored by politicians and closely tied to the parties, these PACs are frequently categorized as nonconnected PACs. They remained scarce until the late 1980s because few members of Congress could raise the money to form them. During the 1990s an increasing number of politicians, including some relatively junior members of Congress, began to sponsor them. Their numbers reached 58 in 1994, 86 in 1996, and 392 in 2010.

The growth in the number of PACs was accompanied by a tremendous increase in their activity. PAC contributions to congressional candidates grew from $12.5 million in 1974 to $403 million in 2010. Corporate and other business-related PACs accounted for most of that growth (see Figure 5-2). In 2010 corporate PACs accounted for more than 37 percent of all PAC contributions to congressional candidates, followed by trade association PACs, which accounted for about 27 percent. Labor PACs gave about 15 percent of all contributions received by congressional candidates, leadership PACs contributed 9 percent, and nonconnected PACs (excluding leadership PACs) gave 8 percent. PACs sponsored by cooperatives and corporations without stock contributed a mere 3 percent.

A very small group of PACs is responsible for most PAC activity. A mere 397 PACs, about 8 percent of the entire PAC community, contributed roughly $285.4 million during the 2010 election cycle, representing approximately two-thirds of all PAC money given in that period (see Table 5-1). Each of these committees, which are clearly the "all-stars" of the PAC community, gave more than $250,000 to congressional candidates. These include PACs sponsored by corporations, trade associations, and unions, such as Honeywell International, the National Association of Realtors, and the Service Employees International Union (SEIU) Committee on Political Education, as well as nonconnected PACs such as the League of Conservation Voters (LCV), which supports pro-environment candidates.

Another 9 percent of all PACs are "major players," each having contributed between $100,001 and $250,000 to candidates during the 2010 election. These committees, which include the Wendy's/Arby's Group PAC (sponsored by the fast food empire); the Wine Institute PAC; the Bakery, Confectionary, Tobacco Workers, and Grain Millers International Union PAC; and Washington

FIGURE 5-2

Growth of PAC Contributions in Congressional Elections, 1974–2010

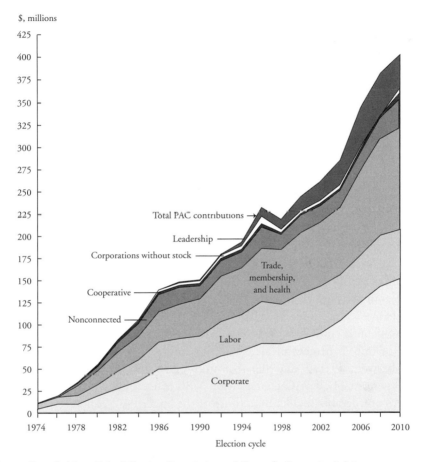

Sources: Compiled from Federal Election Commission and Center for Responsive Politics.

Note: Leadership PAC contributions are separated from contributions made from nonconnected PACs.

PAC (WASHPAC, a pro-Israel group), accounted for 17 percent of all PAC contributions. The all-stars and major players are particularly influential because their wealth enables them to contribute to virtually every candidate whose election is of importance to them.

The "players" are PACs that have the resources to give a significant contribution to many, but not all, of the candidates they wish to support. Comprising 9 percent of all PACs, they include PACs representing the U.S. subsidiary of the Heineken Brewing Company, the American Gaming Association, and the

TABLE 5-1

Concentration of PAC Contributions in the 2010 Election Cycle

	Total contributions by PACs					
	More than $250,000	$100,001– $250,000	$50,001– $100,000	$5,001– $50,000	$1– $5,000	$0
Percentage of all PACs	8	9	9	28	15	30
N	*397*	*458*	*471*	*1,437*	*792*	*1,560*
Percentage of all PAC contributions ($, millions)	67 $285.4	17 $73.8	8 $33.7	7 $29.8	— $1.8	0 $0

Source: Compiled from Federal Election Commission data.

Note: Includes contributions to candidates not up for reelection in 2010.

United Brotherhood of Carpenters and Joiners of New England. Each of the players contributed between $50,001 and $100,000, accounting for roughly 8 percent of all PAC contributions.

The contributions of the next two groups of PACs are clearly constrained by their size. The "junior varsity," comprising PACs that each contributed between $5,001 and $50,000, constitutes 28 percent of all PACs and is the source of only 7 percent of all PAC contributions. The "little league," each giving between $1 and $5,000, accounted for 15 percent of all PACs and less than 1 percent of all PAC contributions. Both sets of PACs make donations that are considerably smaller than those of the larger PACs, and their managers routinely answer requests for contributions by stating that they support the candidate and would like to give a contribution but do not have the money. Finally, 1,560 PACs contributed no money during the 2010 elections. Even though many of these PACs are registered with the FEC, they collected no contributions, paid off no debts, and were otherwise dormant.

527 Committees

Nonprofit interest groups have existed for a long time, but their conspicuous presence in congressional elections is a recent phenomenon. The deteriorating system of regulations governing federal campaign finance led some existing nonprofit entities to use unregulated soft-money to run outside campaigns, comprising coordinated grassroots voter mobilization efforts and independent media expenditures (discussed below) to influence federal elections. Others created new entities for this same purpose. These developments resulted in 527 committees and 501(c) organizations becoming highly visible players in congressional elections.

Traditionally, candidate campaign committees and other groups participating in federal elections were governed by section 527 of the Internal Revenue Code (IRC), which exempts political organizations from paying income taxes. This provision was originally designed to cover candidate campaigns, PACs, and party committees that registered with and disclosed their finances to the FEC, making it unnecessary for the Internal Revenue Service (IRS) to monitor them. Beginning in 1997 some politicians and interest groups created 527 committees solely to raise and spend unregulated soft-money on voter mobilization and candidate-focused issue advocacy advertisements. Issue advocacy ads are similar to independent expenditure ads in that they reference or depict a federal candidate. However, because they do *not expressly* call for a candidate's election or defeat, issue advocacy ads are considered outside the scope of federal campaign finance regulations. Most issue advocacy ads are negative and close with a policy-oriented statement that mentions a politician, such as "Call Senator 'X' and tell him to keep his hands off Social Security and stop gambling with our future."

At first, 527 committees that declined to register with the FEC were not legally obligated to report their financial transactions to any federal agency. Beginning in January 2001 they were required to publicly disclose their funding sources and provide an overview of their expenditures, including those on issue advocacy ads, to the IRS. The BCRA strengthened some reporting requirements for 527s and created a new spending category referred to as "electioneering communications," which, for all practical purposes, are candidate-focused issue advocacy ads that are targeted to a candidate's election constituency and aired thirty days before a primary or sixty days before the general election. Following some FEC rulings and Supreme Court cases, provisions of the BCRA concerning electioneering communications and prohibitions against using soft-money to finance independent expenditures were either weakened or overturned.

Currently, 527 committees are required to provide the IRS with an overview of their activities and the names of their donors (which the agency does not release to the public). They also are obligated to report to the FEC their independent expenditures, electioneering communications, and the names and contributions of any individuals or groups who stipulate that their donations are to be used to finance one of these activities. Thus, the key advantages afforded to 527s are their ability to raise and spend sums from sources and in amounts that are prohibited to PACs and their limited reporting requirements, which do not require public disclosure of donors who help finance a 527's issue advocacy ads (excluding electioneering communications), research, daily operations, or other activities. The disadvantages associated with 527s are prohibitions against their making contributions directly to federal candidates, political parties, or PACs.

Federally oriented 527 committees spent more than $1.1 billion in the 2004 through 2010 elections. Some 338 of them spent $211.6 million with the goal of influencing the 2010 congressional elections. The top spender among federally focused Democratic/liberal-leaning groups was the SEIU at $15.5 million, and the top spender among Republican/conservative-oriented groups was American Solutions for Winning the Future, a group formed by former Republican House Speaker and 2012 presidential candidate Newt Gingrich, which spent $28.4 million. As is the case with PACs, a few groups were responsible for most 527 spending. During the 2010 elections the top ten 527 committees were the source of almost half the spending. Where 527s differed from PACs in 2010 was in the size of the contributions that accounted for much of their revenues. The top personal donations to 527s were given by Fred Eshelman, executive chair of Pharmaceutical Product Development Inc., who contributed $3.4 million to RightChange.com, and Senate candidate Carly Fiorina, R-Calif., whose Carly Fiorina Enterprises contributed $2.5 million to the group Carly for California. The top organizational donor to a 527 was the SEIU, which transferred $18.7 million from its general treasury to its 527 committee.[6]

501(c) Organizations

Tax-exempt organizations defined in section 501(c) of the IRC have become increasingly visible in electoral politics since the 2002 elections and were very active in 2010. As defined, 501(c)(3) organizations are tax-exempt groups organized for charitable purposes. They are prohibited from becoming directly involved in federal campaigns, including endorsing or contributing to candidates or organizing a PAC—a major disadvantage for groups that want to be involved in elections. However, these organizations can conduct research and educational activities, carry out nonpartisan voter registration and get-out-the-vote (GOTV) drives, and sponsor candidate forums. Established in 1957, the League of Women Voters Education Fund is perhaps the quintessential example of a (c)(3) organization that participates in elections. Another example, perhaps more widely known among college students, is Rock the Vote, which was founded in 1990. A group that registers with the IRS as a (c)(3) organization enjoys two major advantages. First, donors can deduct their contributions to the group when filing their federal taxes. Second, the IRS does not disclose the donors' names—an important consideration for those who wish their association with a group to remain anonymous.

The IRC defines 501(c)(4) organizations as nonprofit social welfare organizations. A (c)(4) can engage in partisan political activities, including elections, as long as the activities are not its primary purpose.[7] These organizations are allowed to rate candidates, sponsor PACs, broadcast electioneering communications, and make independent expenditures. Groups with (c)(4) status, similar to (c)(3)s, are prohibited from making campaign contributions, are exempt from federal taxes, and can collect contributions from undisclosed sources. Unlike donors to (c)(3) organizations, donors to (c)(4)s cannot deduct their donations from their federal tax returns. Labor groups that enjoy 501(c)(5) status and trade associations that organize as 501(c)(6)s are allowed to conduct similar activities and receive similar tax benefits as (c)(4) organizations.

The major benefits associated with (c)(4), (c)(5), and (c)(6) organizations concern fundraising. These entities can raise funds from sources and in amounts prohibited to PACs, and the names of the individuals and groups that finance their election activities are generally not made public.[8] One of their disadvantages relative to 527 committees and PACs is the expectation that 501(c)s spend no more than 50 percent of their funds on partisan election activity. However, this may be a relatively minor disadvantage for some groups because the line demarcating partisan activity from nonpartisan (issue-oriented) activity is fuzzy. For example, issue advocacy advertisements (except those that qualify as electioneering communications) are not considered partisan activity or reported to the FEC, even if the ads reference a federal candidate, are targeted to the candidate's district, or have other partisan implications. Consequently, the law provides substantial leeway for 501(c)s to influence elections, and relatively few of these groups find it difficult to avoid exceeding the 50 percent rule of thumb for partisan activity.

It is virtually impossible to determine the exact amounts 501(c)s spend to influence congressional elections because they are required to disclose only some of their election activities to the FEC.[9] However, these groups' spending easily exceeded $100 million in 2010. The top five groups alone spent approximately $95 million on independent expenditures and electioneering communications.[10] They all were associated with conservative Republican-allied groups, which more than hints at the fact that spending by 501(c) organizations provided GOP congressional candidates with a huge advantage over their Democratic opponents.

Super PACs, Corporations, Labor Unions, and Other Groups

Corporations, trade associations, labor unions, and other incorporated groups have long participated in congressional elections. Even though the FECA and the BCRA prohibited them from using treasury funds to contribute to or make independent expenditures for or against federal candidates, it allowed them to use those funds to finance internal political communications to their members. Groups of all types continue to devote portions of their newsletters, e-mails, and other correspondence to endorsing candidates for federal office and urging their members to vote for or contribute to the group's preferred candidates, its PAC, or a party committee. Groups spent $13.4 million on internal political communications during the 2010 congressional elections.[11]

Interest group internal communications are a pittance compared to the new form of spending activity that became available for the first time in 2010. Unleashed by the rulings in *Citizens United v. FEC* and *Speechnow.org v. FEC,* corporations, unions, and other incorporated groups can now use funds from their treasuries to make independent expenditures or to finance separate super PACs created for this purpose.[12] Handed down in January 2010, the *Citizens United* ruling resulted in organizations directly spending $71.8 million from their treasuries on independent expenditures before Election Day. Super PACs spent an additional $59.2 million. Regardless of whether they are funded directly from a group's treasury or by a super PAC, these expenditures and their funding sources must be fully disclosed to the FEC. Of course, and as is the case with a 527, 501(c), or a traditional PAC, a group that organizes a super PAC can give it a name with widespread appeal to mask the narrow interests of its financial backers. The donors to American Crossroads, for example, read like a *Who's Who* of industrialists and corporations, and the supporters of Commonsense Ten are major labor unions.

Independent spending from interest group treasuries or by super PACs offers these organizations some advantages. First, they can be financed with donations from sources and in amounts prohibited to PACs. Second, unlike 501(c) organizations, these organizations do not have to be concerned with spending at least half of their funds on the charitable or educational activities associated with nonprofit organizations. Of course, the main disadvantages associated with super PACs and incorporated groups are associated with their disclosure requirements and prohibitions against their making contributions directly to a federal candidate, party committee, or PAC.

Multifaceted Groups

Some interest groups develop complex interconnected organizational structures to participate aggressively in the political process without violating federal campaign finance law or tax statutes. These groups adapt to changing regulations and political conditions by creating new legal entities to accomplish different purposes. In some ways, interest group organizational development, like party development, is analogous to basic principles of architecture: new needs are met by adding new rooms to existing structures or by building new structures to complement existing ones, and the forms these improvements take are influenced by a group's goals, resources, and regulatory codes.[13] As demonstrated by the preceding review of the advantages associated with the different political entities that participate in elections, the importance of regulatory codes cannot be overstated. A brief comparison of the regulations governing political parties and interest groups reinforces this point. Any party aide or consultant involved in making party independent expenditures is prohibited from discussing them with other party officials. By contrast, coordination is permissible among the personnel associated with a sponsoring interest group. Indeed, it is legal for the same personnel who work for one of an interest group's legal entities to be employed by some or all of the others, including the group's PAC, 501(c) organizations, 527 committee, or super PAC. When this occurs, as is often the case, each participating organization in the group's family pays a portion of the salaries of the overlapping personnel.

The LCV is an example of a group that pursues its mission using several entities. Founded in 1969, the LCV "run[s] tough and effective campaigns to defeat anti-environment candidates, and support those leaders who stand up for a clean, healthy future for America."[14] It is probably best known for its "National Environmental Scorecard," "Environmental Champions," and "Dirty Dozen" lists, which thrust environmental issues onto the political agenda and inform voters of the environmental records of members of Congress. The "LCV Family of Organizations" includes the LCV, its core (c)(4) organization; the LCV Education Fund, a (c)(3) that conducts research and educational activities; the LCV Accountability Project, a (c)(4) that carries out media and grassroots educational campaigns about the environmental records of members of Congress; the LCV Action Fund, the group's PAC; the LCV Victory Fund, a super PAC; and the LCV Political Engagement Fund, a 527 organization that supports the LCV's national election-oriented groups and its thirty-five state-level LCV affiliates (and their local affiliates), freeing these organizations to spend more of their funds to influence elections (see Figure 5-3). Many of the personnel employed by one of the LCV's organizations also work for several of them.[15]

The LCV was fairly active in the 2010 elections. Its PAC gave $390,000 in contributions, 95 percent of which went to Democratic candidates. It also made $653,000 in independent expenditures, 85 percent of which were intended to help Democrats. The remaining 15 percent was spent trying to defeat Sen. Blanche Lincoln in a hotly contested Democratic primary in Arkansas. The LCV's super PAC made an additional $909,000 in independent expenditures—all positive communications and most spent to help the same

FIGURE 5-3

The League of Conservation Voters as an Example of a Multifaceted Interest Group

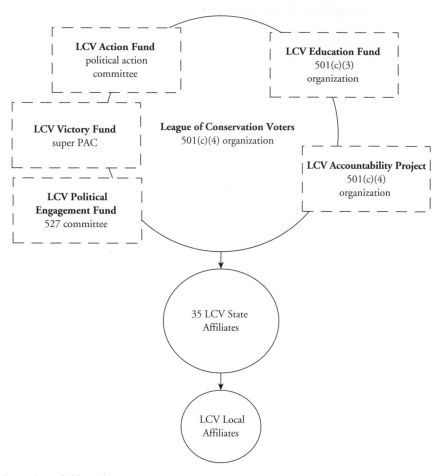

Source: Compiled by author.

Democrats benefiting from the activities of its PAC. In addition, the LCV's 501(c)(4)s spent almost $3.7 million on independent advertising, virtually all of which supported Democratic candidates. Finally, its 527 spent about $1.1 million, most of which was transferred to help other members of the LCV family in pursuit of their common mission. In total, the LCV spent more than $6 million on the 2010 elections.[16]

The LCV demonstrates the organizational complexity of some interest groups that participate in elections. Other groups that possess one or more 501(c) organizations, a PAC, a super PAC, and a 527 committee are the Club for Growth and the Sierra Club. In 2010 entities linked to the Club for Growth spent a total of $8.2 million to promote the candidacies of anti-tax free-market Republicans, and those related to the Sierra Club spent about $1.2 million to help candidates it viewed as pro-environment—almost all Democrats. A number of groups characterized by somewhat less complex interlocking structures had an even bigger financial impact on the 2010 elections. First and foremost were American Crossroads, organized as a super PAC and a 527, and its sister organization, the (c)(4) group Crossroads Grassroots Policy Strategies (often referred to as "Crossroads GPS"), which was created mainly to provide its conservative donors with anonymity.[17] Combined, these Republican-allied groups, founded by former Republican National Committee chair Mike Duncan, former White House adviser Karl Rove, and former RNC chair and White House adviser Ed Gillespie, spent almost $40 million on independent media communications and coordinated grassroots efforts to advance the causes of GOP candidates. Next in line among heavy hitters was the U.S. Chamber of Commerce, which spent an estimated $50 million in 2010, including a mere $104,000 in PAC contributions to candidates and a whopping $32.9 million on electioneering communications made by its 501(c)(6) organization.[18]

The Coin of the Realm

Given that interest groups can use a variety of organizational entities to influence congressional elections, one might want to know about the relative contributions of each. It is impossible to fully assess the impact of some efforts, such as fundraising assistance. It is also impossible to precisely gauge the expenditures of some types of groups because of the limited disclosure requirements imposed on them. Nevertheless, some estimates of the relative expenditures made by different types of groups are possible and provide insights into the changing nature of interest group participation in congressional elections.

Traditional PACs accounted for the lion's share of the $690 million in reported interest group spending in the 2010 congressional elections. PAC campaign contributions to candidates comprised 58 percent of all group spending, and PAC independent expenditures accounted for another 9 percent (see Figure 5-4). Independent expenditures financed by super PACs, 527 committees, or 501(c) organizations, or by funds obtained directly from corporation, union, or other group treasuries accounted for an additional 19 percent. Electioneering communications financed by 501(c) groups and 527 committees constituted an estimated 11 percent. The internal political communications that organizations distribute to their members made up about 2 percent. The final category in Figure 5-4, labeled "unreported spending

FIGURE 5-4

Spending by Different Interest Group Entities in the 2010 Congressional Elections

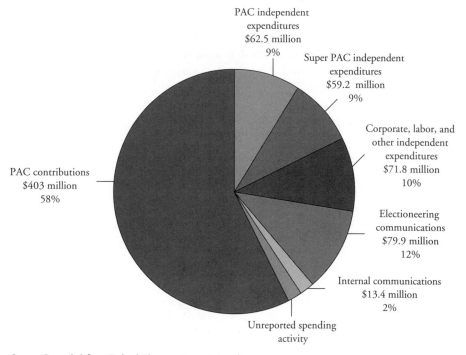

PAC independent
expenditures
$62.5 million
9%

Super PAC independent
expenditures
$59.2 million
9%

Corporate, labor, and
other independent
expenditures
$71.8 million
10%

PAC contributions
$403 million
58%

Electioneering
communications
$79.9 million
12%

Internal communications
$13.4 million
2%

Unreported spending
activity

Source: Compiled from Federal Election Commission data.

activity," is a guesstimate or, more accurately, a place holder for interest group expenditures that are not publicly disclosed.

These percentages underscore the point that one cannot fully measure interest group efforts in congressional elections by focusing solely on PACs. Although they accounted for two-thirds of all reported interest group spending in 2010, the fact that other interest group entities accounted for the remaining third is stunning, given that organized interests had little time to take advantage of the new spending opportunities resulting from the *Citizens United* and *Speechnow.org* decisions. To do so required participating interests to decide which entities to use for their spending efforts, select specific races in which to make expenditures, devise a communications strategy and make media buys, and otherwise adapt to the changed environment. They also required additional financial commitments by organizations and individuals that already had committed substantial amounts to the election.

STRATEGY, DECISION MAKING, AND TARGETING

Once a group decides on the organizational structures and activities it will use to participate in congressional elections, the next step is to devise a strategy for pursuing its goals. Not surprisingly, given the diversity of the causes they champion and the ways in which they participate, interest group goals and strategies are more diverse than are those of the two major parties. Parties are consumed with electing candidates; groups also care about promoting issues and influencing the policy process. Some interest groups follow "ideological" or "electoral" strategies designed to increase the number of legislators who share their broad political perspective or positions on specific, often emotionally charged, issues such as abortion rights. These groups are similar to parties in that they consider congressional elections to be opportunities to alter the composition of Congress and their primary vehicle for changing or reinforcing the direction of public policy.[19] Ideological groups carry out most of their efforts in close contests—primaries and general elections in which they have the best chance of affecting the outcome. However, some groups become involved in uncompetitive contests in order to attract attention to themselves, their issues, or politicians who share their views. By gaining visibility for themselves and their causes, these organizations can more easily raise money and increase their political clout.

PACs that follow ideological strategies usually do not give much money to members of Congress for the sake of gaining access to the legislative process. The issues these PACs support are often linked to values so fundamental that legislators would not be expected to change their views in response to a contribution or visit by a lobbyist. Before giving a contribution, many of these PACs, and some others, require candidates to complete questionnaires that elicit their views on certain issues. Similarly, 501(c)s, 527s, super PACs, and other groups that view elections as their primary vehicle for influencing the federal government research a candidate's views on the issues before mounting an outside campaign to help or harm the candidate's prospects.

Other interest groups pursue "access" or "pragmatic" strategies designed to enable the group to gain at least an audience with members of Congress.[20] These groups, which include PACs sponsored by corporations and trade associations, view an election as an opportunity to shore up relations with members of Congress who work on legislation that is of importance to their sponsoring organization. Elections give these groups an opening to create goodwill with powerful lawmakers, or at least to minimize the enmity of legislators who disagree with them. Because PAC contributions are often delivered by a group's lobbyist (who is usually a member of the PAC's board of directors), these contributions provide opportunities for lobbyists and legislators to mingle with one another. Thus, interactions during elections lay the groundwork for later lobbying efforts.

A group that follows an access strategy is likely to contribute most of its money to incumbents. Members of the House and Senate who chair committees or subcommittees, occupy party leadership positions, or are policy entrepreneurs with influence over legislation are likely to receive large contributions regardless of the competitiveness of their contests.[21] In fact, many access-oriented PACs make contributions to legislators who do not even have opponents. Of course, members of Congress who have supported a group's legislation and who are involved in contests with unpredictable outcomes are singled out for extra support, including large PAC contributions, assistance with fundraising, or independent expenditures. Supporting incumbents also enables interest groups to meet other organizational imperatives, such as backing a large number of winners or contributing to candidates who represent districts that contain many of the group's members.

Access-oriented groups also give significant sums to candidates for open seats. Most of these candidates have good chances of winning but need large amounts of money to run competitive campaigns. Giving an open-seat prospect a large contribution is useful to an access-oriented PAC because it can help elect an ally to Congress or create a foundation for productive relations with a future member of Congress.

Access-oriented groups tend to ignore challengers because most of them are likely to lose. Giving a challenger a contribution is often considered a waste of money and could lead to serious repercussions from an incumbent. Moreover, backing challengers has a high probability of reducing a group's win-loss record and could lead to criticism of the PAC's manager. The managers of access-oriented PACs that decide not to support a challenger or an open-seat candidate know that should the candidate win, they can make amends later by helping to retire a campaign debt or making a contribution early in the next election cycle.

PACs that follow access strategies rarely make independent expenditures because of the publicity these activities can generate. Such efforts could harm a corporation if they anger congressional incumbents, upset some of the group's donors, or call undue attention to the candidate or the group. The publicity also could lead to charges that a group is trying to buy influence and could hinder the achievement of its goals. As discussed later, the corporations and other groups that choose to back such high-profile campaign efforts often reduce the visibility of their involvement by contributing to one or more 527s, 501(c)s, or super PACs. By channeling much of their electoral participation through entities with appealing names, corporations are likely to have a bigger impact on the vote than if they broadcast TV ads or carry out other activities identifying themselves as the sponsors.

Some groups, including most labor unions, practice "mixed" strategies. They support some candidates with contributions, independent expenditures, issue advocacy ads, internal communications, fundraising assistance, or grassroots activities because those candidates share the group's views; they support others because they wish to improve their access to legislators who work on policies the group deems important. Campaign assistance motivated by the former reason is usually distributed to those candidates embroiled in competitive contests. Assistance informed by the latter motive is given to incumbents who are in a position to influence legislation important to the group. In some cases the ideological and access motives clash; for example, when a highly qualified challenger who represents a group's views runs a competitive race against an incumbent in a position of power, groups usually support the incumbent, but sometimes they contribute to both candidates. Groups that follow mixed strategies and groups that are motivated by ideology are more likely than access-oriented groups to make independent expenditures or electioneering communications under their own name.

Interest Group Strategy and the Political Environment

Interest groups, like most other organizations and individuals involved in campaign politics, are strategic actors that respond to their environment in ways that enable them to pursue their goals.[22] During the 1970s most interest group activity was carried out by PACs, and most PACs used electoral strategies that followed partisan lines. They backed candidates who supported the positions to which their organizational sponsors adhered. Most business-oriented PACs, including corporate and trade committees, supported Republican candidates. Labor organizations, which were and continue to be the most consistently partisan of all PACs, regularly gave 90 percent of their contributions to Democrats. In time, many business-oriented committees shifted from ideological to access or mixed strategies. These PACs redirected their support from Republican challengers to incumbents, many of whom were Democrats, out of recognition of the Democratic Party's decades-long control of Congress and a belief that the Democrats would continue to control Congress for the foreseeable future.

Perhaps the clearest strategic response by interest groups takes place after partisan control of one or both chambers of Congress changes hands. When control of the Senate switched from the Democrats to the Republicans in 1981 and back to the Democrats in 1987, many access-oriented PACs switched their contributions to Senate incumbents who belonged to the new majority party. Similarly, after the 1995 GOP takeover of the House and Senate, these PACs gave most of their funds to Republicans, and following the Democrats' takeover of Congress in 2007, the flow of PAC contributions changed direction once again—this time in favor of the Democrats. Given the outcome of the 2010 elections, one should anticipate another shift in PAC contribution patterns—at least in the House.

Because of their desire to influence the composition of Congress, ideologically oriented groups are the most likely to capitalize on the conditions peculiar to a specific election. A group that uses an access strategy, such as a corporate or trade association PAC, is less affected by a particular electoral setting unless changing conditions are almost certain to influence the ability of its lobbyist (or team of lobbyists) to meet with key legislators and their staffs. The strategic changes in PAC behavior that occurred in the early 1980s were the result of PACs learning how to get the most legislative influence for their dollar and the increasing aggressiveness of incumbent fundraising. Changes that occurred following the 1994 and 2006 elections were a response to the change in partisan control of Congress. More recent changes in interest group behavior, particularly the concentration of independent media advertising and grassroots efforts in a small number of extremely close races, represent group responses to the slim majorities determining partisan control of the House and Senate and the weakening of campaign finance regulations.

Making strategic adjustments in anticipation of political change is more difficult. The manager of an access-oriented PAC who believes that a member of Congress is likely to go from having little to major influence in a policy area, for instance, may have difficulty persuading the PAC's board of directors to raise the member's contribution from a token sum to a substantial donation. The manager's prospects of convincing the board that the organization should totally revamp its strategy because partisan control of Congress might change are often slim. For example, prior to the Republican takeover of the House in 2010, many corporate and trade groups, whose support of a pro-business agenda suggests they would want to support Republican nonincumbents who have real prospects for victory, poured more money into the campaigns of Democratic incumbents than their GOP opponents. Some of the managers of these PACs may have been attuned to the fact that a confluence of anti-Washington sentiments, strong challengers, and vulnerable incumbents enhanced the prospects for a switch in partisan control, but their organization's decision-making process made it impossible for them to change its contribution patterns in anticipation of such political change.

Interest Group Decision Making

The decision-making process that an interest group uses to select candidates for support is affected by the group's overall strategy, wealth, organizational structure, and location.[23] Ideological groups spend more time searching for promising challengers to support than do groups that use access or mixed strategies. They also are more likely than others to assist nonincumbents in congressional primaries. Wealthy groups tend to spend more time searching for promising nonincumbents simply because they can afford to participate in more elections.[24] Federated groups whose members and organizational affiliates are spread across the country typically have to respond to the wishes of these constituents when choosing candidates to support.[25] Nonconnected PACs or groups sponsored by a single organization, in contrast, are less constrained by the need to please a diverse and far-flung constituency. Interest groups located in the nation's capital have more insider information available to them about congressional races because they are plugged into more political networks than groups located in the hinterlands.[26] Most interest group decision makers are attuned to the importance of partisanship and look to the parties' congressional and senatorial campaign committees to learn about the competitiveness of various elections and how those races are unfolding.

The influence of a group's organizational structure on its decision making is exemplified by the Realtors PAC (RPAC). Formed in 1969, this large, federated, institutionalized PAC is sponsored by the National Association of Realtors (NAR) and headquartered in Washington, D.C.[27] RPAC receives its money from PACs sponsored by the NAR's 1,800 local affiliates and state associations located in all fifty states plus the District of Columbia, Guam, Puerto Rico, and the Virgin Islands. Realtors give donations to RPAC and to these affiliated PACs, each of which passes 30 percent of its revenues to the national PAC. In 2010 RPAC contributed $3.8 million to candidates, ranking it first among all PACs.

RPAC employs a mixed strategy to advance the goals of the real estate industry. As do most other institutionalized PACs, it has explicit criteria for selecting candidates for support and uses a complex decision-making procedure. Party, incumbency, and electoral competitiveness have major effects on its contributions. Incumbents, who are given preference over challengers, are evaluated on their policy records, activism on behalf of real estate issues, and local realtor support. Members who cosponsor priority NAR legislation, give a speech on behalf of NAR legislation on the House or Senate floor, or write letters to their colleagues in support of such legislation are top priorities. The same is true of those who use their congressional authority to compel the president or an independent regulatory agency to respond to real estate industry concerns, vote for key NAR issues in committee or on the floor, or assist constituents with real estate–related matters. Leaders of both parties and legislators who serve on committees that deal with real estate issues are prime targets for contributions. Nonincumbents who have previously held elective office are judged by their records on real estate issues. Regardless of their prior political experience, most nonincumbents also are interviewed by a local or state NAR member and required to complete a questionnaire to evaluate their political philosophy, background, and campaign skills. The PAC also considers the number and partisanship of realtors who live in the district before making a contribution. Using this information RPAC's staff, trustees, and the NAR's public affairs representatives and lobbyists in Washington select candidates for support. Local realtors are permitted to make separate decisions through RPAC's In-State Reception Program, which allows local NAR members to make separate RPAC contributions with the approval of their state's RPAC affiliate.[28]

Like many interest groups, RPAC's and the NAR's election activities extend beyond the campaign contributions it makes directly to candidates. During the 2010 elections RPAC transferred $689,000 to Democratic and Republican party committees, member-sponsored leadership PACs, and other political action committees. It also made $6 million in independent expenditures to advocate the reelection of fourteen congressional incumbents. The NAR's Congressional Super Fund, its super PAC, spent $1.1 million in expenditures to fund positive ads to provide additional help to five candidates already benefiting from RPAC independent expenditures and contributions. The NAR's 527 committee transferred $808,000 to two of its state affiliates and several nonfederal groups. The NAR also spent $1.8 million in treasury funds on internal communications in support of its preferred candidates, distributed educational and advocacy mailings in close contests, used telephone banks to conduct voter identification and GOTV efforts, and sent some professional organizers to carry out grassroots activities.

The decision-making process of the RPAC and its affiliated organizations is similar to those of other institutionalized committees, such as the U.S. Chamber of Commerce, which also has at least one affiliate in every congressional district; the American Medical Association's PAC (AMPAC); and the organizations belonging to the LCV family.[29] These groups rely on a combination of factual information, local opinion, and national perspective to determine which candidates to support. The requirement that all contributions must be approved through a formal process also is typical, as is the ability to conduct in-house research on individual elections.

At the opposite end of the spectrum from the NAR and RPAC are WASHPAC and other noninstitutionalized PACs. WASHPAC is a nonconnected committee founded in 1980 by Morris J. Amitay, formerly the executive director of the American Israel Public Affairs Committee (AIPAC), to promote a secure Israel and strong American–Israeli relations.[30] WASHPAC spent $132,000 in congressional elections in 2010, contributing the vast majority of its money to incumbents. Noninstitutionalized committees are essentially one-person operations. These PACs conduct limited research and rely on personal contacts with candidates and Washington insiders to guide their contribution decisions. Amitay, who started WASHPAC as a hobby, reviews candidates' public statements and incumbents' voting records and letters to constituents to gauge their support for Israel. He exchanges information about the competitiveness of different elections with other pro-Israel political activists. He listens to the suggestions of WASHPAC's donors but does not base his decisions on them. After all, most of these individuals give to the PAC because they prefer to rely on Amitay's research and judgment rather than their own. Indeed, some use WASHPAC's list of targeted races to guide the contributions they give directly to candidates. The individuals who run noninstitutionalized PACs have much flexibility in choosing candidates for support and are in a better position than those running institutionalized committees to adjust their initial strategies in response to changing electoral conditions. Of course, in the case of very small groups, this is true only as long as their money holds out.

Between the institutionalized PACs and the small, one-person organizations are semi-institutionalized PACs that possess some of the characteristics of the PACs in the other two groups. These PACs usually have staffs of two to four people, which are large enough to allow for a functional division of labor and to require the adoption of some decision rules but small enough to render them dependent on the research provided by others. The decision makers in these groups have less flexibility than the managers of one-person committees and more freedom than the officers of institutionalized PACs.

Lead PACs constitute a final group of committees. These PACs, which include the National Committee for an Effective Congress (NCEC) and the Business-Industry Political Action Committee (BIPAC), are as complex organizationally as the institutionalized PACs.[31] Like the LCV, they are often one part of a larger interlocking group that has several legal entities. These groups are every bit as thorough in their decision making as other institutionalized committees, but they differ in that they operate with an eye toward influencing the decisions of other PACs and individual donors. Much of their research is oriented toward assessing the electability of individual candidates. Like the parties' congressional and senatorial campaign committees, these groups spend much time, money, and energy disseminating information about specific campaigns to others in their networks.

PAC CONTRIBUTIONS

PACs contributed about $403 million to major-party candidates in the 2010 congressional elections (see Figure 5-2). Corporate PACs accounted for $151 million, or 37 percent of all PAC contributions, followed by trade groups, labor committees, leadership PACs, and nonconnected PACs. Corporations without stock contributed the least, giving less than 2 percent. Incumbents have laid claim to the lion's share of PAC money since the PAC boom of the 1970s. Since the mid-1980s, business-related PACs have been among the most incumbent-oriented committees, adhering more closely to an access strategy than do labor, leadership, or ideological PACs.

In 2010 corporate PACs made 89 percent of their House contributions to incumbents involved in major-party contested races (see Table 5-2). More than half of these funds were given to incumbent shoo-ins. Corporate PACs donated a mere 5 percent of their House contributions to challengers and another 5 percent to open-seat candidates. They made only 44 percent of their House contributions to candidates in competitive races. Similarly, corporate PACs distributed 61 percent of their Senate contributions to incumbents, including many incumbents in lopsided contests; 33 percent to open-seat candidates; and 5 percent to challengers (see Table 5-3). PACs sponsored by trade associations, which also represent business interests, also dedicated few resources to challengers. The overall patterns for PAC contributions associated with business interests are consistent with their goal of maintaining good relations with current members and the pressures incumbents place on them for contributions.

Labor PACs have consistently pursued highly partisan, mixed strategies. They contribute the vast majority of their money to Democrats. In 2010 labor PACs favored Democratic incumbents with 81 percent of their contributions to House candidates, including 32 percent to shoo-ins. Labor's contributions to challengers and open-seat candidates, on the other hand, were tilted toward those in competitive races. Labor committees gave 42 percent of their Senate contributions to Democratic incumbents, including 17 percent to Democratic shoo-ins. The rest of their contributions strongly favored nonincumbents in close contests. Labor contributions to candidates in both chambers appear to have been motivated by both access-oriented and election-oriented goals.

TABLE 5-2

Allocation of PAC Contributions to House Candidates in the 2010 Elections

	Corporate	Trade, membership, and health	Labor	Leadership	Non-connected
Democrats					
Incumbents					
In jeopardy	31%	33%	49%	40%	32%
Shoo-ins	21	20	32	2	19
Challengers					
Hopefuls	—	1	4	2	1
Long shots	—	—	2	—	—
Open-seat candidates					
Prospects	1	1	5	4	2
Mismatched	—	1	3	1	1
Republicans					
Incumbents					
In jeopardy	5	5	1	6	5
Shoo-ins	32	27	5	6	23
Challengers					
Hopefuls	5	7	—	27	11
Long shots	—	—	—	—	1
Open-seat candidates					
Prospects	2	2	—	6	2
Mismatched	2	3	—	5	2
Total House contributions ($, thousands)	$110,577	$79,596	$50,656	$24,284	$20,536

Source: Compiled from Federal Election Commission data.

Notes: Figures are for general election candidates in major-party contested races. Corporate PACs included corporations with and without stock. — = less than 0.5 percent. Some columns do not add to 100 percent because of rounding. $N = 812$.

The flow of leadership PAC contributions follows roughly the same pattern as that of party-connected contributions, which also include contributions by candidates, members of Congress not up for reelection, and congressional retirees (discussed in Chapter 4). During the 2010 elections most leadership PAC money flowed to candidates in close races. Leadership PACs associated with Democratic politicians distributed more money to incumbents battling for political survival than to any other group of candidates. Republican politicians,

TABLE 5-3

Allocation of PAC Contributions to Senate Candidates in the 2010 Elections

	Corporate	Trade, membership, and health	Labor	Leadership	Non-connected
Democrats					
Incumbents					
In jeopardy	21%	24%	25%	19%	22%
Shoo-ins	12	10	17	5	15
Challengers					
Hopefuls	—	—	2	—	—
Long shots	1	1	5	3	1
Open-seat candidates					
Prospects	4	6	37	15	12
Mismatched	1	1	11	5	3
Republicans					
Incumbents					
In jeopardy	9	7	—	5	5
Shoo-ins	19	18	1	11	14
Challengers					
Hopefuls	4	6	—	11	4
Long shots	—	—	—	—	—
Open-seat candidates					
Prospects	18	17	1	18	15
Mismatched	9	9	1	7	8
Total Senate contributions ($, thousands)	$31,795	$18,598	$6,201	$10,410	$6,894

Source: Compiled from Federal Election Commission data.

Notes: Figures are for general election candidates in major-party contested races. — = less than 0.5 percent. Some columns do not add to 100 percent because of rounding. $N = 72$. Percentages and totals do not include Lisa Murkowski.

in contrast, contributed the vast majority of their leadership PAC money to nonincumbents, which was consistent with the Republicans' aggressive bid to win control of Congress. As a group, leadership PACs were among the most supportive of challengers and open-seat candidates.

Nonconnected PACs, which have traditionally followed the ideological strategy of spending most of their money in close races, largely continued this pattern in 2010. They made 58 percent of their Senate contributions and 53 percent of their House donations to candidates in close races. Nevertheless, the flow of nonconnected PAC money to Democratic and Republican candidates differed sharply. Nonconnected PACs gave more money to Democratic candidates in competitive than uncompetitive races, and Democratic incumbents in both the House and Senate were the major beneficiaries of these PACs' largesse. When contributing to Republicans, on the other hand, nonconnected PACs targeted relatively more of their resources to nonincumbents.

Several factors influenced nonconnected PACs' giving patterns. The instability of the political environment in 2010—driven by the possibility of a change in partisan control of both chambers of Congress—encouraged liberal PACs to deliver most of their resources to Democratic incumbents, especially those in close contests. However, conservative nonconnected PACs appear to have made donations for both ideological and access reasons. Some of these PACs contributed to competitive challengers and open-seat contestants to help bring about a change in the party controlling Congress. Others contributed to safe incumbents to maintain political access. In more than a few cases, nonconnected PACs may have contributed in response to the requests of safe incumbents, having made the reasonable assumption that these candidates would redistribute some of the funds to candidates on their party's priority list or to a party committee.

CAMPAIGN SERVICES

Although most of the journalistic reporting on interest groups focuses on the money they raise and spend, many groups also carry out activities that have traditionally been conducted by political parties. Some wealthy groups, including some labor unions and the U.S. Chamber of Commerce, try to influence the political agenda in close races. Many ideological organizations, including various groups on both sides of the abortion rights issue, recruit candidates.[32] Others provide candidates with in-kind contributions of polls, issue research, fundraising assistance, or campaign staff. AMPAC, RPAC, and the American Federation of Labor–Congress of Industrial Organizations' (AFL-CIO) PAC, for example, contribute polls to some candidates.[33] The National Federation of Independent Business's PAC hosts campaign training schools and produces media advertisements for many of the candidates it supports.[34] The NCEC gives selected Democratic House and Senate candidates and the Democratic Congressional Campaign Committee and Democratic Senatorial Campaign Committee (DSCC) precinct-level demographic profiles, targeting assistance, and technical advice.[35] The LCV provides research, endorsements—including inclusion on its renowned Environmental Champions list—and other forms of assistance to help pro-environment candidates. Such endorsements can help uninformed voters learn about the issues. Some groups furnish campaign assistance in lieu of, or in addition to, cash contributions because they want to influence how candidates' campaigns are run or leave a candidate with a more enduring impression than one can get from simply handing over a check.

One of the most important forms of assistance that a PAC can give to a candidate, particularly a nonincumbent, is help with fundraising. Lead PACs, such as BIPAC and the NCEC, brief other PACs and individual donors about the campaigns on their watch lists, using techniques similar to those used by the Hill committees. Even some smaller PACs help congressional candidates raise money by cosponsoring fundraising events or serving on candidates' fundraising committees. When PACs solicit donors, they usually provide them with information about their preferred candidates' issue positions and backgrounds. Some also provide contact information about these candidates in their direct mail, e-mails, websites, and social media. ActBlue, which bills itself as "the online clearinghouse for Democratic action," enables donors to contribute to candidates through its website. It directed well in excess of $24 million in contributions to Democratic candidates for Congress in 2010.[36] Other PACs get their members to purchase tickets to candidates' fundraising events, or they "bundle" checks from individual donors and deliver them to the candidate. The maturation of the Washington interest group community has led to the development of several networks of PACs, individual donors, and other organizations, which often assist each other in selecting candidates for support and raising money.

EMILY's List is a pioneer in assisting candidates with fundraising. This nonconnected PAC, whose name stands for "Early Money Is Like Yeast" and whose motto is "It makes the dough rise," helps pro-choice Democratic women candidates raise money in the early days of the election season, including in contested congressional primaries in which contributions typically have several times the impact they have in general elections.[37] EMILY's List requires its members to donate $100 to the PAC and to make minimum contributions of $100 to each of two candidates whom the PAC has designated for support. Originally, members wrote checks to these candidates and sent them to the PAC, which in turn forwarded them with an explanation of the PAC's role in collecting the money. Now EMILY's List members can contribute using the PAC's website. Through bundling, the PAC is able to steer more money to its preferred candidates than it is permitted to contribute directly to them. Bundling works well with individuals who wish to have a candidate acknowledge both their and the group's political support. Groups that bundle, and EMILY's List in particular, have played a major role in persuading individuals who have not previously made congressional contributions to become regular donors.[38] During the 2010 election season, EMILY's List directly contributed $238,000 to candidates in thirty-two races. These contributions were important, but they pale next to the $38.5 million bundled from its more than 600,000 members.

Although not many interest groups are known for bundling, a significant number of them influence the contributions of individuals associated with their group. Individual donors who make significant contributions to congressional candidates—at least one contribution of $200 per election cycle—are a small, fairly elite, and relatively stable group. Many are motivated by political access, ideology, or both. Some also contribute because they enjoy the social aspects of giving, including attending fundraising events. Most are active in political networks, and many rely on business, industry, trade, single-issue, or ideological groups for the information they use to make contribution decisions. Their donations magnify the impact of the groups with which they associate.[39] For example, the financial, insurance, and real estate industries comprise a sector of the economy that makes its influence in congressional elections felt through PAC contributions, contributions to parties, independent expenditures, electioneering communications, and the contributions of individuals working in them. Organizations and individuals connected to these industries seek to influence policies ranging from mortgage regulations to building safety codes to federal appropriations for specific construction projects. Campaign contributions are one of the methods they use. PACs associated with these interests contributed $70.8 million directly to congressional candidates and an additional $14 million to party committees during the 2010 election cycle. Professionals linked to these interests and their families donated another $208.4 million in contributions of $200 or more to congressional candidates and party committees. These figures amply demonstrate that this economic sector brings considerable financial resources to bear on congressional elections.

Other organized interests provide a range of assistance to candidates in congressional elections. Think tanks, such as the Heritage Foundation on the right and the Center for American Progress on the left, provide issue research. Labor unions and church-based organizations in African American and other minority communities have long histories of political activism. Many have made decisive contributions to Democratic candidates' field operations and conducted their own voter registration and GOTV campaigns. Business leaders, including those associated with the Chamber of Commerce and the NAR, have traditionally assisted Republicans. AIPAC is a lobbying organization that provides information about candidates to PACs and individuals who support Israel. Even though it carries out activities similar to those of lead PACs and the Hill committees, this lobbying group gives no cash contributions to congressional candidates, so it does not qualify as a federally registered PAC.

Virtual groups, sometimes referred to as "netroots" associations, are relative newcomers to electoral politics, but they play an increasingly important role in congressional elections. Netroots associations have some similarities to traditional grassroots organizations, but their membership is Internet-based rather than defined by geography. Some groups, such as ActBlue and RightRoots, serve as financial conduits individuals can use to make campaign contributions to their preferred candidates. Others, including Democracy for America and the Progressive Change Campaign Committee, provide websites that, among other things, enable volunteers to download lists of voters for the purpose of making GOTV calls.[40]

OUTSIDE CAMPAIGNS

Interest groups, like political parties, developed outside campaigns as a way to move beyond direct contributions to candidates in their efforts to influence elections. The groups that conduct these campaigns carry out activities similar to those used by the parties, including polling, issue and opposition research, television advertising, direct mail, social media communications, and voter mobilization drives. However, interest groups can fund these activities with large contributions raised from individuals, corporations, unions, and other groups whereas parties only can use funds that originated as relatively modest contributions raised from individuals. Another difference between interest groups and party outside campaigns is that party committees rarely do anything to advantage one nomination candidate over another, but some interest groups are very active in trying to determine who wins the nomination.[41]

Coordinated Grassroots Campaigns

Although an onslaught of interest group–sponsored television attack ads is the most visible impact of the weakening of regulations governing group participation in federal elections, regulatory changes also led to more interest group–sponsored coordinated grassroots campaigns. In 2010 labor unions, the LCV, EMILY's List, and a raft of other left-leaning organizations invested hundreds of millions of dollars and countless volunteer hours registering Democrats and Democratic-leaning voters; informing them of opportunities to vote early or by absentee ballot; and telephoning, e-mailing, or personally visiting them to make sure they cast their votes. For example, the AFL-CIO, a federation of sixty-four unions representing 13 million workers, recruited more than 200,000 union volunteers who knocked on roughly 8.5 million doors, distributed 19.4 million flyers, and sent 24.6 million pieces of mail to mobilize working Americans to support Democratic candidates in close contests.[42] Conservative groups, including the Chamber of Commerce and the National Rifle Association (NRA), also conducted impressive coordinated campaigns; however, they were somewhat less volunteer based. American Crossroads, for example, spent about $10 million on voter mobilization drives in nine targeted states. Part of its efforts involved distributing iPads to campaign workers who used them to locate preselected homes and enter information directly into the group's database.[43]

Finally, some coordinated campaigns are carried out by groups that begin spontaneously as local movements and then loosely affiliate with one another and receive guidance from more structured organizations. The Tea Party movement exemplifies this. Beginning with a few local protests in early 2009, by Election Day there were an estimated 1,400 Tea Party groups. These groups attracted the attention and leadership of former Alaska governor Sarah Palin, Sen. Jim DeMint, R-S.C., Rep. Ron Paul, R-Texas, and Congressional Tea Party Caucus founder Rep. Michele Bachmann, R-Minn. They also received support from several Republican-leaning 501(c)(4) groups and PACs, including the Tea Party Patriots; FreedomWorks, led by former House majority leader Dick Armey; and the Tea Party Express, a bus tour and media campaign associated with a PAC created by a prominent Republican consulting firm in California. The Tea Party's grassroots efforts involved large rallies; small house parties; and the recruitment of multitudes of volunteers who worked on Republican candidates' campaigns, assisted at local GOP headquarters, and ran their own efforts to identify, register, and mobilize voters committed to electing Tea Party candidates. As noted in earlier chapters, the Tea Party movement was very successful in 2010. It had an impact on many Republican primaries, influenced the tenor of the general election, affected the voting behavior of many Republican and independent voters, and helped determine the outcomes of several congressional elections. By providing an outlet for conservative voters, disgruntled Republican Party activists, and independents happy with neither party, the Tea Party was able to channel the energies and votes of these individuals in support of a subset of Republican candidates, thereby contributing to the GOP's success.

Independent Media Campaigns

The emergence of new spending entities had a major impact on the independent media campaigns interest groups waged in the 2010 elections. First, the cost of these campaigns was unprecedented, reaching $287 million—almost five

FIGURE 5-5

Financing of Interest Group Independent Media Campaigns in the 2010 Congressional Elections

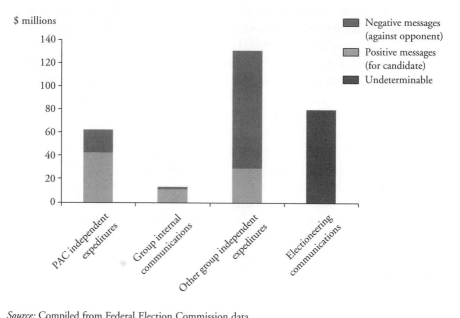

Source: Compiled from Federal Election Commission data.

Notes: Other group independent expenditures include spending by corporations, trade associations, unions, super PACs, and other groups. Electioneering communications include spending by 527 committees and 501(c) organizations.

times more than in the previous midterm election. Second, much of the campaigns' funding came from sources that were previously prohibited. Traditional PACs and interest group internal communications accounted for $62.5 million and $13.4 million, respectively (about 26 percent of the total; see Figure 5-5). Interest group entities that recently became active in federal elections accounted for considerably more: corporations, trade associations, unions, and the super PACs and 501(c) organizations they sponsored made roughly $211 million in independent expenditures and electioneering communications (the remaining 74 percent). Third, the messages disseminated by the new players increased the negativity of outside campaigns. Whereas 68 percent of all independent spending by PACs and 84 percent of all spending on internal communications financed positive messages, the same is true of only 44 percent of the independent expenditures financed by interest group treasuries and the super PACs they financed. Although the disclosure requirements for electioneering communications do not require groups to characterize the tone of the expenditures, the evidence suggests that most of the $70 million spent by conservative groups and the $9 million spent by liberal groups was overwhelmingly negative.[44]

Independent media campaigns were significant in a number of the 2010 elections. There were nine House races in which interest group independent expenditures exceeded the total spending by both candidates and one hundred in which they exceeded the spending of at least one candidate.[45] In forty of those contests, outside spending intended to help one candidate, including negative ads against the opponent, exceeded that candidate's own expenditures. This spending was heavily concentrated in competitive races and divided fairly equally between Democrats and Republicans (see Table 5-4). It also was heavily influenced by the national political agenda. In their attempts to help Republican hopeful challengers ride to victory on the electoral tidal wave they saw forming, pro-Republican groups spent 78 percent of their outside funds on blaming Democratic incumbents for the state of the economy and linking them to unpopular Democratic leaders, policies, and the federal government. The spending pattern for pro-Democratic groups was reversed, as pro-Democratic groups committed 86 percent of their expenditures to preventing Democratic incumbents in jeopardy from being drowned by that same tidal wave, often by attacking the qualifications and experience of competitive GOP challengers. Groups on both sides committed roughly equal sums to the races of open-seat prospects.

Interest group independent media campaigns in the 2010 Senate elections favored the Republicans substantially. For every $1.00 an organization spent to improve the chances of a Democrat, an opposing group spent $2.46 to help a Republican. Interest groups communicated messages in the Senate contests that were similar to those used in races for the House: Republican-leaning groups focused on national issues and Democratic-leaning groups highlighted local concerns. The distribution of outside spending in elections for the upper chamber also was comparable to that for the lower chamber in that most spending to help Democrats was committed to incumbents in competitive contests, and most pro-Republican spending was dedicated to challengers in the same races. One noteworthy difference between the two chambers is that Democratic- and Republican-allied groups spent considerably larger sums in close open-seat contests for the Senate. Another concerns the large sums of pro-Republican spending that occurred in lopsided open-seat contests for the Senate, which were largely the result of the three-way races in Florida and Alaska.

TABLE 5-4

Distribution of Interest Group Independent Media Campaigns in the 2010
Congressional Elections

	House		Senate	
	Democrats	Republicans	Democrats	Republicans
Incumbents				
In jeopardy	86%	8%	60%	2%
Shoo-ins	1	1	1	1
Challengers				
Hopefuls	4	78	—	47
Long shots	—	1	—	—
Open-seat candidates				
Prospects	8	8	34	41
Mismatched	1	3	5	9
($ thousands)	$48,950	$49,570	$28,233	$69,519

Source: Compiled from Federal Election Commission data.

Note: Figures in cells include all independent expenditures designed to help a candidate (i.e., those for the candidate and against the opponent). The categories of candidates are the same as those in Table 1-4. Figures include independent expenditures and internal communications made by PACs, super PACs, 527 organizations, 501(c) committees, and other groups in support of or opposition to major-party general election candidates in contested races. Columns do not add to 100 percent because of rounding. $N = 812$ for the House; $N = 72$ for the Senate.

The heavy concentration of interest group and party spending in the same elections and the overlap in group and party messages come as little surprise. As noted in Chapter 4, the parties have adapted to prohibitions against coordinating their independent media campaigns by going to great lengths to publicize their priority races and the nature of the expenditures they intend to make in them. Such signaling is unnecessary among interest groups because they can legally coordinate their independent media efforts. Many do, and as a result the messages broadcast by allied interest groups are similar to each other and to those broadcast by their preferred candidates and party. In 2010 the "shadow dance" that defines much interest group and party outside spending resulted in party committees reallocating some of their independent expenditure funds in response to interest group media buys. In a few instances, the allied groups beat the parties to the punch, which enabled the parties to deploy their resources elsewhere. Of course, when one party and its allies engage in substantial outside media spending in a set of elections, the opposing party and its allies typically reallocate some of their independent media expenditures in response. The response is usually swiftest and strongest when congressional incumbents come under attack.[46] In this way, interest group and party independent media campaigns spread the field of competition in 2010 and other recent congressional election cycles.

THE IMPACT OF INTEREST GROUP ACTIVITY

How helpful are interest groups in assisting congressional candidates with waging their campaigns? What effects do their outside campaign activities have on election dynamics? Are there specific elections in which their efforts appear to have decided the outcome? The impact of interest groups on congressional elections can be assessed on a number of levels.

Congressional candidates and their campaign aides generally evaluate the help they get from labor, business, other groups, and the PACs they sponsor less favorably than the assistance they get from party committees. The exception to this rule is fundraising: as a function of their sheer numbers and the BCRA's contribution limits, PACs as a group are in a position to contribute more money to a House campaign than are party organizations. The assessments of House campaigners indicate that interest groups play larger roles in the campaigns of Democrats than in those of Republicans. This is especially true for labor unions and labor PACs, which for decades have made large contributions in money and manpower to Democratic campaigns. The Republican candidates' relative lack of dependence on interest groups is also partially a result of their greater reliance on party committees for campaign services.[47] Senate candidates and campaign aides of both parties find PACs and other groups to be helpful in virtually every aspect of campaigning, but not as helpful as the DSCC or NRSC.

Of course, interest group election efforts, like party efforts, are targeted to selected races. The information provided by both House and Senate campaigners indicates that interest group campaign assistance is focused more heavily on competitive contests and is more important to the election efforts of hopeful challengers and open-seat prospects than to incumbents. This is largely the result of incumbents' beginning the election with high levels of name recognition and huge war chests, both of which nonincumbents lack.

Although Rep. Allen Boyd did not set the record for interest group support received in 2010, his reelection campaign in Florida's 2nd district benefited from significant interest group assistance, including the $1.4 million he raised from PACs.[48] Agribusiness, health care, and the finance, insurance, and real estate industries were among his top backers. Lawyers and lobbyists also were very supportive. He raised $730,000 from PACs sponsored by organizations in these economic sectors and another $391,000 from individuals employed in them. Labor PACs accounted for $159,000, but as usually is the case, cash contributions from individual union members were too small to require reporting to the FEC.[49]

Many groups also conducted impressive coordinated grassroots campaigns and independent media campaigns on Boyd's behalf. Several unions, including the American Federation of State, County, and Municipal Employees, the Florida Education Association, and the National Association of Letter Carriers, provided endorsements and drafted volunteers to assist the campaign. More important, they made Boyd the beneficiary of their own GOTV efforts. The efforts were targeted with the assistance of America Votes, a partnership of unions and progressive groups. The endorsements of the National Rifle Association and the Chamber of Commerce were particularly important because they helped burnish Boyd's conservative credentials in a race in which opponents aggressively tied him to Barack Obama, Nancy Pelosi, and the liberal wing of the Democratic Party.

Interest groups spent more than $629,000 on independent media campaigns to bolster Boyd's candidacy. A small number of these ads were positive. The NRA's Political Victory Fund broadcast $22,000 worth of radio ads praising the incumbent for his defense of "the Second Amendment freedoms of law-abiding gun owners, hunters, and sportsmen in Florida and across America."[50] A week before the election, the Chamber of Commerce spent $50,000 on a radio ad praising Boyd for his support of small business. Nevertheless, most of the interest group spending intended to help the incumbent was decidedly negative. The biggest spender, America's Families First Action Fund, a liberal super PAC allied with the Democratic Party, committed $455,000 to a direct mail and cable TV campaign to paint Boyd's opponent, Steve Southerland, as an untenable alternative to the seven-term representative.

However, Southerland also was the beneficiary of substantial interest group support. PACs provided him with $149,000. In contrast to Boyd, Southerland raised no money from labor PACs, but he raised $104,000 from business PACs and hundreds of thousands more from small-business owners and business executives. The Bay Patriots, which Southerland cofounded, the Tea Party movement, and several other organizations helped him recruit hundreds of volunteers. A number of local conservative groups ran their own, largely negative grassroots campaigns, distributing yard signs and other paraphernalia featuring slogans such as "Boyd Void."

Interest groups registered with the FEC spent more than $1.1 million on independent media ads to help Southerland, most of which attacked Boyd. The

60 Plus Association, a 527 group funded largely by the pharmaceutical industry, spent $372,000 criticizing Boyd for his votes on health care reform and his ties to Speaker Pelosi. The Center for Individual Freedom spent $264,000 on TV ads condemning Boyd for supporting the stimulus package. The Faith and Freedom Coalition spent another $210,000 on electioneering communications accusing Boyd of being on the side of Pelosi and Obama, for big government, and against faith and freedom. Virtually all of these ads dovetailed with Southerland's and the Republican Party's anti-Washington messages.

In Nevada, interest groups more than showed their willingness to play a significant role in a Senate election. PACs contributed $5.5 million directly to the candidates. Roughly seventy groups, including PACs, super PACs, 527s, and 501(c) organizations, spent approximately $13 million on outside campaigning to affect the race's outcome.

Democratic senator Harry Reid raised $5.2 million from PACs and millions more from individuals associated with a variety of interest groups. Roughly $4 million of these funds came from corporate and trade association PACs. Ideological PACs accounted for $760,000, and labor accounted for $431,000. Reid's position as majority leader gives him tremendous influence over how the Senate does its business, and it enabled him to raise an enormous amount of money from PACs and individuals associated with many economic sectors. Lawyers and lobbyists were particularly supportive, providing him with almost $4.7 million. In addition to this direct support, interest groups conducted impressive outside campaigns on Reid's behalf. Democratic-oriented interest groups spent almost $1.8 million calling for Reid's election and another $3.2 million advocating opponent Sharron Angle's defeat. Substantial sums were spent by labor unions, environmental groups, and ideological groups that traditionally have been part of the Democratic coalition. Among other things, the unions provided volunteers and concentrated on registering and turning out voters. Patriot Majority, whose various entities spent almost $2.8 million, emerged as the single most significant pro-Reid group in the contest. It aired a series of television ads that attacked Angle's proposal to privatize the U.S. Department of Veterans Affairs and eliminate abortions, and it cast her positions on other issues as "too extreme." The ads were helpful to Reid for a variety of reasons. Most notably, their message and style were consistent with those disseminated by the Reid campaign, which also branded Angle as an extremist. The group's ads, like Reid's, used recordings of Angle's voice to increase their potency.

Interest groups also worked to promote Angle's candidacy. She was able to raise $352,000 from PACs, roughly 80 percent more than the typical Senate challenger. Drawn to her conservative credentials, PACs and individuals associated with the Tea Party and other groups on the right were her biggest backers: they contributed almost $1.9 million. She also received ample support from the business community, including $819,000 in contributions from the financial, real estate, and insurance industries. Nevertheless, these contributions are a drop in the bucket compared to the almost $8 million interest groups spent independently to help Angle's cause. American Crossroads accounted for roughly $4.3 million of the outside spending intended to help Angle, including ads attacking Reid as a Washington insider responsible for "bailouts, deficits, Obamacare," and job losses in Nevada. A variety of other groups also focused on these themes.

As is the case with party independent expenditures, even the best-intentioned interest group independent spending can occasionally create a problem for a candidate. An ad broadcast by Latinos for Reform, a Republican-allied group, exemplifies this point. Prior to the group's airing of its ad, the Angle campaign ran some TV spots on immigration that had racial undertones, raising questions about her views on racial equality in general and Hispanics in particular. The Latinos for Reform ad, intended to deprive Reid of a voting bloc important to his reelection, raised further questions about Angle's candidacy. Broadcast on a Las Vegas Spanish-language radio station, the ad ended with the statement: "Don't vote this November. This is the only way to send them a clear message."[51] The Reid campaign responded to the ad by accusing Angle and her supporters of trying to suppress the Hispanic vote. The combination of Angle's messaging, the group's ad, and the Reid campaign's response helped to solidify Hispanic support for Reid and reinforced the incumbent's strategy of painting Angle as "too extreme" and "too dangerous" to serve in the Senate.

It is impossible to tell whether interest group activities—or party efforts or the candidates' own campaigns—determined the outcomes of the Reid-Angle race, the Boyd-Southerland matchup, or any other hotly contested 2010 congressional election. Nevertheless, it is important to note that PACs, super PACs, 527s, and 501(c)s were responsible for about 29 percent of the spending in the Reid-Angle race and 15 percent of the funds spent in the Boyd-Southerland contest.[52] These elections demonstrate that through their contributions, attempts to influence the political agenda, advertisements touting the strengths and weaknesses of candidates, and voter mobilization efforts, interest groups can have an impact on elections.

SUMMARY

Interest groups, like parties, play important supporting roles in congressional elections. From the mid-1970s until recently, most interest group activity in federal elections was funneled through PACs. Freed from previous legal constraints, a number of groups have begun to use 527 committees, 501(c) organizations, super PACs, or funds from their own treasuries to try to influence the national political agenda or affect the outcomes of specific congressional elections. These activities mark the end of an era when virtually all of the monies spent to influence federal elections originated with a U.S. citizen making a relatively modest voluntary contribution to a federally regulated candidate committee, party, or PAC. Future elections will undoubtedly involve large expenditures originating from the general treasuries of corporations, unions, and other groups that are subject to neither the fundraising limitations nor the disclosure requirements that apply to traditional PACs.

The outside campaigns carried out by these organizations, and the 527s, 501(c)s, and super PACs they support, also may portend a shift in interest group strategies. Most notably, the 2010 election witnessed a bifurcation in the approaches used by some wealthy corporations and trade associations. PACs associated with these groups continued to distribute most of their contributions to congressional leaders and other incumbents of both parties, as is consistent with an access-oriented strategy. However, the 527s, 501(c)s, and super PACs the groups helped finance embraced full-blown, election-oriented strategies consisting of highly partisan, negative outside campaigns that focused on a relatively small number of races, including those involving powerful incumbents.

Increased competition for the control of Congress explains some of these changes, but newly created spending avenues that make it difficult, and in some cases impossible, to identify which interests are propping up which front groups also are important. One of the main results of the abundance of interest group spending in congressional elections is that messages are heard from many sides of the political spectrum, making for a diverse, if not sometimes cacophonous, group of voices competing for voters' attention. In some competitive elections the voices of organized interests actually drown out those of the candidates. The outside campaigns carried out by interest groups and parties have not done away with the candidate-centered system of elections, but they have the potential to confuse voters, reduce accountability, and change the dynamics of close races.

CHAPTER SIX

The Campaign for Resources

Vice President Hubert Humphrey described fundraising as a "disgusting, degrading, demeaning experience."[1] Few politicians would disagree with this sentiment. Yet spending money on political campaigns predates the Constitution. In 1757 George Washington purchased twenty-eight gallons of rum, fifty gallons of spiked punch, forty-six gallons of beer, thirty-four gallons of wine, and a couple gallons of hard cider to help shore up his political base and pry loose the support of enough uncommitted voters to get elected to the Virginia House of Burgesses.[2] Population growth, technological advancements, suburbanization, and other changes associated with the emergence of a modern mass democracy in the United States have driven up the costs of campaigning since Washington launched his political career. Candidates, parties, and interest groups spent more than $3.6 billion on the 2010 elections.[3]

Raising the funds needed to run for Congress has evolved into a campaign in and of itself. Part of this campaign takes place in the candidate's state or district, but many candidates depend on resources that come from party committees and PACs located in and around Washington, D.C., and from wealthy individuals who typically reside in major metropolitan areas.

The campaign for resources begins earlier than the campaign for votes. It requires a candidate to attract the support of sophisticated, goal-oriented groups and individuals who have strong preconceptions about what it takes to win a congressional election. Theoretically, all congressional candidates can turn to the same sources and use the same techniques to gather campaign funds and services; in practice they begin and end on uneven playing fields. The level of success that candidates achieve with different contributors or fundraising techniques depends largely on whether they are incumbents, challengers, or candidates for open seats. It also depends on the candidates' party affiliation and on whether they are running for the House or the Senate, among other factors. In this chapter I analyze the fundraising strategies and successes of different types of candidates.

Virtually every congressional election cycle sets a new record for campaign fundraising and spending; the 2010 elections were no exception. Candidates for the House set a fundraising record of almost $1.1 billion. More than 400 candidates raised more than $1 million each, 41 raised in excess of $3 million, and nine raised more than $5 million. Republican representative Michele Bachmann of Minnesota collected the most of any House candidate—more than $13.5 million.

The Senate elections in 2010 also were record-setting, as candidates raised almost $750 million in those races. Forty-four of the candidates each collected more than $5 million, including twenty-four who raised more than $10 million, thirteen who raised in excess of $15 million, and another six who took in more than $20 million. The top Republican fundraisers were Linda McMahon, who collected $50.3 million, virtually all of it from her own bank account, for an unsuccessful bid for an open seat in Connecticut, and Sharron Angle, who raised $28.4 million in cash and party coordinated expenditures in a failed attempt to defeat Senate majority leader Harry Reid in Nevada. The Democrats' top fundraiser was Sen. Barbara Boxer, who collected $34.1 million in cash and party coordinated expenditures to defeat GOP challenger Carly Fiorina in California. These candidates fell short of the record set by former senator Jon Corzine, D-N.J., who raised almost $63.3 million—$60.2 million from a loan he made to his own campaign—to win an open-seat race for the Senate in 2000.

INEQUALITIES IN RESOURCES

Significant inequalities exist in the resources, including money, loans, and party coordinated expenditures, that candidates are able to raise. The typical House incumbent involved in a two-party contested race raised about $1.6 million in cash and party coordinated expenditures in 2010, which is roughly two and one-half times more than the sum raised by the typical House challenger.[4] Open-seat candidates also gathered significant resources, raising an average of almost $1.2 million.

The resource discrepancies in competitive House races are great. Incumbents in jeopardy raised almost 62 percent more than did hopeful challengers during the 2010 elections (see Figure 6-1). Competitive open-seat contests were much more equal in regard to the amounts raised. The resource discrepancies in

FIGURE 6-1

Average Campaign Resources Raised in Competitive House Elections in 2010

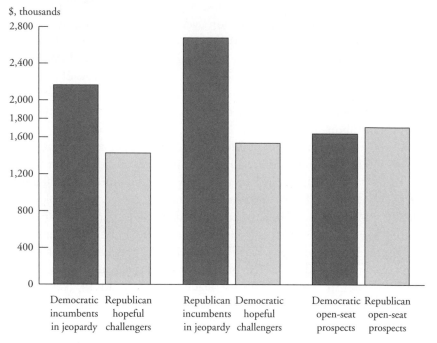

Source: Compiled from Federal Election Commission data.

Notes: Figures include receipts and party coordinated expenditures for all two-party contests that were decided by margins of 20 percent of the vote or less. N = 318.

uncompetitive House contests are even greater than are those in competitive ones. Incumbents, who begin raising funds early—often before they know whom they will face in the general election—collect much more money than do their opponents (see Figure 6-2). Incumbent shoo-ins raised almost nine times more than long-shot challengers in 2010. The spread among open-seat candidates in uncompetitive races is usually much smaller, averaging about $546,000.

The typical Senate incumbent raised about $4.8 million more than the typical challenger during the 2010 election (see Figure 6-3). Open-seat Senate contests were fairly well funded, with contestants spending an average of $9 million. The differences in the amounts raised by Democratic and Republican candidates were unusually significant, favoring Republican contenders by

FIGURE 6-2

Average Campaign Resources Raised in Uncompetitive House Elections in 2010

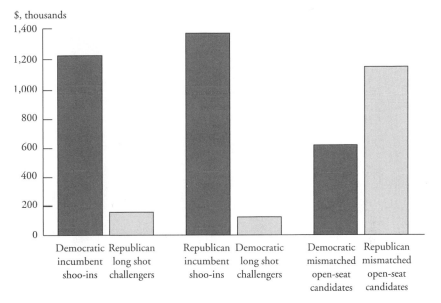

$, thousands

Source: Compiled from Federal Election Commission data.

Notes: Figures include receipts and party coordinated expenditures for all two-party contests that were decided by margins of greater than 20 percent of the vote. *N* = 494.

about $2.8 million, or 41 percent. Finally, electoral competitiveness was impor-
tant in attracting campaign resources. Senate candidates who defeated their
opponents by 20 percent or less of the two-party vote raised more than two
and one-half times as much as candidates involved in one-sided races.

HOUSE INCUMBENTS

Incumbents raise more money than challengers because they tend to be more
visible, popular, and able to exploit the advantages of holding office. This is
reflected both in how incumbents solicit contributions and to whom they turn
for cash. Incumbents rarely hesitate to remind a potential donor that they are
in a position to influence public policy and will more than likely still be in that
position when the next Congress convenes.

FIGURE 6-3

Average Campaign Resources Raised in the 2010 Senate Elections

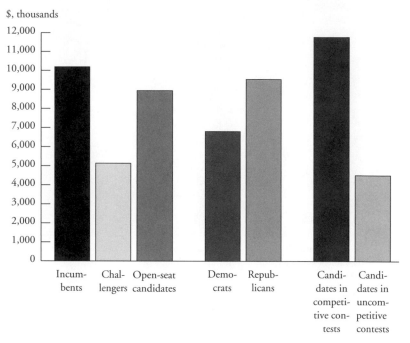

Source: Compiled from Federal Election Commission data.

Notes: Figures include receipts and party coordinated expenditures for all two-party contested races. *N* = 72.

Sources of Funds

Individuals who make contributions of less than $200 are an important source of funds for House incumbents (see Figure 6-4). In 2010 they accounted for about $155,000, or nearly 10 percent, of the typical incumbent's campaign war chest.[5] These contributions are often viewed symbolically as an indicator of grassroots support. Individuals who contributed from $200 to $4,350 accounted for almost $708,000, or 44 percent, of the typical incumbent's funds. These contributions are important for the obvious reason that a candidate needs to gather fewer of them to raise a sum equal to many small contributions. The doubling of the limits for individual contributions that came with the passage of the Bipartisan Campaign Reform Act of 2002 has resulted in House incumbents (and congressional candidates in general) becoming more dependent on large individual contributions.

FIGURE 6-4

Sources of House Incumbents' Campaign Receipts in the 2010 Elections

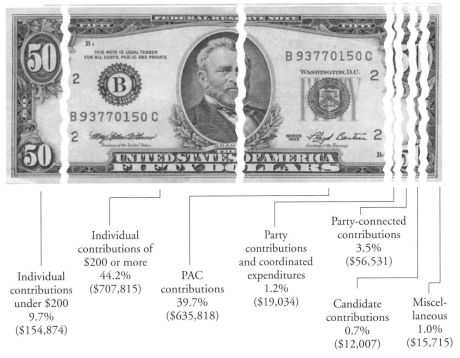

Individual contributions under $200
9.7%
($154,874)

Individual contributions of $200 or more
44.2%
($707,815)

PAC contributions
39.7%
($635,818)

Party contributions and coordinated expenditures
1.2%
($19,034)

Party-connected contributions
3.5%
($56,531)

Candidate contributions
0.7%
($12,007)

Miscellaneous
1.0%
($15,715)

Sources: Compiled from Federal Election Commission and Center for Responsive Politics data.

Notes: The dollar values in parentheses are averages. Candidate contributions include loans candidates made to their own campaigns. PAC contributions exclude contributions by leadership PACs. Party-connected contributions are made up of contributions from leadership PACs, candidates, retired members, and members of Congress not up for reelection in 2010. Miscellaneous sources include interest from savings accounts and revenues from investments. Figures are for general election candidates in major-party contested races. Percentages may not add to 100 percent because of rounding. *N* = 365.

Many individuals made contributions to congressional incumbents (and other candidates) across district or state lines. Individuals living in the Washington, D.C., metropolitan area alone donated almost $152 million to congressional candidates nationwide and to the party committees, PACs, and other groups that participated in the 2010 midterm election. Individuals in the New York metropolitan area came in second at almost $108 million. These contributions, along with the millions distributed by Washington-based parties, PACs, and other groups, have helped to form a national market for campaign contributions.[6]

House incumbents from both parties rely heavily on this market, often fundraising in the same cities. The unequal distribution of wealth across the United States has made crisscrossing the country an important tactic in the campaign for resources. The unequal distribution of power between incumbents and other candidates has made contributing across geographic jurisdictions a prevalent tactic among access-oriented donors. That politicians go where the money is and that money flows to power speaks volumes about the campaign for resources. Because incumbents enjoy greater national recognition and influence, they are positioned to raise more money than are challengers.

PACs provided approximately $636,000, or 40 percent, of a typical House incumbent's campaign bankroll in 2010. Parties delivered much less, accounting for a mere 1 percent of the typical incumbent's total resources. Party-connected contributions from other members, leadership PACs, and congressional retirees accounted for an additional 4 percent. House members contributed even less of their own money to their campaigns. Finally, they raised about $16,000 from miscellaneous sources, including interest and revenues from investments.

Prior to the Republican takeover of Congress in 1995, Democratic House members collected a greater portion of their funds from PACs than did Republicans, who relied more heavily on individual contributors. The Democrats' procedural control of the House gave them greater influence over the substance and scheduling of legislation, which provided them with an overwhelming advantage in collecting PAC money. The 1996 elections brought with them considerable change in this regard. With Republican leaders in charge of the House, GOP incumbents raised substantially more PAC money than did Democratic incumbents in every election cycle—that is, until the Democrats retook control of the chamber in 2007. During the 2010 elections incumbent Democrats typically raised more funds from PACs, and their Republican counterparts raised more from individuals (see Table 6-1). Incumbents in jeopardy from both parties collected substantially more party and party-connected dollars than those in less competitive elections.

Fundraising Activities

Incumbents routinely complain about the time, effort, and indignities associated with fundraising. Their lack of enthusiasm for asking people for money figures prominently in how they raise campaign contributions. A fear of defeat and a disdain for fundraising have two principal effects: they encourage incumbents to raise large sums and to place the bulk of their fundraising in the hands of others, mainly professional consultants. Forty-six percent of all major-party House incumbents spend at least one-fourth of their personal campaign schedule raising funds. Seventeen percent spend more than half of their schedule asking

TABLE 6-1

Sources of Support for House Incumbents in the 2010 Elections

	Democrats		Republicans	
	In jeopardy	Shoo-ins	In jeopardy	Shoo-ins
Individual contributions under $200	$182,561 (9%)	$49,854 (4%)	$698,655 (26%)	$137,379 (10%)
Individual contributions of $200 or more	$916,621 (44%)	$533,028 (45%)	$1,161,821 (44%)	$572,419 (43%)
PAC contributions	$759,080 (37%)	$563,238 (48%)	$648,296 (24%)	$567,414 (43%)
Party contributions and coordinated expenditures	$47,830 (2%)	$2,331 (—)	$24,288 (1%)	$2,451 (—)
Party-connected contributions	$128,156 (6%)	$6,550 (1%)	$108,295 (4%)	$17,081 (1%)
Candidate contributions	$20,937 (1%)	$8,028 (1%)	$0 (—)	$7,883 (1%)
Miscellaneous	$19,124 (1%)	$13,307 (1%)	$9,210 (—)	$15,267 (1%)

Sources: Compiled from Federal Election Commission and Center for Responsive Politics data.

Notes: Figures are averages for general election candidates in major-party contested races. — = less than 0.5 percent. Candidate contributions include loans candidates made to their own campaigns. PAC contributions exclude contributions by leadership PACs. Party-connected contributions are made up of contributions from leadership PACs, candidates, retired members, and members of Congress not up for reelection in 2010. Miscellaneous sources include interest from savings accounts and revenues from investments. Some columns do not add to 100 percent because of rounding. $N = 365$.

others for money.[7] Of course, the money chase is a full-time endeavor for the candidates' consultants.

Most incumbents develop full-time fundraising operations. They hire professional consultants to write direct-mail and telephone appeals, update contributor lists, identify and solicit potentially supportive PACs, and organize fundraising events. These operations enable incumbents to limit their involvement to showing up at events and telephoning potential contributors who insist on a direct conversation prior to making a large contribution.

Incumbents raise small contributions by making appeals through the mail, over the telephone, at fundraising events, and via the Internet. Direct mail can be a relatively reliable method of fundraising for an incumbent because solicitations are usually made from lists of previous donors that indicate which appeals generated earlier contributions.[8] Most successful direct-mail and telephone solicitations garner contributions of less than $100 and are targeted at the candidate's constituents. However, many prominent House members, beginning with the Speaker, have huge direct-mail lists that include hundreds of thousands of citizens who reside across the United States and even a few who live abroad. A significant portion of these individuals contribute large sums. In 2010 Speaker Nancy Pelosi raised more than $401,000 and then–minority leader John Boehner raised more than $2 million in individual contributions of $200 or more from outside their respective states (representing 41 percent and 62 percent, respectively, of these candidates' large individual contributions). Representative Bachmann raised an astounding $2.6 million (69 percent) of her individual contributions of $200 or more from outside her state of Minnesota.

The Internet emerged as an important fundraising tool during the 1998 congressional elections. By 2002, 57 percent of all House candidates in major-party contested races and virtually every Senate candidate used websites or e-mail to solicit funds.[9] Their numbers increased substantially by the 2010 election season. Most candidates' websites enable donors to contribute online using a credit card; virtually all provide instructions for making contributions via mail, phone, or fax.

Some candidates make solicitations using e-mail addresses purchased from Internet providers, other organizations, and individuals who visit their websites. E-mail lists of individuals who share a candidate's issue concerns are a potential source of monetary and volunteer support, especially among computer-literate youth. Facebook, podcasts, and other social media can be used to encourage tech-savvy individuals to contribute to campaigns. The greatest advantage of e-mail and Internet fundraising is that the solicitation is delivered for free, compared with the $3 to $4 it costs to send out one first-class, direct-mail solicitation. The trade-off for e-mail is that it is not always welcome. Mass-distributed e-mails, often referred to as "spam," are frequently deleted without having been read, the electronic equivalent of tossing an unopened piece of direct mail into the trash or hanging up on a telemarketer. The same is true of tweets and other unsolicited communications. Few congressional candidates are able to emulate the electronic fundraising success of presidential contenders, but many high-profile House and Senate contestants are positioned to capitalize on the Internet for some of their fundraising needs.

Traditional fundraising events are another popular means for raising small contributions. Cocktail parties, barbecues, and picnics that are held in the candidate's district, with tickets typically ranging from $10 to $50, are useful ways to raise money. They also are helpful in generating favorable press coverage, energizing political activists, and building goodwill among voters.

Incumbents can ensure the success of local fundraising events by establishing finance committees that include business executives, labor officials, civic leaders, or political activists who live in their districts. These committees often begin with a dozen or so supporters who host "low-dollar" receptions (where individuals usually contribute from $10 to $100) in their homes and make telephone solicitations on the candidate's behalf. Guests at one event are encouraged to become the sponsors of others. In time, small finance committees can grow into large, pyramid-like fundraising networks consisting of dozens of finance committees, each of which makes a substantial contribution to the candidate's reelection efforts. Most House and Senate incumbents have fundraising networks that extend from their district or state to the nation's capital.

Large individual contributions and PAC money also are raised by finance committees, at fundraising events, and through networks of supporters. Events that feature the president, congressional leaders, sports heroes, or other celebrities help attract individuals and groups willing to contribute anywhere from a few hundred dollars to the legal maximum.[10] Some of these events are held in the candidate's state, but most are held in political, financial, and entertainment centers such as Washington, New York City, and Los Angeles. In 2006 the twenty-three Republican House incumbents who were the beneficiaries of one or more visits by President George W. Bush raised 159 percent more than did other GOP incumbents. The House Democrats who received fundraising visits from President Barack Obama in 2010 undoubtedly reaped similar benefits.

Traditional fundraising events can satisfy the goals of a variety of contributors. They give individuals who desire the social benefits of giving, including the proximity to power, the chance to speak and have their picture taken with members of Congress and other celebrity politicians. Persons and groups that contribute for ideological reasons are able to voice their specific issue concerns. Individuals and organizations that are motivated by material gain, such as a tax break or federal funding for a project, often perceive these events as opportunities to build a relationship with members of Congress.[11]

By raising large individual contributions, House members have advantages over challengers that extend beyond the prestige and political clout that come with incumbency and the ability to rely on an existing group of supporters. Lawmakers also benefit from the fact that many wealthy individuals have motives that favor incumbents over challengers. About 25 percent of all individuals who contribute $200 or more to a congressional candidate—usually an incumbent—do so mainly to cultivate access to politicians who are likely to be in a position to influence legislation once the election is over. Roughly 36 percent give contributions primarily for broad, ideological reasons or because of their positions on specific, highly charged issues. These donors tend to rally around incumbents who champion their causes. Another 24 percent are moti-vated to contribute primarily because they enjoy attending fundraising events and mixing with incumbents and other elites who attend these functions. The final 15 percent are not strongly motivated by any one factor. Though they contribute for idiosyncratic reasons, they, like other donors, primarily support incumbents.[12]

Moreover, information disseminated by parties, PACs, and other groups often focuses on incumbents' campaigns, further leading some wealthy indi-viduals to contribute to incumbents in jeopardy rather than to hopeful chal-lengers. The rise of a national economy of campaign finance, complete with organizations and individuals who provide potential donors with decision-making cues, has combined with the ceilings federal law places on campaign contributions to lead to the replacement of one type of fat cat with another. Individuals and groups that gave candidates tens or hundreds of thousands of dollars directly have been replaced by new sets of elites who help candidates raise these sums rather than contribute them directly.

Incumbents consciously use the influence that comes with holding office to raise money from PACs and wealthy individuals who seek political access. Legislators' campaigns first identify the potential donors who are most likely to respond favorably to their solicitations. These include PACs that supported the incumbent in a previous race, lobbyists who agree with an incumbent's positions on specific issues, and others who are affected by legislation the incumbent is in a position to influence. Members of Congress who hold party leadership posi-tions, serve on powerful committees, or are recognized entrepreneurs in certain policy areas can easily collect large amounts of money from many wealthy inter-est group–based financial constituencies. It is no coincidence that all ten of the House incumbents who raised the most PAC money in the 2010 elections, more than $1.4 million each, enjoyed at least one of these assets.[13]

Once an incumbent has identified a financial constituency, the next step is to ask for a contribution. The most effective solicitations describe the member's background, legislative goals, accomplishments, sources of influence (including committee assignments, chairmanships, or party leadership positions), the nature of the electoral competition, and the amount of money needed. Incumbents frequently assemble this information in the packets they mail to PACs. Addressed to a member of the PAC's board of directors, usually a lobbyist, these solicita-tions are customized to tap into the PAC's motives for contributing.

Some PACs require a candidate to meet with one of their representatives, who personally delivers a check. A few require incumbents to complete ques-tionnaires on specific issues, but most PACs rely on members' prior roll-call votes or interest group ratings as measures of their policy proclivities. Some

PACs, particularly ideological committees, want evidence that a representative or senator is facing serious opposition before giving a contribution. Party leaders and Hill committee staff are sometimes called to bear witness to the competitiveness of an incumbent's race.

Parties are another source of money and campaign services. The most important thing incumbents can do to win party support is demonstrate that they are vulnerable. The Hill committees have most of the information they need to make such a determination, but incumbents can give details on the nature of the threat that might not be apparent to a party operative who is unfamiliar with the nuances of a member's seat. The Democratic Congressional Campaign Committee (DCCC) gives incumbents in their Frontline Program the opportunity to make a case for extra party support before a committee of Democratic House members. The National Republican Congressional Committee (NRCC) provides similar opportunities for endangered incumbents enrolled in its Patriot Program. Once a Hill committee has made an incumbent a priority, it will go to great efforts to supply the candidate with money, campaign services, and assistance in collecting money and other resources—that is, as long as the candidate continues to meet the fundraising and other goals the committee has set.

The financing of Rep. Jerrold Nadler's 2010 reelection effort in New York is illustrative of most reelection bids involving safe incumbents. Nadler raised more than $1.3 million and received $84 in in-kind contributions from the DCCC and no party coordinated expenditures, a substantially smaller party supplement than the $48,000 received by the typical Democratic shoo-in incumbent. He collected less than $36,000 (3 percent of his total resources) in small contributions using campaign newsletters, direct-mail solicitations, his website, and low-dollar fundraising events held in the district. He collected another $826,000 (roughly 63 percent) in individual contributions of $200 or more at high-dollar events. Only $97,000 (8 percent) of this money was raised from individuals who reside outside New York.

Nadler raised $416,000 (32 percent) from PACs. Corporate, trade, and other business-related committees contributed about 50 percent of these funds and labor contributed 45 percent.[14] Nonconnected committees accounted for a mere 4 percent of Nadler's PAC dollars. The candidate collected a few token contributions from other members' campaign committees or leadership PACs. Indeed, he contributed about $75,000 from his campaign committee and leadership PAC to other congressional candidates, as well as another $292,000 to other Democrats, various party committees, and other organizations. Most of his PAC money and large individual donations were raised at events held in his New York City district or in Washington and through solicitations coordinated by the candidate's campaign staff. Like most congressional incumbents, Nadler contributed no money to his own reelection effort.

Nadler was successful at capitalizing on his memberships on the House Transportation and Infrastructure and Judiciary Committees. The individuals and groups that are affected by the Transportation Committee's business make up a substantial interest group constituency. Nadler's campaign collected more than $80,000 (20 percent of its PAC funds) from PACs associated with the transportation and construction industries and another $187,000 from labor PACs (45 percent), including many associated with these trades. In addition, it raised $154,000 in contributions of $200 or more from individuals who work in the transportation and construction sector (14 percent of the total he raised from this group). His slot on the Judiciary Committee helped him raise $37,000 from PACs associated with the legal and lobbying professions (8 percent of his total) and another $149,000 in contributions from individuals in those professions (18 percent).[15]

With only two-year terms, House incumbents usually begin raising money almost immediately after they are sworn into office. Sometimes they have debts to retire, but often they use money left over from previous campaigns as seed money for the next election. Almost one-third of all House incumbents began the 2010 election cycle with more than $400,000 left over from their previous campaigns. In turn, almost 28 percent of all successful 2010 House candidates completed their campaigns with more than $400,000 in the bank, including thirty-nine who had amassed more than $1 million. These funds will provide useful seed money for their reelection campaigns in 2012 or bids for some other office.

Early fundraising is carried out for strategic reasons. Incumbents build substantial war chests early in the election cycle to try to deter potential challengers.[16] An incumbent who had to spend several hundreds of thousands or even millions of dollars to win by a narrow margin in the last election will have a greater compulsion to raise money earlier than someone whose previous election was a landslide victory. Once they have raised enough money to reach an initial comfort level, however, incumbents appear to be driven largely by the threat posed by an actual challenger.[17] Incumbents under duress seek to amass huge sums of money regardless of the source, whereas those who face weak opponents may weigh other considerations, such as helping other candidates or their party raise money.

A typical incumbent's campaign—one waged by a candidate who faces stiff competition in neither the primary nor the general election—will generally engage in heavy fundraising early and then allow this activity to taper off as it becomes clear that the candidate is not in jeopardy. The 2010 Nadler campaign exemplifies this pattern. The campaign began the election cycle with more than $578,000 left over from the candidate's last race. Between January 1 and

December 31, 2009, it raised $686,000 (about 52 percent of its total receipts). All of this money was raised before Susan Kone, Nadler's general election opponent, had collected sufficient funds to register her candidacy with the Federal Election Commission. During the next six months, the Nadler campaign began to cut back on its fundraising efforts, collecting about $412,000 (32 percent), perhaps in response to the lackluster fundraising performance of the Kone campaign, which raised only $7,750 during this period. During the next three months, which included New York's August 2nd primary, the Nadler campaign collected an additional $130,000 (10 percent). Between October 1 and November 22 it raised a total of $73,000 (6 percent). The campaign closed out the election year by collecting an additional $4,000 (about 0.3 percent). In its coffers remained $801,000 ready for use in the 2012 election. This war chest could have been substantially larger had Nadler chosen to redistribute fewer funds to others.

Nadler's campaign finances typify a safe incumbent. Money is raised early on to deter a strong primary or general election opponent from entering the race. Like the Nadler campaign, the 2010 campaign of Allen Boyd, at the time the Democratic representative from Florida's 2nd district, also supports the generalization that incumbent fundraising is challenger driven. However, it shows how an incumbent responds to a strong challenge in both the primary and the general election. The campaign began the election cycle with almost $1.2 million in its coffers and raised an additional $2.7 million in contributions and $19,000 in coordinated expenditures, making it the sixteenth most expensive House reelection campaign that year. It raised $1.4 million (54 percent of its total resources) from PACs, excluding leadership PACs, and another $779,000 (29 percent) in individual contributions of $200 or more, 71 percent of which was collected from individuals living in the candidate's home state. The campaign collected a mere $67,000 (3 percent) in individual contributions of less than $200. The Democratic Party provided about $20,000 in coordinated expenditures (about 0.5 percent). Democratic members of Congress and retirees contributed about $108,000, and leadership PACs gave another $239,000 (for a total of 13 percent). Boyd capitalized on his memberships on the House Appropriations and Budget Committees when fundraising. They gave him tremendous advantages in soliciting money from a wide array of PACs, lobbyists, and other individuals who have a financial stake in the decisions these committees reach on government spending and finance. Many of these donors wanted access to Boyd and believed that a campaign contribution would help them get it.[18] Finally, despite the competitiveness of his race, Boyd contributed no money to his campaign. This is typical of incumbent candidates.

Boyd began to solicit contributions early and aggressively in anticipation of a tough primary contest against state senate minority leader Al Lawson. Boyd also recognized that his support for the stimulus program, health care reform, cap-and-trade, and some other salient issues might make him vulnerable in the general election. He began the campaign cycle with almost $1.2 million left over from his 2008 campaign. Between January 1 and December 31, 2009, the Boyd campaign raised $1 million (roughly 37 percent of its receipts). Between January 1 and July 1, 2010, it collected another $656,000 (24 percent). This money was raised in response to both Lawson's highly competitive primary challenge and an anticipated competitive general election. By this point GOP candidate Steve Southerland, who was locked in a competitive primary of his own, also had raised hundreds of thousands of dollars. Lawson's challenge and the prospect of a cliff-hanger of a general election led Boyd to believe he would need to spend more money to hold on to his seat. He greatly stepped up his fundraising efforts, boosting his campaign's resources by an additional $649,000 between July 1 and September 30, 2010 (accounting for 24 percent of his receipts), and $347,000 (13 percent) from October 1 to Election Day. Between his defeat and the close of the calendar year Boyd was able to raise about $7,000 (0.2 percent).

The Boyd campaign's fundraising was driven by a situation the candidate had anticipated: unlike the lack of competition that enabled Nadler to cut back on his fundraising efforts and redistribute substantial sums to others, the stiff competition from Lawson and Southerland encouraged Boyd, the incumbent, to set a personal fundraising record. Unfortunately for him, his fundraising efforts did not bring him victory.

HOUSE CHALLENGERS

Challengers have the greatest need for money, but they encounter the most difficulties raising it. The same factors that make it difficult for challengers to win votes also harm their ability to collect campaign contributions. A lack of name recognition, limited campaign experience, a relatively untested organization, and a high probability of defeat discourage most contributors, especially those who give large amounts in pursuit of access, from supporting challengers. The fact that their opponents are established Washington operators who possess political clout does not make challengers' quests for support any easier.

Sources of Funds

Challengers raise less money than incumbents, and their mix of funding sources differs from that of incumbents. House challengers collect a greater

FIGURE 6-5

Sources of House Challengers' Campaign Receipts in the 2010 Elections

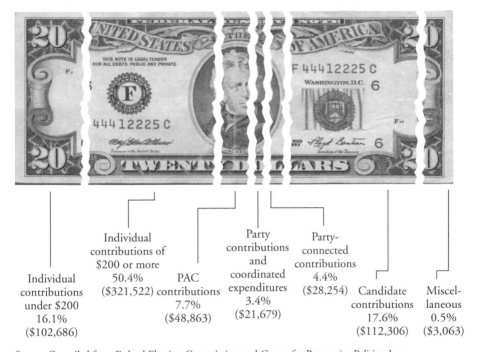

Individual
contributions
under $200
16.1%
($102,686)

Individual
contributions of
$200 or more
50.4%
($321,522)

PAC
contributions
7.7%
($48,863)

Party
contributions
and
coordinated
expenditures
3.4%
($21,679)

Party-
connected
contributions
4.4%
($28,254)

Candidate
contributions
17.6%
($112,306)

Miscel-
laneous
0.5%
($3,063)

Sources: Compiled from Federal Election Commission and Center for Responsive Politics data.

Notes: See notes in Figure 6-4. $N = 365$.

portion of their funds from individuals. Challengers competing in the 2010 elections raised an average of about $103,000, or 16 percent of their campaign budgets, from individual contributions of less than $200 (see Figure 6-5). More than three times as much of their funds came from individual contributions of $200 or more. Both challengers and incumbents raised substantial funds from individuals, but incumbents raised, on average, more than twice as much as did challengers. Moreover, challengers raised a significantly smaller proportion of their funds out of state.

Challengers garnered a mere 8 percent of their money from PACs, trailing incumbents by a ratio of almost 1 to 12 in terms of PAC dollars. Challengers also raised substantially less party-connected money, an average of about $28,000, as opposed to the $57,000 raised by the typical incumbent. The distribution of party contributions and coordinated expenditures, by contrast, was more favorable to challengers, who averaged about $2,000 more than incumbents. Finally, challengers dug far deeper into their own pockets than did incumbents. The typical challenger contributed to or lent the campaign about $112,000—more than nine times the amount provided by the typical incumbent.

Partisanship and competition had significant effects on challenger fundraising. Democratic challengers, particularly those with some realistic hope of victory, raised substantially more money from PACs than did their Republican counterparts (see Table 6-2). Republican hopeful challengers were able to make up for some of this deficit by relying on funds contributed by their party and its members of Congress and investing more in their own campaigns.

Prior political experience also was important. During the 2010 congressional elections House challengers in major-party contested races who had previously

TABLE 6-2

Sources of Support for House Challengers in the 2010 Elections

	Democrats		Republicans	
	Hopefuls	Long shots	Hopefuls	Long shots
Individual contributions under $200	$348,113 (23%)	$24,251 (19%)	$183,123 (13%)	$51,732 (33%)
Individual contributions of $200 or more	$782,849 (52%)	$70,319 (56%)	$698,559 (50%)	$73,435 (47%)
PAC contributions	$153,198 (10%)	$8,860 (7%)	$110,131 (8%)	$2,730 (2%)
Party contributions and coordinated expenditures	$16,345 (1%)	$2,042 (2%)	$58,699 (4%)	$432 (—)
Party-connected contributions	$48,029 (3%)	$1,453 (1%)	$73,331 (5%)	$1,071 (1%)
Candidate contributions	$162,606 (11%)	$19,586 (15%)	$262,432 (19%)	$28,114 (18%)
Miscellaneous	$1,382 (—)	$157 (—)	$8,331 (1%)	$317 (—)

Sources: Compiled from Federal Election Commission and Center for Responsive Politics data.

Notes: Figures are averages for general election candidates in major-party contested races. — = less than 0.5 percent. Candidate contributions include loans candidates made to their own campaigns. PAC contributions exclude contributions by leadership PACs. Party-connected contributions are made up of contributions from leadership PACs, candidates, retired members, and members of Congress not up for reelection in 2010. Miscellaneous sources include interest from savings accounts and revenues from investments. Some columns do not add to 100 percent because of rounding. *N* = 365.

held elective office raised, on average, $792,000 in contributions and coordinated expenditures. This includes $27,000 from party committees and $71,000 in party-connected contributions. Unelected politicians raised an average of $482,000, including $12,000 from party committees and $32,000 in party-connected dollars. Political amateurs raised, on average, only $273,000. Of this, $15,000 came from their party and $12,000 from party-connected sources.

Fundraising Activities

Incumbents may find fundraising a disagreeable chore, but at least their efforts usually meet with success. Challengers put in just as many long, hard hours on the money chase as do incumbents.[19] Yet, as noted above, they clearly have less to show for their efforts. Most challengers start raising early money at home. They begin by donating or lending their campaigns the initial funds needed to solicit contributions from others. They then turn to relatives, friends, professional colleagues, local political activists, and virtually every individual whose name is in their personal organizer or, even better, on their holiday card list. Some of these people are asked to chair fundraising committees or host fundraising events. Candidates who have previously run for office are able to turn to past contributors for support. Competitive challengers frequently obtain lists of contributors from private vendors or hire fundraising consultants who provide their own. In some cases these challengers receive lists from party committees, PACs, or other candidates; however, most of those supporters mail fundraising letters on behalf of selected candidates rather than turn over their contributor lists.

Only after enjoying some local fundraising success do most nonincumbents set their sights on Washington. Seed money raised from individuals is especially helpful in attracting funds from PACs, particularly for candidates who have not held elective office.[20] The endorsements of local business, labor, party, or civic leaders have a similar effect, especially if they can be persuaded to serve on a fundraising committee. If the assistance of congressional leaders or members of a candidate's state delegation can be obtained, it can be helpful to challengers who hope to raise money from their party's congressional campaign committee, PACs, or individuals who make large contributions. When powerful incumbents organize luncheons, attend "meet-and-greets," and appear at fundraising events for nonincumbents, contributors usually respond positively. Designation as a Red to Blue candidate or Young Gun, which conveys such benefits as well as an aura of viability that is rare for challengers, provided positive results for candidates of both parties in 2010. Red to Blue challengers, on average, raised $2.3 million in total contributions and party coordinated expenditures, almost twenty times more than other Democratic challengers. Young Guns raised an average of $1.9 million, above two and one-half times more than other Republican challengers. Candidates who had significant unelected political experience (such as working as a political aide or party official) or no political experience at all (political amateurs) benefited the most from these party recognitions because prospective donors customarily pay more attention to candidates who have previous office-holding experience, particularly those they have supported in the past.

Contributors also look favorably on events attended by high-ranking executive branch officials, particularly the president. The few Republican challengers who benefited from a campaign visit by President Bush in 2006 raised ten times more than other Republican challengers. The same is undoubtedly true of the Democratic challengers who received fundraising visits from President Obama in 2010. Unfortunately for most challengers, their long odds of success make it difficult for them to enlist the help of a president, party leader, or even rank-and-file congressional incumbents. Political leaders focus their efforts on candidates who have strong electoral prospects and some day may be in a position to return the favor by supporting the member's leadership aspirations or legislative goals in Congress.

A knowledge of how donors make contribution decisions can improve a challenger's fundraising prospects. Political experience and a professional campaign staff often come together, and they are particularly helpful in this regard.[21] Candidates who put together feasible campaign plans, hire reputable consultants, and can present polling figures indicating that they enjoy a reasonable level of name recognition usually attract the attention of party officials, PAC managers, individuals who make large contributions, and the inside-the-Beltway journalists who handicap elections. Political amateurs who wage largely volunteer efforts usually cannot.

One way in which challengers can increase their chances of success in raising money from PACs is to identify the few committees likely to give them support. For example, Democratic challengers can improve their prospects of attracting labor PAC money by showing they have strong ties to the labor community, have previously supported labor issues in the state legislature, or support labor's current goals.[22] Challengers of both parties may be able to attract contributions from PACs, particularly ideological committees, by demonstrating their support for the group's cause. Many challengers, and in fact many nonincumbents, can demonstrate this support by pointing to roll-call votes they cast in the state legislature, the backing of a PAC's donors or affiliated PACs located in their state or district, or the support of Washington-based organizations that share some of the PAC's views. Properly completing a PAC's questionnaire or having a successful interview with a PAC manager also is extremely important. Taking these steps can help a challenger obtain a contribution and endorsement from a PAC, as well as gain assistance in raising money from individuals and other PACs with shared policy concerns.

Ideological causes have been at the forefront of many candidates' fundraising strategies during the past few decades. Pro-choice women challengers are able to capitalize on their gender and attract large amounts of money and campaign assistance from EMILY's List. The WISH List (the Republican counterpart of EMILY's List) provides support for female pro-choice GOP candidates. By taking a side on emotionally laden issues, such as handgun control or support for Israel, some challengers are able to attract the contributions of ideological PACs and individuals who identify with those causes. The same is true of challengers who attach themselves to a broader political movement, as many Republicans did with the Tea Party in the 2010 election.

A perception of competitiveness is critical to challenger fundraising, and a scandal involving an incumbent can help a challenger become financially competitive. In 2010 it helped Hansen Clarke raise the $576,000 he used to defeat Rep. Carolyn Cheeks Kilpatrick in the Democratic primary in Michigan's 13th district and best John Hauler in the general election.

Kone's and Southerland's experiences demonstrate the effect that perceptions of competitiveness have on challenger fundraising. Almost from the beginning, Kone's campaign to unseat Nadler encountered the fundraising doldrums that plague most House challengers, particularly those who would be classified as long-shots. Her campaign began collecting money more than a year after her opponent did, which is typical in most incumbent-challenger races, and it got off to a very slow start. By September 30, 2010, it had raised just over $23,000 (53 percent of its total). It collected about $20,000 (47 percent) between October 1 and November 22, leaving it unable to run a financially viable campaign. The campaign had no debt to retire and raised no money between November 22 and the year's end.

Besides getting a late start in raising funds, the Kone campaign suffered from having no professional operation to solicit contributions. It had difficulty raising PAC money—collecting only one PAC contribution of $1,500. The Republican Party provided no contributions or coordinated expenditures, and the same is true of Republican members of Congress and their leadership PACs. Kone donated $210 to her campaign and raised $41,000 (95 percent of its total) from individuals, including $31,000 in contributions of $200 or more—almost three-fourths of which were given by New Yorkers.

The Southerland campaign exemplifies the fundraising dynamics of most hopeful challengers. As a result of his strong connections with local business owners and party activists and prominence in the Republicans' Young Guns Program, Southerland was able to solicit money from a broad array of individuals and groups. Notoriety, party assistance, a strong professional organization, grassroots support, and an effective strategy enabled him to raise almost $1.3 million in contributions and $85,000 in party coordinated expenditures. Southerland collected almost $149,000 from PACs (excluding leadership PACs, 11 percent of the total), $90,000 from his party (7 percent), $120,000 in party-connected contributions (9 percent), and $951,000 in individual contributions (69 percent of his resources). Almost $822,000 of his large individual contributions were given in amounts of $200 or more—86 percent of which were donated by Floridians. Southerland donated $28,500 to his own campaign (about 2 percent).

The Southerland campaign, unlike the Kone organization, began collecting money early in the election season. By December 31, 2009, it had amassed $54,000 (4 percent of its funding). With the help of Republican leaders and the party's donor network, the campaign took in an additional $313,000 (24 percent) during the next six months. The campaign's fundraising took off once Southerland won the Republican nomination, and it collected $913,000 (71 percent) by November 22 and another $12,000 to close out the calendar year.

Boyd's plummeting popularity and Southerland's strong fit to the district and strong party backing helped the challenger attract the support of party committees, PACs, and individual donors who were eager to wrest a seat held by a senior Democrat. Boyd and his supporters also responded to the competitiveness of the race, resulting in the incumbent raising more than twice as much as his opponent. The dynamics of the race were typical of a close incumbent-challenger contest, except that the incumbent was forced to spend heavily in both the primary and the general election.

CANDIDATES FOR HOUSE OPEN-SEATS

Candidates for open seats possess few of the fundraising advantages of incumbents, but they also lack the liabilities of challengers. Open-seat candidates rely on many of the same fundraising strategies as challengers but usually have considerably more success. Because most open-seat contests are competitive, they receive a great deal of attention from parties, PACs, and other informed contributors, particularly individuals who make large contributions. This attention places open-seat candidates in a position to convince Washington insiders and other elites that their campaigns are worthy of support.

Sources of Funds

The campaign receipts of open-seat candidates bear some similarity to those of incumbents and challengers. Open-seat candidates typically raise about as much as incumbents. Like challengers, however, they usually collect less money from out-of-state donors, invest more heavily in their own campaigns, and garner more support from parties and party-connected sources (see Figure 6-6). The typical open-seat candidate's PAC receipts lie between those amassed by incumbents and those gathered by challengers.

Following the GOP takeover of Congress in 1994, more PACs became disposed to support Republican open-seat candidates—a trend that continued until the Democrats reclaimed control of the House in 2007. In 2010 Democratic open-seat prospects typically raised slightly less PAC money than

FIGURE 6-6

Sources of House Open-Seat Candidates' Campaign Receipts in the 2010 Elections

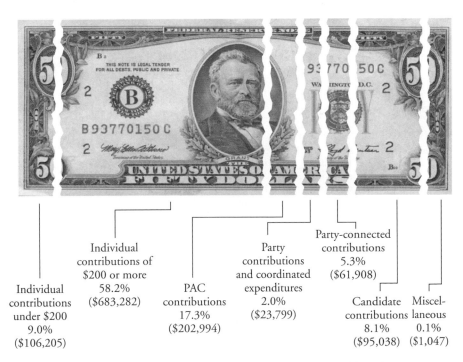

Sources: Compiled from Federal Election Commission and Center for Responsive Politics data.

Notes: See notes in Figure 6-4. N = 82.

their Republican opponents, and Republican candidates in mismatched open-seat contests collected substantially more PAC money than the Democrats, mainly because the national environment helped most of them establish strong leads in their races (see Table 6-3). Republican candidates received slightly more party and party-connected money than did their Democratic counter-parts, as one might expect given the Democratic Party's emphasis on incumbent retention and the Republican Party's focus on picking up new seats. Although candidates of both parties bankrolled portions of their own campaigns, Republicans typically contributed more personal funds than Democrats.

TABLE 6-3

Sources of Support for House Open-Seat Candidates in the 2010 Elections

	Democrats		Republicans	
	Prospects	Mismatched	Prospects	Mismatched
Individual contributions under $200	$164,339 (10%)	$61,623 (10%)	$161,009 (10%)	$78,506 (7%)
Individual contributions of $200 or more	$953,986 (60%)	$359,423 (60%)	$928,445 (55%)	$676,986 (59%)
PAC contributions	$276,229 (17%)	$95,882 (16%)	$286,211 (17%)	$209,977 (18%)
Party contributions and coordinated expenditures	$44,266 (3%)	$7,580 (1%)	$45,897 (3%)	$12,776 (1%)
Party-connected contributions	$92,525 (6%)	$16,937 (3%)	$112,020 (7%)	$55,212 (5%)
Candidate contributions	$67,781 (4%)	$60,825 (10%)	$150,735 (9%)	$111,049 (10%)
Miscellaneous	$1,950 (—)	$778 (—)	$777 (—)	$911 (—)

Sources: Compiled from Federal Election Commission and Center for Responsive Politics data.

Notes: Figures are averages for general election candidates in major-party contested races. — = less than 0.5 percent. Candidate contributions include loans candidates made to their own campaigns. PAC contributions exclude contributions by leadership PACs. Party-connected contributions are made up of contributions from leadership PACs, candidates, retired members, and members of Congress not up for reelection in 2010. Miscellaneous sources include interest from savings accounts and revenues from investments. Some columns do not add to 100 percent because of rounding. $N = 82$.

Among open-seat candidates, elected politicians raised the most money in 2010, averaging almost $1.3 million, about $200,000 more than the amounts raised by unelected politicians and political amateurs. Elected officials did not do particularly well when it came to raising money from party committees, averaging about $27,000, which was about the same as amateurs and more than unelected politicians. Elected officials did, however, raise considerable amounts in party-connected contributions—averaging about $79,000, $37,000 more than unelected politicians and $30,000 more than political amateurs.

Fundraising Activities

Candidates for open seats put in the longest fundraising hours of all House contestants and, as noted above, with considerable success. Just over 60 percent devote more than one-fourth of their personal campaign schedule to attending fundraising events, meeting in person with potential donors, and dialing for dollars.[23] These candidates help their cause by informing potential contributors of their political experience and the assets their campaign organization brings to the race.

Winning support from PACs can be a little more challenging. Although open-seat candidates use the same techniques as challengers to identify interest group constituencies and campaign for PAC support, they usually have greater success. Because their odds of victory are better, open-seat candidates have an easier time gaining an audience with PAC managers and are able to raise more PAC money. Similarly, open-seat candidates point to the same types of information as challengers to make the case that their campaigns will be competitive. Experienced open-seat contestants and those who wage professional campaigns collect more PAC money than do amateurs.[24]

Like challengers, open-seat candidates can improve their prospects in the campaign for resources by impressing congressional leaders. Candidates whose initial campaign efforts enabled them to attain Red to Blue or Young Gun status raised about three times more than others running for open seats in 2010. Nonincumbents clearly benefit when their party signals they are mounting strong campaigns. The ability to pick up the support of a broad political movement also can help. Despite the fact that Tea Party candidates for open seats raised no more than other GOP challengers, it is safe to assume the group's endorsement helped them collect contributions from Tea Party activists.

The fundraising experiences of the candidates in Illinois' 10th district mirror those of most open-seat candidates in competitive races. Both candidates built up considerable war chests. Dan Seals raised about $2.9 million and received an additional $63,000 in Democratic Party coordinated expenditures.

He collected $2.4 million from individuals (83 percent of his total), almost all of it from in state, and $311,000 (11 percent) from PACs.[25] Labor committees gave Seals about $160,000. PACs sponsored by trade associations, corporations, and cooperatives provided an additional $123,000. Liberal nonconnected committees gave him $26,000. Individuals and groups associated with legal and lobbying firms were especially supportive, providing him with $425,000 in contributions. In addition to the $63,000 Seals received in coordinated expenditures from the Democratic Party, he collected $12,000 in party contributions and $120,000 in party-connected contributions. Party and party-connected money accounted for about 5 percent of his resources. Much of Seals's fundraising success stems from the ties he forged in his previous two runs for Congress and his designation as a Red to Blue candidate. He provided no funds of his own.

The Republican Bob Dold had not previously held elective office or run for Congress, but his experience working for the House provided him with plenty of political contacts and more than a basic knowledge of electoral politics. As a Young Gun he benefited from a great deal of fundraising assistance. He raised more than $2.9 million; most of it (84 percent) came in the form of individual contributions from Illinois voters. He collected $324,000 (11 percent of his total resources) from PACs, receiving $286,000 from trade association, corporate, and cooperative PACs. Conservative nonconnected PACs contributed another $38,000.[26] Individuals and PACs connected to the finance, insurance, and real estate industries were particularly supportive of Dold, providing him with $673,000 in contributions. Not surprisingly, Dold received no support from PACs affiliated with organized labor. Dold raised less party and party-connected money than Seals. The NRCC contributed $5,000 and Republican members of Congress and retirees contributed $30,000 from their campaign committees and $82,000 from their leadership PACs (totaling 4 percent of his receipts). Unlike Seals, Dold invested $10,500 of his own funds to jumpstart his campaign.

As is the case with most competitive open-seat contests, the candidates in Illinois' 10th district race attracted a great deal of attention from potential contributors and were able to raise large amounts of money once they began fundraising in earnest. Between July 1 and December 31, 2009, Seals and Dold collected $303,000 and $258,000, respectively (accounting for roughly 10 percent of their respective campaign receipts). During the next nine months, when both candidates were involved in hotly contested primaries, they each raised an additional $2 million (about 70 percent). The candidates continued their frenetic fundraising between October 1 and November 22, with a slight advantage going to Dold, who collected another $597,000 compared to Seals's $582,000 (about 20 percent). During the remaining days of 2010, the victorious Dold collected about $44,000 and ended the election cycle with $6,000 cash on hand, while the defeated Seals raised less than $6,000 and his campaign was $5,000 in debt.

SENATE CAMPAIGNS

The differences in the campaigns for resources waged by Senate and House candidates are consistent with other differences that exist between House and Senate elections. Candidates for the Senate need more money, start requesting support earlier, and devote more time to asking for it. About 57 percent of all candidates spend more than one-fourth of their campaign schedule asking potential donors for funds.[27] They often meet with party officials, PAC managers, wealthy individuals, and other sources of money or fundraising assistance three years before they plan to run. Most Senate candidates also attempt to raise money on a more national scale than do House contestants. This monumental task requires Senate candidates to rely more on others for fundraising assistance. Nonincumbent Senate candidates are more likely than their House counterparts to hire professional consultants to manage their direct-mail and event-based solicitation programs.

Senate candidates raised an average of $3.8 million in large individual contributions in 2010—about 49 percent of their campaign resources (see Figure 6-7). Many of these donations came from out of state. Small individual contributions accounted for 16 percent of their resources, PACs for another 12 percent, and party contributions and coordinated expenditures for 6 percent. Party-connected contributions accounted for a mere 2 percent, mostly because each party has limited numbers of senators to contribute to one another. The candidates themselves provided roughly 14 percent of the money spent directly on Senate campaigns. Compared with candidates for the House, candidates for the upper chamber rely more heavily on individuals and formal party organizations and less on PACs and their colleagues for their funding.

Party affiliation affects fundraising for the upper chamber of Congress less than it does for the lower chamber. Democratic Senate candidates raised slightly more funds in the form of large individual contributions and Republicans collected slightly more from PACs (see Table 6-4). The biggest difference is that Republican candidates contributed more personal funds to their own campaigns than did the Democrats. However, this is largely due to the fact that the GOP fielded both more challengers and more challengers who were willing to invest their own substantial wealth. Indeed, self-funding accounted for one-fifth of

FIGURE 6-7

Sources of Senate Candidates' Campaign Receipts in the 2010 Elections

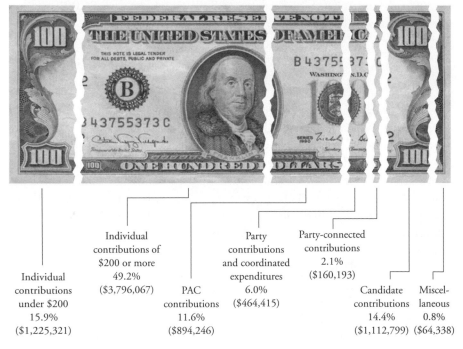

Individual contributions under $200
15.9%
($1,225,321)

Individual contributions of $200 or more
49.2%
($3,796,067)

PAC contributions
11.6%
($894,246)

Party contributions and coordinated expenditures
6.0%
($464,415)

Party-connected contributions
2.1%
($160,193)

Candidate contributions
14.4%
($1,112,799)

Miscellaneous
0.8%
($64,338)

Sources: Compiled from Federal Election Commission and Center for Responsive Politics data.

Notes: See notes in Figure 6-4. $N = 72$.

challengers' resources, almost one-fourth of open-seat candidates' resources, and less than one-half of 1 percent of incumbents' resources. Other funding differences involve resources raised from individuals, parties, party-connected committees, and PACs. Incumbents raised more money than challengers from each of these sources except for individuals who make small contributions, where the difference is relatively inconsequential. A comparison between open-seat candidates and challengers shows virtually the same set of differences.

Underlying these patterns are the fundraising advantages enjoyed by Senate incumbents. Senators, like House members, often begin their quest for reelection with significant sums left over from their previous campaigns, and they start raising money early. Twelve senators each had more than $2 million prior to the start of the 2010 campaign season, and six had in excess of $3 million. Four senators scheduled for reelection in 2012 had each raised more than $2 million by March 31, 2011. Sen. Richard Lugar, R-Ind., led the pack with

TABLE 6-4
Sources of Support for Senate Candidates in the 2010 Elections

	Party		Status			Competitiveness	
	Democrats	Republicans	Incumbents	Challengers	Open-seat candidates	Competitive	Uncompetitive
Individual contributions under $200	$875,396 (14%)	$1,575,247 (17%)	$1,264,294 (14%)	$1,287,029 (26%)	$1,154,845 (13%)	$1,902,523 (17%)	$548,120 (13%)
Individual contributions of $200 or more	$3,891,902 (60%)	$3,700,232 (41%)	$5,291,372 (58%)	$2,086,022 (41%)	$3,946,386 (46%)	$5,175,226 (46%)	$2,416,909 (58%)
PAC contributions	$854,134 (13%)	$934,359 (10%)	$1,799,615 (20%)	$195,101 (4%)	$749,890 (9%)	$1,060,837 (9%)	$727,656 (17%)
Party contributions and coordinated expenditures	$406,485 (6%)	$522,344 (6%)	$411,584 (4%)	$388,958 (8%)	$554,216 (6%)	$789,921 (7%)	$138,908 (3%)
Party-connected contributions	$155,389 (2%)	$164,997 (2%)	$219,955 (2%)	$73,187 (1%)	$179,264 (2%)	$216,234 (2%)	$104,152 (2%)
Candidate contributions	$179,016 (3%)	$2,046,583 (23%)	$43,093 (—)	$998,281 (20%)	$1,941,757 (23%)	$2,076,790 (18%)	$148,809 (4%)
Miscellaneous	$70,919 (1%)	$57,758 (1%)	$159,499 (2%)	$1,265 (—)	$41,878 (—)	$25,913 (—)	$102,764 (2%)

Sources: Compiled from Federal Election Commission and Center for Responsive Politics data.

Note: Figures are averages for general election candidates in major-party contested races. Candidate contributions include loans candidates made to their own campaigns. PAC contributions exclude contributions by leadership PACs. Party-connected contributions are made up of contributions from leadership PACs, candidates, retired members, and members of Congress not up for reelection in 2010. Miscellaneous sources include interest from savings accounts and revenues from investments. Some columns do not add to 100 percent because of rounding. $N = 72$.

a war chest of more than $3 million. Senators, like House members, are able to raise these large sums because of their political clout, which few challengers possess. For example, in 2010 Sen. Harry Reid was able to raise $5.2 million from PACs and $17.5 million from individuals, $16.1 million of which came from contributions of $200 or more. Reid's position as Senate majority leader gives his fundraising apparatus a long reach. About 77 percent of his large individual contributions came from donors who live outside Nevada. Individuals and PACs from across the nation and representing a variety of economic sectors committed several million dollars to his campaign. Donors from the finance, insurance, and real estate sectors provided $3.6 million; those from the health care sector contributed $1.8 million; and those in communications and electronics donated $1.4 million. Perhaps most telling is that lawyers and lobbyists, many of whose livelihoods are affected by their ability to influence the Senate's actions, accounted for $4.7 million in contributions to the Reid campaign.

SUMMARY

The campaign for resources is an important aspect of contemporary congressional elections. It requires candidates and campaign strategists to identify groups of sympathetic potential donors and fashion a pitch that will appeal to them. The campaign for resources is a campaign among unequals. Incumbents typically begin the election season with more money in the bank than challengers, who usually start fundraising much later. The levels of skill and resources that incumbents and challengers bring to bear on the fundraising process, including their prospects for success and political clout, also differ markedly. As a result, incumbents raise more money than challengers, and incumbents raise proportionately more funds from PACs and individuals interested in directly influencing the legislative process. Candidates for open seats typically raise about the same as, if not slightly more than, incumbents, and open-seat candidates are more likely to wage campaigns that are financially competitive with that of their opponent. Nonincumbents who have significant political experience typically raise more money than do amateur candidates. Candidates who associate themselves with a broad-based group or movement, such as a labor union or the Tea Party, also can derive some fundraising advantages. However, these pale next to the benefits of formal recognition as a top contender by a Hill committee, which are especially pronounced among unelected politicians and amateurs.

CHAPTER SEVEN

Campaign Strategy

The campaign for votes involves voter targeting, message development, communications, and mobilization. During the heyday of the parties, party organizations formulated and executed campaign strategies. Party leaders, candidates, and activists talked with neighbors to learn about their concerns, disseminated campaign communications to address those concerns, and turned out the vote on Election Day. The predisposition of voters to support their party's candidates was strong and was frequently rewarded with government jobs, contracts, and other forms of patronage.

Contemporary campaigns also involve many of these aspects of campaigning. Successful candidates craft a message with broad appeal, set the agenda that defines voters' choices, and get their supporters to the polls to vote. During years in which there is a presidential election, that contest dominates the news and greatly influences most people's thinking about politics. Candidates who stake out positions that correspond to the national political agenda often have an advantage over those who do not, especially during nationalized (or wave) elections, which are dominated by national issues rather than local concerns.

In this chapter I focus on how voters decide to cast their ballots in congressional elections and on the strategies and tactics that campaigns use to affect those decisions. The primary topics are voting behavior, strategy, public opinion research, voter targeting, and the message.

VOTING BEHAVIOR

Traditional democratic theory holds that citizens should make informed choices when voting in elections. It contends that they should be knowledgeable about the candidates, be aware of the major issues, and take the time to discern which candidate is more likely to represent their views and govern in the nation's best interests. The weight of the evidence, however, suggests that the vast majority of voters in congressional elections fall short of those expectations.[1]

Most voters make their congressional voting decisions on the basis of relatively little information. In a typical House contest between an incumbent and a challenger, for example, only about one in ten voters can recall the names of the two major-party candidates. In House open-seat contests, about 37 percent of all voters can remember both candidates' names.[2] Voters tend to possess more information about contestants in Senate elections: roughly one-third can recall the names of both candidates in contests involving an incumbent and a challenger, and about two-thirds can identify both candidates in open-seat races.[3]

A less stringent test of political awareness involves merely recognizing the names of the candidates. About 60 percent of voters recognize the names of both major-party contestants in an incumbent-challenger race, and 80 percent of voters recognize the names of both candidates in open-seat contests. The levels of name recognition are higher in Senate contests: roughly four out of five recognize the names of the incumbent and the challenger, and more than nine in ten recognize the names of candidates in open-seat races.[4] More important are the percentages of voters who fail to recognize the names of the candidates and the even greater percentages of voters who cannot recall them because these are substantially larger than the vote margins that decide many House and Senate elections. Clearly, many voters lack the information needed to make what might be referred to as an informed vote choice.

The inability to recall or recognize the candidates' names is indicative of the overall lack of substantive information in congressional elections. Most House election campaigns are low-key affairs that do not convey much information about the candidates' ideological orientations or policy positions.[5] Information on House challengers, most of whom wage underfunded campaigns, is usually scarce. Campaign communications, voters' assessments of the issues, and candidates' qualifications become important only in hard-fought contests.[6]

Incumbency and Voter Information

By and large, the candidates who suffer most from lack of voter interest are House challengers. Whereas nine out of ten voters recognize their House member's name, fewer than 60 percent usually recognize the name of the challenger. Incumbents tend to be viewed favorably. Typically more than half of the voters who recognize their representative's name indicate that they like something about that person; roughly one-third mention something they dislike. The corresponding figures for House challengers are 35 percent and 32 percent.[7] As the high reelection rate for House members indicates, the name recognition and voter approval levels of most incumbents are difficult for opponents to overcome. Only challengers who can overcome their "invisibility problem" and create a favorable image stand a chance of winning.

Senate challengers tend to be less handicapped by voter inattentiveness. They enjoy better name recognition because of their political experience, skill, superior campaign organizations, party backing, and greater campaign spending. The newsworthiness of their campaigns also attracts media attention and voter interest. Voters learn more about the ideological orientations and issue positions of Senate challengers than those of their House counterparts.[8] Even though the name recognition of Senate challengers is lower than the near-universal recognition enjoyed by Senate incumbents, it is high enough to make the typical incumbent-challenger race competitive. This helps explain why more electoral turnover occurs in the upper than in the lower chamber of Congress.

The inequalities in candidate information that characterize most incumbent-challenger races generally do not exist in open-seat contests. The major-party candidates in an open-seat race for a marginal seat begin the campaign with similar opportunities to increase their name recognition and convey their messages to voters. Because these contests are more competitive, they receive more press coverage, which helps both candidates become better known to voters. Thus, more voters make informed choices in open-seat races than in incumbent-challenger contests.

Voting Decisions

Given their lack of knowledge of the candidates and issues, how do most voters make a decision on Election Day? Only those voters who know something about the background, political qualifications, party affiliation, and issue stances of both candidates are in a position to sift through the information, weigh the benefits of voting for one candidate over another, and cast their ballots in accordance with classical democratic theory.[9]

Nevertheless, voters who fall short of that ideal level of awareness may respond to the campaign information that candidates and the news media disseminate. Competitive, high-intensity elections that fill the airwaves, newspapers, and voters' mailboxes and e-mail accounts with campaign information provide some voters—especially those with an interest in politics—with enough information to form summary judgments about the candidates, which they tend to rely on when deciding which candidate to support.[10]

In the absence of a spirited, high-intensity election in their state or congressional district, most voters use "voting cues"—shortcuts that enable them to cast a ballot without engaging in a lengthy decision-making process. The most frequently used voting cue is incumbency. Knowing only an incumbent's name is sufficient for an individual to cast an adequately informed vote, some scholars argue.[11] Reasoning that the incumbent should be held accountable for the government's performance, the state of the economy, the nation's foreign involvements, or other issues, these voters quickly determine whether to support the status quo and vote for the incumbent or to advocate change and cast their ballot for the challenger.

Other voters pin the responsibility for the state of the nation on the president. When they are satisfied with how things are being run in Washington, those who use the president as a voting cue are inclined to support the congressional candidate who belongs to the president's party. When these voters are dissatisfied with the state of the nation's affairs, they often vote for the candidate whose party does not occupy the White House. Even though the party connection can have a positive impact on the fortunes of congressional candidates whose party is led by a popular president, belonging to the president's party often has a more harmful influence, especially in midterm elections.[12] Membership in the party that controls the House or Senate also can help or harm a congressional candidate.[13] The party cue, like the incumbency cue, enables voters to make retrospective voting choices without having much knowledge about the candidates or their issue positions. Under conditions of unified government, party cues are stronger because voters can more readily assign credit or blame for the state of the nation to the party that controls both the executive and legislative branches.[14] Political leaders of both parties attribute the massive turnover in the 2010 elections to the Democrats' control of Congress and the presidency in a time of major economic unrest.[15] The power-sharing arrangements of divided government, in contrast, obscure political responsibility because they enable politicians to blame others in power.

The party cue also enables voters to speculate about a candidate's ideological orientation and issue positions. Republicans are generally identified as more conservative than Democrats and are associated with free-market economics, deregulation, lower taxes, traditional family values, hawkish foreign policy, and the wealthier elements of society. Most Republicans profess to be for limited government, and some campaign as though they are antigovernment. Democrats are often viewed as the party of government. They are associated with greater economic intervention, the social safety net, environmental protection, public education, acceptance of alternative lifestyles, and a more dovish foreign policy, as well as protecting the interests of senior citizens, minorities, the poor, and working people. Some voters project the parties' images onto candidates and use those projections to guide their congressional voting decisions.[16] Others habitually support a party's nominees regardless of their credentials, issue positions, or opponents.

Partisanship and incumbency can affect the voting decisions of people who possess even less political information than the individuals described above. The voting behavior of people who go to the polls out of a sense of civic responsibility or habit and who lack much interest in or knowledge about politics can, in many ways, be equated with the behavior of shoppers at a supermarket. Individuals in both situations select a product—either a consumer good or a congressional candidate—with relatively little information. Except for first-time shoppers and newly enfranchised voters, the individuals have made similar selections before. Previous decisions and established preferences often strongly influence their current decisions. Shoppers lacking a good reason to try a new product, such as a sale or a two-for-one giveaway, are likely to purchase the same brand-name product that they previously purchased. Similarly, voters are likely to cast a ballot for the candidate or party that they supported in previous elections.[17] If a voter recognizes one candidate's name, which is almost always the incumbent's, that candidate usually gets the individual's vote. If the voter recognizes neither candidate but tends to be favorably predisposed toward one party, then most often the person votes for that party's candidate. Situations in which voters have little information, then, usually work to the advantage of incumbents and candidates who belong to the district's or state's dominant party.

However, if the recognized candidate or favored party is associated with scandal or a domestic or foreign policy failure, many relatively uninformed voters, as well as some who are informed, break old habits and cast their ballots against that candidate or party, or they may not vote at all. During the elections of the 1990s, for example, many challengers, with the support of Washington-based party committees and interest groups, sought to make control of Congress itself a major campaign issue. That strategy is credited with enabling the Republicans to take over Congress in 1994 and end forty uninterrupted years of Democratic control of the House. Attacking the performance of Congress and the Bush administration also was a major tactic for many in 2006 and 2008. It helped Democratic candidates wrest control of Congress back from the GOP in the former election and increase their majorities in the latter. Of course, a similar set of appeals—but aimed at holding President Barack Obama and the Democrats accountable—was critical to the Republicans winning back the House and increasing their presence in the Senate in 2010. Regardless of which party has been in control, attacking Congress has contributed to the electoral success of many challengers, and some incumbents, for much of recent history.

VOTERS AND CAMPAIGN STRATEGY

Candidates and political consultants generally do not plan election campaigns on the basis of abstract political theories, but they do draw on a body of knowledge about how people make their voting decisions. Politicians' notions about voting behavior have some ideas in common with the findings of scholarly research. Among them are the following: (1) most voters have only limited information about the candidates, their ideologies, and the issues; (2) voters are generally more familiar with and favorably predisposed toward incumbents than they are toward challengers; and (3) voters tend to cast their ballots in ways that reflect their party identification or previous voting behavior. Candidates and consultants also believe that a campaign sharply focused on issues can be used to motivate supporters to show up at the polls and to win the support of undecided voters. They try to set the campaign agenda so that their candidate's most popular issues are the ones a majority of voters use to make their voting decisions. Of course, candidates and consultants recognize that the nature of a given election cycle influences their ability to shape the local political agenda. As discussed in Chapter 1, congressional candidates running during so-called status quo (or normal) election cycles have more control over the issues than those running in nationalized (or wave) elections that are defined by political, economic, or social issues that dominate the political discussion nationwide.

Politicians' and consultants' beliefs account for some of the differences among the campaigns waged by incumbents, challengers, and open-seat candidates, as well as many of the differences between House and Senate campaigns. Generally, members of Congress use strategies that capitalize on the advantages of incumbency. They discuss the services and the federal projects they have delivered to their constituencies.[18] They focus on elements of their public persona that have helped make them popular with constituents and draw on strategies that they have used successfully in previous campaigns.[19]

Some incumbents capitalize on their advantages in name recognition and voter approval by virtually ignoring their opponents. They deluge the district with direct mail, e-mail, radio advertisements, television commercials, yard signs, podcasts, or other communications that make no mention of their opponent in order to minimize the attention the challenger gets from the local media and voters. An alternative strategy is to take advantage of a challenger's relative invisibility by attacking his or her qualifications, performance while holding a prior office, or issue positions early in the campaign. Incumbents who succeed in defining their opponents leave them in the unenviable position of being invisible to most voters and negatively perceived by others.

Democratic incumbent Jerrold Nadler's campaign pursued the former strategy, treating Republican challenger Susan Kone as if her candidacy would have no impact on the outcome of their 2010 New York City House race. He refused to debate Kone, and not one of the articles or press releases posted on his website even mentioned her name. The campaign waged by Democratic Senate majority leader Harry Reid in Nevada used the latter strategy. He began criticizing his opponent, Sharron Angle, as "extreme" and "dangerous" within days of her winning the GOP nomination.

House challengers are in the least enviable position of any candidate. Not only are they less well known and less experienced, they also lack the campaign resources of their opponents. To win, challengers must force their way into voters' consciousness and project a message that will give voters a reason to cast a ballot for a little-known commodity.

Many challengers try to make the election a referendum on some negative aspect of the incumbent's performance. They portray the incumbent as incompetent, corrupt, or out of touch with the district. They magnify the impact of any unpopular policy or scandal with which the incumbent can be associated. Challengers often try to link the current officeholder to unpopular political leaders, programs, or trends and present themselves as agents of change, often using negative or comparative ads to do so. Running for a seat in a district that includes the World Trade Center site and has a large Jewish population, Kone zeroed in on Nadler's support for a mosque and Islamic community center to be built there and questioned his support for Israel. Angle painted Reid as a Washington insider responsible for Nevada's and the nation's immigration and economic problems. Both challengers offered themselves as a better alternative to the incumbent. The goals of this approach are to win the backing of undecided voters and individuals who previously voted for the incumbent and to discourage the incumbent's supporters from going to the polls.

Without the advantages of an incumbent or the disadvantages of a challenger, both candidates in an open-seat race face the challenges of making themselves familiar to voters and becoming associated with themes and issues that will attract electoral support. Both also have the opportunity to define their opponent. Some open-seat candidates seek to define themselves on the basis of their policy positions or performance in another office. Others, particularly those running in districts that favor their party, emphasize partisan or ideological cues. The candidates in Illinois' 10th district shaped their messages to appeal to a constituency that was wealthy, economically conservative, and socially liberal, and whose partisanship provided opportunities for both of them. The GOP candidate, Robert Dold, positioned himself as a fiscally conservative, tax-cutting political outsider in order to appeal to economically conservative voters. He also campaigned as the candidate for change. The Democratic nominee, Dan Seals, focused mainly on the social safety net issues and social issues designed to appeal to liberal voters. Not surprisingly, given the district's affluence, the impact of the economic downturn on local voters, and the importance of the economy on the political dialogue nationwide, Dold was the more successful of the two candidates in framing the debate and creating more positive associations for himself among voters.[20]

GAUGING PUBLIC OPINION

Campaigns use many approaches to take the public's pulse. Election returns from previous contests are analyzed to locate pockets of potential strength or weakness. Geodemographic analysis enables campaigns to identify individuals who voted in previous elections and classify them according to their gender, age, ethnicity, race, religion, occupation, and income. By combining geodemographic information with polling data, consumer information, and election returns, campaigns are able to identify potential supporters and formulate messages that will appeal to them. Many candidates send volunteers to knock on these voters' doors to discern whether they are indeed supporters, or to find out how to motivate potential supporters to vote for their candidate. With the assistance of party committees and some interest groups, some have employed lists developed through microtargeting. These approaches, discussed in Chapter 4, enable campaigns to concentrate their efforts on supporters or persuadable voters.

Polls are among the most common means of gauging public opinion. Virtually every Senate campaign and roughly seven out of ten House campaigns take at least one poll to learn about voters. Benchmark polls, which are taken early in the election season, inform candidates about the issue positions, partisanship, and initial voting preferences of people living in their state or district. House campaigns typically commission benchmarks one year prior to the election, and Senate campaigns have been known to commission them as early as three years before Election Day. Benchmark polls also measure the levels of name recognition and support that the candidates and their opponents or prospective opponents enjoy. They help campaigns learn about the types of candidates voters prefer, the messages likely to attract support, and to whom they should direct specific campaign communications.

Campaigns also use benchmark polls to generate support. Challenger and open-seat candidates disseminate favorable benchmarks to attract media coverage and the support of campaign volunteers and contributors. Incumbents typically publicize benchmarks to discourage potential challengers. When poll results show a member of Congress to be in trouble, however, the incumbent quietly uses them to convince parties, PACs, and other potential contributors that he or she needs extra help to win.

Trend polls are taken intermittently throughout the campaign season to discover changes in voters' attitudes. Some senators use them to chart their public approval throughout their six-year term. These polls are more narrowly focused than benchmarks typically are. They feature detailed questions designed to reveal whether a campaign has been successful in getting voters to associate its candidate with a specific issue or theme. Trend polls help campaigns determine whether they have been gaining or losing ground with particular segments of the electorate. They can reassure a campaign that its strategy is working or indicate that a change in message is needed.

Whereas trend and benchmark polls present "snapshots" of public opinion, tracking polls provide campaigns with a "motion picture" overview. Tracking polls typically ask samples of 150 to 200 voters per night to discuss their reactions to a few key advertisements, issue statements, or campaign events. The interviews are pooled and used to calculate rolling averages based on the responses from the three most recent nights. Changes in rolling averages can be used to reformulate a campaign's appeals. Because tracking polls are expensive, most House campaigns wait until late in the election cycle to use them.

Candidates may supplement their polling with focus groups. Focus groups usually consist of one to two dozen participants and a professional facilitator who meet for two to three hours. The participants are selected not as a scientifically representative sample but to represent segments of the population whose support the campaign needs to reinforce or attract. Campaigns use focus groups to learn how voters can be expected to respond to different issues and messages. They are especially useful for gauging voters' emotional responses to TV ads and other communications. Some high-priced consultants, such as Wirthlin Worldwide, a prominent Republican firm, employ computerized audience response techniques to obtain a precise record of how focus group participants react to specific portions of campaign advertisements.[21] These techniques enable an analyst to plot onto the ad itself a line that represents the participants' reactions, pinpointing exactly which portions of an ad the participants liked or disliked. Focus group research is useful in fine-tuning the visuals and narratives in television communications.

Finally, candidates learn about public opinion through a variety of approaches that do not require the services of public opinion experts. Newspaper, magazine, radio, and television news stories provide information about voters' positions on major issues. Exchanges with local party leaders, journalists, political activists, and voters can also help candidates get a sense of the public mood.

Blogs are also now used to learn about and influence the views of politically engaged, computer-savvy voters.

When asked about the significance of different forms of information, House candidates and campaign aides typically rank direct contact with voters first, indicating that they consider it very important to extremely important (see Table 7-1). Voter contact is followed by public opinion polls, which are generally considered moderately helpful to very helpful in learning about voters' opinions. News stories come next, followed by discussions with local party activists and mail from voters. Although their role is bigger than those of PACs and other interest groups, national party officials and the materials they publish are less important than local information sources.

TABLE 7-1

Campaigners' Perceptions of the Importance of Different Sources of
Information for Gauging Public Opinion in House Campaigns

	All	Incumbents		Challengers		Open-seat candidates	
		In jeopardy	Shoo-ins	Hope-fuls	Long shots	Pros-pects	Mis-matched
Candidate contact with voters	4.37	4.23	4.41	4.44	4.44	4.16	4.59
Public opinion surveys	3.53	4.23	3.54	3.68	2.88	3.96	3.09
Newspaper, radio, TV	3.05	2.69	3.13	3.08	3.27	2.86	3.17
Local party activists	2.63	2.78	2.74	2.69	2.41	2.45	2.80
Mail from voters	2.45	2.65	3.43	2.19	1.99	2.00	2.29
National party publications	2.28	1.83	1.96	2.39	2.75	2.12	2.65
National party leaders	2.14	1.80	1.94	2.31	2.32	2.20	2.30

Source: "1992 Congressional Campaign Study," Center for American Politics and Citizenship, University of Maryland.

Notes: Candidates and campaign aides were asked to assess the importance of each source on the following scale: 1 = not important or not used; 2 = slightly important; 3 = moderately important; 4 = very important; 5 = extremely important. The values listed are the arithmetic means of the scores. Figures are for major-party candidates in contested general elections, excluding a small number of atypical races. N = 325.

Incumbents and candidates for open seats make greater use of polls than do challengers. Candidates in competitive contests of all types make greater use of them than do those in lopsided races. Challengers and open-seat candidates in one-sided contests often cannot afford to buy polls and must rely heavily on news reports, party publications, and the advice of national party leaders. Incumbents, who are often sensitized to issues by the constituent mail that floods their offices, value letters as a significant indicator of public sentiment more than other candidates do. Incumbents in safe seats show a greater preference than others for learning about public opinion through the mail and other forms of unmediated voter contact.

VOTER TARGETING

Campaigns are not designed to reach everyone. Targeting involves categorizing different groups of voters, identifying their political preferences, and designing appeals to which they are likely to respond. Targeting is the foundation of virtually every aspect of campaign strategy. Candidates and their advisers consider many factors when devising targeting strategies, including the underlying partisan and candidate loyalties of the groups that reside in the district, the size and turnout levels of those groups, and the types of issues and appeals that will attract their support.[22] Using this information, they formulate a strategy designed to build a winning coalition.

Partisanship is the number one consideration in the voter targeting of most campaigns; it subsumes all other factors. Almost one-half of all campaigns focus on individuals who identify with their party, independent voters, or both (see Table 7-2). About 2 percent of campaigns primarily target voters who identify with the opposing party. The campaigns of former Republican representative Constance Morella, who represented Maryland's strongly Democratic-leaning 8th district, are examples of those. Morella was able to hold her seat for eight terms by building bipartisan support. Like many incumbents, she routinely sent letters of congratulation to constituents who had recently registered to vote in her district. Unlike most other incumbents, however, she often sent letters to voters who had registered in the opposing party—in this case as Democrats.[23]

Campaigns by challengers are the most likely to target voters who identify with the opposing party. Many of these candidates recognize that the one-sidedness of their district makes it impossible for them to compete without winning some of the opposing party's supporters. For example, as a Republican challenger, Steve Southerland, who ran against the Democratic incumbent Allen Boyd, focused on his Republican base and voters who resided in

TABLE 7-2

Partisan Components of Targeting Strategies in House Campaigns

	All	Incumbents		Challengers		Open-seat candidates	
		In jeopardy	Shoo-ins	Hope-fuls	Long shots	Pros-pects	Mis-matched
Own party	9%	17%	9%	9%	7%	9%	17%
Opposing party	2	—	1	6	2	—	—
Independents	3	3	1	3	5	—	6
Both parties	2	—	—	—	2	3	6
Own party and independents	36	35	43	38	30	40	39
Opposing party and independents	2	7	—	3	2	3	5
All voters	45	38	46	41	50	43	28
Did not target	1	—	—	—	2	3	—

Source: "2002 Congressional Campaign Study," Center for American Politics and Citizenship, University of Maryland.

Notes: Figures are for general election candidates in major-party contested races, excluding those in incumbent-versus-incumbent races. — = less than 0.5 percent. Some columns do not add to 100 percent because of rounding. $N = 320$.

"split homes"—those in which families had members registered with both major parties. Some challengers do not have the resources to carry out even a basic, party-oriented targeting strategy. Lacking a poll or a precinct-by-precinct breakdown of where Republican, Democratic, and independent voters reside, some amateurs resort to unorthodox strategies, such as focusing on the precincts that had the highest turnout in the previous election.

Other factors that campaigns consider when designing targeting strategies include demography and voters' political attitudes. Sixty-two percent of all House campaigns target demographic, geographic, or occupational groups; 53 percent concentrate on specific ethnic, racial, religious, gender, or age groups; 4 percent focus on counties, suburbs, cities, or other geographic locations; and 5 percent target union members, blue-collar workers, small-business owners, or voters involved in particular industries.[24] Political attitudes, including partisanship and support for various issues, are central to the targeting strategies of roughly 36 percent of all campaigns.

Group-oriented and attitude-oriented targeting strategies offer campaigns distinct advantages. The group-oriented, or geodemographic, approach is based on the idea that there are identifiable segments of the population whose support the campaign needs to attract and that specific communications can be tailored to win that support. Just as soliciting money from a readily identifiable fundraising constituency is important in the campaign for resources, communicating a message to identifiable groups of supporters and undecided voters is important in the campaign for votes. Group-based targeting strategies emphasize different aspects of the campaign's message, depending on the intended audience for a particular campaign advertisement. By tailoring their messages to attract the votes of specific population groups, campaigns hope to attract enough supporters to win. In recent years, many campaigns have stressed the effect of the economy on children and families in literature mailed to women, whereas they emphasized tax cuts and economic growth issues in literature sent to business executives and upper-class and upper-middle-class voters. Tailoring messages to particular groups can help persuade some group members to support a candidate and boost the group's turnout.[25]

Candidates focus on many groups, reflecting the diverse constituencies that are represented by the two major parties.[26] More Democrats than Republicans target single women and racial and ethnic minorities; Democratic candidates target senior citizens more than any other segment of the population. More Republicans focus on frequent churchgoers and rural voters.[27] The 2010 contest between Seals and Dold lends insight into the dynamics of targeting. Seals anticipated winning support from the Democratic base and independents. As an African American, he expected to win the district's black vote. His campaign focused much of its efforts on Democratic women, minorities, and senior citizens. Dold aggressively courted Republican voters and independents. He targeted local business owners, affluent voters, and other voters affected by the economic downturn. Both candidates courted the district's large Jewish community. An overlap of targets is typical of a close election because both campaigns pursue the same swing voters.

The issue- or attitude-oriented strategy is based on the premise that issues and ideas should drive the campaign. Campaigns that target on the basis of specific policies or a broad ideology, such as conservatism or progressivism, hope to win the support of single-issue or ideological voters who favor those positions. In many cases one or two specific issues are emphasized to attract swing voters whose support a candidate believes will be a deciding factor in the election outcome. Some candidates target pro-life or pro-choice voters, believing their ballots will be decisive. Others target pro-environment or anti–gun control voters. Republicans who employ such strategies focus mainly on voters who are concerned about moral values, taxes, the size and role of the federal government, and crime. Democrats who use them focus on voters who care about public education, jobs, the environment, and health care, and the protections and services that government provides for the elderly, children, and underprivileged groups. In 2010 Republicans also targeted voters especially concerned about the anemic economic recovery, disappearing jobs, the deficit, and health care reform. Many Democrats focused on constituencies who were concerned about the environment or maintaining adequate funding for government programs. Most Democratic incumbents tried to focus on their record of serving the district.

Targeting strategies based on voter attitudes lend themselves better to the communication of a coherent campaign message than do group-oriented strategies. They are especially effective at mobilizing single-issue voters and political activists who have strong ideological predispositions. But they run the risk of alienating moderate voters who agree with the candidate on most policy matters but disagree on the issues the campaign has chosen to emphasize. Campaigns waged by policy amateurs and ideologues are the most likely to suffer from this problem. Often these candidates become boxed in by their own message, are labeled "ultra-liberals" or "right wingers" by their opponents, and ultimately lose.

Incumbents target demographic, geographic, and occupational groups more than challengers and open-seat candidates. Most incumbents have a detailed knowledge of the voting blocs that supported them in the past and target constituents who belong to those groups. Many challengers, especially those unable to mount competitive campaigns, do not have this information. Lacking good voter files and recognizing that they need to peel away some of their opponent's supporters, they emphasize specific issues with the hope of appealing to specific groups.

THE MESSAGE

A candidate's message gives substance to a campaign. It helps to shape the political agenda, mobilize backers, and win swing voters and a few converts.[28] In a well-run campaign, the same coherent message pervades every aspect of the candidate's communications, from paid television advertisements to impromptu remarks. Campaign messages can be an essential ingredient for victory in close elections because they activate supporters and strongly influence the decisions of persuadable voters.

Campaign messages rely heavily on imagery. The most successful campaigns weave the candidate's persona, values, and policy stances into thematic messages.[29] These frame the image the candidate seeks to project. According to Joel Bradshaw, president of the Democratic consulting firm Campaign Design

Group, good campaign messages are clear and easy to communicate, are short, convey a sense of emotional urgency, reflect voters' perceptions of political reality, establish clear differences between the candidate and the opponent, and are credible.[30]

The precise mix of candidate characteristics, issues, and broad themes that campaigns project depends on their political views, the groups they target, and the messages that they anticipate their opponents will communicate. Good strategic positioning results in the transmission of a message that will resonate with most voters; when both candidates achieve this result an election becomes a "battle for the middle ground."[31] In designing a message, campaign decision makers consider a variety of factors, which J. Toscano, a partner in the Democratic media firm Greer, Margolis, Mitchell, and Burns, refers to as "the five Cs of strategy": commitments on issues that drive votes; competence, as exhibited by the candidate's professional accomplishments; cultural connections that "shortcut" voters' need for information; a core message that describes the values that drive the candidate, often exemplified by the candidate's personal experiences; and contrast with opponents to foster a clear choice.[32] Ladonna Lee, a leading Republican political strategist, emphasizes the importance of consistency.[33] The different components of the message must add up to a coherent public image. Otherwise, a campaign's communications will get lost in an environment that is saturated by commercial advertisers that spend billions every year finding new, interesting, and entertaining ways to engage audiences.

Campaigns endeavor to create a favorable image for their candidates by identifying them with decency, loyalty, honesty, hard work, and other cherished values.[34] Campaign communications interweave anecdotes about a candidate's personal accomplishments, professional success, family, or ability to overcome humble origins to portray him or her as the living embodiment of the American dream—someone whom voters should be proud to have represent them in Washington. Campaigns frequently emphasize elements of their candidate's persona that point to an opponent's weakness. In 2006 and 2008 many veterans used their military experience to increase the credibility of their positions on the Iraq War and raise questions about the qualifications of their opponents on this key voting issue. Many challengers and open-seat candidates responded to the anti-Washington mood of the electorate in 2010 by emphasizing their outsider status rather than their political experience.

Incumbents frequently convey image-oriented messages. They seek to reinforce or expand their base of support by concentrating on those aspects of their persona that make them popular with constituents. Their messages convey images of competent, caring individuals who work tirelessly in Washington to improve the lives of the folks back home they represent. Incumbents' campaign messages often describe how they have helped constituents resolve problems, brought federal programs and projects to the district, and introduced or cosponsored popular legislation. Some discuss their efforts to prevent a military base or factory from closing. Those whose districts have experienced the ravages of floods, earthquakes, riots, or other disasters almost always highlight their roles in bringing federal relief to victims.

Many challengers and open-seat contestants also portray themselves as caring, hardworking, and experienced. Nonincumbents who have held elective office frequently contrast their accomplishments with those of their opponent. During the elections held at the dawn of the twenty-first century, many challengers who were state legislators blamed their opponents for contributing to the federal deficit while pointing to their own budget-cutting efforts.

Political amateurs usually discuss their successes outside of politics, seeking to make a virtue of their lack of political experience. Many blame the "mess in Washington" on the "career politicians" and discuss how someone who has succeeded in the private sector is needed to make government work for the people again. This was a popular theme among nonincumbents in 2010. For example, Kone's website, streaming video, press releases, and other communications, conveyed the message, *"I am not a professional politican, but I am a professional. I have real world experience*—not Washington experience. I earn my living by bringing people together with creative, common sense solutions*"* [emphasis in original].[35] Her message dovetailed with most Republican Party and candidate communications. Still, a challenger who focuses solely on experience rarely wins. As one consultant explained, "By virtue of their being the current officeholder an incumbent can 'out-experience' a challenger to death."

Of course, smart campaigners consider the national mood when formulating a message, regardless of whether a candidate is an incumbent, challenger, or candidate for an open seat. In most nationalized elections, strategic candidates who belong to the party out of power endeavor to ride a wave of voter dissatisfaction by making national issues the core of their local congressional campaigns. In 2010 many Republican candidates sought to tap into voter dissatisfaction with the slow pace of the economic recovery and the new government initiatives passed by a Democratic administration and Democratic-controlled Congress. Challenger Steve Southerland was among them. He built his primary and general election campaigns around the slogan, "Have you had enough?" It appeared on little red stickers his campaign workers placed on each seat prior to rallies, debates, and other events, and on signs, T-shirts, and other campaign paraphernalia. He repeated his slogan when discussing the recession and related problems and laying blame for the hardships felt by voters locally and nationwide on the incumbent Allen Boyd and the Democrats. By drawing these connections

Southerland argued that the economic downturn had led to layoffs of local workers and the devaluation of homes, and that the Democrats' health care reform program exacerbated these problems by forcing the closure of local businesses. He attacked Boyd's vote for cap-and-trade (the environmental protections program) for its potential to harm the district's pine tree industries, "raising our energy costs, killing jobs, increasing debt and transferring American's [sic] sovereignty."[36] He accused Boyd of flip-flopping on the stimulus package and health care reform. He attacked the conservative Blue Dog Boyd for catching the "Washington bug" and becoming too closely tied to House Speaker Pelosi and special interests. Southerland's slogan was repeated by the local media, embraced by disgruntled voters, and used as a rallying cry for his supporters. It was an effective message to make the case that Boyd no longer represented the interests of Northwestern Floridians.

Issues

Most House candidates and campaign aides maintain that the bulk of their messages focus on policy concerns rather than the candidate's personality, a claim borne out by examinations of their campaign materials.[37] More than half of all House campaigns make issues—either their own issue positions or their opponents'—the primary focus of their message; 44 percent, mostly incumbent campaigns, emphasize candidate imagery (see Table 7-3). Challengers and open-seat candidates run the most issue-oriented campaigns, reflecting the belief that taking policy stances is a useful way to draw support away from their opponents. Challengers run the most opposition-oriented campaigns. They point to incumbents' ethical lapses, congressional roll-call votes that are not in accord with constituents' views, or federal policies that have harmed local voters or the national interest. About 24 percent of all challengers try to make their opponent or their opponent's actions in office a defining campaign issue. A few incumbents holding marginal seats respond in kind by pointing to unpopular aspects of their challenger's background or policy stances. Twelve percent of open-seat candidates in close contests also make their opponent the central focus of their message.

Almost all candidates associate themselves with "valence" issues, which are universally viewed in a favorable light.[38] These issues include peace, prosperity, and national security. When both candidates make valence issues the centerpiece of their campaign the dialogue can be like a debate between Tweedledum and Tweedledee, the identical twins from *Alice in Wonderland* who know each other so well that they finish each other's sentences. In reality, elections are rarely characterized by high levels of issue convergence because most candidates

TABLE 7-3

Major Focus of Advertising in House Campaigns

	All	Incumbents In jeopardy	Incumbents Shoo- ins	Challengers Hope- fuls	Challengers Long shots	Open-seat candidates Pros- pects	Open-seat candidates Mis- matched
Candidate's image	39%	54%	58%	31%	22%	44%	50%
Candidate's issue positions	47	42	39	31	59	44	44
Opponent's image	5	—	1	6	9	6	6
Opponent's issue positions	9	4	1	31	11	6	—

Source: "2002 Congressional Campaign Study," Center for American Politics and Citizenship, University of Maryland.

Notes: Figures are for general election candidates in major-party contested races, excluding those in incumbent-versus-incumbent races. — = less than 0.5 percent. Some columns do not add to 100 percent because of rounding. $N = 308$.

campaign on policy positions that are favorably associated with their party. Consequently, they are on opposing sides on most issues.[39]

When candidates communicate dissimilar stands on the issues, political debate becomes more meaningful. "Position" issues (sometimes referred to as "wedge" issues) including abortion, civil rights, tax cuts, immigration, and health care reform have the potential to draw the attention of voters and influence whom they choose to represent them in Congress. "Government performance" issues such as the economy, corruption, and the prosecution of international conflicts can have similar effects. Jobs, the economy, and the failures of the federal government were front and center on the national political agenda in 2008 and 2010, favoring the Democrats in the former election and the Republicans in the latter.

Challengers are especially likely to benefit from emphasizing position and government performance issues. By stressing points of disagreement between themselves and the incumbent, challengers can crystallize their image, attract media attention, and strip away some of their opponent's support.[40] Incumbents may not derive the same electoral benefits from running on position issues because they are usually evaluated in personal terms.[41] Candidates who campaign on position issues hope to attract the support of ideological voters or to overcome some weakness in their image. Some liberal Democrats emphasize crime fighting or their war records to project "tougher" images. To show their compassionate side, some conservative Republicans discuss the need to protect the Social Security Trust Fund. Both groups of candidates seek to convince the voters that they share their concerns. Candidates try to anticipate the issues their opponents will emphasize before taking a strong policy stance. Candidates who run against police officers rarely mount "law-and-order" campaigns because of the obvious disparities in credibility between themselves and their opponents on crime-related issues.[42] Only the most inexperienced or ideologically driven candidates ignore major local concerns or the national political agenda when selecting their campaign's core issues.

Dold focused on a variety of issues that traditionally favor Republican candidates. On taxes, he championed extending the Bush tax cuts for all income levels; to address the deficit, he called for reduced government spending; and in order to stimulate the economy, he proposed increasing the availability of credit for small businesses. Seals focused on issues that traditionally have worked to the advantage of his party, including advocating more funding for Medicare and Social Security and supporting abortion rights, gay rights, and immigration reform.

Angle tried to hold Reid responsible for the economic recession and problems associated with illegal immigration. She presented a battery of dismal unemployment, foreclosure, and other statistics to highlight the downward spiral of Nevada's and the nation's economies during Reid's tenure as Senate majority leader. She also criticized him for the nation's immigration policy by trying to brand him as "the best friend an illegal alien ever had." Reid sought to make the election a choice between two candidates rather than a referendum on himself. He used Angle's statements about the unemployed, Social Security, Medicare, veterans' health care, and a host of other issues to paint her as too far from the American mainstream to serve in the Senate.[43]

Candidates who learn that their opponent is vulnerable on a salient issue generally make it a major focus of the campaign to try to win the support of independents or pry voters from their opponent's camp. Many Democrats lure women's votes by making abortion rights a major part of their campaign platforms. Democrats who adopt this position during presidential election years typically receive the added benefit of being able to coordinate their message with their party's presidential campaign. Divisions within the Republican Party have made abortion rights an issue to avoid for GOP candidates from the Northeast and other less conservative areas in presidential election years.

Economic issues—inflation, unemployment, taxes, jobs, the federal budget, or the national deficit—have been the number-one concern of voters in most elections since the Great Depression. Virtually all candidates make some aspect of the economy part of their campaign message. Democratic candidates often discuss the economy as a fairness issue. In 2010 many tried to remind voters that the nation's economic collapse took place under a Republican administration and after years of GOP control of Congress. Some also attacked the increased tax burdens that Bush administration policies placed on the middle class and the tax breaks Republicans gave to wealthy Americans.

Republican candidates usually focus on economic growth and the deficit. Throughout the 1980s and early 1990s they sought to blame the economic woes of the country on wasteful government subsidies, excessive regulation, and profligate pork-barrel spending approved by the Democratic-controlled Congress. Their message gained traction in 2010 when President Obama and congressional Democrats were unable to reverse the economic recession and enacted a variety of policies that the Republicans claimed exacerbated it, including health care reform and environmental regulations.

Political reform also has been an important issue for both Democrats and Republicans, reflecting the anti-Washington mood of the country. Many House challengers raise corruption in government and the role of special interests as campaign issues by criticizing incumbents who accept congressional pay raises, take junkets paid for by wealthy lobbyists, or depend on PAC contributions. Incumbents address political reform differently. Some seek to defend Congress, whereas others try to impress upon voters that they are part of the solution and not the problem. One House member said he "neutralized" the reform issue by arguing that he "was constructively working to improve government from the inside, while [his opponent] was content to merely lob stones from a distance." Another popular incumbent strategy is to campaign for reelection to Congress by attacking the institution itself.[44]

Most candidates prefer to be the ones whom voters associate with valence issues, but candidates also can find it profitable to take strong stands on position issues. That is especially true when their stances are welcomed by voters in their district or occupy a prominent place on the national agenda. The 2010 election was nationalized on several domestic issues on which most Democrats and Republicans took opposite sides.[45] Perhaps the most powerful debate was about government spending and mismanagement as they related to the economic recovery and the deficit. Other prominent domestic policy debates involved immigration reform, the environment, abortion and other so-called moral issues, the increasing gap between the rich and the middle class, and social safety net issues such as health care, Medicare, and the solvency of Social Security. There was some debate over homeland security in the elections following the attacks on the World Trade Center and the Pentagon, but these issues had faded in importance by 2010.

Partisanship, incumbency, and geography are critical in determining whether a candidate makes an issue a priority in the campaign, as well as the position he or she takes on it.[46] Most candidates' issue priorities and substantive issue positions dovetail with those of their party's core voters. Thus, in 2010 most Republican candidates focused on jobs, the economy, health care reform, and other unpopular Democratic legislation. More Democratic than Republican candidates, on the other hand, sought to make the election about the candidates' qualifications, public service records, and local concerns. Elected officials are notorious for capitalizing on the stature that comes with holding office and "wrapping themselves in the flag" during times of crisis. Geography and local political culture also are important. Candidates from the Midwest focus more on agricultural issues than those from coastal areas, who emphasize the fishing industry and tourism. Locally reinforced policy divisions pose obstacles to the nationalization of congressional elections, but their importance subsides when such elections occur.

Partisanship, Populism, and Progressivism

Candidates who run in districts made up overwhelmingly of people who identify with their party normally emphasize partisan themes and messages. They frequently mention their party in speeches and campaign literature. Campaigns in "hostile" or divided districts typically use nonpartisan strategies, avoiding mention of party affiliation.

Progressive strategies have become increasingly popular with Democrats, who run as agents of change. These candidates avoid the term "liberal" because voters associate it with government regulations and high taxes, which are unpopular.[47] They instead choose to call themselves "progressives" or "new Democrats."

Many candidates of both parties use populist strategies. Republican populists, like those associated with the Tea Party movement, rail against the government, taxes, and special interests in Washington, even when they are in control of the government. Democratic populists also champion the cause of ordinary Americans. Rather than oppose big government, however, these candidates run against big business. For example, Democrat Byron Dorgan, who was elected North Dakota's at-large representative in 1980 and its junior senator in 1992, earned his populist credentials when, as state tax commissioner, he sued out-of-state corporations doing business in North Dakota to force them to pay state taxes.[48] Running campaigns based on populism served Dorgan well: he made a career in Congress for three decades prior to retiring in 2010.

Negative Campaigning

Negative campaigning has always been, and will probably always be, a part of U.S. elections. Just as positive campaigning attempts to build up a candidate, negative campaigning endeavors to tear down an opponent. Negative campaigning has the potential to increase voter knowledge and otherwise enhance the electoral process. Campaign ads that question a candidate's qualifications or point to unpopular, wasteful, or unethical practices bring a measure of accountability to the political system.[49] Still, much negative campaigning amounts to little more than character assassination and mudslinging. Whether negative campaigning turns off voters and discourages them from participating in elections or captures voters' attention and stimulates voter turnout may be of interest to academics, but it is of little concern to candidates.[50] What matters to them is that more of their supporters than their opponent's show up at the polls.

One or both candidates use negative campaigning in almost three-quarters of all House contests and virtually every Senate election. As Election Day approaches the probability increases that someone will attack his or her opponent.[51] The sense of urgency that pervades a close contest encourages the contestants to figuratively tar and feather each other because it is easier to discredit an opponent than to build loyalty.[52]

Attack ads can be an important component of challenger campaigns because they can help break voters of the habit of casting their ballots for the incumbent.[53] However, many incumbents have made negative advertising a central element of their strategies in recent years, using early attacks to define their challengers before the challengers can define themselves.[54] Because of their competitiveness, open-seat campaigns tend to be the most negative of all. Negative ads criticize an opponent's integrity, credentials, policy positions, or association with other political leaders, including the head of their party. Some are meant to evoke negative emotions and are accompanied by ominous music. Others are light and comical.

Opposition research provides the foundation for negative campaigning. Campaigns begin with a thorough examination of the opponent's public record. Challengers often study their opponent's attendance record, roll-call votes, and speeches. The defeat of fifty-eight House members and four senators in 2010 poignantly demonstrates that what an incumbent does in office can become a liability. If an opponent has never held office, a campaign will usually turn to newspaper or trade magazine accounts of speeches made to civic organizations, trade associations, or other groups.

An opponent's professional and personal background are explored next. Employment histories are often a matter of public record. The same is true of many business arrangements, divorce proceedings, and legal violations. The backgrounds of challengers and open-seat candidates are often open to question, especially if a candidate who has no political experience has pursued a career that most constituents would view with skepticism. Junk bond traders and dog catchers, for example, are at risk of being labeled unqualified because of their professions. Of course, the same is true of "deadbeat dads," tax evaders, and criminals.

Virtually all campaigns search for evidence of illegal and unethical behavior. Recent elections provided many candidates with a mountain of dirt they could throw at their opponents. Some incumbents became vulnerable because of their own actions. Among the misdeeds that cost members of Congress reelection are assaulting a Capitol Hill police officer, bribery, using racial epithets, adultery, and improper sexual advances toward congressional employees. Of course, some challengers and open-seat candidates are guilty of similar offences and experience a similar demise. Moreover, a few politicians lose as a result of guilt by association, including Rep. Carolyn Cheeks Kilpatrick of Michigan, the mother of the Detroit mayor who was convicted of corruption charges.

Campaigns need to be careful they do not go too far when criticizing an opponent. Attacks that focus on a private matter unrelated to politics, such as youthful indiscretion, can backfire and make the candidate leveling the charges look dishonest, mean-spirited, or just plain foolish. The hazards of crossing the line are something that Democrat Jack Conway, who was running in Kentucky to fill an open seat in the Senate, learned the hard way. Conway's campaign aired a negative TV ad that raised the following questions about his opponent Rand Paul's alleged sophomoric activities in college: "Why was Rand Paul a member of a secret society that called the Holy Bible 'a hoax'— that was banned for mocking Christianity and Christ?" and "Why did Rand Paul once tie a woman up? Tell her to bow down before a false idol and say his God was 'Aqua Buddha'?" The ad was intended to undercut Paul's support among Bible Belt voters, but it backfired heavily. An internal Republican poll showed that 69 percent of Kentucky voters believed the ad had gone too far, including 50 percent who identified themselves as Democrats. The ad is believed to have caused Conway to plummet in the polls, and it probably cost him the election.[55]

Although the information that can be dug up from public records or interviews with former business partners and neighbors can make for a riveting attack ad, most opposition research is tedious. Researchers scour the *Congressional Record*, search records of the floor proceedings of state legislatures, scan old newspapers, surf the Internet, or pore over campaign finance reports to make the case that a candidate is out of touch with voters; has flip-flopped on an issue or committed some other questionable act; or is too beholden to PACs, wealthy individuals from out of state, or donors with questionable reputations to represent the views of constituents.

Tracking is a somewhat more glamorous form of political espionage. As mentioned in Chapter 4, this involves following an opponent with a video recorder in an attempt to capture a misstatement, an embarrassing moment, or some other impolitic situation that can be incorporated into an attack ad. Perhaps the most well-known case of tracking occurred in 2006 when Sen. George Allen, R-Va., called a student volunteer for Allen's opponent Democrat James Webb a "macaca" (a racial epithet). The incident made the national headlines and is credited with costing Allen his seat and killing his aspirations to the presidency. Trackers collected many of the impolitic remarks made by Angle that were used by the Reid campaign, the Democratic Senatorial Campaign Committee, and supportive interest groups to make the case that Angle was dangerous and an extremist. In some recent elections, trackers have taken things a step further by ambushing a candidate with an aggressive line of questioning designed to provoke a misstep on the candidate's part. Tracking contributed to the 2010 defeat of Rep. Bob Etheridge, D-N.C., who was caught on videotape roughing up a student who began to engage him in what appeared to be a partisan line of questioning.

The widespread use of negative advertising also has encouraged most campaigns to search for their own candidate's weaknesses. As J. Toscano explains, "A campaign needs to be prepared for the worst. We spend a lot of time looking for the things an opponent may try to use against one of our candidates."[56] Some campaigns go as far as putting a positive spin on a potential liability before an opponent has had a chance to raise it. Preemption is an effective tactic for "inoculating" a candidate against an attack. Another approach is to hire one of the consulting firms that stake their reputation on the ability to prepare a televised response to an attack in less than half a day. Many well-financed Senate and House contenders in tight races even record television commercials that present responses to particular charges before an opponent has actually made them.

When an incumbent loses a congressional election, negative advertising usually contributes to that outcome. One of the lessons to be drawn from the elections of the past three decades is that, if used skillfully, negative campaigning can be a potent weapon.

SUMMARY

The campaign for votes, like the campaign for resources, requires candidates and strategists to identify groups of loyalists and potential supporters and communicate a message they will find appealing. Campaign strategists recognize that most voters have little interest in politics, possess little information about congressional candidates, are more familiar with incumbents than challengers, and know more about candidates for the Senate than for the House. They also understand that voters tend to cast their ballots for candidates whom they have previously supported or who share their party identification.

Candidates and their advisers consider these factors when plotting strategies. Most campaigns use voting histories, census data, and polls to target voters. Demography and geography are often major considerations; sometimes micro-targeting techniques are used. Campaigns consider the advantages associated with specific policy stances, the positions likely to be staked out by the opponent, the opinions of the blocs of supporters they need to mobilize, and the views of undecided voters they need to win. Most candidates make issues a major component of their message, but incumbents have a greater tendency to focus on imagery and their performance in office. Most candidates also seek to hold their opponent accountable for perceived weaknesses in the person's public record or private life. However, competitive election campaigns are usually the most negative. The combination of issues, images, and attacks incorporated into a candidate's message depends on many factors, including incumbency, party affiliation, the closeness of the race, and the concerns of local voters. In nationalized election cycles, such as 2010, powerful issues that transcend congressional districts and state boundaries also influence campaign messages.

CHAPTER EIGHT

Campaign Communications

Campaign communications range from attention-grabbing television advertisements, sophisticated websites, and social media to old-fashioned knocking on doors. The resources at a candidate's disposal, the types of media available, and the competitiveness of the election are the factors that most strongly influence how campaigns reach voters. In this chapter I examine the techniques that campaigns use to disseminate their messages and get their supporters to the polls.

Campaign communications are meant to accomplish six objectives: improve a candidate's name recognition, project a favorable image, set the campaign agenda, exploit the issues, undermine an opponent's credibility or support, and defend the candidate against attacks. These objectives, of course, are designed to advance the campaign's broader goals of shoring up and expanding its base of support and getting its supporters sufficiently interested in the election to vote.

Campaign communications usually proceed through four short phases. In the first, often called the biography phase, candidates introduce themselves to voters by highlighting their experience and personal background. Next, in the issue phase, candidates use policy stances to attract the support of uncommitted voters, energize their supporters, and further define themselves to the public. The attack phase often begins when one candidate learns that he or she is slipping in the polls and is desperate to advance on an opponent. During this phase, candidates contrast themselves with their opponent, point to inconsistencies between an opponent's rhetoric and actions, try to exploit unpopular positions the opponent has taken, or just plain sling mud at one another. In the final weeks of the campaign, most candidates pull their message together by reminding voters who they are, why they are running, and why they are more worthy of being elected than their opponent. During this summation phase, they commonly emphasize phrases and symbols presented earlier in the campaign.

TELEVISION ADVERTISING

Virtually every household in the United States possesses at least one television set, and the average adult watches three and one-half to four hours of television per day.[1] More than three-fourths of all Americans get their news from television.[2] These factors make television an important vehicle for campaign communications and have encouraged congressional campaigners in cheap, moderately priced, and sometimes extremely expensive media markets to utilize it.

In 2010 candidates, political parties, and interest groups aired well in excess of 1.5 million ads on broadcast and national cable TV stations.[3] Voters in states and districts with competitive elections were undoubtedly exposed to hundreds of TV ads during the final weeks of the campaign. Television is the best medium for conveying image-related information to a mass audience. It is also extremely useful for setting the campaign agenda and associating a candidate with popular issues.[4] Television ads enable candidates to transmit action-oriented visuals that convey leadership and other desirable qualities. Images of candidates meeting with voters or attending groundbreaking ceremonies convey more powerfully than written or verbal statements the message that these individuals are actively involved in community affairs and have close ties to voters. Images also have a stronger emotional impact than words. Republican strategist Robert Teeter explains that "80 or 90 percent of what people retain from a TV ad is visual. . . . If you have the visual right, you have the commercial right. If you don't, it almost doesn't matter what you're saying."[5] Television advertisements have the extra advantage of enabling a campaign to control its message. Unlike interactive modes of communication such as debates and speeches, paid advertisements do not allow an opponent or disgruntled voter to interrupt. Message control makes TV a potent means for increasing name recognition.[6]

Roughly nine out of ten Senate campaigns and 65 percent of House campaigns use either broadcast or cable television, and the percentage would be larger if the costs were not so high.[7] Although candidates pay lower rates than political parties, interest groups, and commercial advertisers, these ads still can be prohibitively expensive. In November 2010 Democratic representative Jerrold Nadler or his Republican opponent, Susan Kone, would have had to spend $90,000 to broadcast a single thirty-second advertisement at 9:00 p.m., during the airing of the popular TV show *Grey's Anatomy,* to reach voters in New York's 8th congressional district. This exorbitant cost is due to the seat's location in a media market that spans the entire New York City metropolitan area. By contrast, Allen Boyd or Steve Southerland would only have paid $4,800 to air an ad that would blanket Florida's 2nd district during that same time slot. Dan Seals and Robert Dold would have paid $30,000 to cover Illinois' 10th district. Of course, some campaigns, including many in major metropolitan areas, save money and improve targeting by substituting cable TV ads for broadcast ads. They also post ads in the form of streaming video on the Internet.

High costs and the misalignment of the boundaries of media markets and congressional districts discourage House candidates in the highly urbanized areas of the mid-Atlantic, the West Coast, and southern New England from using television advertising. The distribution of media markets and relatively low advertising rates in most southwestern states and many rural areas, how-ever, enable many House candidates there to use television extensively.[8] Senate candidates tend to make greater use of television than candidates for the House because the configurations of state borders and media markets make television relatively cost-efficient in statewide contests. Senate campaigns' greater finan-cial resources and public expectations also contribute to the more frequent use of television in contests for the upper chamber.

Televised campaign advertisements have come a long way since the days when candidates appeared as talking heads spouting their political qualifica-tions and issue positions. Six trends define the evolution of the modern televi-sion campaign commercial: a movement toward greater emphasis on imagery, the use of action-oriented themes and pictures, the employment of emotion-ally laden messages, a decrease in the length of ads, an increase in negative advertising, and a reduction in the amount of time required to create an ad.[9] Gimmicky ten- and fifteen-second spots punctuated by brief messages have become popular with congressional candidates and political groups. The abil-ity to counterattack rapidly has become a selling point for the nation's top media firms. Campaign advertisements broadcast in the guise of independent expen-ditures, electioneering communications, and issue advocacy ads by parties and interest groups are a relatively recent phenomenon, but they are abundant in many close elections.[10]

During the biography phase of the campaign, incumbents' ads typically depict them as experienced leaders who know and care about their constitu-ents. Challengers and candidates for open seats also try to present themselves as capable and honorable by pointing to their accomplishments in public ser-vice, family life, or the private sector. Regardless of incumbency, good cam-paigns broadcast advertisements that display their candidate's core values and help the candidate connect with voters. Most repeatedly mention and display their names in order to boost their name recognition. Federal law requires that candidates state who paid for the ad; that statement frequently comes last.

Candidates who have led remarkable lives, come from humble origins, or compiled impressive records of public service often broadcast "mini-docudramas" to showcase their war record, community activism, or road to professional success. The ad a campaign selects to introduce its candidate depends on the background of the candidate and the opponent.

Southerland, who ran against the incumbent Boyd in Florida, was relatively well known among voters for a challenger who had no previous electoral experience. His family has lived in the area for more than 100 years, his local relatives number in the thousands, and his family-run funeral business has connected him with hundreds of thousands of people in their time of need. According to his campaign director, Southerland is personable, telegenic, and a good communicator. His first television advertisement, a thirty-second biography spot, was narrated by his wife, Susan. In it, she testified that "Steve's passions, values, and beliefs are genuine." The ad recounted that they have known each other since first grade and have been married for twenty-three years. Featuring video taken of the Southerland family and at campaign stops in the district, the ad helped to burnish the candidate's image as a "family man" and community leader.[11]

Boyd had little reason to introduce himself to voters because of his seven terms representing the district. He did, however, need to remind them of his accomplishments and record of service. His early television spots portrayed him as a tireless worker on behalf of the district. Featuring images of the candidate and the district, these spots highlighted the popular votes the representative had cast and his success in securing federal funds. The ads were designed to reinforce the positive image Boyd had cultivated over the previous fourteen years and to reconnect him with the different constituencies that had benefited from his efforts. Such "community action" spots are frequently used by incumbents. Many employ the testimonials of constituents to demonstrate the candidate's knowledge, empathy, and ability to improve the quality of life in the district.

"Feel-good" ads are virtually devoid of issues and are designed to appeal to the electorate's sense of community pride or nationalism. They feature visuals of a candidate marching in parades, serving food at backyard cookouts, or involved in some other popular local activity. "Passing the torch" ads manipulate symbols to depict the concept of succession in order to make the case that a candidate is the right person for the job. The most effective spot of this kind in decades was broadcast in 1992 by a presidential rather than congressional candidate. It featured then-teenager Bill Clinton shaking hands with President John F. Kennedy on the grounds of the White House.

During the issue phase, campaign ads communicate candidates' policy stances on valence, position, or government-performance issues.[12] The Southerland campaign used them to drive home its candidate's economic and anti-establishment message. Drawing from his ubiquitous slogan, "Have you had enough?" a typical Southerland TV ad proclaimed the candidate's opposition to "out-of-control government spending, like 'Obamacare' [and] high taxes " and pledged he would "fight to create jobs, lower taxes, and rein in the Obama/Boyd/Pelosi spending spree."[13] Boyd's ads linked his issue positions to local improvements that resulted from his efforts. They focused on increased funding for military installations, to attract the support of members of the armed forces and veterans; federal support for Florida's universities, to shore up support among teachers and students; and federal subsidies for highways, to appeal to voters who commute to work.[14]

In the attack phase of the campaign, candidates use TV ads to point to their opponent's shortcomings. Television is ideally suited to comparative ads because it enables candidates to present pictures of themselves and their opponent side by side and roll lists of issues down the screen to show themselves on the popular side of salient policies and their opponent on the unpopular side. It's an understatement to say that less-than-flattering pictures of the opponent are usually used. Sometimes the opponent's head is reduced in size, "phased out," or distorted, to keep voters' attention and subtly imply that faulty issue positions are only the beginning of the opponent's inadequacies. Advertisements that feature images of the opponent somersaulting back and forth across the screen or debating himself or herself are useful for highlighting inconsistencies among an opponent's speeches, campaign positions, or congressional roll-call votes. Ominous or flighty music is often used to reinforce the visuals and language.

The most effective negative ads are grounded in fact, document their sources, focus on some aspect of the opponent's policy views, use ridicule, are delivered by a surrogate, and avoid discussing the plight of unfortunate citizens.[15] Many negative ads feature actors depicting incumbents embracing unpopular politicians, voting themselves pay raises, or attending lavish parties with lobbyists. Some use fancy graphics to show opponents literally "flip-flopping" when the ads discuss the issues. Ridicule is a powerful weapon in politics because it is difficult for people to vote for a candidate they have just laughed at.

One of the most effective negative ads in 2010, "Seals for Dold," was aired by the Dold campaign. The ad opens with a deep voice saying, "And now, a very special political endorsement," and the phrase, "A very special political endorsement" printed in white letters on a black background. Next, there is a loud cry of a bird and, as playful, up-tempo music begins, a gray seal looks into the camera. As its mouth moves up and down through digital animation a voice feigning conviction states, "Dan Seals is a proud resident of the tenth district." A knowledgeable-sounding male voice cuts in and responds, "Actually he's not." The seal replies, "What? He's not?" and the voice yells "Cut!" Next, the seal says, "Dan Seals is a tax fighter," and the voice debunks this too, saying, "No, he's all about raising your taxes and increasing government spending." "Uh! For real, broheim?" the seal says, tilting its head back in a sign of frustration. The seal begins anew with, "Dan Seals is a fresh new candidate," only to be interrupted again as the voice says, "No. He's run, like, two times already and lost. I think he was running since before there were, like, iPods." The seal responds with, "What the . . . !" and then, apparently having been persuaded by the voice, says, "Look if you want common-sense leadership in Congress, lower taxes, and more jobs, just vote for Robert Dold. Alrighty. Arf arf. Where's my fish treat?" At this point, the ad closes with a picture of the seal, the phrase "SEALS FOR DOLD," and the Dold campaign website printed at the bottom. The audio features a man singing a catchy tune used in other Dold ads: "It's Dold with a 'D' not an 'E.'"[16] In addition to getting a few laughs and attracting substantial media coverage, the ad portrayed Seals, who won his primary race in part by positioning himself as a political outsider, as the political insider in the general election.

Of course, candidates are not responsible for all comparative and negative advertising. In close elections, much of it also comes from party and interest group independent media campaigns. All three—candidates, parties, and interest groups—broadcast attack ads in the Boyd-Southerland, Dold-Seals, and Reid-Angle contests. Indeed, in many races these three sources broadcast TV ads that used the same themes, examples, and phrases. Some of these similarities are the result of different organizations using the same information sources, partly because they are posted on the Internet. Others are the result of a party committee signaling to its interest group allies the themes and issues it believes will be the most helpful to its candidates and networks of interest groups coordinating their communication efforts, as noted in Chapters 4 and 5.

Finally, in the summation phase of the campaign, eleventh-hour television blitzes are used to solidify a candidate's message in the minds of voters. Key phrases and visuals from earlier commercials are repeated, as candidates who are ahead shore up support and those running behind appeal to undecided voters. Sometimes these TV spots are supplemented by party and interest group ads.

RADIO ADVERTISING

Radio is an extremely popular medium for congressional campaign communications. Almost two-thirds of all House candidates and virtually all Senate contestants purchase radio ads.[17] During the last week of a congressional midterm election, voters typically hear four to five radio ads per day.[18] Inexpensive to record and broadcast, radio commercials are ideal for building a candidate's name recognition. Another advantage is that some candidates—who may be intimidated by the television camera, not telegenic, or novices to the spotlight— perform better on radio. For many incumbents, taping radio commercials is an easy extension of the prerecorded radio shows they routinely transmit to stations in their district. Like television, radio is an excellent vehicle for emotional messages.[19]

Radio enables candidates to target voters with great precision. Radio stations broadcast to smaller, more homogeneous audiences than television stations, enabling campaigns to tailor their messages to different population groups. Campaigns can reach Hispanic voters in the Southwest, Florida, or the inner cities of the Northeast and Midwest by advertising on Spanish-language stations. "Golden oldies" stations, which feature music from the 1960s and 1970s, are ideal for reaching voters in the fifty- and sixty-year-old age group. Radio talk programs, such as the *Rush Limbaugh Show,* are excellent vehicles for reaching voters who are committed to a particular ideology. Commuting hours furnish near-captive audiences of suburbanites who travel to work.

NEWSPAPER ADVERTISING

Newspaper advertisements dominated campaign communications for much of American history but became less important with the decline of the partisan press in the late 1800s.[20] Congressional campaigns still purchase newspaper ads, but they are not as widely used as radio and many other media. Sixty-three percent of all House and 80 percent of all Senate campaigns purchase ads in local or statewide newspapers.[21]

Newspapers have some advantages but many shortcomings as a campaign medium. Their major advantages are that they provide plenty of opportunity to deliver a detailed message, and their readers are educated and likely to vote. On the other hand, newspapers do not communicate images or convey emotions as well as television. They also cannot be used to deliver a personalized message. Moreover, only a few congressional districts and states have minority communities large enough to sustain independent newspapers that can be used to target communications to those groups. The effectiveness of campaign advertisements that appear in newspapers is also somewhat limited.[22]

If such shortcomings exist, why do most campaigns place ads in newspapers? One reason is that they are inexpensive. Newspaper advertisements cost less than ads transmitted via television, radio, mail, or virtually any other medium. Newspaper ads also can be useful for announcing the times and locations of campaign events, which can help attract coverage by other media. Finally, some candidates and campaign aides believe that purchasing advertising space from a local newspaper can help secure the paper's endorsement.

DIRECT MAIL AND NEWSLETTERS

Newsletters and direct mail can be used to raise money, convey a message, or encourage people to vote, but the key to success in all three areas is a good mailing list. A good fundraising list is made up of previous donors or persons who have a history of contributing to like-minded candidates; a good advertising list includes supporters and persuadable voters; and a good voter mobilization list includes only those who intend to vote for the candidate.

Direct-mail pieces and newsletters (sometimes referred to as "persuasion" or "mobilization" mail, depending on its main purpose) are among the most widely used methods of campaign advertising in congressional elections. Roughly 80 percent of all House candidates and virtually all Senate candidates use them.[23] Voters who reside in congressional districts or states featuring competitive contests typically receive dozens of pieces of direct mail. Most of those who live in areas that only feature one-sided contests receive at least a few pieces. In a typical election year, roughly 70 percent of all registered voters receive at least one piece of direct mail.[24] Mail is a one-way communications tool that offers significant advantages in message control and delivery. Precise targeting is its main advantage. Campaigns can purchase lists that include information such as a voter's name, address, gender, age, race or ethnicity, employment status, party registration, voting history, and estimated income.[25] This information enables campaigns to tailor the candidate profiles, issue positions, and photographs they include in their mailings to appeal to specific segments of the population. Lists developed through microtargeting, which include a variety of consumer preference data, enable a campaign to fine-tune its message to individual voters. The ability to narrowcast a message makes mail excellent for staking out position issues and for campaigning in heterogeneous states or districts. Campaigns in highly diverse areas, such as New York's 12th district, which is 49 percent Hispanic and includes most of Chinatown, often use the mail to campaign in more than one language.

Another advantage of mail is that it is relatively inexpensive. Letters produced using personal computers and laser printers can be mailed to voters for little more than the price of a stamp. Campaigns also can take advantage of postal service discounts for presorted mailings. Finally, mail campaigns often fly under the radar for a while. As long as an adversary does not detect them, his or her campaign will not respond.

Nevertheless, direct mail has some disadvantages, including the fact that it is often tossed out as junk mail. Another disadvantage is that it rests principally on the power of the printed word. Whereas television and radio enable campaigns to embellish their messages with visual images, music, or sound effects, mail depends primarily on written copy to hold voters' attention and get a message across. This makes it a less effective medium for communicating image-related information.

Direct-mail experts rely on many techniques to combat the weaknesses of their medium. Personalized salutations, graphs, and pictures are often used to capture and hold voters' attention. Other gimmicks include the use of postscripts designed to look as though they were handwritten.

Direct mail is an especially powerful medium for challengers and candidates who have strong ideological positions because it is ideal for negative advertising or making appeals that stir voters' emotions. Yet mail also offers some advantages to incumbents. Many members of Congress send out letters early in the election cycle as a low-cost way to reinforce voter support.[26] These mailings often include messages that reinforce the ones that incumbents communicate in congressionally franked mass mailings to constituents, which are prohibited during the ninety days before a primary or general election for House members and the sixty days before an election for senators.

TELEPHONE CALLS

Just over 70 percent of all House campaigns and most Senate campaigns use mass telephone calls to communicate with voters.[27] Campaigns make personal calls, referred to as "telemarketing" in the business world, for a variety of reasons, including identifying voters' political predispositions and candidate preferences. This information is often added to an existing database so that core supporters and swing voters can be contacted later. Campaigns that can afford it, or that receive the assistance of a party committee or interest group equipped with the appropriate resources, use microtargeting to make this outreach more effective. Telephone calls also are used to try to win the support of undecided voters and to contact supporters to ask them to volunteer, make a contribution, or attend an event. Of course, a major purpose of mass telephone calls is voter mobilization. Automated mass telephone calls, sometimes referred to as "robo-calls," can provide a less labor-intensive alternative to person-to-person calls for voter mobilization. In a typical midterm election season almost two-thirds of all registered voters receive at least one robo-call, and another 24 percent receive phone calls from a live person.[28]

Voters who reside in a district or state that is hosting one or more competitive elections are often bombarded with personal calls and robo-calls. Voters living in congressional districts that allow them to participate in both a hotly contested House race and an unpredictable Senate contest, such as those residing in Florida's 2nd or Illinois' 10th district, are the recipients of dozens of waves of targeted calls, most of them made during the final week of the election. Some of these calls originate with a candidate's campaign; some are components of a party committee's or interest group's coordinated grassroots campaign.

Although personal calls are much more effective than recorded ones and can be made by volunteers, recorded messages also can be effective in mobilizing voters. Some candidates, particularly challengers, ask prominent politicians for assistance with these. During the congressional elections held early in George W. Bush's presidency, many Republican candidates in close races benefited from prerecorded voter mobilization messages featuring President Bush and other GOP leaders. During the 2008 and 2010 elections Barack Obama, Hillary Rodham Clinton, former president Bill Clinton, and other Democratic leaders lent their voices to some candidates' causes. In many cases party committees financed these efforts.

Live and prerecorded telephone calls also have been used for less noble purposes. Campaigns have been known to leave prerecorded messages attempting to implicate an opponent in a scandal or mislead an opponent's supporters about the hours of operation of their polling place. They also have been known to hire telephone firms to conduct "push polls," which seem to be normal telephone surveys used for collecting information but soon degenerate into allegations and attacks phrased as questions. Another "dirty trick" involves making automated phone calls in the middle of the night in the name of an opposing candidate. These types of activities are intended to keep voters away from the polls rather than to learn about or mobilize them.

THE INTERNET AND SOCIAL MEDIA

Although rarely used in politics during the 1990s, the Internet is now used by many contemporary political campaigns, party committees, other political organizations, and activists. The best websites are integrated into the candidate's campaign. They provide a convenient and reliable place for voters to collect information that is often spread across many locations. They help meet the needs of the roughly 60 percent of Americans who get some of their news online.[29] Campaigns save money and effort—and prevent careless mistakes—when they direct voter, donor, and press inquiries to their website. Given that more than half of all adults watch streaming video, campaigns can expect to increase the audiences for their television and radio advertisements, speeches, and other recorded events when they post them online.[30]

Good campaign websites are easy to navigate, feature attractive home pages that immediately tell voters about the candidate and his or her reasons for running, present the candidate's issue positions, display attractive photographs and video, post the candidate's schedule, and are updated regularly. They enable individuals to volunteer for campaign activities, make a contribution, learn how to register to vote, look up directions to their polling place, or sign up for the campaign's contact list—which itself is a valuable communications tool. These data are usually integrated into the campaign's computerized volunteer and campaign finance databases.[31] Campaigns that create Facebook pages, post blogs, send out tweets, and use other social media can regale supporters with their candidate's experiences on the campaign trail or answer voters' questions. Some political websites encourage "viral" campaigning, which often takes place with limited or no guidance from the candidate's campaign organization. They feature information that voters can distribute to their friends or use to write op-ed articles, send letters to the editor, or raise on radio call-in talk shows. The inclusion of the names, addresses, and telephone numbers of local media outlets further encourages political activists to publicly express their support for a candidate. Campaigns also can use social media to stimulate "meet-ups," house parties, and other grassroots activities. Opportunities for interactivity are particularly useful in helping a candidate attract a coterie of web-savvy supporters, many of whom are young people.

Blogs sponsored by a candidate's supporters also are usually very helpful, but because they are not the property of the campaign, it has less control over the online conversation. Independent blogs, ranging from the widely read and influential Daily Kos to a teenager's postings on MySpace or Blogger, afford the campaign no influence over their content. As is the case with other forms of free media (discussed below), the best a campaign typically can do in response to a negative posting is to request that its rebuttal be posted.

How widespread is Internet use in congressional elections? During the 2010 elections almost every major-party general election candidate for Congress had a campaign website. Candidate websites are far from identical. A number of factors, including cost, have a noteworthy impact on website quality and features. Nevertheless, a campaign can spend less than $20,000 to create an effective website. The content and tone of the information posted on House candidates' websites also vary according to incumbency and competitiveness. Although few incumbents post information about their standings in the polls, substantial numbers of open-seat candidates and challengers in close contests do, presumably because the nonincumbents recognize that this information can help generate more voter and donor support and can attract additional media coverage. Candidates in neck-and-neck races, particularly challengers, are the most likely to post comparative and negative information about their opponents. Recall from Chapter 7 that this information can be useful in peeling away support from sitting members of Congress. Of course, incumbents who are in danger of losing the election are liable to perceive advantages in going on the offensive online. Websites and social media may be the most cutting-edge technological innovation in campaign politics, but a large number of contemporary campaigns use them to enhance traditional grassroots efforts. Almost all congressional campaigns use the Internet to recruit campaign volunteers, and most use it to provide supporters with information about how to register to vote and locate their polling place.[32]

FREE MEDIA

One of the major goals of any campaign is to generate free, or "earned," media—radio, television, newspaper, or magazine coverage that candidates receive when news editors consider their activities newsworthy. The coverage has other advantages besides its lack of cost. Because it is delivered by a neutral observer, it has greater credibility than campaign-generated communications.[33] Its major disadvantage is that campaigns cannot control what news correspondents report. Also, misstatements and blunders are more likely to appear in the news than in the candidate's major policy speeches.

News coverage of congressional elections consists of stories based on press releases that campaigns issue; stories about events, issues, campaign ads, or the time that a reporter has spent with a candidate; and analytical or editorial stories about a candidate or campaign.[34] Most analysis focuses on the "horse race" aspect of the election. The stories that go beyond handicapping the race usually discuss a candidate's political qualifications, personal characteristics, or campaign strategy. Fewer stories focus on the issues.[35] Coverage by television and radio tends to be shorter, more action oriented, and less detailed than print journalism.

Most journalists strive to cover politics objectively, but that does not mean that all candidates are treated the same. Reporters follow certain norms when pursuing leads and researching and writing their stories—norms that usually work to the advantage of incumbents.[36] Moreover, editorials are largely exempt from the norms of objectivity that apply to news stories. Newspaper owners and their editorial boards do not hesitate to voice their opinions on the editorial page. Radio and television stations also air programs that feature pundits discussing the virtues and foibles of specific candidates. Most voters have come to expect newspaper editors, political talk show hosts, and bloggers to endorse specific candidates shortly before the election. Media endorsements and campaign coverage can have a significant impact on the outcome.[37]

Attracting Coverage

Attracting media coverage requires planning and assertiveness. Besides issuing streams of press releases, campaign offices distribute copies of the candidate's schedule to correspondents, invite them to campaign events, and make special efforts to grant interviews. Candidates also submit themselves to interrogations by panels of newspaper editors, with the goal of generating good press coverage or winning an endorsement.

Successful campaigns carefully play to the needs of different news media. Media releases that feature strong leads, have news value, provide relevant facts, and contain enough background information for an entire story are faxed or e-mailed to print reporters. Advance notice of major campaign events, including information about predicted crowd size, acoustics, and visual backdrops, goes to television and radio correspondents in the hope that the event will be one of the few they cover.[38] Interpretive information is provided to journalists in all the news media to try to generate campaign stories with a favorable news spin. News organizations are willing to report stories based on materials distributed by congressional campaigns because few of them have the resources to research or even verify the information.

Newspapers and radio stations are more likely than television stations to give candidates free coverage. Television stations devote little time to covering congressional elections, particularly House races. Television news shows occasionally discuss the horse race aspect of campaigns, cover small portions of campaign debates, or analyze controversial campaign ads, but few are willing to give candidates air time to discuss issues. Radio stations are more generous with air time. Many invite candidates to participate in call-in shows and public forums. Newspapers usually give the most detailed campaign coverage. Small, understaffed newspapers frequently print portions of candidates' press releases and debate transcripts verbatim.

Senate candidates attract more free media coverage than House candidates. Incumbents and open-seat contestants usually get more—and more favorable—press coverage than challengers, regardless of whether they are running for the

House or the Senate. Inequities in campaign coverage are due to the professional norms that guide news journalists and to inequalities among candidates and their campaigns. The preoccupation of journalists with candidates' personalities, qualifications, campaign organizations, and probable success is to the advantage of incumbents because they are almost always better known, more qualified, in possession of more professional organizations, and more likely to win than their opponents.[39]

Newspaper coverage in House contests between an incumbent and a challenger is so unequal that veteran Democratic political adviser Anita Dunn believes "the local press is the unindicted coconspirator in the alleged 'permanent incumbency.'" As Dunn explains,

> A vicious circle develops for challengers—if early on they don't have money, standing in the polls, endorsements, and the backing of political insiders, they—and the race—are written off, not covered, which means the likelihood of a competitive race developing is almost nonexistent.[40]

The experience of Kone, the long-shot challenger who ran in a district in New York City, is fairly typical. Unable to attract any coverage from local Manhattan-based newspapers, she received only scant attention from press outlets covering Brooklyn.

The reporting policies of many news outlets combine with state election laws to contribute to high incumbent retention rates. Newspapers that provide no coverage of challengers in uncontested primaries until the actual primary date has passed and the general election begins are particularly harmful to candidates in states that hold late primaries. In states in which primaries are held only a couple of months before Election Day, it is virtually impossible for challengers to receive sufficient free media to become viable candidates.

Although many challengers can usually count on getting only four stories—the announcement of their candidacy, coverage of their primary victory, a candidate profile, and the announcement of their defeat—it is still worth pursuing free media coverage. Those few challengers who are able to make the case to journalists that they have the capacity to mount a strong campaign are able to attract significant coverage, often enough to become known among the local voters. Challengers who have held elective office or had other significant political experience, or who have assembled professional campaign organizations and raised substantial funds, are in a better position to make this case than those who have not. The same is true of candidates in the Democratic Congressional Campaign Committee's Red to Blue Program, the National Republican Congressional Committee's Young Guns Program, and those who are designated priority contestants by a national party organization. These candidates typically receive extra press coverage, which helps them raise more money, hire additional help, become more competitive, and attract even greater attention from the media.[41] A similar set of relationships exists for open-seat candidates, except that it is usually easier for them to make the case that they are involved in a close contest.

Scandal can help candidates attract more media coverage. Underdogs are taken more seriously when their opponent has been accused of breaking the law or ethical misconduct. As noted in Chapter 7, candidates who are either directly implicated in a scandal or publicly associated with a person who has come under a cloud of accusations can be put on the defensive and thrown off message. Scandal also can result in a little-known contender's receiving enough favorable media coverage to become competitive and eventually win. Scandal was critical in helping state legislator Mike Oliverio attract the news coverage needed to defeat Rep. Alan Mollohan in West Virginia's 2010 Democratic primary, as observed in Chapter 2. It also helped Michigan Democrat Hansen Clarke attract the media attention needed to vault him from a likely congressional "also-ran" to a U.S. House member.

Campaign Debates

Debates are among the few campaign activities that receive extensive press coverage and can place a challenger on equal footing with an incumbent. The decision to participate in a debate is a strategic one. Front-runners, who are usually incumbents, generally prefer to avoid debating because they understand that debates have the potential to do them more harm than good. Nevertheless, incumbents recognize that the public expects them to debate; most participate in at least one debate in order to avoid being blasted for shirking their civic responsibility. Candidates who are running behind, usually challengers, have the most to gain from debating. They prefer to engage in as many debates as possible and to hold them when they will attract the most media coverage.

Before debates are scheduled, the candidates or their representatives negotiate certain matters. In addition to the number and timing of debates, candidates must agree on whether independent or minor-party candidates will participate, on the format, and on where the debate or debates will be held. All these factors can influence who, if anyone, is considered the winner.[42] Negotiations about debates can become heated but are almost always successfully resolved. Roughly nine out of ten House and Senate contestants debate their opponents.[43] The few who refuse usually enjoy insurmountable leads, lack verbal agility, or both.

Media Bias

House challengers and incumbents disagree over the nature of the coverage the news media give to House campaigns (see Table 8-1).[44] Challengers, particularly those in uncompetitive contests, are the most likely to perceive a bias for the incumbent, reflecting the one-sided nature of press coverage in elections for safe seats. To some extent these perceptions are a product of the norms that guide the distribution of media endorsements, which favor incumbents by almost nine to one.[45]

Partisan differences also exist in perceptions about media coverage. More Republican campaigners than Democrats maintain that the press gives more coverage and endorsements to their opponent, reflecting an opinion widely shared among Republican politicians and voters that the media corps is made up of members of a liberal establishment. Nevertheless, equal numbers of campaigners from each party believe the media covered their campaign fairly. That almost four out of ten campaigners from both parties believe that the news media are biased against them, however, highlights the adversarial relationship that exists between politicians and the press.[46] It also explains why increasing numbers of politicians and voters of both parties seek out radio and cable TV talk shows and other information providers recognized for having a partisan tilt.

TABLE 8-1

Campaigners' Perceptions of Media Coverage in House Campaigns

	All	Incumbents		Challengers		Open-seat candidates	
		In jeopardy	Shoo-ins	Hope-fuls	Long shots	Pros-pects	Mis-matched
Favored your campaign	9%	—	11%	10%	9%	12%	12%
Favored your opponent's campaign	37	18%	5	48	62	24	47
Equally fair	54	82	84	42	29	65	41

Sources: "2002 Congressional Campaign Study," Center for American Politics and Citizenship, University of Maryland.

Notes: Figures are for general election candidates in major-party contested races, excluding those in incumbent-versus-incumbent races. — = less than 0.5 percent. Some columns do not add to 100 percent because of rounding. *N* = 312.

FIELD WORK

Field work involves voter registration and get-out-the-vote (GOTV) drives, literature drops, the distribution of yard signs and bumper stickers, and other grassroots activities. It also includes candidate appearances at town hall meetings and in parades, speeches to rotary clubs and other civic groups, door-to-door campaigning, and other forms of direct voter contact. Grassroots politics was the major means of campaigning during the golden age of parties, and it remains important in modern congressional elections. Sophisticated targeting plans—similar to those used in direct mail, mass e-mails, and mass telephone calling—guide many grassroots activities. They are particularly important in getting a candidate's supporters to the polls.[47]

Field work is the most labor-intensive and volunteer-dependent aspect of congressional elections. Candidates, their supporters, and local party workers or interest group members knock on doors and make telephone calls to learn whether citizens intend to vote, whom they support, and whether they have any specific concerns they would like the candidate to address. In competitive contests, this information is often fed directly into a campaign database, sometimes using an iPad or some other web-based tool. Regardless of how the information is recorded, it is used to guide follow-up contacts. Supporters and potential supporters who express an interest in a policy area, need to register to vote, desire help in getting to the polls, state a preference for casting an absentee or early ballot, or are willing to work in the campaign typically receive follow-up contacts to address these issues. Everyone who is coded as a supporter gets numerous reminders to vote. Such direct voter contact boosts election turnout.[48]

Person-to-person communication is probably the most effective means of political persuasion and boosting turnout, especially when it's directly between the candidate and a voter. It also provides a campaign with useful feedback. Candidates routinely draw on conversations with people they meet along the campaign trail to develop anecdotes that humanize issues.

Field work is relatively inexpensive because volunteers can carry out much of the actual labor. Local party activists and other volunteers are often called on to deliver campaign literature, register voters, or drive voters to the polls. In 2006 more than four out of ten registered voters received a phone call or visit at home from a volunteer or someone hired by a campaign during the election season.[49] Because of the increased number of competitive elections in the 2010 election season, just as many, if not more, voters were probably contacted then. Party and interest group coordinated grassroots campaigns allow many congressional candidates to rely, in part, on outside organizations to carry out their field work— that is, when these organizations believe the candidate has at least a fighting chance.[50] Most House campaigners report that local party committees are especially helpful: 60 percent state they played a moderately to extremely important role in their registration and GOTV drives, and almost 75 percent maintain they were a moderately to extremely important source of campaign volunteers.[51] The most positive assessments are provided by those involved in hotly contested races. Not surprisingly, the Dold and Seals campaigns in Illinois and the Boyd and Southerland campaigns in Florida benefited from extensive party and interest group grassroots campaigning. The Kone campaign in New York, conversely, was unable to raise the money to conduct a major GOTV drive on its own and could not rally party or interest group support for this purpose. Kone's opponent, the incumbent Nadler, did not feel the need to invest in a monumental voter mobilization effort and did not attract the levels of party and interest group involvement that characterize most competitive elections.

THE IMPORTANCE OF DIFFERENT COMMUNICATIONS TECHNIQUES

Congressional campaigns disseminate their messages through a variety of media, each of which has advantages and disadvantages. Door-to-door campaigning is inexpensive but requires a corps of committed volunteers. Television advertising can present voters with a compelling image of a candidate, but it is rarely cheap. Direct mail and mass telephone calls make few demands on a candidate but require accurate targeting to be effective. Websites enable a campaign to attractively package a large quantity of material and collect contributions, among other things, but voters must take the initiative to visit them.

Most campaigners believe that direct contact with voters is the best way to win votes (see Table 8-2). A firm handshake and a warm smile, accompanied by an explanation of why one wants to serve in Congress, perhaps followed by a direct response to a voter's question, are the best ways to convey politically relevant information and build trust—two ingredients key to winning votes.[52] However, with the typical congressional district containing approximately 700,000 residents, candidates who wish to run competitive races cannot rely solely on direct voter contact, to say nothing of the challenges faced by Senate candidates, who must win the support of half their state's voters.

The next most popular communications techniques among candidates in close races are broadcast television, newsletters, direct mail, and free media. Incumbents find television (broadcast or cable) more important than challengers do, reflecting the fact that more incumbents can afford TV commercials. But open-seat candidates most consistently evaluate television as very important, if not essential, to their campaigns. As shown in Chapter 6, the overwhelming

TABLE 8-2

Campaigners' Perceptions of the Importance of Different Communications Techniques in House Campaigns

	All	Incumbents		Challengers		Open-seat candidates	
		In jeopardy	Shoo-ins	Hope-fuls	Long shots	Pros-pects	Mis-matched
Direct contact with voters	91%	86%	92%	91%	91%	94%	94%
Broadcast TV ads	50	72	47	84	23	91	72
Cable TV ads	36	55	32	52	23	58	47
Newsletters or direct mail	70	83	83	84	51	77	83
Radio ads	50	69	51	66	38	57	65
Newspaper ads	33	17	30	38	35	34	53
Free media	77	83	83	81	71	76	76
Door-to-door campaigning	68	72	54	81	69	77	78
Mass telephone calls	54	79	54	62	39	77	56
Billboards or yard signs	65	59	67	72	62	60	88
Debates and forums	52	48	36	72	54	63	56
Internet websites or e-mail	62	38	48	62	77	54	67

Sources: "2002 Congressional Campaign Study," Center for American Politics and Citizenship, University of Maryland.

Notes: Figures are for general election candidates in major-party contested races, excluding those in incumbent-versus-incumbent races, responding that a technique was moderately, very, or extremely important. The number of cases varies slightly because some respondents did not answer every question. $N = 318$.

majority of open-seat candidates can afford the high cost of broadcast time, and their races are usually competitive enough to warrant purchasing it.

Incumbents (regardless of the closeness of their elections), competitive challengers, and open-seat candidates also rely heavily on direct mail, newsletters, mass telephone calls, and free media to get out their message. Door-to-door campaigning, newspaper ads, candidate debates and forums, and websites and e-mail are favored more by challengers and open-seat campaigns than by incumbents. Presumably, nonincumbents depend more on door-to-door campaigning and newspaper ads because they are inexpensive. Similarly, they look to debates and forums because they are free and enable voters to make side-by-side comparisons between them and their opponent.

District characteristics and campaign strategy also affect how candidates use media. Television is a more important communication medium for House campaigns in rural districts than for those in urban and suburban settings because of cost and the mismatch between media markets and House districts in metropolitan areas. Greater population density enables campaigns waged in urban and suburban districts to make greater use of field activities, including distributing campaign literature and canvassing door to door, than campaigns in rural areas. Campaigns that target individuals who live in particular neighborhoods, work in certain occupations, or belong to specific demographic groups (such as women, the elderly, and racial or ethnic minorities) make greater use of direct mail than do campaigns that focus their efforts on less easily identifiable groups, such as single-issue voters.[53]

OUTSIDE CAMPAIGNS

Not all of the communications that influence congressional elections are under a candidate's control. The outside campaigns waged by party committees and interest groups also can influence the messages voters receive. Indeed, parties and interest groups spent an estimated $470 million on independent media campaigns and $88 million on coordinated grassroots campaigns, representing about 16 percent of the funds spent on the 2010 congressional elections.[54] Of course, outside campaigns are not carried out in every election. Their influence is felt primarily in competitive contests, even as parties and interest groups seek to broaden the field of competition. Incumbent shoo-ins, long-shot challengers, and open-seat candidates competing in similarly lopsided elections typically maintain that independent media spending by outside groups has no impact on their campaign.[55] Candidates in close races, by contrast, hold a different point of view. About two-thirds of them typically state that parties and interest groups sought to influence the campaign agenda, and about one-half report that such organizations' efforts either helped or harmed their candidacy.[56] Open-seat contestants were significantly more likely than incumbents and challengers to describe party and interest group independent media communications as having had an impact on the campaign agenda in their races. Similarly, and as noted in Chapters 4 and 5, the impact of voter mobilization efforts that are at the heart of party and interest group coordinated grassroots campaigns are most evident in competitive open-seat races and hard-fought incumbent-challenger contests.

SUMMARY

Campaign communications are central to any bid for elective office. Congressional candidates disseminate their messages using a variety of media. Television and radio enable candidates to powerfully convey emotional messages. Direct mail and e-mail enable campaigns to disseminate targeted, customized messages. Websites and social media can convey a great deal of information, and they have the potential to reach thousands of voters in minutes, but these technologies are limited by the population—albeit a growing one—who use them. Free media coverage is highly sought after, but it can be difficult for some candidates to attract, and it affords campaigns less control over their message than other communications methods. Old-fashioned, person-to-person contacts between candidates, campaign volunteers, and voters, augmented by sophisticated data collection and targeting methods, are among the most effective means of communication.

Of course, the specific media mix that a campaign uses depends on the size of its war chest, the match between the district's boundaries and those of local media markets, the talents and preferences of the individual candidate, and the recommendations of the campaign's advisers. The roles that political parties and interest groups choose to play in an election also are important. Candidates whose elections attract significant party or interest group outside campaign activity have to compete not only with their opponent but also with these organizations to draw voters' attention. Regardless of the media used or the roles of outside groups, it is important to reinforce the point that, as is the case in most aspects of congressional elections, incumbents enjoy tremendous advantages in communicating with voters.

CHAPTER NINE

Candidates, Campaigns, and Electoral Success

During the golden age of parties, party loyalties dominated the voting decisions of the vast majority of citizens and were the chief determinants of the outcome of most congressional elections. Since then, incumbency has become increasingly important in influencing congressional voting. The decline of voter partisanship in the 1960s and 1970s led to the partial replacement of party-based voting cues with cues based on incumbency.[1] Incumbents' better use of the perks of office also contributed to their increased reelection rates.[2] During the 1980s the growth in the number of congressional districts dominated by voters of one party and the increased inequalities in financial and other campaign resources available to incumbents and challengers further contributed to high reelection rates. As a result of these developments, better than 90 percent of all House members who seek reelection routinely win. Senators' reelection rates are somewhat lower, but impressive just the same. Although challenger victories are relatively rare, the types of campaigns that individual candidates mount, especially in open-seat contests, often make the difference between victory and defeat.

In most congressional elections incumbency, money, district partisanship, and other factors pertaining to individual candidates and their campaigns are usually the major determinants of who wins. Challengers have long odds of victory. This is especially the case in status quo election years that produce little partisan change. In other years national forces can be very powerful, however. This was the situation in 1994 and 2002 when congressional elections were nationalized in favor of the Republicans, it was the case in 2006 and 2008 when national conditions benefited the Democrats, and it was the case again in 2010 when the political environment again favored the Republicans. During these wave elections, the political climate strongly favored one party, and a larger than usual number of that party's challengers had an opportunity to navigate a path to victory. Challengers who waged well-funded and strategic campaigns benefited from substantial outside campaign spending and a sub-set of them went on to win, but many others joined the scores of challengers who waged weak campaigns in defeat. Of course, incumbents' responses to national conditions also have an impact on challenger success. Incumbents who build huge war chests often deter potentially strong challengers, and those who make other strategic adjustments can usually protect themselves from an impending national partisan tide. In 2010 a pro-Republican environment led to an 18-point voter enthusiasm gap that manifested as an increased turnout of voters generally supportive of GOP candidates and depressed turnout among traditional Democratic supporters. It also led to a large swing by inde-pendent voters in the direction of the Republican Party. The political land-scape contributed to the election of fifty-eight House and four Senate challengers—almost all of them Republicans.[3] Assisted by the national mood and efforts of parties and other groups, Republicans who ran strong campaigns also won the overwhelming majority of open seats in both chambers of Congress. Despite all of this turnover, better than four out of five members of Congress seeking reelection kept their seats.

Regardless of whether an election is dominated by local candidates and themes or national issues and events, the decisions of candidates and others who are active in campaigns have a major impact on their outcomes. Thus, it makes sense to ask what separates winners from losers in contemporary congressional elections. How great an impact do candidate characteristics, political conditions, campaign strategy, campaign effort, media coverage, and party and interest group activities have on the percentage of the votes that candidates receive? Do these factors affect incumbents, challengers, and open-seat contestants equally? Or do different candidates need to do different things to win elections? This chapter addresses these questions. It also contains a discussion of the differences between what winners and losers think determines the outcomes of elections.

HOUSE INCUMBENT CAMPAIGNS

Incumbency is extremely important to the types of campaigns that candidates wage, and it is the most significant determinant of congressional election outcomes.[4] Virtually all House incumbents begin the general election campaign with higher name recognition and voter approval levels, greater political experience, more money, and a better campaign organization than their opponent. Nearly all incumbents also benefit from the fact that most constituents and political elites in Washington expect them to win and act accordingly. For the most part, voters cast ballots, volunteers donate time, contributors give money, and news correspondents provide coverage in ways that favor incumbents. Most strategic politicians also behave in ways that contribute to high incumbent success rates. They usually wait until a seat becomes open rather than take on a sitting incumbent and risk a loss that could harm their political career.

The big leads most incumbents enjoy at the beginning of the election season make defending those leads the major objective of their campaigns. Incumbent campaigns usually focus more on reinforcing and mobilizing existing bases of support than on winning new ones. The overwhelming advantages that most members of Congress possess make incumbency an accurate predictor of election outcomes in more than nine out of ten House races and three-quarters of all Senate races in which incumbents seek reelection.

Incumbency advantages are sometimes reduced in post-redistricting House elections. This is especially the case when incumbents are forced to compete against one another, run in a newly created district, or compete in a district that has been heavily redrawn, sometimes to their disadvantage. Like challengers, these members must introduce themselves to large numbers of voters who are unfamiliar with their records.

Even in elections that do not follow a redrawing of districts, some incumbents find themselves in jeopardy, and a few challengers have realistic chances of winning. Incumbents who are implicated in a scandal, have cast roll-call votes that are not in accord with constituent opinions, or possess other liabilities need to run more aggressive campaigns. They must begin campaigning early to reinforce their popularity among supporters, to remind voters of their accomplishments in office, and to set the campaign agenda. They also must be prepared to counter the campaigns of the strong challengers who are nominated to run against them and the coordinated grassroots and independent media campaigns that party committees and interest groups wage in support of those challengers. Many incumbents in jeopardy face experienced challengers, some of whom amass sufficient financial and organizational resources to conduct a serious campaign. A few of the challengers capitalize on their opponent's weaknesses and win.

Because most incumbents have established a firm hold on their district, there is little they can do to increase their victory margins. Incumbents as a group, whether Democrat or Republican; Caucasian, Hispanic, African American, or Asian American; old or young; male or female, have tremendously favorable odds of being reelected. Few variables (those identified as such in Table 9-1) have a significant, direct effect on the percentage of the vote that incumbents win. Such characteristics as gender, age, race, ethnicity, and occupation, which

TABLE 9-1

Significant Predictors of House Incumbents' Vote Shares

	Percentage of Vote
Base vote	57.28
District is very different or completely new	−1.96
Partisan bias (per 1-point advantage in party registration)	+0.15
Ideological strength	+0.92
Incumbent implicated in scandal	−3.71
Challenger spending on campaign communications (per $100,000)	−0.69
Incumbent received most endorsements from local media	+5.22
National partisan tide	+2.02

Sources: "2002 Congressional Campaign Study," Federal Election Commission and CQ MoneyLine.

Notes: The figures were generated using ordinary least squares regression to analyze data for general election candidates in major-party contested races, excluding those in incumbent-versus-incumbent races. Complete regression statistics are presented in note 7. $N = 97$.

Chapter 2 showed to be so influential in separating House candidates from the general population, typically have no impact on the votes incumbents receive.[5] Primary challenges by members of their own party rarely harm the reelection prospects of House incumbents who retain the nomination. Moreover, incumbents' targeting strategies, issue stances, and spending on campaign communications and voter mobilization do not significantly increase their share of the vote in the general election.[6] Party and interest group outside campaign efforts also rarely spell the difference between success and defeat in incumbent-challenger races.

The first figure in Table 9-1, labeled the base vote, represents the percentage of the vote that a House incumbent in a typical, two-party contested race would have received if all the other factors were set to zero.[7] That is, a hypothetical incumbent who runs for reelection in a district that was not recently altered by redistricting and is composed of roughly equal numbers of registered Democratic and Republican voters, has developed a reputation as a moderate member of Congress, spends no money, is not endorsed by most local editorial boards, faces a challenger who spends no money, and is in a race not affected by a national partisan tide would win about 57 percent of the vote.

Certain districts and states lend themselves to the election of particular types of candidates. Districts that are heavily affected by redistricting are usually less favorable to incumbents. Incumbents who run in newly drawn districts or ones that are very different from those in which they previously competed typically suffer a net loss of about 2 percentage points of the vote, which is not experienced by incumbents who run for seats that are largely unchanged by redistricting.

Partisanship also is important. In recent congressional elections, the vast majority of voters, more than 90 percent in 2010, cast their ballots for congressional candidates who represent their party.[8] Districts populated mainly by Democratic voters (often urban districts that are home to many lower-middle-class, poor, or minority voters) typically elect Democrats; those populated by Republican voters (frequently rural, suburban, and more affluent districts) usually elect Republicans. The partisan bias of the district (the difference between the percentage of registered voters that belong to a candidate's party and the percentage that belong to the opponent's party) has a positive impact on incumbents' electoral prospects.[9] As the third figure in Table 9-1 indicates, for every 1 percent increase in the partisan advantage that incumbents enjoy among registered voters, they receive a 0.15 percent boost at the polls (controlling for the other factors in the table). A Democratic incumbent who represents a one-sided district, with seventy-five registered Democratic voters for every twenty-five registered Republicans, typically starts out the election with a 7.5 percentage point (a 50-point advantage in party registration multiplied by 0.15) vote advantage over a Democratic incumbent in a district that is evenly split between Democratic and Republican voters. Partisan bias is an important source of incumbency advantage because most House members represent districts that are populated primarily by members of their party. Incumbents who represent districts that are closely divided along partisan lines or have many swing voters are among the most vulnerable in elections in which the political environment favors neither party. They also are the most likely to be swept out of office in a nationalized election that favors the opposing party.

Most incumbents begin the general election campaign relatively well known and liked by their constituents. Many voters have a general sense of where their House member falls on the ideological spectrum. Like Jerrold Nadler, the shoo-in incumbent in New York's 8th district, most House members come from districts made up primarily of individuals who share their party and ideological preferences. These incumbents rarely face a strong general election challenge from the opposing party, though some Democratic members must be concerned with facing a stiff primary test from the left, and their Republican counterparts must be wary of a challenge from the right.[10] It is moderate members of Congress who represent less ideologically consistent, more middle-of-the-road constituencies who are at greatest risk in the general election. They need to build broad electoral coalitions, and they often face challengers who are able to position themselves to compete aggressively for the same swing voters.

In nationalized election years that favor the challenger's party, swing voters may defect in droves. In 2010 their defections contributed to Rep. Allen Boyd's defeat in Florida's 2nd district and to the outcomes of most other House and Senate elections in which Democratic incumbents were defeated.[11] These representational dynamics work to the advantage of staunch liberals, such as Nadler and most Democratic House leaders, and unabashedly conservative Republicans, including most GOP congressional leaders. They collect about 3 points more than do moderate House incumbents of either party.[12]

Of course, not all incumbents begin their reelection campaigns with clean slates. Members of Congress who are caught up in a scandal run the risk of angering or disappointing constituents, attracting strong opposition, or both. Some scandals involve many members of Congress. In a 1992 House banking scandal, for example, revelations that more than 325 House members had made 8,331 overdrafts at the House bank undermined the reelection campaigns of many of them. Other scandals involve only one or a few legislators. Some of these involve extramarital affairs or abuses of office, such as the receipt of vacations, meals, and other gifts from lobbyists. Congressional leaders and other members, such as former representative Carolyn Cheeks Kilpatrick, can pay a price for covering up a scandal or being connected to someone involved in one. Incumbents lose an average of about 4 percentage points at the polls if they are implicated in or closely associated with a scandal.

Scandal, ideology, and district conditions (usually in place before the start of the campaign season) can be important in determining an incumbent's vote share. But most aspects of incumbent campaigning do not have much influence on the outcomes of their races. The targeting approaches that incumbents use and the themes and issues they stress do not significantly affect their vote margins. Nor do the dollars incumbents spend on direct mail; television, radio, and newspaper advertising; or websites, social media, field work, or other communications make a significant contribution to the percentage of the vote that they win.[13]

Following the usual pattern, incumbent spending in 2010 increased in direct response to the closeness of the race.[14] Shoo-ins, such as Nadler, who ran against underfunded challengers, undertook fairly modest reelection efforts by incumbents' standards, assembling relatively small organizations and spending moderate sums of money reaching out to voters. Those who were pitted against well-funded challengers, however, followed Boyd's example and organized high-spending, professionally run campaigns.

Although the communications expenditures and other campaign activities of incumbents are not significantly related to higher vote margins, they are not inconsequential. A more accurate interpretation is that incumbent campaigning generally works to reinforce, rather than to expand, a candidate's existing base of support. Incumbents who are in the most trouble—because they represent marginal districts, have been redistricted in ways that do not favor them, have been implicated in a scandal, have failed to keep in touch with voters, or have cast controversial votes that are out of step with their constituents—usually spend the most. Most either succeed in reinforcing their electoral bases or watch their share of the vote dip slightly from those of previous years. Others watch their victory margins become perilously low. The high-powered campaigns these incumbents wage might make the difference between winning and losing. In a few cases probably no amount of spending would make a difference. Scandal, an adverse political agenda, or some other factors simply put reelection beyond the reach of some House members. Whether an incumbent in a close race wins or loses, however, that individual would undoubtedly have done worse without an extensive campaign effort.

House challengers' expenditures do reduce incumbents' vote shares somewhat. The typical challenger spent roughly $610,000 campaigning in 2010, shaving about 4 percentage points more off the typical incumbent's vote share than a challenger who spent no money or just a few thousand dollars.[15] Strong challengers who ran against weak incumbents were able to raise and spend substantially more. Hopeful challengers committed an average of $1.3 million to campaigning communications, which drove down the portion of the vote won by the typical incumbent in jeopardy by about 9 percentage points. Individual challengers who spent even more generally drew greater numbers of votes away from incumbents, although the impact of campaign spending may diminish in the most expensive races.[16]

Obtaining favorable media coverage can help an incumbent's reelection efforts. Editorial endorsements in local newspapers can be extremely influential because many voters read them and some take them into the voting booth. Incumbents who receive the lion's share of the endorsements from local media outlets are likely to benefit at the polls.[17] Roughly 85 percent of incumbents in races against major-party challengers benefit from this advantage. It typically improves their electoral performance by roughly 5 points over incumbents who do not enjoy such positive relations with journalists. The efforts that House candidates and their press secretaries make to cultivate relationships with news correspondents are clearly worthwhile.

National partisan tides, which are beyond any one candidate's control, can affect how an incumbent fares in an election. The terrorist attacks of September 11, 2001, and the war in Afghanistan encouraged voters to focus on national security, which worked to the advantage of Republicans in 2002 and 2004. The unpopularity of the war in Iraq, growing numbers of American fatalities in the

Middle East, and perceptions of widespread corruption and mismanagement in the Republican-controlled Congress and executive branch hung like an albatross around the necks of GOP candidates in 2006. The economic collapse brought further bad news to Republican incumbents in 2008. However, the same economic woes that harmed the Republicans in 2008 worked against Democratic members of Congress in 2010. National partisan tides gave Republican incumbents a 2-point boost in 2002 and presumably a similar lift in the subsequent election. They worked against GOP House members in 2006 and 2008, but they helped all but two Republican incumbents claim victory in the 2010 general elections. Indeed, candidates, party officials, and opinion leaders associated with both parties, as well as more neutral observers of politics, widely agree that economic unrest was the source of energy behind the tidal wave that washed away large numbers of Democratic members of Congress.[18]

These generalizations hold for the vast majority of incumbent campaigns waged throughout the 1990s and 2000s. However, a relatively small but important group of incumbent-challenger races illustrate the power of outside campaigning. As described in Chapters 4 and 5, the coordinated grassroots and independent media campaigns conducted by political parties and interest groups are, by and large, beyond a candidate's control. These campaigns often involve significant sums and are characterized by barrages of direct mail, broadcast and cable TV spots, radio advertising, phone calls, and other communications directed at voters. These efforts can change the dynamics of individual campaigns because they force candidates to compete with other organizations, as well as with each other, when trying to set the election agenda, influence the political debate, and mobilize their supporters. Party and interest group communications often result in contests becoming more competitive and contentious.

About 33 percent of all major-party contested incumbent-challenger races in 2010 were characterized by a significant amount of independent campaigning by parties, PACs, super PACs, and other groups. Parties and interest groups spent more than $35,000 in independent expenditures, internal communications, and electioneering communications ads in each of them. As demonstrated in Chapter 5, most outside campaigning took place in competitive contests: 17 percent of competitive incumbent-challenger elections witnessed in excess of $1 million in outside spending and 10 percent, including the Boyd-Southerland race, drew more than $2 million. Moreover, there were eighty-seven contests in which party and interest group independent spending exceeded the spending of at least one candidate (almost always the challenger). Among these races were six elections in which outside spending exceeded the total expenditures of both candidates, and thirty in which outside spending intended to help one candidate (including negative ads against an opponent) exceeded that candidate's own spending. In all but two elections, the balance of the outside spending favored the challenger rather than the incumbent.[19]

Party and interest group outside spending has a variety of effects on the dynamics of incumbent-challenger races—few of which work to the advantage of incumbents.[20] First, it directly drives down incumbents' vote shares. Second, it heightens the impact of challenger expenditures while doing nothing to increase the effect of incumbent spending. Third, it results in newspaper endorsements bringing incumbents somewhat fewer benefits, presumably because the plethora of political advertising to which voters are exposed weakens the endorsements' effects, as well as the influence of an incumbent's own campaign expenditures. And fourth, even outside media advertisements intended to help incumbents may not have the desired effect. Similar to incumbent spending, outside spending may add little to an incumbent's vote share because it mainly reinforces the decisions of existing supporters. Moreover, when outside campaigns are "off message"—that is, they are inconsistent with an incumbent's own campaign communications—they can cloud voters' perceptions of the candidates and cost the incumbent votes. In short, outside spending is more likely to harm than help incumbents, who generally win when elections are low-key affairs that are ignored by national party committees and interest groups. This certainly was the case in 2010 when outside spending shifted the balance of expenditures in favor of Republican House candidates in many elections, including some contests in which Democratic incumbents' vote shares hovered at around 50 percent.[21] Leaders of both parties agreed that outside spending was extremely helpful to the many underfunded Republican challengers in these races.[22] By running attack ads focusing on the flagging economy; Democratic incumbents' support for unpopular policy initiatives; and their ties to President Barack Obama, Democratic congressional leaders, and the Washington establishment, outside campaigns reinforced the Republican Party's overall message and freed GOP candidates to focus on more positive communications. Although campaigns are complex efforts with many moving parts, it is safe to conclude that pro-GOP spending had a significant role in bringing about the defeat of many Democratic incumbents in 2010.

HOUSE CHALLENGER CAMPAIGNS

Most challengers begin the general election at a disadvantage. Lacking a broad base of support, these candidates must build one. Challengers need to mount aggressive campaigns to become visible, build name recognition, give voters reasons to support them, and overcome the initial advantages of their opponent. Most challenger campaigns must communicate messages that not only will attract uncommitted voters but also will persuade some voters to abandon their pro-incumbent loyalties in favor of the challenger. The typical House challenger is in a position similar to that of a novice athlete pitted against a world-class sprinter. The incumbent has experience, talent, professional handlers, funding, equipment, and crowd support. The challenger has few, if any, of these assets and has a monumental task to accomplish in a limited amount of time. Predictably, most challengers end up eating their opponent's dust. Still, not every novice athlete or every congressional challenger is destined to suffer the agony of defeat. A strong challenger who is able to assemble the money and organization to devise and carry out a good game plan may be able to win if the incumbent stumbles. The odds of this occurring increase in a nationalized election year that favors the challenger's party.

Even though the vast majority of challengers ultimately lose, the experience and resources that they bring to their races have an impact on their ability to win votes. In short, challenger campaigning matters. The figures in Table 9-2 reveal that challengers' nomination contests, election expenditures, targeting, strategies, campaign messages, and media relations affect their vote shares in meaningful ways.[23] The same is true of national forces that may work to favor the candidates of one party over the candidates of the other.

Table 9-2 shows that a hypothetical House challenger will finish with about 25 percent of the vote—far from victory—under the following circumstances: the candidate runs in a district that is evenly split between registered Republicans and Democrats, is handed a major-party nomination without a primary fight, uses an unorthodox targeting strategy, fails to offer voters a clear choice on the issues, runs a race virtually bereft of candidate campaign spending, receives few endorsements from the local news media, and is in a contest unaffected by national partisan forces.

Challengers who run under more favorable circumstances fare better. In most cases the partisan composition of the district works to the advantage of the incumbent, but a few challengers are fortunate enough to run in districts that include more members of their party. Challengers in districts in which the balance of registered voters favors their party by 10 percentage points begin the general election with a 1.3-point advantage over those who run in neutral districts. Those few challengers who run in districts that favor their party by 20 percent possess an advantage of between 2 and 3 percent of the vote.

Political experience has indirect effects on a challenger's ability to win votes. As explained in Chapters 2 and 3, challengers with office-holding or significant nonelective political experience are more likely than political amateurs to

TABLE 9-2

Significant Predictors of House Challengers' Vote Shares

	Percentage of vote
Base vote	25.29
Partisan bias (per 1-point advantage in party registration)	+0.13
Contested primary	+2.46
Targeted own party members, independents, or both	+2.50
Challenger spending on campaign communications (per $100,000)	+0.31
Opponent spending on campaign communications (per $100,000)	+0.56
Challenger received most endorsements from local media	+5.50
National partisan tide	+2.50

Sources: "2002 Congressional Campaign Study," Federal Election Commission and CQ MoneyLine.

Notes: The figures were generated using ordinary least squares regression to analyze data for general election candidates in major-party contested races. Communications expenditures are expressed in 2010 constant dollars. Complete regression statistics are presented in note 23. $N = 138$.

run when their odds of winning are best, to capture their party's nomination, and to assemble organizations that draw on the expertise of salaried professionals and political consultants. Moreover, political experience and campaign professionalism help challengers obtain recognition as one of their party's top contenders, as demonstrated by their achieving Red to Blue or Young Gun status. All of these factors help them raise money, as Chapter 6 demonstrated. They also help challengers gain free media coverage and endorsements, as well as favorable outside communications by party committees and interest groups, as shown in Chapters 4 and 5. Challenger campaigns that are staffed with experienced political operatives also are presumably better at targeting, message development, communications, and attracting outside spending by parties and interest groups than those run by amateurs.[24]

Contested primaries, which only rarely have negative general election consequences for incumbents, have a positive impact on the prospects of general election challengers for the House. It should be recalled from Chapter 2 that primaries in which an incumbent is challenged are often hotly contested when the incumbent is perceived to be vulnerable, and they are usually won by strategic candidates who know how to wage strong campaigns. The organizational effort, campaign activities, and media coverage associated with contested primaries provide the winners with greater visibility and support than they would have attained had the primary not been contested. The momentum that House challengers get from contested primaries and the incumbent weaknesses that give rise to these primaries in the first place lead to stronger performances in general elections. Challengers who have had to defeat one or more opponents in a primary typically wind up winning between 2 and 3 percentage points more than challengers who were merely handed their party's nomination.

General election campaign strategy is critical. Challengers who target members of their own party, independents, or both gain, on average, between 2 and 3 more points than those who use less conventional strategies, such as targeting all registered voters or some other unorthodox approach. Challengers who run issue-oriented campaigns that spotlight their policy stances or their opponent's stances and congressional voting record enjoy a 2-percentage-point boost over those who focus on character, political experience, or fail to deliver a clear campaign message. In 2010, for example, Republican challengers benefited from zeroing in on health care reform, the stimulus package, or the Troubled Asset Relief Program, especially when they could hold their opponent accountable for voting for them.[25] The experience of Steve Southerland, who successfully challenged the incumbent, Allen Boyd, is typical. Southerland worked aggressively to turn out his Republican base and swing voters, and appeal to some disgruntled Democrats. His message centered on the economic recession and job losses he attributed to Democrat-backed programs that Boyd voted for in Congress. His campaign slogan "Have you had enough?" helped voters draw sharp distinctions between him and the incumbent. It was particularly appealing to voters who identified with the Tea Party movement.

Not surprisingly, campaign spending is another factor that has a significant impact on the vote shares challengers receive. For every $100,000 that House challengers spent on television, radio, literature, direct mail, mass telephone calls, the Internet, or some other campaign effort, they won an additional 0.25 percent of the vote. Challengers in 2010 spent an average of $610,000 on campaigning, garnering the typical challenger a boost of 1.5 percentage points. Incumbent campaign expenditures, largely a reaction to the closeness of the race and the efforts of strong challengers and their supporters, have an even stronger association with challengers' vote shares.

Large expenditures by both candidates are strongly associated with closely decided incumbent-challenger races. Boyd spent $2.8 million and Southerland spent approximately $842,000 on campaign communications and outreach in their 2010 contest. Campaign spending undoubtedly played an important role in Southerland's 13-percentage-point victory. Low-spending incumbent-challenger campaigns tend to produce very lopsided results. Susan Kone spent less than $25,000 on advertising and outreach to voters in her 50-point loss to the incumbent Nadler, who spent about $265,000 on these activities in their

New York House race. That the typical 2010 House challenger spent less than $700,000 on reaching out to voters helps to explain why so few of them won and why challengers generally fare poorly.

Media relations, which involve a courtship of sorts between candidates and local media outlets, also can have significant consequences for an election. Southerland and the other 5 percent or so of all House challengers who are endorsed by the local press typically watch their vote shares increase between 5 and 6 points. National partisan tides, over which challengers have no control, can be important. The pro-Republican tide of 2002 provided the typical GOP challenger with an extra 2 to 3 percentage points; the Republican tidal wave of 2010 also gave Republican challengers a boost.

How best to allocate scarce financial resources is a constant concern for strategists in challenger campaigns. Are radio or television commercials more effective than campaign literature? How effective is direct mail at influencing voters compared with less precisely tailored and less precisely targeted forms of advertising? Is it worthwhile to invest money in newspaper ads or the grassroots activities commonly referred to as "campaign field work?" Untangling the effects of different types of campaign expenditures is complicated. However, it is possible to estimate the cost-effectiveness of various campaign activities. Direct mail and campaign literature have the strongest association with increases in challengers' vote shares. This is largely because of their low cost, personalized messages, and goal of mobilizing supporters and others who previously indicated an interest in the candidate. Because television ads are considerably more expensive than mail and literature and are targeted with less precision and to broader audiences, they bring somewhat lower direct returns. However, they are very important because they can help set the election agenda and frame the messages that are delivered using other media. Radio ads, which fall between direct mail and television in terms of targeting, can have a positive impact on some challenger races, but they generally do not register as having a significant impact on challengers' vote shares. Newspaper advertisements, purchased by little more than half of all challenger campaigns, are typically a low-priority, low-budget item that provides no net increase in vote returns. Field work is the most labor-intensive form of electioneering and virtually impossible to assess in terms of a cost-benefit analysis. It differs from direct mail and television advertising in that, if done properly, it requires both skillful targeting and a corps of committed campaign workers, usually volunteers. It also is performed in cooperation with parties and interest groups.

Finally, party and interest group outside campaigns can significantly boost a challenger's prospects. Challengers in elections in which the balance of outside spending favors their campaign do substantially better at the polls than challengers in general.[26] In 2010 a substantial number went on to win. Despite the benefits challengers gain from these party and group efforts, some are ambivalent about them, and with good reason. Outside spending takes control away from the campaign and puts it in the hands of others, sometimes blurring the message the campaign wishes to convey or making the election more negative than the candidate would prefer. Moreover, when independent communications deviate from a challenger's message, they have the potential to neutralize the effects of some important elements of challenger strategy, including those associated with voter targeting and campaign advertising, and, as noted earlier, they can cause serious damage when they backfire.

In sum, most House challengers lose because the odds are so heavily stacked against them. Those few who run in favorable or competitive districts, compete against a vulnerable incumbent, assemble the resources needed to communicate with voters, develop and implement a sound campaign strategy that blends partisan targeting with an issue-oriented message, and spend their money wisely win more votes than those who do not. The same is true of those who curry favor with the media and benefit from party and interest group outside campaigning. Despite their situational advantages and shrewd decision making, these challengers rarely win enough votes to defeat an incumbent. The partisan composition of most House districts, the preelection activities that incumbents undertake to cultivate the support of constituents, and their success in warding off talented and well-funded challengers are critical in determining the outcome of most incumbent-challenger races.

Nevertheless, politics is a game that is often played at the margins. Not all House incumbents begin the general election as shoo-ins and go on to win. The few who hold competitive seats, are implicated in scandal, are out of step with their constituents, draw a strong major-party opponent, or are targeted for defeat by the opposing party and independent-spending interest groups often find themselves in a precarious position. Many of these incumbents spend huge sums of money, sometimes to no avail. If the challengers who run against them are able to apply the lessons learned while working in politics (or imparted by a political consultant) and assemble the money and organizational resources to wage a strong campaign, they can put their opponents on the defensive. Challengers have some chance of winning if they set the campaign agenda; carefully target their base and groups of potential supporters; tailor their messages to appeal to those voters; and communicate their messages through paid ads, free media, and strong field operations. Challengers who can attract newspaper endorsements and considerable outside spending by parties and interest groups have even better odds. A win by a challenger is typically the result of both incumbent failure and a strong challenger campaign. Numerous

House members were anxious about their reelection prospects before the 2010 campaign season got under way. Some incumbents retired. Others sought reelection, and more than fifty of those—mostly Democrats—were defeated. The challengers who beat an incumbent were successful primarily as a result of their own efforts, including their successful campaigns for resources and their successful campaigns for votes. Party and interest group outside campaigns and a strong national partisan tide also helped Republican challengers defeat Democratic incumbents in the 2010 general election.

HOUSE OPEN-SEAT CAMPAIGNS

Elections for House open seats are usually won by much smaller margins than incumbent-challenger races. Once a seat becomes open, several factors come into play. The partisanship of the district and the skills and resources of the candidates and their organizations have a greater influence on elections when there is no incumbent who can draw on established voter loyalties. Because voters usually lack strong personal loyalties to either candidate, campaigning becomes more important. The same is true of local media endorsements and national partisan trends. The factors that significantly affect the outcome of open-seat House races are listed in Table 9-3.[27]

The partisan bias of open seats is important. Candidates who run for open seats where the balance of voter registration favors their party do much better than others. Those who run for open seats in districts where the registration balance favors their party by 10 percent have, on average, a 1.7 percent vote advantage over those who compete in districts with the same number of Democrats and Republicans.

Campaign strategy is critical to the outcome of an open-seat contest. Campaigns that target party members, independents, or both typically increase their votes by 5 percentage points over those that do not consider partisanship when formulating their targeting plans. Candidates' issue positions also have a large impact. Unlike incumbents, open-seat candidates do not have to defend a congressional voting record, nor are they in a position to emphasize their performance in office. Unlike challengers, they cannot attack a sitting House member for failing to adequately tend to constituents' needs, nor can they use a member's congressional roll-call votes to contrast the incumbent's issue positions with their own. Open-seat candidates are usually best served when they put together an issue-based message that is powerful enough to inspire a strong turnout by voters who identify with their party and to win the support of swing voters. In 2002 Republicans who campaigned on homeland security,

TABLE 9-3

Significant Predictors of House Open-Seat Candidates' Vote Shares

	Percentage of Vote
Base vote	32.58
Partisan bias (per 1-point advantage in party registration)	+0.17
Targeted own party members, independents, or both	+4.68
Republican ran on Republican issues	+7.42
Open-seat candidate spending on campaign communications:	
$400,000	+21.02
$600,000	+22.93
$800,000	+23.21
$1,000,000	+23.91
$2,000,000	+26.09
$3,000,000	+27.36
Opponent spending on campaign communications:	
$400,000	−16.91
$600,000	−17.93
$800,000	−18.66
$1,000,000	−19.23
$2,000,000	−20.98
$3,000,000	−22.01
Candidate received most endorsements from local media	+6.70
Republican national partisan tide	+8.52

Sources: "2002 Congressional Campaign Study," Federal Election Commission and CQ MoneyLine.

Notes: The figures were generated using ordinary least squares regression to analyze data for general election candidates in major-party contested races, excluding those in incumbent-versus-incumbent races. Communications expenditures are expressed in 2010 constant dollars. Complete regression statistics are presented in note 27. $N = 50$.

defense-related issues, or taxes—issues that are favorably associated with the GOP—performed better than Republicans who focused on other issues. In 2006 Democrats who focused on the Iraq War, jobs and the economy, health care reform, government corruption and mismanagement, and other Democratic position and government performance issues also were very successful in garnering votes. In 2008 and 2010 jobs and the economy were once again critical, working to the advantage of Democrats in the former year and Republicans in the latter. This is to be expected given the salience of these issues and the impact they had on individuals' voting decisions (discussed in Chapter 4). In 2010 Illinois Republican Robert Dold was in a strong position to mobilize his party's base and win the support of swing voters because he championed retaining the tax cuts enacted during George W. Bush's administration and instituting business tax credits to stimulate economic growth and job creation. His Democratic opponent, Dan Seals, was disadvantaged by his campaign's focus on abortion rights, gay rights, and increased funding for Medicare and other social safety net programs, which were secondary concerns to most voters.[28]

Candidates in open-seat elections stand to make large gains in name recognition and voter support through their campaign communications. In contrast to candidates in incumbent-challenger races, both candidates in open-seat elections clearly benefit from spending on campaign advertising and voter contact. A campaign's initial expenditures are particularly influential because they help voters become aware of a candidate and his or her message. Further expenditures, although still important, have a lower rate of return; as more voters learn about the candidates and their issue positions, the effects of campaign spending diminish. An open-seat candidate facing an opponent who spends virtually no money gains, on average, an additional 21 percent above the base vote of 33 percent for the first $400,000 spent to communicate with voters. That same candidate gains an additional 1.9 percent of the vote (a total increase of almost 23 percent) when spending is increased by $200,000. An expenditure of $3 million would increase a candidate's vote share by about 1.2 percent over the amount gained for the first $2 million in communications expenditures—a smaller increase in votes than is associated with increasing spending from $400,000 to $600,000.

Lopsided spending is unusual in open-seat contests; rarely does a candidate spend $3 million, $2 million, $600,000, or even $100,000 against an opponent who spends virtually nothing. More often, these elections feature two well-funded opponents. When the campaigns spend nearly the same amount on communications, their expenditures come close to offsetting each other. Once the campaigns have completely saturated the airwaves, overstuffed the mailboxes, and left about half a dozen or so voicemail and e-mail messages, the quality and timing of their communications may have a bigger influence on the election outcome than the dollars each ultimately spends to reach out to voters. In the 2010 race between Dold and Seals, for example, each candidate spent about $1.7 million on campaign communications, making it likely that Dold's 2-point victory was the result of something other than campaign spending.[29]

The amounts that open-seat campaigns spend on most forms of campaign communication are positively related to the number of votes they receive, but the precise effects of the communications are difficult to evaluate because relatively few open-seat contests take place in any given election year. It is possible, however, to make some generalizations about the relative importance of the techniques open-seat candidates use to get out their message. Open-seat candidates spend substantial portions of their campaign budgets on campaign literature, direct mail, TV, and radio. Of these, literature, direct mail, and radio—which can be directed to specific individuals or voting blocs—have the greatest electoral impact.[30]

The mass media also play an important role in open-seat House races. Experienced politicians who have strong campaign organizations and run for open seats in districts that are made up mostly of voters who belong to their party usually receive better treatment from the media than do their opponents. Open-seat candidates, such as Dold, who win the endorsements of the local press typically pick up an additional 7 percent at the polls.

The partisan tides that lift many House candidates in incumbent-challenger races have an even greater influence on campaigns for open seats. Republican open-seat candidates in 2002 benefited from an 8- to 9-point boost in their vote shares, giving them a considerable edge over their Democratic opponents. Eight years later, the tsunami that took with it many House Democratic incumbents also gave many Republican candidates for open seats a substantial boost. A favorable issue agenda, a highly motivated Republican base, and an energetic turnout by Tea Party voters helped the GOP capture fourteen open seats previously occupied by Democrats, while only one Democrat managed to wrest an open seat from the Republicans.

Competitive open-seat contests usually witness substantial party and interest group outside campaign activity. During the 2010 elections 59 percent of these contests attracted more than $35,000 in outside spending, 44 percent attracted more than $1 million, and 30 percent drew in excess of $2 million. Moreover, in thirteen of forty-one two-party contested open-seat races, party and interest group outside spending exceeded the spending of at least one candidate. Among these races were three elections in which outside spending exceeded the total expenditures of both candidates and ten in which outside spending intended to help one candidate (including negative ads against an opponent) exceeded that candidate's own spending. Voters in Illinois' 10th congressional district, for example, were exposed to appreciably more campaign activities than voters nationally in 2010. In addition to the communications and mobilization efforts of the Seals and Dold campaigns, some nineteen organizations also sought to influence the decisions of voters. The top spenders supporting Seals were the Democratic Congressional Campaign Committee, America's Families First Action Fund, and several labor unions. Leading the effort to help Dold were the American Action Network, the National Republican Congressional Committee, the New Prosperity Foundation, and the U.S. Chamber of Commerce. Most of these groups' expenditures occurred during the last few weeks before the election. One of the main effects of outside spending is that even many of the least politically engaged voters learn something about the election; another effect is that most voters become weary of being bombarded with negative advertisements and look forward to the election being over.

Just as party and interest group coordinated grassroots and independent media campaigns can change the dynamics of incumbent-challenger races, they can influence open-seat elections.[31] Outside spending rewards candidates whose campaigns target on the basis of partisanship and emphasize party-owned issues. Republicans campaigning in contests featuring a high volume of party and interest group activity in 2002 and 2004 reaped greater electoral benefits from emphasizing pro-Republican issues than GOP candidates who did so in elections free of outside spending. The same lesson appears to have applied in 2010: Republican open-seat candidates in races that attracted a great deal of outside spending and who campaigned on Republican position issues, such as tax cuts or reducing the role of government, received a boost at the polls that was not enjoyed by GOP candidates whose campaigns also stressed these issues but whose elections did not involve much party or interest group outside campaigning. This suggests outside campaigning can help open-seat candidates ride the wave in a nationalized election. That is, candidates who belong to the ascendant party benefit when they, party committees, and other groups emphasize campaign themes that are consistent with the national political agenda.

SENATE CAMPAIGNS

The small number of Senate elections that occur in a given election year and the differences in the size and politics of the states in which they take place make it difficult to generalize about Senate campaigns. Nevertheless, a few broad statements are possible. Chief among them is that incumbents possess substantial advantages over challengers. The advantages of incumbency in Senate elections are similar to those it bestows in House elections. Most Senate incumbents enjoy fundraising advantages, greater name recognition, and more political experience—particularly in running a statewide campaign—than their opponents.

Yet the advantages that senators enjoy are not as great as those that House members have over their opponents. Most Senate challengers and open-seat candidates then House nonincumbents have previously served in the House, as governor, or in some other public capacity. Thus, they tend to be more formidable opponents than their House counterparts. Their greater previous political experience helps Senate challengers assemble the financial and organizational resources and gain the media coverage needed to run a competitive campaign.[32]

One of the most important differences between Senate and House contests is the effect of incumbent expenditures on election outcomes. Although increased challenger spending has a negative effect on incumbents' margins in both Senate and House elections, it is only in Senate races that spending by incumbents is positively related to the number of votes they receive. Incumbent expenditures on campaign communications are not as important as challenger expenditures, but the amounts that both sides spend are influential in determining the victor in Senate elections.[33] This difference is due to four major factors. First, because Senate challengers are usually better qualified, Senate elections tend to be closer than House contests. Second, senators' six-year terms and greater responsibilities in Washington result in their meeting less frequently with voters than House members do, so the bonds that they establish with their constituents are not as strong. Third, senators' larger constituencies also have a similar effect on their constituent relations. Fourth, the greater diversity of their constituencies means that senators are more likely to offend some voters in the course of their legislative activities. Because of these differences, campaign spending and campaigning in general are more likely to affect the electoral prospects of Senate than House incumbents.

Senate elections bear further comparison with House contests. Scandal and the partisan bias of the constituency influence the results of elections for both the upper and lower chambers. Senate campaigns' targeting strategies and issue selection also are believed to be important.[34] Primary challenges, which have no detrimental effects on the election prospects of House incumbents, harm those of incumbents in Senate campaigns.[35]

The 2010 Senate election in Nevada illustrates many of the preceding generalizations. In particular, it highlights how a masterful campaign can enable an endangered incumbent to overcome a superior-funded challenger in a hostile environment.[36] Despite the harsh economic decline in Nevada and the nation, widespread anger at the federal government and the Democrats for failing to quickly reverse the situation, and millions of dollars in independent media advertising blaming the situation on Democratic leaders, including Senate majority leader Harry Reid, Reid was able to defeat former Republican state legislator and Tea Party candidate Sharron Angle in one of the most costly and closely watched elections in the nation. He did so in a state that routinely elects statewide officeholders of both parties.

Reid's path to victory began in the primary season. Facing token opposition, he easily defeated three Democrats, none of whom raised more than $5,000. Things were not so straightforward in the Republican nominating contest. Scared off by Reid's aggressive fundraising and concerned about the sex scandal enveloping Nevada GOP senator John Ensign, none of the state's top-tier

Republicans entered the race. This left a dozen lesser candidates to battle for the nomination. The race narrowed to Sue Lowden, a television reporter who had served a term in the state Senate and as state party chair, and Angle. Although Lowden was the preferred candidate of the state's Republican establishment, her campaign began to self-destruct after a video tracker recorded her responding to a question about health care reform by suggesting that people should barter chickens to pay for needed medical attention. Attack ads against Lowden by the Club for Growth and the Tea Party Express helped seal Angle's primary victory.

Reid's general election strategy was to frame the race as a contest between himself and an opponent he characterized as too extreme and dangerous to serve in the Senate. His campaign went to great lengths to mobilize its base and attract the support of demographic groups it considered essential to building a winning coalition. In addition to scheduling appearances by President Obama, former president Bill Clinton, and other party luminaries to excite core Democrats, his campaign brought in other party leaders to energize specific voting blocs. These included U.S. Secretary of Commerce Gary Locke, to appeal to Asian Americans, and Dolores Huerta, cofounder of the United Farm Workers of America, to solidify the backing of Hispanics. The campaign also took full advantage of the many mistakes made by Angle and her campaign team, portraying them as evidence of her being too out of step to represent Nevadans in the Senate.

In contrast to Reid, Angle sought to make the election a referendum on the poor economy, the growth of the federal government, and Reid's leadership in Washington. Her campaign targeted Republicans, Tea Party voters, and other conservatives, as well as independents. Like Reid, she benefited from visits by prominent party leaders. As is often the case with second-tier candidates who have not previously contested a statewide race, Angle made some missteps. As noted in previous chapters, there was a great deal of tension within her campaign organization, she had a tendency to go off message, and some of her campaign ads—particularly those concerned with immigration—resulted in unwanted controversy. An independent expenditure by a Republican-allied group that urged Hispanics not to vote helped to reinforce Reid's argument that Angle was an extremist. Simply stated, Angle's campaign was not as well run as Reid's.

Political parties and interest groups were very active in the Nevada race, as discussed in Chapters 4 and 5. In addition to the millions in contributions, coordinated expenditures, and party-connected contributions they provided directly to candidates, party committees spent millions on independent expenditures and transfers to state party organizations. These financed television, radio, and direct mail advertisements as well as voter identification, registration, and get-out-the-vote efforts. Interest groups also directly contributed millions of dollars through their PACs, but they spent substantially more on independent media campaign ads and coordinated grassroots activities. Indeed, parties and interest groups were responsible for about $18.7 million in outside spending, roughly 26 percent of the total spent in the race.

It is impossible to tell exactly what contributions specific factors made to the outcome of a race decided by less than 6 percentage points. The candidates' experience, public records, and the quality of their campaigns were important. The same is true of the efforts of political parties and interest groups.

CLAIMING CREDIT AND PLACING BLAME

Once the election is over, candidates and their campaign staffs have a chance to reflect. Their main interest, naturally, is what caused the election to turn out as it did. Winners and losers have very different ideas about what factors influence congressional election outcomes. Some differences are obvious. Losing candidates almost always obsess about money, particularly the funds that they and their opponents spent on campaigning. Unsuccessful candidates for the House generally considered the funds that they and their opponents spent to have been very important in determining the outcome of their elections, whereas the winners believed money was only moderately important (see Table 9-4).[37] Defeated candidates also placed greater emphasis on the impact of party and interest group spending on their elections than did winners. Some had strong beliefs about the influence of the parties' and groups' outside campaigns.

Unsuccessful candidates frequently assert that if they had had more money—or if their party or interest group allies had spent more money on their behalf—they would have reached more voters and won more votes. The almost 3 to 1 advantage in campaign resources that victorious House incumbents had over losing challengers in 2010 supports their point (see Figure 9-1). The spending advantage that successful open-seat candidates had over their opponents is not as large, but it also lends credence to the view that money matters. The fact that successful House challengers in two-party contested races spent almost $1.8 million, on average, in the 2010 elections demonstrates that the cost of admission is fairly high.

The patterns of spending in competitive House elections further reinforce the importance of money (see Figure 9-2). Moreover, they show that some of these contests receive substantial attention from outside groups. Incumbents in jeopardy who managed to hold on to their seats attracted, on average, about

TABLE 9-4

Winners' and Losers' Opinions of the Determinants of House Elections

	Winners	Losers
Money spent by campaigns	2.95	3.90
Money spent by political parties	2.11	2.97
Money spent by advocacy groups	1.79	2.60
Candidate's image and personality	4.53	3.53
Incumbent's record	4.10	2.79
Incumbency advantages	3.51	4.51
Local issues	3.53	2.74
National domestic issues	3.69	3.05
Foreign affairs and defense	3.36	2.96
Party loyalty	3.11	3.65
Newspaper endorsements	2.23	2.25
U.S. Senate election	1.96	2.58
State or local elections	1.96	2.55
Negative campaigning	1.86	2.04
Debates	1.72	1.85
Political scandal in own race	1.36	1.47

Sources: "1998 and 2002 Congressional Campaign Studies," Center for American Politics and Citizenship, University of Maryland.

Notes: Candidates and campaign aides were asked to assess the importance of each factor on the following scale: 1 = not important; 2 = slightly important; 3 = moderately important; 4 = very important; 5 = extremely important. The values listed are arithmetic means. Figures for the impact of incumbents' record and incumbency advantages exclude responses from candidates and campaign aides from open seats. Figures are for general election candidates in major-party contested races, excluding those in incumbent-versus-incumbent races. See note 37 for more details.

$116,000 in favorable outside spending.[38] These candidates also benefited from close to $62,000 that outside organizations spent to harm their opponents. The hopeful challengers who lost to these candidates benefited from similar amounts of outside spending, which helped them compensate for the better than 70 percent spending advantage enjoyed by the incumbents. Candidate and outside spending were considerably higher in the races in which a challenger defeated a House incumbent, such as the Southerland-Boyd contest, but even in those cases incumbents and their allies typically held a substantial advantage. Not surprisingly, elections between open-seat prospects, who are usually equally matched in many respects, draw considerable outside spending. Still, the winners of these contests usually are advantaged in terms of their own spending and that of outside groups over those they defeated. The patterns for Senate elections further corroborate the importance of money in elections and

FIGURE 9-1

Average Campaign Expenditures in Competitive House Elections in 2010

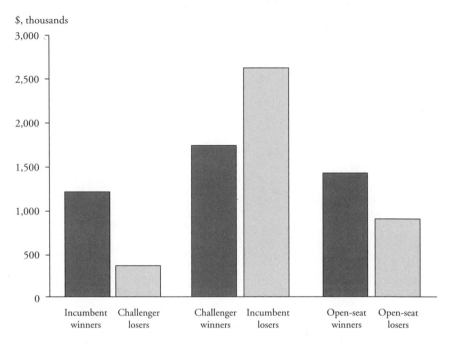

Source: Compiled from Federal Election Commission data.

Notes: Figures are for major-party candidates in contested general elections. They include candidate expenditures and party coordinated expenditures; they exclude funds candidates donated to other candidates and party committees. $N = 812$.

substantiate the claim that outside spending can help level the playing field between candidates (see Figure 9-3). In 2010 outside spending was particularly important in contests in which a Senate challenger emerged victorious. It also enabled the open-seat contestants who eventually won their contests to reach spending parity with those whom they defeated.

There are differences of opinion about the extent to which factors other than money influence election outcomes. Successful House candidates have a strong tendency to credit their victories to their own attributes and matters largely under their campaign's control. They believe that the candidate's image was the most important determinant of their election. Successful incumbents credit their record in office next. They also acknowledge the advantages they derived from incumbency.

FIGURE 9-2

Average Campaign Spending in Competitive House Elections in 2010

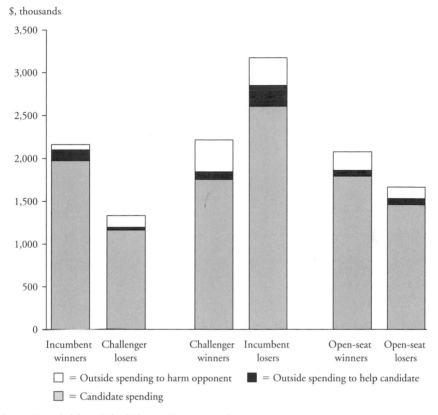

$, thousands

Incumbent winners Challenger losers Challenger winners Incumbent losers Open-seat winners Open-seat losers

□ = Outside spending to harm opponent   ■ = Outside spending to help candidate
□ = Candidate spending

Source: Compiled from Federal Election Commission data.

Notes: Figures are for major-party candidates in contested general elections. Candidate spending includes candidate expenditures and party coordinated expenditures (over which candidates exercise some influence); they exclude funds candidates donated to other candidates and party committees. Outside spending includes independent expenditures and interest group internal communications to members, either to help a candidate or harm an opponent. $N = 318$.

The winners of House races rank issues as moderately to very influential in producing the outcomes of their elections. Democratic winners in recent elections believed that they benefited from focusing on Social Security, Medicare and health care generally, education, the environment, and other traditional Democratic issues. Many successful Republican candidates believed they helped themselves by concentrating on tax cuts, the deficit, moral values, national defense, and other issues that have traditionally formed the core of

FIGURE 9-3

Average Campaign Spending in Competitive Senate Elections in 2010

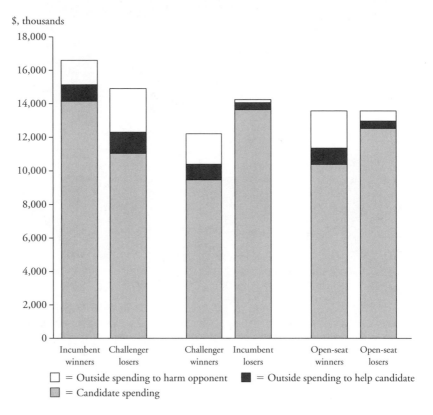

$, thousands

Source: Compiled from Federal Election Commission data.

Notes: Figures are for major-party candidates in contested general elections. Candidate spending includes candidate expenditures and party coordinated expenditures (over which candidates exercise some influence); they exclude funds candidates donated to other candidates and party committees. Outside spending includes independent expenditures and interest group internal communications to members, either to help a candidate or harm an opponent. $N = 36$.

the GOP's communication efforts. During the 2006 and 2008 elections Democrats felt they were advantaged by the economy and various government performance issues, whereas it was the Republicans who reaped the benefits of these issues in 2010. Candidates of both parties considered local concerns to have been roughly as important as national domestic issues, followed by foreign affairs or defense. Winning candidates rate the partisan loyalties of voters in their districts as moderately important.

Finally, winners generally believe newspaper endorsements, the influence of U.S. Senate, state, or local elections, as well as; negative campaigning, debates, and political scandal, were much less important to the outcome of their contests. The winners' opinions reflect a tendency to attribute their victories to their own efforts and the wisdom of voters.[39] These beliefs stand in stark contrast to political science theories that suggest that congressional election outcomes are primarily a function of national conditions and events.[40]

Defeated House candidates have very different views about what caused their elections to conclude as they did. First and foremost, losing challengers point to the incumbent's perquisites of office, which they believe to have been very to extremely important. Next, unsuccessful candidates point to money—specifically, their opponent's financial advantages. They rank the partisanship of voters in their district third. Candidate images come in fourth, followed by national domestic issues, foreign affairs and defense-related issues, and party and interest group spending.

Unsuccessful candidates tend to believe that local issues and debates are less important than these other factors. They place more emphasis on the influence of Senate, state, and local elections than do winners. Defeated candidates prefer to rationalize their defeats by blaming them on factors over which neither they nor their campaigns had any control.[41] Boyd, for example, blamed Democratic leaders, particularly Democratic House Speaker Nancy Pelosi, for moving the Democratic agenda too far to the left for his conservative Florida constituents. The challenger Kone of New York was highly critical of the local media for failing to adequately cover her race.[42] The losers' views bear similarities to political science theories that downplay the importance of individual candidates and campaigns.[43]

Senate candidates have a somewhat different view of the causes of their election outcomes than do House contestants. Both the winners and losers in Senate contests emphasize factors that are largely under their control. Contestants generally believe that the images they projected to the voters were the number-one determinant of the election outcome. Winners typically maintain that candidate imagery was extremely important, whereas losers believe it was moderately important. Winners are more likely to emphasize the importance of issues, ranking them second only to imagery. Losing challengers, conversely, believe that the advantages of office holding are substantially more important. Winning and losing incumbents are equally likely to view incumbency as a two-edged sword, agreeing that the anger that many voters direct at Washington reduces their vote margins.

Senate incumbents place greater emphasis on the importance of their voting records than do Senate challengers, but both acknowledge that job performance was at least a moderately important determinant of the outcome of Senate elections. Both winners and losers also place moderate importance on the partisan loyalties of state voters. Senate candidates attribute less influence to debates, negative campaigning, local issues, and state and local elections than do House contestants.

SUMMARY

The efforts that candidates make to communicate with voters can have an impact on congressional elections, but they are especially important for House challengers and open-seat contestants. Challengers who carefully target their campaign resources, run on issues that draw distinctions between themselves and the House members they seek to unseat, spend significant sums on campaign advertising and voter mobilization, and win local media endorsements can significantly increase the number of votes they receive. House challengers who must defeat an opponent to secure their party's nomination, who run in districts that have many members of their party, who oppose vulnerable incumbents, and who attract significant outside campaigning by their party and supportive interest groups also increase their share of the vote. House incumbents can do little to substantially increase their standing in the polls. The efforts they make to serve their constituents and deter a strong challenger result in most incumbents' beginning and ending their campaigns with a commanding lead. Most House incumbent campaign spending, like most incumbent fundraising, is driven by the threat that an opponent poses and directed at solidifying the candidate's existing support. Campaigns for House open seats are usually very competitive. Voter targeting, issue selection, and candidate communications can be decisive in these races, even in districts that are inundated by outside campaign advertisements aired by parties and interest groups. Senate elections bear many similarities to House contests, but they are usually both more expensive and more competitive. Moreover, although contested primaries hurt Senate incumbents and incumbents' spending has a positive impact on their vote shares, these factors do not have the same effects on House incumbents' shares of the vote.

Congressional campaigners have divergent views about the causes of their election outcomes. Successful campaigners credit their candidates' abilities and their organizations' strategic and tactical efforts for their wins. House losers focus on money, incumbents' perks of office, voter partisanship, and other factors outside of their control. Senate losers are somewhat more likely to acknowledge that candidate characteristics and some aspects of their campaigns contributed to their loss.

CHAPTER TEN

Elections and Governance

"The election is over, and now the fun begins."[1] Those were the words of one new House member shortly after being elected to Congress. Others have more sober, if not more realistic, visions of what lies ahead. Although getting elected to Congress is difficult, especially for those who have to topple an incumbent, staying there also requires great effort. The high reelection rates that members of Congress enjoy are not guarantees; they are the results of hard work, the strategic deployment of the resources that Congress makes available to its members, and the campaign dynamics discussed in previous chapters.

This chapter addresses the question: What impact does the electoral process have on the activities of members of Congress and the operation of Congress as a policy-making institution? It examines the efforts that members of Congress make to stay in office and the resources and strategies they use to shore up their electoral coalitions and participate in the legislative process. First, I discuss the goals and activities of members of Congress and their congressional staffs. I then discuss the committees, issue caucuses, party organizations, and other groups that influence congressional activity. Finally, I comment on the policy-making process.

THE PERMANENT CAMPAIGN

As locally elected officials who make national policy, members of Congress almost lead double lives. The main focus of their existence in Washington, D.C., is framing and enacting legislation, overseeing the executive branch, and carrying out other activities of national importance. Attending local functions, ascertaining the needs and preferences of constituents, and explaining their

Washington activities are what legislators do at home. Home is where members of Congress acquire their legitimacy to participate in the legislative process. The central elements of legislators' lives both at home and in Washington are representing the voters who elected them, winning federally funded projects for their state or district, and resolving difficulties that constituents encounter when dealing with the federal government. The two aspects of members' professional lives are unified by the fact that much of what representatives do in Washington is concerned with getting reelected, and a good deal of what they do at home directly affects the policies and interests they seek to advance in Washington.[2] Some reelection activities, including fundraising and meeting with political supporters, occur in both locations. In a great many respects, the job of legislator resembles a permanent reelection campaign.

Members of Congress develop home styles that help them to reinforce or expand their bases of electoral support. One common element of these home styles concerns how legislators present themselves to voters. Members build bonds of trust between themselves and voters by demonstrating that they are capable of handling the job, that they care about their constituents, and that they are living up to their campaign promises.[3]

A second component of home style is concerned with discussing the Washington side of the job. Members describe, interpret, and justify what they do in the nation's capital to convey the message that they are working relentlessly on their constituents' behalf.[4] Many respond to the low opinion that people have of Congress by trying to separate themselves from the institution in the minds of voters. Members frequently portray themselves as protectors of the national interest locked in combat with powerful lobbyists and feckless colleagues.

Members of Congress and their staffs spend immense amounts of time, energy, and resources advertising the legislator's name among constituents, claiming credit for favorable governmental actions, and taking strong but often symbolic issue positions to please constituents.[5] Their offices provide them with abundant resources for these purposes. House members are entitled to roughly $1.5 million for office expenses annually, including funds for staff, travel, and one or more district offices. They also get a suite of offices in the Capitol complex and virtually unlimited long-distance telephone privileges. Members who are assigned to certain committees, occupy committee chairs, or hold party leadership positions receive extra staff, office space, and operating funds. Senators are allowed even greater budgets, reflecting their larger constituencies and the greater responsibilities associated with representing an entire state. Senators' staffs, office space, and budget allocations are determined by their state's population and by their committee assignments. The annual administrative and clerical allowance for a senator ranges from $3.1 million to $4.9 million.[6]

Although few legislators consume all the resources they are allocated, many come close. The average House member hires approximately fifteen full-time aides; the average senator hires about thirty-four.[7] Among these aides are administrative assistants, legislative assistants, legislative correspondents, schedulers, office managers, caseworkers, press secretaries, receptionists, staff assistants, and interns. Each performs a different set of functions, but nearly all are somehow related to building political support among constituents. Legislative correspondents and legislative assistants are highly conscious of the electoral connection when they send franked mail to constituents or assist with their member's legislative agenda. Caseworkers help constituents resolve problems with the federal bureaucracy knowing that their performance can directly affect the reelection prospects of the legislator for whom they work. Receptionists, staff assistants, and schedulers are well aware that the tours they arrange for visitors to Washington contribute to the support their member maintains in the district. Those who forget that constituents come first are quickly reminded of this by the member's administrative assistant, who is responsible for making sure that the office runs smoothly and frequently serves as the member's chief political adviser.

The most reelection-oriented staffers tend to be congressional press secretaries (sometimes called communications directors). Most members of Congress have at least one press secretary, and some have two or more aides on their communications team.[8] The press secretary is the chief public relations officer in a congressional office. Press secretaries write newsletters and press releases and are heavily involved in crafting the targeted mass mailings that most legislators send to constituents. They also help produce the content of radio ads, television spots, website postings, and social media communications.[9] Press secretaries help organize town hall meetings, arrange interviews with correspondents, and disseminate transcripts and videotapes of their boss's floor and committee speeches. A good press secretary is often able to arrange for local media outlets to print or air a legislator's remarks verbatim or with minimal editing.

Many factors led to the emergence of the press secretary as a key congressional aide, including the election since the mid-1970s of highly media-conscious members, increased television coverage of politics, the opening of Congress to greater media scrutiny, the growth in the size of the congressional press corps, and the availability of new communications technologies. These changes created both pressures and opportunities to increase the public relations side of congressional offices. Members of Congress, who work in a resource-rich institution, responded by allowing themselves to hire specialized staff who could help them advance their political careers.

Congress also has allowed its members to exploit new technologies to firm up their relations with voters. Legislative aides use computerized databases to target large volumes of mail to specific audiences. Information about constituents who write, telephone, e-mail, or contact their legislator using social networking sites is routinely entered into a database that includes the constituent's name, contact information, and the subject of his or her communication. These individuals are then sent periodic updates on what their legislator is doing in the area of concern. Constituents who contact members' offices using one communications medium may receive correspondence through that and a variety of other media.

Subsidized House and Senate recording studios and party-owned recording facilities also help legislators reach out to voters. Many members use the studios to record radio shows and television briefings or to edit floor speeches for local media outlets. Some make use of satellite technology to hold live "town meetings" with constituents located on the other side of the country. Streaming video that is posted on the member's website or disseminated via social media is among the latest tools legislators use to stay in touch with supporters.

A DECENTRALIZED CONGRESS

The candidate-centered nature of congressional elections provides the foundation for an individualized, fragmented style of legislative politics. Legislators are largely self-recruited, are nominated and elected principally as a result of their own efforts, and know that they bear the principal responsibility for ensuring their own reelection. Local party organizations, Washington-based party committees, political action committees, and other groups and individuals may have helped convince them to run for office and assisted with fundraising and campaign communications, but politicians arrive in Congress believing that their election is a direct result of the efforts they made on their own.

Reelection Constituencies

Legislators' first loyalties are to their constituents, and most members staff their offices, decide which committee assignments to pursue, and choose areas of policy expertise with an eye toward maintaining voter support. Campaign contributors, including those who live outside a legislator's district or state, form another important constituency. Local elites and interest groups that provide campaign support or political advice routinely receive access to members of Congress, further encouraging legislators to respond to forces outside of the institution rather than within.[10] Other personal goals, including advancing specific policies, accruing more power in the legislature, or positioning themselves to run for higher office, also have a decentralizing effect on the legislative process.[11] Much of the work done to advance these goals—conducting policy research, drafting bills, attending committee meetings, overseeing the bureaucracy, maintaining a media presence, and meeting with constituents and lobbyists— is done by staffers who owe their jobs and their loyalties to individual legislators more than to the institution.[12] This, in turn, makes their bosses less dependent on congressional leaders and encourages members to march to their own beat.

Congressional Committees

The dispersal of legislative authority among 21 committees and their 104 subcommittees in the House, 20 committees and their 68 subcommittees in the Senate, and 4 joint committees in each chamber adds to the centrifugal tendencies that originate from candidate-centered elections. Each committee and subcommittee is authorized to act within a defined jurisdiction. A chair and a ranking member, who are among the majority and minority parties' senior policy experts, head each committee and subcommittee. Each committee and subcommittee has its own professional staff, suite of offices, and budget to help it carry out its business.

The committee system was designed to enable Congress to function more efficiently. Committees enable Congress to investigate simultaneously a multitude of issues and to oversee a range of executive branch agencies. Although committees and subcommittees are Congress's main bodies for making national policy, much of what they do revolves around local issues, the distribution of federal grants and programs, and activities that could boost the reelection of individual legislators. Most members of Congress serve on at least one committee or subcommittee with jurisdiction over policies of importance to their constituents. Members use their committee assignments to develop expertise in policy areas, to actively promote their constituents' interests, to build reputations as champions of popular issues, and to attract political support.

Congressional committees can be categorized according to the objectives they enable members to pursue: reelection, prestige, and policy.[13] *Reelection committees,* such as the House Transportation and Infrastructure Committee and the Senate Environment and Public Works Committee, enable members to work directly on the policy areas that are most important to their constituents.

Reelection committees usually rank high among the assignments that new members of Congress seek. About 60 percent of all first-term House members seek appointment to one or more of them.[14]

Prestige committees give their members influence over legislative activities that are of extraordinary importance to their congressional colleagues. The House and Senate Appropriations Committees are the ultimate prestige, or power, committees. They are responsible for funding federal agencies and programs and have the ability to initiate, expand, contract, or discontinue the flow of federal money to projects located across the country. This gives their members the power to affect the lives of the beneficiaries of those programs and the ability to influence the reelection prospects of legislators who represent them. The House Ways and Means and Senate Finance Committees' jurisdiction over tax-related matters, particularly their ability to give tax breaks to various interests, gives members of these panels sway with their colleagues. Members of prestige committees can help their constituents by acting directly through the committee's work or indirectly by wielding their clout with other legislators. Sitting on one of the appropriating or tax-writing committees is particularly helpful when it comes to raising campaign funds from individuals and PACs associated with a wide array of economic interests.

In contrast to reelection and prestige committees, *policy committees,* such as those that deal with criminal justice, education, or labor issues, are sought by legislators who have a strong interest in a particular policy area. These committees are among the most divisive because they are responsible for some highly charged issues, such as sentencing guidelines, standardized testing requirements, and regulations on workplace equality. Many members use them to stake out conservative or liberal stands. Ambitious legislators who seek a career beyond Congress often use policy committees as platforms for developing a national reputation on salient issues. Thus, the committee system gives expression to the differing goals and viewpoints of representatives and senators and their constituents. By doing so, it decentralizes Congress.

Congressional Caucuses

Congressional caucuses—informal groups of members who share legislative interests—have a similar but less powerful effect on Congress then do committees. Even though caucuses have been prohibited from having their own congressional staffs and office space since the 104th Congress, they continue to function as competing policy centers, alternative suppliers of information, and additional sources of legislative decision-making cues.[15] Groups such as the Congressional Black Caucus and the Congressional

Women's Caucus are recognized as advocates for specific segments of the population. The Northeast–Midwest Senate Coalition, Western States Senate Coalition, and other geographically based groups seek to increase the clout of legislators from particular regions. Steel, auto, and textile caucuses have ties to outside industries and work to promote their interests in Congress. Although they do not hold any formal legislative powers, caucuses further add to the fragmentation of Congress by advancing disparate goals.

Interest Groups

Privately funded interest groups, which form an important part of the political environment with which Congress interacts, also have decentralizing effects on the legislative process. Like caucuses, interest groups are sources of influence that compete with congressional leaders for the loyalty of legislators on certain issues. Roughly 13,000 registered lobbyists work in the Washington area. They are assisted by tens of thousands of others in trade associations, public relations firms, and other agencies who work to advance the political interests of particular groups, and Congress is their number-one target. With expenditures of $3.5 billion in 2010 alone, lobbying is big business in the nation's capital.[16]

Interest groups work to influence the legislative process in many ways. Participation in elections is usually considered an important first step. It should be recalled from Chapter 5 that access-oriented groups make campaign contributions, provide campaign services, or carry out other campaign activities to create or maintain strong relationships with legislators. Ideological groups primarily become involved to elect members of Congress who share their views about the role of government or positions on visceral issues. Groups motivated by both ideological and access concerns participate in elections to influence the membership of Congress and to advance relations with the legislators they consider key to the achievement of their organization's goals.

Once the election is over, groups use many methods to influence the legislative process.[17] Some groups advertise on television, on radio, in newspapers, on the Internet, or through the mail to influence the political agenda or stimulate grassroots support for or opposition to specific legislation. Their efforts often resemble election campaigns in that they involve both targeted and mass communications to influence the policy-making process. Most groups advocate their positions in less visible ways that are designed to play to the legislative and electoral needs of individual members of Congress. Group representatives testify at committee hearings and meet with legislators at their offices and informally at social events. Lobbyists use a variety of forums to provide members and their staffs with technical information, impact statements of how congressional activity (or inactivity) can affect their constituents, and insights into where other legislators stand on the issues. Sometimes they go so far as to draft a bill or help design a strategy to promote its enactment.[18] Many groups supplement these insider techniques with approaches that focus more directly on the electoral connection. Trade and business associations ask their members to contact their legislators. Labor unions, churches, and other groups with large memberships frequently organize telephone and letter-writing campaigns. These communications show members of Congress that important blocs of voters and their advocates are watching how they vote on specific legislation.[19] Interest group–sponsored issue advocacy advertising intended to influence the legislative process or elections has resulted in some groups contributing to the permanent campaigns that consume a significant portion of the professional lives of members of Congress. Interest groups, congressional subcommittee members, and executive branch officials form collegial decision-making groups, which are frequently referred to as "iron triangles," "issue networks," or "policy subgovernments."[20] These issue experts often focus on the minutiae of arcane, highly specialized areas of public policy. Because they form small regimes within a government, they further contribute to the decentralization of Congress.

One of the most powerful groups in American politics is the U.S. Chamber of Commerce. Representing the interests of more than three million businesses across the United States, it has state and local affiliates in every major city, county, and congressional district across the nation. Its members are the owners of predominantly small- and medium-sized businesses that span virtually every economic sector.[21] The Chamber's wealth, reputation, highly skilled and experienced staff, election activities, and lobbying efforts combine with its dispersed, diverse, and relatively elite membership to make it one of the heaviest hitters in American politics. In 2010 alone the group spent more than $132 million to directly lobby the U.S. government. Almost all of these funds were used to pay lobbyists.[22] These expenditures are in addition to the approximately $50 million it spent in 2010 on campaign contributions, electioneering communications, and other election-related efforts. They do not include the millions of grassroots volunteers the Chamber routinely recruits to make its case on policy matters to members of Congress or participate in voter mobilization efforts in election years.

The Chamber presses its pro-business agenda on policies ranging from reform of the banking and financial industries to health care to issues dealing with corporate taxes, international trade, energy, and virtually every area in which government spending, regulations, or revenue collection affect American businesses and business owners. It makes its influence felt in Congress, various parts of the executive branch, and the courts. Its impact is readily visible in the bills it helps to pass, the concessions it gets inserted into bills it is unable to defeat, and the large number of bills it and its allies prevent from reaching the House or Senate floor for a vote. It has helped to create an overall environment in the United States that is much more business friendly than in most other industrialized democracies. Among its most prominent victories were the passage of President George W. Bush's tax cuts in 2001 and the extension of those tax cuts ten years later—with a Democrat in the White House and the Democrats in control of the Senate. Although few organizations can claim the Chamber's electoral or lobbying clout, this example amply demonstrates the resources and techniques that interest groups bring to bear on the legislative process. The disparate demands placed on its members by the interest group community are among the most powerful forces that fragment Congress. They can make it difficult for the legislature to act.

POLITICAL PARTIES AS CENTRALIZING AGENTS

Unlike the structural, organizational, and political factors that work to decentralize Congress, political parties act as a glue—albeit sometimes a weak one—to bond members together. A party's ability to unite its members in support of a legislative program, or even a single bill, depends on the situation, especially the partisan balance of power. A party's prospects for success are better when it controls both chambers of Congress and the White House and the individuals holding these offices share a common agenda and ideological perspective.[23] However, from the 1940s until the turn of the twenty-first century, when many moderates served in both parties, party leaders were able to look beyond the ranks of their own members to build support for important legislation.[24] More recently, the polarization of Congress has resulted in party leaders relying mostly on their own members to enact important bills.[25]

Congressional parties lay the foundation for cooperation among their members through a number of activities. They socialize new members to Congress's norms and folkways, distribute committee assignments, set the legislative agenda, disseminate information, and carry out other tasks that are essential to Congress's lawmaking, oversight, and representative functions. Although they are not the central actors in elections, party committees help individual candidates develop their campaign messages. Party campaign efforts on behalf of individual candidates and election agenda-setting efforts encourage members to vote for bills that are at the core of their party's agenda when Congress is in session.[26] Party issue advocacy and other communications that focus on salient policies outside the campaign season are used to influence legislators' votes on specific bills and, in some situations, damage the reputations of members of the opposing party. Party leaders sometimes turn to allied interest groups to supplement their efforts.

Congressional party leadership organizations are structured similarly to those of legislative parties in other countries. The Democrats and Republicans are headed by a leader in each chamber—the Speaker and minority leader in the House and the majority and minority leaders in the Senate. Each party has several officers and an extensive whip system to facilitate communications between congressional party leaders and rank-and-file legislators. Legislative parties convene caucuses and task forces to help formulate policy positions and legislative strategy. Providing campaign assistance, giving out committee assignments and other perks, setting the congressional agenda, structuring debate, and persuading legislators that specific bills are in the best interests of their constituents and the nation are among the approaches legislative party leaders in representative democracies use to build coalitions.[27]

Nevertheless, U.S. congressional party leaders have less control over the policy-making process than do their counterparts in other Western-style democracies.[28] The persuasive powers of congressional leaders are usually insufficient to sway members' votes when party policy positions clash with the preferences of legislators' constituents and campaign supporters. Recognizing the primacy of the electoral connection, party leaders generally tell legislators to respond to constituents rather than "toe the party line" when the latter could endanger their chances of reelection. The reality is that party leaders and shared partisan motives are important, but other matters also influence congressional behavior.[29] Commonalities in the political outlooks of a party's legislators and similarities among these legislators' constituents may be even more influential.[30]

The nomination of candidates by partisans whose views are ideologically extreme has contributed to the polarization of Congress in recent years. The election of more conservative Republicans, more liberal Democrats, and declining numbers of moderates in both parties encouraged ideologically motivated members of Congress, particularly in the House, to enhance the power of congressional leaders to facilitate the majority party's policy and electoral goals. When strong House Speakers, such as Newt Gingrich, Dennis Hastert, and Nancy Pelosi, exploit these powers, they are able to structure the congressional debate and dominate political outcomes. The result is a dramatic increase in the support members of Congress provide for their party's legislative goals and an equally dramatic decline in their support for the opposing party's agenda.[31]

Party leaders are most able to overcome the forces that fragment Congress when they propose policies that have widespread bipartisan support or when the majority party possesses many more seats than the opposition and proposes popular legislation that advances its core principles. As the historic

104th Congress shows, a change in party control also can act as a catalyst for party unity. Members of the new House and Senate majorities in 1995 were aware that their accomplishments as a party would directly influence their individual reelection campaigns and their party's ability to maintain control of Congress. They empowered their leaders to use extraordinary measures to encourage party discipline. The leadership, in turn, cut the number of House committees, subcommittees, and committee aides; enacted term limits for committee chairs and the Speaker; and made other formal changes aimed at centralizing power. The House Republican leadership also reduced minority party influence by relying on party task forces instead of the normal committee process to write several major bills, using highly restrictive rules to prevent Democrats (and others) from amending them, and holding some roll-call votes open for hours beyond their allotted time until they had enough votes to pass the legislation. Although some of these tactics had been used before, including by Democratic-controlled Congresses, the Republicans took them to new lengths. The GOP's "right in" rather than a "center out" approach to coalition building led to extraordinarily high levels of party unity.[32]

Following their takeover of Congress, the Democrats pledged to return to a more open and inclusive style of legislating that respected the rights of the minority party. However, before House Democrats kept that promise, they used a series of restrictive rules to pass their so-called "6 for '06" policy agenda. The Republicans put forward a similar message and took similar action after taking control of the House in 2010. One of their first acts was to grant the Budget Committee chair unilateral authority to enact spending and revenue limits on interim budgets until 2012 by merely publishing them in the *Congressional Record*. Commenting on the rule, Congress expert Norm Ornstein noted it "takes away the accountability, openness and deliberation that a regular budget process provides. . . . Members, by voting in lockstep to enact a package of rules, will implicitly vote for a budget they have never seen."[33] Turnover in control provides incoming majority party leaders with the opportunities to rewrite some of the rules governing their chamber and unify their members in support of their core policy agenda. It also helps minority party leaders bring together their members in opposition. These aspects of parties that promote centralization have contributed to recent Congresses displaying record levels of party unity.

RESPONSIVENESS, RESPONSIBILITY, AND PUBLIC POLICY

In representative democracies, elections are the principal means of ensuring that governments respond to the will of the people and promote their interests.

Voters hold public officials accountable for their actions and for the state of the nation. Elections are a blunt but powerful instrument of control that enables people to inform their individual representatives, or the government collectively, of how political action or inaction has affected the quality of their lives. Elections are the primary means that democracies use to empower or remove political leaders at all levels of government. Campaigns help to establish standards by which officeholders are judged. Other paths of influence, such as contacting members of Congress and giving campaign contributions, are usually used to advance narrower goals, are more demanding, and are in practice less democratic.

Despite the extensive resources for building and maintaining relationships with constituents that Congress puts at their disposal, its members cannot fully insulate themselves or Congress as an institution from the impact of electoral forces. As the nationalized election of 2010 amply demonstrated, voters occasionally expel large numbers of incumbents, leading to changes in the membership, leadership, operations, and output of Congress. Individuals whose public service is contingent on being reelected often straddle the fuzzy line that demarcates responsiveness and responsibility in government. On some occasions, legislators are highly responsive, functioning as delegates who advance their constituents' views. On others, they take the role of trustee, relying on their own judgment, sometimes informed by cues from their party, to protect the welfare of their constituents or the nation.[34] Responsible legislators must occasionally vote against their constituents' wishes to best serve the interests of the nation.

Election Systems and Public Policy

The type of political system in which public officials serve influences to whom they answer. The U.S. candidate-centered system is unique and encourages elected officeholders to respond to those who helped elect them. It leads to a style of governance that contrasts sharply with the parliamentary systems that govern most democracies. Elections in parliamentary systems focus almost exclusively on political parties and national politics; the characteristics of legislative candidates and local concerns figure little into parliamentary campaigns and individuals' voting decisions.[35] As a result, members of the British Parliament, for example, vote for legislation fashioned to please national rather than local constituencies. They support party initiatives because they know that their prospects for reelection are tied closely to their party's ability to enact its legislative program. The candidate-centered nature of the U.S. system, in contrast, motivates elected officials to respond to the desires of local voters and then consider the appeals of others, including campaign contributors. Pressures by these constituencies sometimes lead members of Congress to oppose legislation backed by their party's leadership. The separation of powers reinforces members' predispositions to represent local voters and campaign supporters when making public policy.

Even when one party controls both chambers of Congress and the White House it may find it difficult to unify its legislators around a policy agenda because these officials can disagree without fear of losing their seats or control of government. Members of the majority party in Congress cast roll-call votes secure in the knowledge that they will remain in office for their full two- or six-year terms even if their party suffers a major legislative defeat. In parliamentary systems, by contrast, members of the governing party (or ruling coalition) understand that a substantial policy defeat can lead to a vote of no confidence and force an election that could turn them out of office in less than a month. Political institutions also influence the behavior of legislators in the minority party. Few members of parliament will cross party lines solely to support a bill that benefits their local constituents, especially if sticking with their party could lead to a smashing legislative defeat for the governing party that is followed by a snap election that could put their party in the majority. Although members of Congress prefer to vote with their party, and usually do, the rules and norms governing elections and representation result in their routinely putting their constituents first when participating in the legislative process.

The fate of President Barack Obama's immigration policy in the 111th Congress demonstrates the difficulties that U.S. parties encounter when they try to overcome the centrifugal forces that influence Congress.[36] Obama, who had made immigration reform one of his major campaign promises, was unable to get his program enacted, despite Democratic majorities in the House and Senate, and his aggressive campaigning for congressional Democrats. Obama urged legislators to enact comprehensive reform that would have provided a path to citizenship for illegal immigrants and strengthened border security, among other things. However, congressional Democrats were unwilling to fully cooperate. Democratic leaders in the House said they would only consider comprehensive immigration reform if the Senate acted first. Sen. Robert Menendez, D-N.J., introduced a reform package encompassing the president's proposals in September 2010, but the bill stalled because of opposition among conservative Democrats and most Republicans. Sensing that an overhaul of immigration policy was not possible, Democratic leaders in both chambers sought to enact some narrower initiatives. They succeeded in passing only one: a $600 million supplemental appropriation for border security. They failed on several others, including one their most high-profile initiatives, the so-called DREAM Act. This bill would have made it possible for illegal immigrants under thirty years of age who had lived in the United States for five or more years to obtain a green card and eventually citizenship. The bill passed the House, but it fell short of the necessary sixty votes to end debate and bring it to a vote in the Senate. Five Democrats voted against cloture and another opted not to vote. All six largely responded to constituent pressures. Had five of these legislators agreed to allow the bill to come to a floor vote, it would have become law.

Most legislative outcomes do not involve a major presidential initiative involving a politically sensitive and salient issue. However, the outcome is often the same. The separation of powers, bicameralism, federalism, and the election system make it difficult for legislators to enact many policy changes, especially long-term ones that affect national programs. Members of Congress who believe that their individual images, issue stances, and public records were decisive in their election are less likely than legislators in party-centered democracies to vote against the opinions of large numbers of local voters or compromise on highly visible issues in order to enact policies advocated by party leaders. House members, who must run for reelection every two years, and members of both chambers who hold competitive seats respond strongly to parochial concerns. This makes it difficult to enact sweeping changes in public policy.

The effects of parochialism are most apparent in distributive politics, which provide tangible benefits to private individuals and groups. Building coalitions in support of spending on roads, bridges, universities, museums, and other projects is relatively simple in a decentralized legislature such as the U.S. Congress. Bill sponsors have traditionally added new programs and projects, referred to as "earmarks," as a way to win enough legislative supporters to pass their plan.[37] A farm advocate who is hoping to subsidize northern sugar beets, for example, might build support for this cause by expanding the number of subsidized crops in a bill to include sugar cane, rice, corn, wheat, and even tobacco, thereby expanding support that began with representatives from Minnesota to include colleagues from Hawaii, Massachusetts, virtually every southern state, and the states of the Midwest.[38] Subsidies for ostrich farmers can be left out because they will not draw many legislative votes, but food stamps can be added to attract the support of legislators from poor urban districts.[39] Trading subsidies for votes is a simple example of logrolling. Other deals are cut over tax breaks, budget votes, and even appointments to the federal judiciary.

Logrolling and other forms of compromise usually do not allow individual legislators to get all the federal "pork" they would like for their constituents. Nevertheless, these compromises enable most legislators to insert enough pork into a bill to claim credit for doing something to help their constituents. A broadly supported distributive bill is an easy candidate for congressional enactment because, like a Christmas tree decorated by a group of friends, all can see their handiwork in it and find something to admire in the finished product.

Distributive politics are problematic because they are practiced with both eyes focused on short-term gain and little attention to long-range consequences. Broadening programs that were originally intended to provide benefits to one group to include others usually causes the programs to become ineffectively targeted, watered down, and too expensive. When large sums are spent to benefit many groups, overall spending rises, and fewer funds remain available to help the group originally selected for assistance. This does little to promote the original goals of a bill and leads to deficit spending.[40] Pork-barrel spending and logrolling, which are at the heart of distributive politics, contribute heavily to the U.S. national debt. Distributive politics exemplify what happens when independently elected officials seek to promote the interests of their constituents and campaign supporters without giving much thought to the effect of their collective actions on the nation. Members of Congress enthusiastically take on the task of distributing pork, and despite attempts at reining in government spending, more than 9,400 earmarks were introduced in fiscal year 2010.[41] Wrangling over tax cuts, military spending, and other federal programs has historically hindered attempts at debt reduction. Recently, the wars in Afghanistan and Iraq, investments in homeland security, and actions taken to address the economic recession also have contributed to the national debt, which had ballooned to more than $14 trillion as of September 2011.

Policy Gridlock and Political Cycles

Parochialism also leads to a reactive style of government and incremental policy making. Congress is better at making short-term fixes than at developing long-term initiatives. Congressional leaders often find it difficult to develop a vision for the future. Since the 1980s House Democrats took steps to outline, publicize, and act on a partisan agenda. Parts of this effort were successful, but much of it was not. Differences in legislators' political philosophies, the diversity of their constituencies, and the limited resources available to party leaders made it difficult to develop and implement a Democratic plan for the nation's future.[42] House Republicans also tried on several occasions since the 1980s to develop a partisan agenda, but prior to the *Contract with America* they, too, enjoyed only limited success.[43]

Under most circumstances, election outcomes, constituent demands, interest group pressures, and White House initiatives support the continuation of the status quo or suggest only small changes in public policies. One of the major reasons for the persistence of the status quo is that the interests that dominate a policy realm at a given time also dominated it earlier. Thus, having already achieved most of their policy goals, these interests focus on protecting them.[44] When pressure for change becomes strong enough to prompt Congress to act, it generally initiates limited reform. On some occasions, however, the federal government enacts comprehensive programs that significantly affect people's lives.

Major policy change is most likely to occur during periods of economic, social, or political turmoil, and it is frequently associated with nationalized elections that are followed by partisan realignments. Realignments traditionally occur when a critical event polarizes voters on a major issue, the two major parties take clear and opposing stands on that issue, and one party succeeds in capturing the White House and large majorities in both the House and Senate. The ascendant party then has an electoral mandate to enact major policy change.[45]

The events leading up to and continuing through Franklin Roosevelt's presidency exemplify federal policy making during a period of crisis. The seeds of Roosevelt's New Deal programs were sown in the Great Depression of the 1930s. Republicans controlled the White House, the House of Representatives, and the Senate when the stock market crashed in 1929. The Democrats made a major campaign issue out of the Republicans' failure to initiate economic reforms to reverse the Depression. After winning the White House and both chambers of Congress, the Democrats used their mandate to replace laissez-faire economics with a Keynesian approach, which relied on government intervention to revive the economy. Other partisan and policy realignments took place during the late 1820s, the Civil War era, and the 1890s.

Some major policy changes have been instituted in the absence of partisan realignments, but most of those were less sweeping. The civil rights and Great Society programs of the 1960s and the U.S. withdrawal from Vietnam are examples of major policy changes that occurred in the absence of a partisan realignment. The tax cuts, welfare reform, reductions in long-running federal programs, regulations, and mandates on the states that followed the GOP's takeover of Congress in 1995 also appear to have occurred in the absence of a partisan realignment—though the change in partisan control did mark the end of the Democrats' long-term hegemony. This change, and Bush's election in 2000, also shifted the policy debate from how to improve the efficiency and performance of the federal government to how to decrease the government's size and scope. The Democrats' reclaiming congressional majorities following the 2006 election and capturing the White House in 2008 also led to some important policy changes. Most notably the enactment of the Patient Protection and Affordable Health Care Act created the United States' first-ever national health care program. Of course the future of this program, like all federal programs and policies, depends on many factors, including the outcomes of future congressional elections. Given GOP attempts to overturn and defund the program, its likelihood of continuing in its current form would be slim in the event that the Republicans win control of all three branches of the federal government.

Elections that result in a shift in partisan control and the swearing in of many new members can be catalysts for Congress to overcome its normal state of decentralization, especially when a widespread consensus for change exists among the American people. When such partisan turnover occurs, congressional parties in the United States resemble both parliamentary parties in other countries and an idealized system of responsible party government.[46] However, once public support for sweeping change erodes, the centrifugal forces that customarily dominate Congress reassert themselves, and the legislature returns to its normal, incremental mode of policy making. The natural parochialism of members of Congress, bicameralism, the internal decentralization of the House and Senate, and other centrifugal forces encourage political cycles of long periods of incremental policy making followed by short periods of centralized power and major policy change.

SUMMARY

The candidate-centered congressional election system has a major impact on how Congress functions. The electoral connection encourages members of Congress to develop home styles that result in their building bonds of trust with local voters. Congress, as an institution, provides its members with resources to help them accomplish this objective. The candidate-centered system also finds expression in the individualistic legislative behavior exhibited by most representatives and senators and in Congress's decentralized style of operation. Although political parties can overcome the legislature's naturally fragmented state, the centrifugal forces exerted on Congress by constituents, campaign contributors, interest groups, committees, and other organizations within Congress itself eventually cause the institution to return to its normal, decentralized operation. Congressional procedures combine with the overall design of the political system to result in national policy making that is characterized by prolonged periods of small policy adjustments followed by brief episodes of sweeping policy change.

CHAPTER ELEVEN

Campaign Reform

Congress has come under fire in recent years for its inability to solve some of the nation's most pressing problems, its perceived shortcomings in representing the general public, and its failure to keep its own house in order. Gridlock, economic meltdowns, deficit spending, scandal, partisan polarization, and a belief among many that Congress has been captured by special interests have led to calls for congressional reform.[1] Reformers have advocated a variety of changes, ranging from internal reforms, such as consolidating the authorizing committees that create federal programs with the appropriations committees that fund them, to term limits, which would restructure the political careers of members and would-be members. Campaign reform falls somewhere between these measures: it requires the passage of new legislation but does not require a constitutional amendment. Given that it only requires a bill to survive the legislative process, one might ask: Why aren't campaign reforms enacted more often? And why isn't the process Americans use to elect their national legislators better? I address these questions by first reviewing the politics surrounding the enactment and implementation of the Bipartisan Campaign Reform Act of 2002 (BCRA), the last major campaign finance reform signed into law, and the failure of the Democracy Is Strengthened by Casting Light on Spending in Elections (DISCLOSE) Act, the most recent attempt at campaign finance reform. I also comment on how recent federal court decisions overturning parts of the law affect elections. This is followed by a discussion of some additional reform proposals and their prospects for passage.

THE CASE FOR REFORM

Numerous arguments are routinely made for reforming congressional elections. Some proposals are quite sweeping, revolving around the question: Is this any way to elect a member of Congress? When this question was put to major-party candidates and campaign aides competing in congressional elections, 35 percent responded that the campaign process prepares candidates "poorly" or "not at all" for holding office. The defeated candidates were more critical than the winners, but 24 percent of the winners also shared that view. Similarly, 58 percent of the campaigners agreed with the statement, "There are only a few important connections between being a good candidate and being a good public official," and 21 percent maintained that "there is little or no connection" between the two roles. Only one out of five candidates felt that "the best candidates are usually the best public officials." Only 28 percent of the winners took the position that the best congressional candidates make the best members of Congress, and losers perceived even fewer links between campaigning and governing.[2]

These respondents also voiced skepticism about the substantive policy links between campaigning and governing. Ten percent agreed that "issues raised in political campaigns are almost never the most important for future governing," and another 60 percent held that campaign issues are "occasionally" the most important. Only 30 percent felt they were "usually" the most important. Moreover, the winners were no more likely than the losers to maintain that issues raised in campaigns were usually the most important for governing.[3]

Congressional contestants' dissatisfaction with the limited connections between campaigning and governing are important, but they are too amorphous to provide a basis for reform. How does one begin to write a law to ensure that the issues candidates discuss on the campaign trail are the same issues they act on when in office? Elections are the means voters use to hold government office-holders accountable. The disenchantment that politicians feel about the campaign process may be important, but most political reformers are consumed with more concrete shortcomings. Many reformers point out that the campaign system stacks the cards so much against challengers that incumbents almost always win, sometimes calling attention to congressional perks and the politics of redistricting. Even more reformers zero in on money and politics, taking issue with the large sums routinely spent in congressional elections; bemoaning the fact that most of the money comes from wealthy individuals and interest groups; and, more recently, complaining that in many cases it is impossible to tell who is funding the growing number of negative campaign ads. That most incumbents raise and spend so much money, making it virtually impossible for their opponents to compete, is another frequent complaint.

Enterprising politicians, party leaders, interest group executives, and political consultants have found ways to work around federal campaign finance laws,

TABLE 11-1

Assessments of the Campaign Finance System by Congressional Candidates, Significant Donors, and the General Public

	Congressional candidates	Significant donors	General public
It is broken and needs to be replaced	40%	32%	12%
It has problems and needs to be changed	39	46	70
It has some problems but is basically sound	21	21	14
It is all right just the way it is and should not be changed	1	2	4
N	*326*	*1,027*	*807*

Sources: Peter L. Francia, John C. Green, Paul S. Herrnson, Lynda W. Powell, and Clyde Wilcox, *The Financiers of Congressional Elections* (New York: Columbia University Press, 2003), 291–292; Campaign Assessment and Candidate Outreach Project, Center for American Politics and Citizenship, University of Maryland, 2000 survey.

Notes: Congressional candidates include 2000 major-party primary and general election candidates. Significant donors are individuals who contributed $200 or more to a congressional candidate. Some columns do not add to 100 percent because of rounding. $N = 326$ for the candidates; $N = 1,027$ for the donors; $N = 807$ for the public.

including both the BCRA and its predecessor, the Federal Election Campaign Act (FECA). Both laws were progressively weakened by court decisions and administrative rulings, leading many critics to become more vociferous in their objections to the campaign finance system. More than eight out of ten members of the public agreed with the statement that the campaign finance system "is broken and needs to be replaced" or that "it has problems and needs to be changed"; fewer than two out of ten said that "it has some problems but is basically sound" or that "it is all right just the way it is and should not be changed" (see Table 11-1). Individuals who were significant participants in the campaign finance system—those who contributed $200 or more to at least one congressional candidate—were as critical of the system as the rest of the public, if not more so. Among the criticisms that contributors to congressional campaigns routinely levied were that "donors regularly pressure officeholders for favors," "officeholders regularly pressure donors for money," and "money has too big an impact on the outcomes of elections." Congressional candidates are among the most disparaging of election financing. Of course, voters, donors, and candidates of different political parties were critical of different aspects of the system. The same was true of incumbents, challengers, and candidates for open seats.[4]

OBSTACLES TO REFORM

Enacting legislation is never easy, but it is particularly challenging when a bill promises to affect the political careers and livelihoods of those whose support is required to pass it. Mustering sufficient backing to pass the FECA and its amendments in the 1970s and the BCRA decades later was difficult, and passing any future reform will be similarly challenging. It requires winning the approval of individuals who have succeeded under the current campaign finance system, who view politics in light of their personal experiences, and who consider themselves experts on campaigns and elections. Members of Congress and the party and interest group officials who participate in campaigns possess a keen understanding of the provisions of the election system that work to their advantage or disadvantage. They can readily speculate on how different reform packages may affect their ability to participate in elections and influence the policy-making process. Although these individuals often portray themselves as reformers, they frequently advocate changes that reflect their self-interest. Not surprisingly, incumbents and challengers are likely to endorse different reform packages, at least until the challengers become incumbents. Republicans and Democrats also take different positions. Members of the GOP favor high contribution limits or no limits at all, which would enable them to take advantage of their superior fundraising prowess and larger donor base. Democrats are more favorably disposed toward public funding for campaigns and free media time and postage, which would reduce the impact of the Republicans' traditional financial advantages.[5] Some of the differences are based on philosophical orientation: Republicans tend to favor marketplace approaches with few limits on campaign contributions; Democrats generally prefer regulatory measures and government programs, such as limits on contributions accompanied by public subsidies.

Additional differences of opinion originate with the demands that campaigning makes on different types of candidates. Because of the dissimilarities in their term lengths and the sizes of their constituencies, as well as other structural factors, members of the House and Senate disagree on some issues. Many women, African Americans and other ethnic minorities, and members of other traditionally underrepresented groups who depend on national donor networks hold preferences different from those of most white male candidates. Candidates from wealthy urban districts tend to have fundraising opportunities, spending needs, and views on reform that differ from those of candidates from poor rural states or districts.

The diversity of views and the complexity of the issue make it difficult for legislators to find the common ground needed to pass meaningful campaign reform. The sometimes questionable recommendations and inflammatory public relations campaigns of reform groups often widen, rather than close, gaps between members of Congress. Not surprisingly, legislators often find it challenging to move beyond public posturing and engage in serious reform efforts. Since the late 1970s House members and senators of both parties have introduced comprehensive packages that they knew would never be adopted by their respective chambers, survive a conference committee, and be signed into law by the president. Their efforts were geared more toward providing themselves with political cover than enacting meaningful reform.

The BCRA and the DISCLOSE Act

The BCRA and the DISCLOSE Act are instructive examples of the politics of campaign finance reform. They demonstrate that success is most likely to occur when a bill is limited in scope, and it requires somewhat unique circumstances and the use of unusual legislative procedures. The intent of the BCRA was to close some of the loopholes that resulted from the weakening of FECA. It sought to prevent political parties and interest groups from circumventing federal contribution and expenditure limits and avoiding federal disclosure requirements. It also aimed to reduce corruption and the appearance of corruption associated with federal candidates' raising huge, unregulated donations from wealthy interests.[6] The goal of the DISCLOSE Act was to readdress some of those issues following the Supreme Court's rulings in a number of cases, most notably *Citizens United v. FEC*.[7] The act sought to expand the definitions of "independent expenditure" and "electioneering communication" to include the political advertisements corporations, unions, super PACs, and 527 and 501(c) organizations disseminated by so that those groups would be subject to the same disclosure rules and other requirements as candidates, parties, and traditional PACs. It also sought to prohibit certain government contractors and organizations controlled by foreign nationals from making contributions or expenditures in federal elections.[8]

The BCRA's enactment was made possible by a confluence of factors. They included public pressure arising from political scandal and the growing amount of unregulated soft-money spent in politics, skillful bipartisan coalition building and the use of unorthodox approaches to lawmaking, resourceful insider lobbying and outside grassroots mobilization by reform groups, and sympathetic portrayal of the struggle for reform by the mass media.[9] The efforts, over several Congresses, of the BCRA's sponsors, Sens. John McCain, R-Ariz., and Russell Feingold, D-Wis., and Reps. Christopher Shays, R-Conn., and Martin Meehan, D-Mass., were essential to its passage.

The political setting was critical. The Democrats' reclaiming control of the Senate in the 107th Congress and a small but important increase in the number of legislators in support of reform improved its prospects. McCain's discussion of campaign finance reform during the 2000 Republican presidential nominating contest and a major corporate scandal involving the now-defunct energy giant Enron raised the issue's profile. These factors increased the number of legislators who believed a vote for the BCRA was a good vehicle for showing their willingness to act against corporate abuse and corruption in general.

The sequencing of events also was extremely important. In both the 105th and 106th Congresses the House had passed a campaign reform package first, with a significant number of signatories to the bill, anticipating that the Senate would scuttle it. In the 107th Congress the Senate passed the BCRA first. Because President George W. Bush had previously announced that if given the opportunity he would sign a campaign finance reform bill into law, it was up to the House to determine the bill's future. The House Republican leadership fiercely opposed the reform, but when the BCRA's supporters gathered backing sufficient for a discharge petition to force a floor vote, the leadership relented. This left representatives who had previously voted for reform but did not actually want the BCRA to become law in an awkward position. They could cast their votes consistently and in support of the bill and live with the consequences of the new law, or they could reverse their positions on previous votes, deny the bill passage, and look like hypocrites. Most chose to support reform. After the House voted to pass a slightly different version of the bill than had been passed by the Senate, McCain and Feingold successfully pressed their colleagues to accept the House version as a substitute for the Senate version, to prevent the bill from dying in a conference committee or in a new round of voting on a revised version in either chamber. On March 27, 2002, President Bush signed the BCRA into law.

Like the BCRA, the DISCLOSE Act had a limited, well-defined set of goals. However, the DISCLOSE Act differed from the BCRA in that it was proposed in response to a court case, not a major scandal. The case drew attention in political, legal, and academic circles, but it did not generate anywhere near the public attention and anger as did the Enron or Watergate scandals, which motivated legislators to pass the BCRA and the FECA. It also did not generate as much sympathetic media coverage as those other bills because journalists recognized that it would probably be more helpful to Democrats than to Republicans. Moreover, powerful interest groups were more sharply divided over the DISCLOSE Act than the BCRA. Finally, partisanship played a major role in the defeat of the DISCLOSE Act. It passed the House with the votes of most Democrats but of only two Republicans, and it died in the Senate after the Republicans filibustered it twice and Democratic leaders recognized there was no legislative avenue to overcome the will of a united Republican minority. Even if the bill had been enacted, it may not have survived the scrutiny of the courts.

The Courts Weigh In

The enactment of a reform usually marks the end of a major political battle, but it does not necessarily mean that the war over a policy issue has been concluded. Just as the FECA of 1974 was challenged in the courts less than three months after it became law, those who opposed the BCRA prepared to contest it before it was officially enacted. Leading the charge was Sen. Mitch McConnell, R-Ky., who, while still filibustering against the reform, stated, "Should the bill become law, I will be the lead plaintiff."[10] Among the dozens of others who joined the effort to overturn the law were the Republican National Committee (RNC), then–House Speaker Dennis Hastert, the Cato Institute, the American Civil Liberties Union (ACLU), the American Federation of Labor and Congress of Industrial Organizations, the National Rifle Association, and eight state attorneys general. These plaintiffs maintained that the law's ban on issue advocacy advertising and restrictions on party financial activity were violations of the right to free speech. The National Voting Rights Institute, the U.S. Public Interest Research Group (associated with consumer advocate Ralph Nader), and some other voter groups joined the suit for a different reason, claiming that its increased contribution limits were unconstitutional because they favored the wealthy. Writing in defense of the law were the Committee on Economic Development (composed of many of the nation's business leaders), almost every living former member of the ACLU leadership, and twenty-one state attorneys general.[11]

In addition to legal wrangling that was destined to find its way to the U.S. Supreme Court on a number of occasions, the BCRA encountered another set of challenges when the Federal Election Commission (FEC) began drafting the regulations for administering the law. The BCRA was not warmly received by some members of the FEC, including Chair David Mason and Commissioner Bradley Smith, who had made speeches and released statements challenging the bill during the congressional debate.[12] Numerous party committees, interest groups, and other supporters and opponents of the law worked to influence the rule-making process. Some provisions of the law that were weakened by the resulting FEC regulations were designed to prevent soft-money from influencing federal campaigns. Among these were rules exempting Internet communications from the law's soft-money prohibitions and allowing federal candidates to participate in soft-money fundraising events held by state parties.

Fourteen months after the BCRA's enactment, a special three-judge panel of the U.S. District Court for the District of Columbia handed down a verdict in *McConnell v. FEC* that upheld most of the BCRA's main provisions.[13] Next, the case moved to the Supreme Court. In a 5–4 decision the Court ruled in favor of most of the BCRA but overturned the law's prohibition against a political party making both coordinated and independent expenditures in conjunction with one campaign, freeing the parties to do both. It also overturned the BCRA's prohibition against contributions by minors, allowing infants, toddlers, and other children (perhaps with the influence of their parents) to once again contribute to the candidates of their choice.

Four years later, the act was significantly weakened by a ruling of a differently constituted Supreme Court. In a combined decision addressing *FEC v. Wisconsin Right to Life* and *McCain et al. v. Wisconsin Right to Life* (jointly referred to as *"WRTL"*), the Court overturned part of the law that regulated soft-money spending by interest groups.[14] Specifically, the Court ruled unconstitutional the law's prohibitions against the use of soft-money to finance broadcast electioneering communications featuring the name or likeness of a federal candidate during the last thirty days leading up to a primary or the sixty days preceding the general election. In justifying the ruling Chief Justice John Roberts argued that such advertisements might be about issues, as opposed to the sham candidate-focused ads that were one of the reasons for the BCRA's enactment, and "where the First Amendment is implicated, the tie goes to the speaker, not the censor." Ironically, on the same day that the Court ruled in favor of the speech rights of wealthy corporations, unions, and other groups, it limited the free speech of ordinary citizens when, in *Morse v. Frederick,* it held that high school student Joseph Frederick had no right to display a cheap, handmade banner proclaiming "Bong Hits 4 Jesus."[15] Perhaps if Frederick had written "and vote for Frederick for President" underneath his original message the Court would have upheld his speech rights, too.

In 2010 the Supreme Court dealt another blow to the BCRA when in *Citizens United v. FEC* it struck down the law's prohibition against corporations using their general treasuries to finance independent expenditure ads that expressly advocate the election or defeat of a candidate. In making this ruling the Roberts Court overturned several decades of campaign finance law, as well as some of its forerunners' precedents, and it spurred a heated debate over whether the Court had correctly interpreted the Constitution. Most important for corporations and other groups that had been prohibited from spending treasury funds on independent expenditures, or were wary of using those funds to help finance electioneering communications or issue advocacy ads, the ruling gave them a green light to do so.

As discussed in Chapter 5, the practical effect of *Citizens United* and other recent federal court decisions has been to increase the opportunities for corporations, trade associations, unions, and other wealthy groups to make their views known in politics. As a practical matter, this has reduced the ability of others to have their views heard. Traditional PACs and political parties have lost some of their ability to influence elections because they can only raise and spend hard-money contributions that originate as voluntary donations from U.S. citizens. The same is true of congressional and other candidates whose messages are sometimes drowned out by front groups with innocuous, sometimes patriotic-sounding names that are created and funded by corporations and other groups. Further, the rulings signal to those intent on eviscerating laws that regulate the role of money in politics that the Court has a sympathetic ear. Indeed, shortly after the ruling in the *Citizens United* case was handed down, Theodore Olson, the lawyer representing the group, filed an appeal on behalf of the RNC arguing that the logic of *Citizens United* should be used to overturn the BCRA's prohibition of corporate contributions to political parties and its ceilings on individual contributions to parties.[16]

THE EVOLVING STATE OF CAMPAIGN FINANCE

The Supreme Court's rulings in the *McConnell, WRTL,* and *Citizens United* cases had some predictable and some not-so-predictable effects on the financing of congressional elections. Following these decisions candidates, political parties, interest groups, and individual donors scrambled to take advantage of the new regulatory situations or protect themselves from them. One can analyze the immediate effects of these decisions, but their long-term impact is more difficult to recognize because of the time it takes for some groups and individuals to adapt to regulatory change. Nevertheless, some speculation is possible.

Political Parties

The *McConnell* case's overturning of the BCRA's prohibitions against a political party making both coordinated and independent expenditures led both parties to dramatically increase their independent expenditures. Democratic independent spending increased from a mere $1.7 million in the 2002 midterm elections to $108.1 million in 2006 before leveling off at about $106.4 million in 2010. Republican spending increased from $1.9 million to $115.6 million before dropping off to only $71.9 million in 2010. However, the decline in GOP independent expenditures was likely a short-term phenomenon resulting from the lost revenues caused by the fundraising scandals that plagued the party during the 2010 elections and the siphoning off of funds from the Republican donor pool by conservative interest groups, discussed in Chapters 4 and 5. The massive increase in the parties' independent expenditure campaigns was accompanied by decreases in their issue advocacy spending, which had been funded largely by soft-money. Barring another major regulatory change it is likely that these changes in party spending will be long lasting, and party contributions and coordinated expenditures will continue to make up only a small portion of the parties' electioneering efforts. Moreover, it is just as likely that parties will adapt to *Citizens United* and other recent cases by encouraging the formation of new allied 527 and 501(c) groups and super PACs similar to American Crossroads, Crossroads GPS, and America Votes.

Interest Groups

The BCRA's goal of channeling more interest group activity through PACs may, to some degree, have been undermined by an unanticipated consequence of the law itself. Rather than reducing their spending in federal elections, some existing 527 groups, such as EMILY's List and the Club for Growth, were able to increase their spending by raising funds from former party soft-money donors. The same is true of some new groups, including the pro-Democratic America Votes and the pro-Republican Progress for America. Groups headed by former party leaders, like American Crossroads and Crossroads GPS (led by former RNC chairs Mike Duncan and Ed Gillespie and former White House adviser Karl Rove), are especially well positioned to raise such funds.

The Supreme Court's ruling in *Citizens United* contributed to the growth of non-PAC outside spending. As a result, 527 and 501(c) organizations have spent hundreds of millions of dollars to influence congressional elections.[17] In the ten months between the ruling and Election Day 2010, the corporations, trade associations, unions, and super PACs that were freed to use group treasury monies matched the independent spending of traditional PACs. Given that the ruling was handed down in the middle of that election cycle, it is likely that spending by these recent entrants into federal campaign finance will increase substantially in upcoming elections. The 2010 experience suggests that many interest groups will continue to make most of their PAC contributions to incumbents for the purpose of maintaining or gaining access to powerful lawmakers, but they may use super PACs and other organizations to make independent media expenditures to try to defeat incumbents. Because the limited disclosure requirements governing 527 and 501(c) committees make it difficult to identify the sources of these organizations' funds, it is likely that these groups will become the primary vehicles for such expenditures.

Individual Donors

Few members of the public contribute to political campaigns. Roughly 7 percent of all voters claim to have made a contribution to any candidate for public office, and only 0.2 percent donated $200 or more to a congressional candidate. The average individual contribution is less than $75, and the top 1 percent of all individual donors account for roughly 10 percent of all individual donations. The BCRA's ban on party soft-money, its limits on interest group issue advocacy advertising, and its increased ceilings for individual contributions led some party organizations, PACs, and candidates to broaden their donor bases and increase the number of small and medium individual contributions they solicit. This may have led to a small increase in the number of individuals who make such contributions, but it is just as likely that heightened political competition and the use of the Internet, social media, and other fundraising innovations are equally responsible for any increase. Moreover, nearly four-fifths of all the individual contributions to congressional candidates in 2010 were made in amounts of $200 or more, and House and Senate incumbents continued to be the major beneficiaries of these contributions. Clearly, the BCRA did not lead to a wide-scale democratization of the financing of congressional elections, nor did it increase the financial competitiveness of those contests. There is no reason to anticipate that the recent weakening of federal campaign finance law will change this.

Congressional Candidates

One of the immediate effects of the BCRA was to inspire a major jump in the fundraising activity of congressional candidates. It is doubtful that this was one of the reformers' goals, but it is not surprising, given that most politicians tend to be cautious and like to protect themselves from the impact of change. House candidates raised almost 37 percent more money in the 2006 elections than in the 2002 cycle. Senate candidates increased their take by a whopping 71 percent. The recent court decisions unleashing interest groups to spend more funds in new ways has had a similar impact. Candidates for the House raised about 26 percent more in the 2010 midterm elections than they did in 2006, and candidates for the Senate increased their fundraising by 34 percent. Incumbents, particularly those who were attacked by parties or interest groups in a previous election or anticipate a close contest that will attract substantial outside spending, are the most likely to step up their fundraising efforts. It is likely that campaign spending will grow even faster in upcoming elections.

The Public

An underlying objective of all campaign finance reforms is the restoration of public trust in the campaign finance system and in politics more generally. Most voters do not understand the differences between hard and soft-money or independent expenditures, coordinated expenditures, electioneering communications, and other issue advocacy ads. They know little, at best, about campaign finance statutes or the court rulings that uphold or overturn them. The distinctions that lawyers, politicians, and scholars draw among 527 committees, 501(c) groups, traditional PACs, super PACs, political parties, party independent expenditure groups, and perhaps even candidates' campaigns are indistinguishable to most of the voters who receive these organizations' communications. Rather, most voters adhere to broadly preconceived notions about the role of money in politics. News stories about campaign spending, lavish fundraising events, and the power of high-priced lobbyists feed these negative preconceptions. Public opinion is difficult to change, and Americans traditionally have had a healthy skepticism about money and politics.

The growing disconnection between the campaign for votes and the campaign for resources contributes to voters' skepticism. During the golden age of parties, when local party activists were among the most important campaign resources, an intimate connection existed between the two campaigns. Elections were neighborhood affairs, and campaigns involved personal contact between candidates, party activists, other volunteers, and voters. Parties facilitated ongoing relationships among ordinary voters, politicians, and others who participated in politics before, during, and after the election season. Often these relationships revolved around jobs, contracts, social clubs, and opportunities to improve oneself or one's neighborhood. They helped to humanize government for voters and to build bonds of trust between people and political institutions.[18]

Contemporary campaigns encourage fewer meaningful ties between voters and candidates. Despite the efforts of political parties, interest groups, and candidate organizations, the campaign for votes is still relatively impersonal, consisting largely of television, radio, direct mail, mass telephone calls, e-mails, Internet postings, and the free media they generate. Fleeting contacts occasionally take place among citizens, candidates, and party and campaign activists, but they rarely lead to enduring personal relationships. Moreover, campaigns for resources rarely focus on ordinary voters, turning instead toward national party organizations, PACs, and wealthy individuals in a position to provide the wherewithal needed to mount a contemporary campaign. Corporations, unions, and other organizations that finance coordinated grassroots and independent media campaigns also have become important targets in the campaign for resources.

Many voters believe that the elite special interests that spend large sums in elections, rather than the individuals who vote in them, possess the strongest and most beneficial relationships with members of Congress and others in government.[19] Because members of Congress have relatively little patronage, few government contracts, and hardly any opportunities for social advancement to distribute to their constituents, many voters have come to believe that these "goodies" are being distributed instead to wealthy campaign contributors in Washington and the nation's other financial centers. Transformations in the way that campaigns are conducted at home and in Washington have contributed to the public's belief that the operation of the federal government has changed in ways that favor special interests in Washington over the folks back home.

SOME IDEAS FOR REFORM

Over the last several decades a variety of proposals have been floated to reform congressional elections. These include banning PACs, prohibiting bundling, requiring candidates to raise at least 60 percent of their funds from within their state, and offering candidates free television time and reduced postage in exchange for voluntary spending limits—all of which were part of the original BCRA introduced by Sens. McCain and Feingold. The law that was enacted fell short of the sponsors' original goal of limiting the influence of wealthy individuals and groups in elections. Other reform measures that have been proposed include term limits, the revival of multimember House districts, and public funding for candidates and parties.[20]

Among the reforms that have received more serious consideration are improved disclosure of campaign contributions and expenditures; free or subsidized campaign communications for candidates and political parties; tax credits for individual contributors; restructuring of the FEC; revamping state redistricting processes; measures to increase voter turnout; and initiatives to improve voting machines, ballots, and other aspects of election administration.

Regardless of their goals, reformers should base their proposals on an understanding that elections are fought primarily between candidates and that party committees, interest groups, and individual donors have important supplemental roles in them. Reformers need to appreciate the different goals and resources that individuals and groups bring to elections and consider how their proposals would affect them.

Campaign reform should be predicated on the assumption that highly participatory, competitive elections are desirable because they are the best way to hold elected officials accountable to voters and to enhance representation.

Reform should make congressional elections more competitive by encouraging talented candidates to run and by improving the ability of candidates, particularly nonincumbents, to communicate with voters. Campaign reform should also seek to increase the number of people who vote and contribute to campaigns. It should attempt to minimize the amount of unregulated money spent to influence federal elections. The recommendations that follow are not a comprehensive reform package but a series of proposals intended to make congressional elections more participatory, more competitive, and perhaps eventually instill greater public confidence in the political system.

Disclosure

One of the most important and broadly supported provisions of the original FECA and its amendments concerns the full disclosure of receipts and expenditures made in federal elections. Disclosure makes it possible for the public to track the money flow in election campaigns. Timely publication of a campaign's financial transactions enables voters to hold candidates accountable for where they raise their funds and how they spend them, making it possible for campaign financing to become an issue in an election. Moreover, combined with information about legislators' roll-call votes, candidates' campaign finances provide citizens with information they can use to gauge whether an incumbent appears to be held captive by one or more specific interests. Similarly, publication of a party committee's, PAC's, or other organization's receipts, contributions, and expenditures enables interested voters to develop a sense of whom these organizations depend on for their resources and how they seek to influence elections, legislators, and policy making in general.

Since 1976 federal law has been largely successful in enabling voters to follow the money trail in federal elections. Watchdog groups, particularly the Center for Responsive Politics, improved on the FEC's disclosure efforts by making it possible for individuals to easily visit a website containing detailed information about candidates' reliance on various organizations and interests for their campaign funds. This has resulted in news reports on campaign finance becoming at least as prevalent as stories about substantive campaign issues.

However, the emergence of soft-money and outside spending by interest groups weakened disclosure. The expenditures that some interest groups undertake to influence congressional and other elections, and the sources of their revenues, are largely hidden from the public and, in some cases, the corporate stockholders and group members whose funds are being spent. One downside is that the general treasury funds these groups spend on politics are not voluntarily contributed for that purpose. Such spending is likely to distort the representation of the political preferences of stockholders and dues-paying group members. A lack of public accountability is the root of another set of shortcomings. Because stockholders, group members, and ordinary voters cannot identify the sources of some groups' funding, they are deprived of the opportunity to change their political, economic, or social behavior in response to such information. The lack of transparency becomes especially problematic when interests attempt to hide their identities by contributing to or forming shadow groups like Crossroads GPS, the 60 Plus Association, and America's Families First Action Fund. These groups' limited disclosure makes it even more difficult for the public to track the sources and flow of interest group spending in elections. Whether individuals would change their investment portfolios, consumer purchases, or group memberships if they knew who was financing the attack ads they viewed on TV is an open question. However, they should be provided with enough information to have this option. Current regulations could be improved by requiring that all funds intended to influence elections, and perhaps lobbying and other political activities, be voluntarily donated and subject to strict disclosure, regardless of a group's designation under federal election law or the Internal Revenue Code.

Free or Subsidized Communications

Free or subsidized campaign communications—whether in the form of postage, television or radio time, or communications vouchers—would give nonincumbents, particularly challengers, opportunities to present their messages to the public. Given the promise of free or heavily discounted communications resources, better candidates might run for Congress.[21] This could provide a foundation for increased competition and result in nonincumbents raising money from more PACs and individual donors. Arming quality challengers and open-seat candidates with some of the resources needed to reach out to voters can expand the field of competition in congressional elections.

Parties also could be offered free or subsidized communications resources to mobilize current supporters and attract new ones. Minor parties and their candidates, as well as candidates who run as independents, could be given free postage if they persuaded a threshold number of voters to register under their label prior to the current election, if the candidates had received a minimum number of votes in the previous contest, or if they met some other threshold requirement. Minor parties, their candidates, and independent candidates also could be reimbursed if they reached some threshold level of votes in the current election. Providing free or subsidized communications to candidates and parties could be justified by the fact that it would contribute to the education of citizens—the same argument used to justify congressional franked mail and reduced postage for party committees and nonprofit groups.

Another approach involving campaign communications would require local broadcasters to provide candidates, and perhaps parties, with free television or radio time. This could be justified by the fact that airwaves are public property, and one of the conditions of using them is that broadcasters "serve the public interest, convenience, and necessity."[22] The United States is the only major industrialized democracy that does not require broadcasters to contribute air time to candidates for public office—a distinction that should be eliminated.[23] Cable and satellite television operators also could be required to distribute advertising time to House and Senate candidates and parties because their signals also pass through the public airwaves at some point.

Tax Incentives

Tax incentives should be used to broaden the base of campaign contributors and to offset the impact of funds collected from wealthy and well-organized segments of society. Prior to the tax reforms introduced in 1986, individuals were able to claim a tax credit of $50 if they contributed $100 or more to federal candidates. (Couples who contributed $200 could claim a tax credit of $100.) Although some taxpayers took advantage of these credits, the credits themselves were not sufficient to encourage many citizens to contribute to campaigns.[24]

A system of graduated tax credits similar to those used in some other Western democracies might accomplish this goal.[25] If they could claim a 100 percent tax credit for up to $100 in campaign contributions, individuals would be more likely to contribute. Credits of 75 percent for the next $100 and 50 percent for the following $100 would encourage further contributions. Tax credits would encourage candidates and parties to pursue small and moderate contributions more aggressively. Because being asked is one of the most important determinants of who actually makes a contribution, tax credits for individual donations are likely to have a positive impact on the number of taxpayers who make them.[26] Using taxpayer dollars to increase the number of individuals who give money to federal candidates is an expensive proposition, but it would probably be the most effective way to increase the number of people who participate in the financing of congressional elections. Increasing the base of small contributors is the best way to offset the influence of individuals and groups that make large contributions while maintaining a tie between a candidate's levels of popular and financial support.

The Federal Election Commission

The FEC should be strengthened. The commission is currently unable to investigate many of the complaints brought before it, has a backlog of cases, and has been criticized for its failure to dispense quickly with frivolous cases and pursue more important ones. Some of these shortcomings are the result of underfunding and micromanagement by its oversight committees in Congress. Other shortcomings are due to the FEC's structure—it has three Democratic and three Republican commissioners, all of whom are political appointees. In recent years the commissioners also have ignored the opinions of the FEC's professional legal staff. All of this has led to indecision and stalemate.[27]

It is essential that the FEC be restructured so that it operates in a more decisive fashion. Only strong enforcement by the FEC, with backup from the Justice Department and a specially appointed independent counsel on appropriate cases, can discourage unscrupulous individuals, including politicians, from violating the law. Recent failures by the FEC to enforce the law adequately have encouraged Congress to spend tens of millions of dollars on partisan investigations. Although these may be useful for embarrassing political opponents, they are an inadequate substitute for impartial administration of the law.

Redistricting

As a result of redistricting, the 2002 elections set a contemporary record for the number of uncompetitive House races. Deals cut between Democratic and Republican House members have resulted in an absence of competition in most incumbent-challenger races. Only a few states, most notably Iowa, feature a significant number of competitive House races in most election years. The contrast between Iowa and most other states suggests that competition would increase if more states emulated Iowa's redistricting commission, which does not take into account partisanship or incumbency when drawing congressional districts.

Another reform related to redistricting is to prohibit state legislatures from redrawing House seats following the initial redistricting that takes place after reapportionment. Republicans in Texas and Colorado sought to do precisely that after they won control of both the legislature and the governorship in those states in the 2002 elections. The GOP initially succeeded in both states, but the Colorado plan was overruled because the state's constitution explicitly mandates that congressional seats only be drawn once per decade. Midcycle redistricting is a bad idea. Allowing politicians to create new district boundaries any time—including whenever party control of a state's government changes hands—rather than wait until the normal census, reapportionment, and redistricting cycle runs its course, can only inject more discord into an already conflict-ridden process and increase the number of lawsuits that accompany the drawing of congressional districts.

Voter Turnout Initiatives

Campaign reform should address low voter turnout in elections. In the 2010 congressional elections about 42 percent of all eligible voters cast their ballots—an unimpressive figure, but one that is slightly higher than other recent midterm elections.[28] Citizen apathy and disenchantment with the political system are probably responsible for some voter abstention, but voter registration laws are believed to depress turnout by about 9 percent.[29] The "motor-voter" law, enacted in 1993, has eased some barriers to voter registration. Requiring all states to include a check-off box on their income tax forms to enable citizens to register to vote when they file their tax returns could further reduce the barriers to voting.

Other measures that make it easier for voters to exercise the franchise also should be considered. Making Election Day a national holiday is one possibility. Wider use of mail-in ballots, such as those used exclusively in Oregon, is another. Early, countywide, and mobile voting procedures also should be considered. These enable voters to cast their ballots prior to Election Day and, in some cases, at numerous locations in the county in which they are registered, including at some mobile units that are dispatched to parks and other popular locations on weekends. Another innovation involves allowing voters to print out an official ballot from the Internet and mail it back to election board headquarters for processing. Introduced statewide in Maryland during the 2010 elections, this reform improves opportunities for military personnel in the field, Americans living abroad, and transient domestic voters, including college students, to exercise their right to vote.[30]

Measures that make it more convenient to register to vote or cast a ballot will not cause a groundswell in voter turnout, but they should increase it, especially when combined with increased competition and greater efforts by candidates and parties to mobilize voters.[31]

Improving the Way Americans Vote

The 2000 presidential election was a wake-up call for voters, election administrators, and candidates for public office. It showed that something was amiss with the way Americans vote. Between 4 million and 6 million presidential votes and as many as 3.5 million senatorial and gubernatorial votes were lost in the balloting process. Approximately 7.4 percent of the 40 million registered voters who did not vote stated that they did not cast a ballot because of problems with their registration. An additional 2.8 percent of all registered voters who did not vote attributed their lack of participation to long lines at the polls, inopportune hours for voting, or inconveniently located polling places.[32]

Discussions of "butterfly ballots," "chads," "undervotes," "overvotes," and partisan decision making by election officials and the courts also left many people unsettled. Reports that substantial numbers of the poor and members of minority groups were supplied with faulty information about their proper polling place, subjected to intimidation, or turned away at the polls raised alarm among civil rights groups. Evidence that the votes cast by members of these groups were less likely to be counted than votes cast by wealthy or middle-class white voters raised concerns about adherence to the principle of one person, one vote. Learning about the absence of clearly delineated procedures for vote recounts in many states and localities also was cause for some anxiety. The fact that 1960s technology was still being widely used in twenty-first-century elections was another cause of voter dissatisfaction.[33]

Congress responded to public pressure for reform by passing the Help America Vote Act (HAVA), which President Bush signed into law on October 29, 2002. The HAVA requires the states to replace outdated voting machines, employ computerized voting registration systems, and improve poll worker training, among other things, and it authorizes federal subsidies for these purposes. Each polling place is required to have at least one voting system that is accessible to individuals with disabilities. All polling places are to provide provisional ballots to individuals whose names do not appear on the voter rolls, and to count those ballots once the voter's registration is verified. The law also requires first-time voters who registered by mail to provide identification the first time they show up to cast their ballots.

The HAVA depends on state governments, and ultimately the county governments that administer elections in most states, for implementation. Thus, its success depends largely on the capabilities and resources of those governments. Complicating the picture is the fact that these governments depend on private manufacturers and vendors for voting equipment, poll worker training, and much of the software to run new voting machines and manage voter rolls. Most of the voting systems currently available for purchase perform well. Nevertheless, there is room for improvement, including improvement of paper ballot/optical scan systems and "direct recording electronic" systems that employ touch screens, buttons, or other interface features. One step that could improve voter satisfaction, reduce voters' need for help, and increase voters' ability to cast their ballots as intended would be to do away with ballots that have a straight-party-voting option.[34] Another possibility for improving voter satisfaction is to recruit younger, more technologically proficient poll workers—perhaps by providing higher pay or allowing citizens to substitute duty as poll workers for jury duty.[35] The HAVA is an important step in improving how Americans vote, but actions must be taken by many governmental and private institutions for it to be effective. As the 2000 elections demonstrated, voting technology, ballot design, and election administration are important, especially when elections are competitive.

SUMMARY

The rules and norms that govern congressional elections resemble those that structure any activity: they favor some individuals and groups at the expense of others. In recent years the number of Americans who believe that the electoral process is out of balance and provides too many advantages to incumbents, interest groups, wealthy individuals, and other insiders has grown tremendously. Their views are evident in growing citizen distrust of government, the sense of powerlessness expressed by many voters, and the public's willingness to follow the lead of insurgent candidates and reformers without scrutinizing their qualifications or objectives. These are signs that the prestige and power of Congress are in danger. They also are signs that meaningful campaign reform is in order.

Campaign reform should make congressional elections more competitive and increase the number of citizens who participate in them, both as voters and financial contributors. Campaign reform should enable candidates to spend less time campaigning for resources and more time campaigning for votes. Reform also should seek to enhance representation, accountability, and trust in government.

Without major campaign reform, incumbency will remain the defining element of most congressional elections. Challengers, particularly those who run for the House, will continue to struggle to raise money and attract the attention of the news media and voters. The dialogues in House incumbent-challenger contests will remain largely one-sided, whereas those in open-seat contests and Senate races will be more even. Interest groups will continue to conceal their identities and spend outside money to influence elections. Party and interest group independent media campaigns will probably continue to compete with and even overshadow the election activities of candidates in very close races. Congress, elections, and other institutions of government will remain targets for attack both by those who have a sincere wish to improve the political process and by those seeking short-term partisan gain.

Elections are the most important avenue of political influence afforded to the citizens of a representative democracy. They give voters the opportunity to support politicians they favor, oppose those with whom they disagree, and hold those serving in public office accountable for their actions. Respect for human rights and political processes that allow for citizen input are what make democratic systems of government superior to others. Yet all systems of government have their imperfections, and some of these are embodied in their electoral processes. Sometimes the imperfections are serious enough to warrant significant change. Such change should bring the electoral process closer in line with broadly supported notions of liberty, equality, and democracy, as well as with the other values that bind the nation. The current state of congressional elections demonstrates that change is warranted in the way Americans elect those who serve in Congress.

Notes

1. Abraham Lincoln, "The Gettysburg Address," November 19, 1863.
2. 558 U.S. 08-205 (2010).
3. Prior to the ruling these organizations needed to establish PACs—separate, segregated accounts composed of individual contributions—in order to spend money in federal elections.

1. THE STRATEGIC CONTEXT

1. Leon D. Epstein, *Political Parties in Western Democracies* (New York: Praeger, 1967), chap. 8.
2. Kenneth Martis, *The Historical Atlas of U.S. Congressional Districts, 1789–1983* (New York: Free Press, 1982), 5–6.
3. See, for example, Frank J. Sorauf, "Political Parties and Political Action Committees," *Arizona Law Review* 22 (1980): 445–64.
4. Jerrold B. Rusk, "The Effect of the Australian Ballot Reform on Split Ticket Voting," *American Political Science Review* 64 (1970): 1220–83.
5. See, for example, V. O. Key, *Politics, Parties, and Pressure Groups* (New York: Thomas Y. Crowell, 1964), 371.
6. Ibid., 389–91.
7. Committee on Political Parties, American Political Science Association, "Toward a More Responsible Two-Party System," *American Political Science Association Review* 44, no. 3, part 2 (1950): 21.
8. The exception to this is so-called Levin funds, contributions to state and local parties of up to $10,000 per donor per year from sources and in amounts that are permissible under a state's laws. These funds can be used for voter registration, identification, and mobilization activities. The ratio of federally regulated funds and Levin funds that can be spent in a given election is based on an allocation formula determined by the Federal Election Commission.
9. Contributions of $200 or less constitute an exception to the law's reporting and disclosure requirements.
10. Arthur B. Gunlicks, "Introduction," in *Campaign and Party Finance in North America and Western Europe,* ed. Arthur B. Gunlicks (Boulder, Colo.: Westview Press, 1993), 6.

11. Paul S. Herrnson, *Party Campaigning in the 1980s* (Cambridge: Harvard University Press, 1988), 82.

12. 599 F.3d 686, 689 (D.C. Cir. 2010).

13. Figure includes contributions, transfers, independent expenditures, electioneering communications, and internal communications by traditional PACs, 501(c) organizations, 527 committees, and super PACs. Compiled from data collected by the FEC and the Center for Responsive Politics.

14. Paul S. Herrnson, "The Roles of Party Organizations, Party-Connected Committees, and Party Allies in Elections," *Journal of Politics* 71 (2009): 1207–24.

15. Louis Hartz, *The Liberal Tradition in America* (New York: Harcourt, Brace, 1955).

16. See, for example, Herbert McClosky and John Zaller, *The American Ethos* (Cambridge: Harvard University Press, 1984), 62–100.

17. See Rusk, "The Effect of the Australian Ballot."

18. Key, *Politics, Parties, and Pressure Groups,* 342, 386; Nelson W. Polsby, *The Consequences of Party Reform* (Oxford: Oxford University Press, 1983), 72–74.

19. Lee Ann Elliot, "Political Action Committees—Precincts of the '80s," *Arizona Law Review* 22 (1980): 539–54; Kay Lehman Schlozman and John T. Tierney, *Organized Interests and American Democracy* (New York: Harper and Row, 1986), 75–78.

20. John R. Petrocik, *Party Coalitions* (Chicago: University of Chicago Press, 1981), chaps. 8 and 9; Paul Allen Beck, "A Socialization Theory of Partisan Realignment," in *Controversies in American Voting Behavior,* ed. Richard G. Niemi and Herbert F. Weisberg (Washington, D.C.: CQ Press, 1984), 396–411; Martin P. Wattenberg, *The Decline of American Political Parties, 1952–1988* (Cambridge: Harvard University Press, 1990), chap. 4.

21. Jack Dennis, "Support for the Party System by the Mass Public," *American Political Science Review* 60 (1966): 605.

22. Bruce E. Keith, David B. Magleby, Candice J. Nelson, Elizabeth Orr, Mark C. Westlye, and Raymond E. Wolfinger, *The Myth of the Independent Voter* (Berkeley: University of California Press, 1992), 8.

23. Pew Research Center, "Independents Oppose Party in Power . . . Again," September 23, 2010, http://people-press.org.

24. This group includes independents who "lean" toward one of the parties.

25. Sorauf, "Political Parties and Political Action Committees," 447.

26. Robert Agranoff, "Introduction," in *The New Style in Election Campaigns,* ed. Robert Agranoff (Boston: Holbrook Press, 1972), 3–50; Larry J. Sabato, *The Rise of the Political Consultants* (New York: Basic Books, 1981).

27. Dennis W. Johnson, *Campaigning in the Twenty-First Century* (New York: Routledge, 2011), 11–27.

28. Sorauf, "Political Parties and Political Action Committees."

29. Cornelius P. Cotter and John F. Bibby, "Institutional Development and the Thesis of Party Decline," *Political Science Quarterly* 95 (1980): 1–27; Herrnson, *Party Campaigning,* chaps. 3 and 4; Herrnson, "The Roles of Party Organizations."

30. Alan Abramowitz, Brad Alexander, and Matthew Gunning, "Incumbency, Redistricting, and the Decline of Competition in U.S. House Elections," *Journal of Politics* 68 (2006): 75–88; Bruce Oppenheimer, "Deep Red and Blue Congressional Districts: The Causes and Consequences of Declining Party Competitiveness," in *Congress Reconsidered,* ed. Lawrence C. Dodd and Bruce Oppenheimer (Washington, D.C.: CQ Press), 135–57.

31. See Bruce E. Cain and Thomas E. Mann, eds., *Party Lines: Competition, Partisanship, and Congressional Redistricting* (Washington, D.C.: Brookings Institution Press), 2005.

32. California created a new commission to redistrict its U.S. House seats prior to the 2012 election.

33. Bruce I. Oppenheimer, James A. Stimson, and Richard W. Waterman, "Interpreting U.S. Congressional Elections," *Legislative Studies Quarterly* 11 (1986): 227–47; James E. Campbell, *The Presidential Pulse of Congressional Elections* (Lexington: University of Kentucky Press, 1993), 7–11.

34. Michael S. Lewis-Beck and Tom W. Rice, *Forecasting Elections* (Washington, D.C.: CQ Press, 1992), chaps. 4–6.

35. On coattail effects, see Barry C. Burden and David C. Kimball, *Why Americans Split Their Tickets* (Ann Arbor: University of Michigan Press, 2002), esp. 78–96, 134–38.

36. Edward R. Tufte, "Determinants of the Outcomes of Midterm Congressional Elections," *American Political Science Review* 69 (1975): 812–26; Lewis-Beck and Rice, *Forecasting Elections,* 60–75.

37. Gary C. Jacobson, "Does the Economy Matter in Midterm Elections?" *American Journal of Political Science* 34 (1990): 400–4. For an alternative interpretation, see Patrick G. Lynch, "Midterm Elections and Economic Fluctuations," *Legislative Studies Quarterly* 227 (2002): 265–94.

38. Morris P. Fiorina, *Retrospective Voting in American National Elections* (New Haven: Yale University Press, 1981), 165.

39. Norman Nie and Kristi Andersen, "Mass Belief Systems Revisited," *Journal of Politics* 36 (1974): 540–91; Crotty, *American Parties in Decline,* 49–50.

40. David R. Mayhew, *Congress: The Electoral Connection* (New Haven: Yale University Press, 1974); Morris P. Fiorina, *Congress: Keystone of the Washington Establishment* (New Haven: Yale University Press, 1978), 19–21, 41–49, 56–62; Bruce Cain, John Ferejohn, and Morris Fiorina, *The Personal Vote* (Cambridge: Harvard University Press, 1987), 103–6.

41. Harrison W. Fox and Susan Webb Hammond, *Congressional Staffs* (New York: Free Press, 1977), 88–99, 154–55.

42. *Thornburg v. Gingles,* 478 U.S. 30 (1986).

43. Richard F. Fenno Jr., *Home Style* (Boston: Little, Brown, 1978), 164–68.

44. John R. Hibbing and Elizabeth Theiss-Morse, *Congress as Public Enemy: Public Attitudes toward American Political Institutions* (Cambridge: Cambridge University Press, 1995), 31–33, 69–71, 96–100; The Pew Center for the People & the Press, "Distrust, Discontent, Anger, and Partisan Rancor: The People and Their Government," April 18, 2010, http://people-press.org.

45. David R. Jones, "Partisan Polarization and Congressional Accountability in House Elections," *American Journal of Political Science* 54 (2010): 323–37.

46. Philip A. Klinkner, ed., *Midterm: The 1994 Elections in Perspective* (Boulder Colo.: Westview Press, 1996); James G. Gimpel, *Fulfilling the Contract* (Boston: Allyn & Bacon, 1996).

47. Richard F. Fenno Jr., "If, as Ralph Nader Says, Congress Is 'The Broken Branch,' How Come We Love Our Congressmen So Much?" in *Congress in Change,* ed. Norman J. Ornstein (New York: Praeger, 1975).

48. Paul S. Herrnson and Irwin L. Morris, "Presidential Campaigning in the 2002 Congressional Elections," *Legislative Studies Quarterly* 32 (2007): 629–48.

49. The figure for the House includes the seat formerly occupied by Independent Bernard Sanders of Vermont; the figure for the Senate includes the seat occupied by Joseph I. Lieberman of Connecticut who, although technically an Independent, caucuses with the Democrats.

50. See, for example, Jonathan Mummolo, "Nimble Giants: How National Interest Groups Worked to Harness Grassroots Tea Party Enthusiasm," in *Interest Groups Unleashed,* ed. Paul S. Herrnson, Clyde Wilcox, and Christopher J. Deering (Washington, D.C.: CQ Press, in press).

51. Twenty percent is an appropriate victory margin given the heightened level of uncertainty in contemporary congressional elections. A narrower margin, such as 15 percent, would have eliminated campaigns that were competitive for part of the election season but were ultimately decided by more than 15 percent of the vote. Slightly changing the boundaries for the competitiveness measure does not substantively change the results. Moreover, the 20-point classification produces results similar to the forecasts of political journalists who handicap congressional elections. When the seats the *Cook Political Report* classifies as "lean," "likely," or "toss-up" races (based on twelve reports from September 2, 2010, through November 2, 2010) are combined into one category, 94.2 percent of those races fall into the 20-point classification for competitiveness used here. For more discussion of the classification scheme, see the Appendix to the first edition of this book.

52. After Bennett placed third at the Utah Republican Convention, he was ineligible to participate in the primary.

53. Kelly Ayotte, R-N.H., Michael Lee, R-Utah, and Rand Paul, R-Ky., had not previously held at least one elective office, but each had significant unelected experience: Ayotte served as the attorney general of New Hampshire; Lee as U.S. solicitor general in the Reagan administration; and Paul, the son of Texas House member and 2008 and 2012 candidate for the Republican presidential nomination Ron Paul, was founder and chair of the anti-tax organization Kentucky Taxpayers United.

2. CANDIDATES AND NOMINATIONS

1. E. E. Schattschneider, *Party Government* (New York: Holt, Rinehart & Winston, 1942), 99–106.

2. See, for example, L. Sandy Maisel, Walter J. Stone, and Cherie Maestas, "Quality Challengers to Congressional Incumbents," in *Playing Hardball,* ed. Paul S. Herrnson (Upper Saddle River, N.J.: Prentice Hall, 2001), 12–40.

3. Gary C. Jacobson and Samuel Kernell, *Strategy and Choice in Congressional Elections* (New Haven: Yale University Press, 1983), chap. 3; David T. Canon, *Actors, Athletes, and Astronauts* (Chicago: University of Chicago Press, 1990), 76–79.

4. Jamie L. Carson, "Strategy, Selection, and Candidate Competition in U.S. House and Senate Elections," *Journal of Politics* 67 (2005): 1–28; Cherie D. Maestas, Sarah Fulton, L. Sandy Maisel, and Walter J. Stone, "When to Risk It? Institutions, Ambitions, and the Decision to Run for the U.S. House," *American Political Science Review* 100 (2006): 195–208.

5. Canon, *Actors, Athletes, and Astronauts,* 106–8; Scott Ashworth and Ethan Bueno de Mesquita, "Electoral Selection, Strategic Challenger Entry, and the Incumbency Advantage," *Journal of Politics* 70 (2008): 1006–25.

6. Roger H. Davidson, Walter J. Oleszek, and Frances E. Lee, *Congress and Its Members,* 12th ed. (Washington, D.C.: CQ Press, 2010), 65.

7. Richard F. Fenno Jr., *Home Style* (Boston: Little, Brown, 1978), 164–68.

8. Janet M. Box-Steffensmeier, "A Dynamic Analysis of the Role of War Chests in Campaign Strategy," *American Journal of Political Science* 40 (1996): 352–71. For another viewpoint, see Jay Goodliffe, "The Effect of War Chests on Challenger Entry in U.S. House Elections," *American Journal of Political Science* 45 (2001): 830–44.

9. Sara Fritz and Dwight Morris, *Gold-Plated Politics* (Washington, D.C.: Congressional Quarterly, 1992), esp. chap. 2.

10. On redistricting, see Antoine Yoshinaka and Chad Murphy, "The Paradox of Redistricting: How Partisan Mapmakers Foster Competition but Disrupt Representation," *Political Research Quarterly* 20 (2010): 1–13.

11. Michael K. Moore and John R. Hibbing, "Is Serving in Congress Fun Again?" *American Journal of Political Science* 36 (1992): 824–28; Jennifer Wolak, "Strategic Retirements: The Influence of Public Preferences on Voluntary Departures from Congress," *Legislative Studies Quarterly* 32 (2007): 285–308.

12. Rep. Chris Van Hollen, chair, DCCC, interview, November 30, 2010; Brian Walsh, political director, NRCC, interview, November 22, 2010.

13. Joseph Cooper and William West, "The Congressional Career in the 1970s," in *Congress Reconsidered,* ed. Lawrence Dodd and Bruce Oppenheimer (Washington, D.C.: CQ Press, 1981); John R. Hibbing, "Voluntary Retirement from the U.S. House," *Legislative Studies Quarterly* 8 (1982): 57–74.

14. Walter Stone, Sarah A. Fulton, Cherie D. Maestas, and L. Sandy Maisel, "Incumbency Reconsidered: Prospects, Strategic Retirement, and Incumbent Quality in U.S. House Elections," *Journal of Politics* 72 (2010): 178–90.

15. Mike Allen and Josh Kraushaar, "Rep. Bart Stupak Won't Seek Reelection," *Politico,* April 9, 2010, www.politico.com.

16. Jim Gallaway, "John Linder Endorses Former Chief of Staff to Replace Him," *Atlanta Journal-Constitution,* April 13, 2010, http://blogs.ajc.com/political-insider-jim-galloway.

17. Darrell M. West and John Orman, *Celebrity Politics* (Upper Saddle River, N.J.: Prentice Hall, 2003), 2–4.

18. Jeffrey Lazarus, "Buying In: Testing the Rational Model of Candidate Entry," *Journal of Politics* 70 (2008): 837–50.

19. On the impact of term limits, see Richard J. Powell, "The Impact of Term Limits on the Candidacy Decisions of State Legislators in U.S. House Elections," *Legislative Studies Quarterly* 25 (2000): 645–61; on the number of states with term limits, see National Conference of State Legislatures, "The Term Limited States," June 2009, www.ncsl.org.

20. On ambitious, policy, experience-seeking, or hopeless amateurs, see Canon, *Actors, Athletes, and Astronauts,* xv, 26–32.

21. Susan Kone, Republican candidate for Congress, interview, March 28, 2011.

22. Cherie D. Maestas and Cynthia R. Rugeley, "Assessing the 'Experience Bonus' through Examining Strategic Entry, Candidate Quality, and Campaign Receipts in U.S. House Elections," *American Journal of Political Science* 52 (2008): 520–35.

23. Throughout this chapter, seats are categorized according to their status (open or incumbent occupied) at the beginning of the election cycle. Seats that began the election cycle as incumbent occupied but featured two nonincumbents in the general election are classified as open from Chapter 3 forward.

24. Some states, including Texas, are exceptions in that they allow an individual to appear on the ballot for two offices simultaneously.

25. Harold D. Lasswell, *Power and Personality* (Boston: Norton, 1948), 39–41.

26. The generalizations that follow are drawn from responses to the 1992 Congressional Campaign Study. See also Paul S. Herrnson, *Party Campaigning in the 1980s* (Cambridge: Harvard University Press, 1988), 86.

27. Thomas A. Kazee and Mary C. Thornberry, "Where's the Party? Congressional Candidate Recruitment and American Party Organizations," *Western Political Quarterly* 43 (1990): 61–80; Steven H. Haeberle, "Closed Primaries and Party Support in Congress," *American Politics Quarterly* 13 (1985): 341–52.

28. Herrnson, *Party Campaigning,* 51–56.

29. Van Hollen, interview, November 30, 2010.

30. Walsh, interview, November 22, 2010.

31. See, for example, Linda L. Fowler and Robert D. McClure, *Political Ambition* (New Haven: Yale University Press, 1989), 205–7.

32. On WISH List, see Mark J. Rozell, "WISH List," in *After the Revolution: PACs and Lobbies in the New Republican Congress,* ed. Robert Biersack, Paul S. Herrnson, and Clyde Wilcox (Boston: Allyn & Bacon, 1991), 184–91. See also Christine L. Day and Charles D. Hadley, *Women's PACs* (Upper Saddle River, N.J.: Prentice Hall, 2005).

33. Walter J. Stone and L. Sandy Maisel, "The Not So Simple Calculus of Winning," *Journal of Politics* 65 (2003): 951–77; Walter J. Stone, L. Sandy Maisel, and Cherie D. Maestas, "Quality Counts: Extending the Strategic Politician Model of Incumbent Deterrence," *American Journal of Political Science* 48 (2004): 479–95.

34. Fenno, *Home Style,* 176–89.

35. See, for example, Schlesinger, *Ambition and Politics: Political Careers in the United States* (Chicago: Rand McNally, 1966), 99; Canon, *Actors, Athletes, and Astronauts,* 50–53, 56–58; Maisel et al., "Quality Challengers to Congressional Incumbents."

36. "West Virginia District 1; Rep. Alan Mollohan (D)," *National Journal*, www.nationaljournal
.com.

37. Tharuni Jayaraman, "West Virginia's First Congressional District," unpublished paper, University
of Pennsylvania, December 9, 2010.

38. Ibid.

39. The discussion of the congressional election in Illinois' 10th district draws from Allyson
Gasdaska, "Illinois' 10th District: Congressional Midterm Election 2010," unpublished paper,
University of Pennsylvania, December 9, 2010, and the candidates' websites and advertisements.

40. Tea Party candidates were identified using the following websites: "ABC News Guidebook to
Tea Party Candidates," http://abcnews.go.com/Politics/2010_Elections; "Election 2010: The Tea
Party Movement," *Washington Post*, www.washingtonpost.com; "Where Tea Party Candidates Are
Running," *New York Times*, www.nytimes.com.

41. Jennifer E. Manning, *Membership of the 112th Congress: A Profile* (Washington, D.C.:
Congressional Research Service, 2011), www.crs.gov.

42. *CQ Roll Call*, "The 50 Richest Members of Congress (2010)," http://innovation.cq.com.

43. Richard L. Fox and Jennifer L. Lawless, "Gendered Perceptions and Political Candidacies: A
Central Barrier to Women's Equality in Electoral Politics," *American Journal of Political Science* 55
(2011): 59–73.

44. Linda L. Fowler, *Candidates, Congress, and the American Democracy* (Ann Arbor: University of
Michigan Press, 1993), 127–36.

45. Jennifer L. Lawless and Kathryn Pearson, "The Primary Reason for Women's Underrepresentation? Reevaluating the Conventional Wisdom," *Journal of Politics* 70 (2008): 67–79.

46. Richard L. Fox and Jennifer L. Lawless, "If Only They'd Ask: Gender, Recruitment, and
Political Ambition," *Journal of Politics* 72 (2010): 310–26.

47. On the impact of religious participation on the development of political and civic skills, see
Sidney Verba, Kay Lehman Schlozman, and Henry E. Brady, *Voice and Equality* (Cambridge: Harvard
University Press, 1995), 333.

48. On the effect of race on candidate selection, see Fox and Lawless, "To Run or Not to Run for
Office," *American Journal of Political Science* 49 (2005): 642–59; Fowler, *Candidates, Congress, and the
American Democracy*, 136–42.

49. Kevin A. Hill, "Does the Creation of Majority Black Districts Aid Republicans?" *Journal of
Politics* 57 (1995): 384–401; Charles Cameron, David Epstein, and Sharyn O'Halloran, "Do
Majority-Minority Districts Maximize Substantive Black Representation in Congress?" *American
Political Science Review* 90 (1996): 794–812.

50. Ortiz was defeated by a Caucasian and Kilpatrick by a candidate who is part African
American.

51. David T. Cannon, *Race, Redistricting, and Representation* (Chicago: University of Chicago
Press, 1999).

52. *CQ Roll Call*, "The 50 Richest Members."

53. *Biographical Directory of the United States Congress*, http://bioguide.congress.gov.

54. Beginning with the U.S. House, and proceeding in the order listed, only the highest office is
included.

55. This includes Connecticut senator Joseph Lieberman, who was defeated in the Democratic
primary by Ned Lamont in 2006 but successfully ran as an Independent in the general election.

56. Chris LaCivita, political director, NRSC, interview, November 17, 2010; Reid Wilson, "Like
GOP, Dems Struggle to Woo Top-Notch Recruits," *The Hill*, April 28, 2009.

57. This generalization is drawn from responses to question 18 of the 1992 Congressional
Campaign Study; see the Appendix to the first edition of this book and the book's website, http://
herrnson.cqpress.com.

3. THE ANATOMY OF A CAMPAIGN

1. See, for example, Edie N. Goldenberg and Michael W. Traugott, *Campaigning for Congress* (Washington, D.C.: CQ Press, 1984), 19–24.

2. Committee on Political Parties, American Political Science Association, "Toward a More Responsible Two-Party System," *American Political Science Association Review* 44, no. 3, part 2 (1950): 21; Larry J. Sabato, *The Rise of the Political Consultants* (New York: Basic Books, 1981).

3. R. Sam Garrett, Paul S. Herrnson, and James A. Thurber, "Perspectives on Campaign Ethics," in *The Electoral Challenge,* ed. Stephen C. Craig (Washington, D.C.: CQ Press, 2006), 203–26.

4. Unless otherwise noted, all campaign finance data were furnished by the Center for Responsive Politics (www.opensecrets.org) or the Federal Election Commission (http://fec.gov/).

5. Figures from the Center for Responsive Politics, www.opensecrets.org.

6. There have been important exceptions to this generalization in recent years. See David T. Canon, *Actors, Athletes, and Astronauts* (Chicago: University of Chicago Press, 1990), 3, 36.

7. Paul S. Herrnson, *Party Campaigning in the 1980s* (Cambridge: Harvard University Press, 1988), 61–63, 92–94.

8. "Charities on the Hill," *Washington Post,* March 7, 2006, Sec. A.

9. Peter L. Francia, John C. Green, Paul S. Herrnson, Lynda W. Powell, and Clyde Wilcox, *The Financiers of Congressional Elections* (New York: Columbia University Press, 2003), 69–98.

10. James N. Druckman, Martin J. Kifer, and Michael Parkin, "Campaign Communications in U.S. Congressional Elections," *American Political Science Review* 103 (2009): 343–66.

11. As noted in Chapter 8, virtually every major-party general election candidate possesses a website and uses it for many purposes.

12. This finding supports Fenno's observation that the explanatory power of challenger quality and political experience is largely the result of the quality of the candidates' campaign organizations. See Richard F. Fenno Jr., *Senators on the Campaign Trail: The Politics of Representation* (Norman: University of Oklahoma Press, 1996), 100.

13. "The List," *Campaigns & Elections,* December 2006.

14. Susan Kone, Republican candidate for Congress, interview, March 28, 2011.

15. The discussion of the congressional election in Florida's 2nd district draws from Lauren M. Harding, "The Funeral Home Director Buries the Blue Dog," unpublished paper, University of Pennsylvania, December 9, 2010.

16. The discussion of the Dold-Seals election in Illinois' 10th district draws from Allyson Gasdaska, "Illinois' 10th District: Congressional Midterm Election 2010," unpublished paper, University of Pennsylvania, December 9, 2010.

17. The discussion of the Reid-Angle election draws from David F. Damore, "Reid vs. Angle in Nevada's Senate Race," in *Cases in Congressional Campaigns,* ed. Randall E. Adkins and David A. Dulio (New York: Routledge, 2010), 32–54.

18. In states with only one representative, House campaigns must reach out to as many voters as Senate campaigns.

4. THE PARTIES CAMPAIGN

1. Frank J. Sorauf, "Political Parties and Political Action Committees," *Arizona Law Review* 22 (1980): 447.

2. See, for example, Robert Agranoff, "Introduction," in *The New Style in Election Campaigns,* ed. Robert Agranoff (Boston: Holbrook Press, 1972), 3–50.

3. Joseph A. Schlesinger, "The New American Political Party," *American Political Science Review* 79 (1985): 1151–69; Paul S. Herrnson, *Party Campaigning in the 1980s* (Cambridge: Harvard University Press, 1988), chaps. 2–3.

4. Herrnson, *Party Campaigning,* chap. 2.

5. Paul S. Herrnson, "The Roles of Party Organizations, Party-Connected Committees, and Party Allies in Elections," *Journal of Politics* 71 (2009): 1207–24.

6. For more on the concept of party issue ownership, see John R. Petrocik, "Issue Ownership in Presidential Elections, with a 1980 Case Study," *American Journal of Political Science* 40 (1996): 825–50; George Rabinowitz and Stuart McDonald, "A Directional Theory of Voting," *American Political Science Review* 65 (1989): 93–122.

7. Paul S. Herrnson, Kelly D. Patterson, and John J. Pitney Jr., "From Ward Heelers to Public Relations Experts," in *Broken Contract? Changing Relationships between Citizens and Government in the United States,* ed. Stephen C. Craig (Boulder, Colo.: Westview Press, 1996), 251–67.

8. James G. Gimpel, *Fulfilling the Contract* (Boston: Allyn & Bacon, 1996); Robin Kolodny, "The Contract with America in the 104th Congress," in *The State of the Parties,* ed. John C. Green and Daniel M. Shea (Lanham, Md.: Rowman and Littlefield, 1996), 314–27.

9. Paul S. Herrnson and Irwin L. Morris, "Presidential Campaigning in the 2002 Congressional Elections," *Legislative Studies Quarterly* 32 (2007): 629–48.

10. Greenberg Quinlan Rosner Research, "Election 2006," www.americanprogress.org.

11. Ken Spain, communications director, NRCC, interview, November 17, 2010.

12. Trend lines for presidential ratings are available at www.gallup.com/poll/124922/Presidential-Approval-Center.aspx.

13. Brian Walsh, political director, NRCC, interview, November 22, 2010; Spain, interview, November 17, 2010.

14. Rep. Chris Van Hollen, chair, DCCC, presentation, University of Maryland, November 15, 2010.

15. "Kaiser Health Tracking Poll, November 2010," Henry J. Kaiser Family Foundation, www.kff.org/.

16. Even though the reports that candidates filed with the FEC indicate that some received large national committee contributions and coordinated expenditures, this spending is almost always directed by a congressional or senatorial campaign committee's election strategy.

17. The term *Hill committees* probably originated in the days when the congressional and senatorial campaign committees were located in congressional office space on Capitol Hill.

18. The Democrats raised a total of $600.4 million, the Republicans a total of $549 million. To avoid double counting, these figures exclude funds transferred among party committees. Unless otherwise noted, all campaign finance data were furnished by the Center for Responsive Politics (www.opensecrets.org) or the Federal Election Commission (http://fec.gov/).

19. Anna Palmer and Steven T. Dennis, "Pelosi Puts Heat on Chairmen," *Roll Call,* September 28, 2010; Chris Van Hollen, chair, DCCC, interview, November 30, 2010.

20. Steven T. Dennis and Lauren W. Whittington, "Van Hollen Offers Up Another $800,000 to Boost Party," *Roll Call,* October 21, 2010.

21. Michael Luo, "Campaign Donors Betting on a Big Step for Boehner," *New York Times,* October 21, 2010.

22. On party donor networks, see Peter L. Francia, John C. Green, Paul S. Herrnson, Lynda W. Powell, and Clyde Wilcox, *The Financiers of Congressional Elections* (New York: Columbia University Press, 2003).

23. Herrnson, "The Roles of Party Organizations."

24. Gary C. Jacobson, "Party Organization and Campaign Resources in 1982," *Political Science Quarterly* 100 (1985–1986): 604–25.

25. On the use of congressional and senatorial campaign committee chairmanships as vehicles for advancing in the congressional leadership, see Paul S. Herrnson, "Political Leadership and Organizational Change at the National Committees," in *Politics, Professionalism, and Power,* ed. John Green (Lanham, Md.: University Press of America, 1993), 186–202; Robin Kolodny, *Pursuing Majorities* (Norman: University of Oklahoma Press, 1998), 175–95.

26. Gary C. Jacobson and Samuel Kernell, *Strategy and Choice in Congressional Elections* (New Haven: Yale University Press, 1983), 39–43, 76–84.

27. The information on committee strategy, decision making, and targeting is from numerous interviews conducted with high-ranking officials of the congressional and senatorial campaign committees before, during, and after various election cycles dating back to 1984. See previous editions of this book.

28. Ibid.

29. The categorizations of political journalists who handicap congressional elections are similar to those of party leaders. See Chapter 1, note 48.

30. Rep. Chris Van Hollen, chair, DCCC, interview, March 26, 2007.

31. Brian Walsh, political director, NRCC interview, November 22, 2010; Spain, interview, November 17, 2010.

32. Van Hollen, interview, November 30, 2010; Van Hollen, memorandum to Democratic colleagues, November 18, 2010.

33. These are considered separate elections under the BCRA. Party committees usually give contributions only to general election candidates.

34. The coordinated expenditure limit for states with only one House member was originally set at $20,000 and reached $87,000 in 2010.

35. Herrnson, *Party Campaigning,* 43–44.

36. For information about prior elections see the previous editions of this book.

37. Ross K. Baker, *The New Fat Cats: Members of Congress as Political Benefactors* (New York: Priority Press, 1989), 31.

38. Herrnson, "The Roles of Party Organizations."

39. The coverage of these topics draws from Herrnson, *Party Campaigning,* chaps. 4 and 5.

40. Andrew Grossman, political director, DSCC, interview, February 27, 2003.

41. Guy Cecil, DSCC, interview, December 4, 2006. Cecil served as political director in the 2006 election cycle and was appointed executive director for the 2012 cycle.

42. Information provided by Johanna Berkhart, DCCC, November 30, 2010.

43. Information provided by Lisa Boothe, assistant press secretary, NRSC, November 30, 2010.

44. Chris LaCivita, political director, NRSC, interview, November 17, 2010.

45. This amount includes funds to pay staff and for subscriptions; Boothe, November 30, 2010.

46. Van Hollen, interview, November 30, 2010; Van Hollen, "Political Update," memorandum to Democratic colleagues, November 18, 2010.

47. Mark Stephens, NRSC executive director, interview, December 13, 2006.

48. Spain, interview, November 17, 2010; LaCivita, interview, November 17, 2010; Van Hollen, interview, November 30, 2010.

49. LaCivita, interview, November 17, 2010; Spain, interview, November 17, 2010; Van Hollen, interview, November 30, 2010.

50. Typical PAC kits include information about the candidate's personal background, political experience, campaign staff, support in the district, endorsements, issue positions, and campaign strategy.

51. David Maraniss and Michael Weisskopf, "Speaker and His Directors Make the Cash Flow Right," *Washington Post,* November 27, 1995.

52. Quote from Curt Anderson, RNC, in Dan Balz and David S. Broder, "Close Election Turns on Voter Turnout," *Washington Post,* November 1, 2002.

53. Other convenience voting options include electronic voting and voting by fax. Estimate based on the fact that in 2008, 30 percent used some form of convenience voting. See Paul Gronke, Eva Galanes-Rosenbaum, Peter A. Miller, and Daniel Toffey, "Convenience Voting," *Annual Review of Political Science* 11 (2008): 437–55.

54. Jason McBride, RNC deputy political director, interview, December 15, 2010.

55. Eliza Newlin Carney, "Rules of the Game," *National Journal,* October 12, 2010.

56. 518 U.S. 604, 116 S.Ct. 2309 (1996).

57. Ken Goldstein and Paul Freedman, "Campaign Advertising and Voter Turnout," *Journal of Politics* 64 (2002): 721–40; Deborah Jordan Brooks and John G. Geer, "Beyond Negativity," *American Journal of Political Science* 51 (2007): 1–16; Deborah Jordan Brooks, "The Resilient Voter: Moving toward Closure in the Debate over Negative Campaigning and Turnout," *Journal of Politics* 68 (2006): 684–96.

58. Kim Fridkin Kahn and Patrick J. Kenney, *No Holds Barred: Negativity in U.S. Senate Campaigns* (Upper Saddle River, N.J.: Prentice Hall, 2004), 74–84, 91–107.

59. Van Hollen, interview, November 30, 2010, and "Political Update"; Walsh, interview, November 22, 2010; LaCivita, interview, November 17, 2010.

60. "Harold Ford . . . Call Me," YouTube video, 0:31, posted by "llehman84," June 13, 2010, www.youtube.com.

61. These generalizations are drawn from responses to questions VI.1 through VI.7 of the "2002 Congressional Campaign Study," Center for American Politics and Citizenship, University of Maryland.

62. To some degree these assessments are influenced by the propensities of candidates and campaign aides to consider themselves at the center of all campaign activity and to understate the contributions of others, including party committees.

63. The discussion of the congressional election in Florida's 2nd district draws heavily from Lauren M. Harding, "The Funeral Home Director Buries the Blue Dog," unpublished paper, University of Pennsylvania, December 9, 2010.

64. See note 61.

65. "Two Candidates," YouTube video, 0:31, posted by "dscclive," October 27, 2010, www.youtube.com.

66. "NRSC Nevada IE Ad: Ritz," YouTube video, 0:33, posted by "TheNRSC," October 19, 2010, www.youtube.com.

67. Figures include party contributions, coordinated expenditures, independent expenditures, and party-connected contributions. For the Senate race, they also include the total transfers from the congressional, senatorial, and national campaign committees (which would influence voter turnout statewide), and for the House race they include 10 percent of those transfers (a conservative estimate based on the number of competitive races in the state). The figures underestimate the party's impact on the race because they do not include expenditures made by party committees that influence state and local elections and do not report to the FEC, nor do they include the PAC and individual contributions the parties stimulate.

5. THE INTERESTS CAMPAIGN

1. It should be recognized that these advantages are subject to change in response to FEC decisions, federal court rulings, and the somewhat unlikely enactment of campaign finance reform legislation.

2. It should be noted that some PACs also participate in state and local elections.

3. PACs that do not meet these requirements are subject to the same $1,000 contribution limit as are individuals.

4. 424 U.S. 1 (1976).

5. The number of nonconnected PACs excludes leadership PACs.

6. Center for Responsive Politics, www.opensecrets.org.

7. The IRS uses a "totality of the circumstances" analysis that includes an organization's expenditures, self-defined purpose, and other factors when determining the organization's primary purpose. The IRS does not have a definitive rule on expenditures. However, the information in this and the following paragraph is based on the advice that many tax lawyers, including FEC employees and former FEC commissioners, report they provide to 501(c) organizations. See also Federal Election Commission, 11 C.F.R. 100 (2007).

8. The exception is that a 501(c) organization that accepts a contribution earmarked for an independent expenditure or electioneering communication must publicly disclose the source of that contribution to the FEC.

9. See, for example, Stephen R. Weissman and Kara D. Ryan, *Soft Money in the 2006 Election and the Outlook for 2008: The Changing Nonprofits Landscape* (Washington, D.C.: Campaign Finance Institute, 2007).

10. Based on figures compiled by the Center for Responsive Politics, www.opensecrets.org.

11. Unless otherwise noted, all campaign finance data were furnished by the Center for Responsive Politics (www.opensecrets.org) or the Federal Election Commission (http://fec.gov/).

12. *Citizens United v. FEC,* 558 U.S, 08-205 (2010), *Speechnow.org v. FEC,* 599 F.3d 686, 689 (D.C. Cir. 2010).

13. Herrnson, "The Roles of Party Organizations, Party-Connected Committees, and Party Allies in Elections," *Journal of Politics* 71 (2009): 1207–24.

14. The League of Conservation Voters, www.lcv.org/about/mission/.

15. Ibid., and Ronald G. Shaiko, "It Wasn't Easy Being Green in 2010: The League of Conservation Voters and the Uphill Battle to Make the Environment Matter," in Paul S. Herrnson, Clyde Wilcox, and Christopher J. Deering, eds., *Interest Groups Unleashed* (Washington, D.C.: CQ Press, in press).

16. The figures add to more than $6 million because of transfers among LCV-related organizations.

17. John J. Pitney Jr., "American Crossroads and Crossroads GPS," in Herrnson et al., *Interest Groups Unleashed.*

18. Robert Boatwright, "The U.S. Chamber and the 2010 Elections," in Herrnson et al., *Interest Groups Unleashed*

19. J. David Gopoian, "What Makes PACs Tick," *American Journal of Political Science* 28 (May 1984): 259–81; Craig Humphries, "Corporations, PACs, and the Strategic Link between Contributions and Lobbying Activities," *Western Political Quarterly* 44 (1991): 353–72; and the case studies in Biersack, Herrnson, and Wilcox, eds., *Risky Business? PAC Decision Making in Congressional Elections* (Armonk, N.Y.: M. E. Sharpe, 1994).

20. Richard Hall and Frank Wayman, "Buying Time," *American Political Science Review* 84 (1990): 797–820; Richard Hall and Alan V. Deardorff, "Lobbying as Legislative Subsidy," *American Political Science Review* 100 (2006): 69–84.

21. Thomas Romer and James M. Snyder Jr., "An Empirical Investigation of the Dynamics of PAC Contributions," *American Journal of Political Science* 38 (1994): 745–69; Andrew J. Taylor, "Conditional Party Government and Campaign Contributions," *American Journal of Political Science* 57 (2003): 293–304; Kevin M. Esterling, "Buying Expertise," *American Political Science Review* 101 (2007): 93–109.

22. Gary C. Jacobson and Samuel Kernell, *Strategy and Choice in Congressional Elections* (New Haven: Yale University Press, 1983), esp. chap. 4.

23. See the case studies in Biersack et al., *Risky Business?;* Robert Biersack, Paul S. Herrnson, and Clyde Wilcox, eds., *After the Revolution: PACs and Lobbies in the New Republican Congress* (Boston: Allyn & Bacon, 1991).

24. Clyde Wilcox, "Organizational Variables and the Contribution Behavior of Large PACs: A Longitudinal Analysis," *Political Behavior* 11 (1989): 157–73.

25. John Wright, "PACs, Contributions, and Roll Calls," *American Political Science Review* 79 (1985): 400–14.

26. Robert Biersack, "Introduction," in Biersack et al., *Risky Business?*, 3–15.

27. The information on the Realtors PAC is from Anne H. Bedlington, "The Realtors Political Action Committee," in Biersack et al., *After the Revolution,* 170–83.

28. Challenger contributions also require the formal approval of both state and national RPAC trustees.

29. On AMPAC, see Michael K. Gusmano, "The AMA in the 1990s," in Biersack et al., *After the Revolution,* 47–65.

30. The information on WASHPAC is from Barbara Levick-Segnatelli, "The Washington PAC," in Biersack et al., *Risky Business?*, 202–13.

31. On lead PACs, see the Introduction to Part I in Biersack et al., *Risky Business?*, 17–18. On the NCEC, see Paul S. Herrnson, "The National Committee for an Effective Congress," in Biersack et al., *Risky Business?*, 39–55. On BIPAC, see Candice J. Nelson and Robert Biersack, "BIPAC," in Biersack et al., *After the Revolution,* 36–46.

32. On abortion rights PACs, see, for example, Christine L. Day and Charles D. Hadley, *Women's PACs* (Upper Saddle River, N.J.: Prentice Hall, 2005).

33. Linda L. Fowler and Robert D. McClure, *Political Ambition* (New Haven: Yale University Press, 1989), 205–207.

34. Ronald G. Shaiko and Marc A. Wallace, "From Wall Street to Main Street," in *After the Revolution,* 18–35.

35. Herrnson, "The National Committee for an Effective Congress," in *Risky Business?*, 39–55.

36. Emma Shapiro, communications assistant, EMILY's List, interview, June 7, 2011.

37. Peter L. Francia, "Early Fundraising by Nonincumbent Female Congressional Candidates," *Women & Politics* 23 (2001): 7–20; Day and Hadley, *Women's PACs.*

38. Peter L. Francia, John C. Green, Paul S. Herrnson, Lynda W. Powell, and Clyde Wilcox, *The Financiers of Congressional Elections* (New York: Columbia University Press, 2003), 116.

39. Francia et al., *The Financiers of Congressional Elections,* 42, 87–89.

40. See http://calloutthevote.com/.

41. An exception is party support for incumbents in competitive primaries, as discussed in Chapter 4.

42. "UWUA Joins AFL-CIO Campaign to Get Out the Vote in 2010 Elections," http://uwua.net/.

43. Pitney, "American Crossroads and Crossroads GPS."

44. On the tone of the ads, see Michael M. Franz, Erika Franklin Fowler, and Travis N. Ridout, "Citizens United and Campaign Advertising in 2010," paper presented at the Annual Conference of the Midwest Political Science Association, Chicago, March 31–April 3, 2011.

45. The analysis excludes electioneering communications and other issue advocacy ads because of the limited information disclosed about these expenditures.

46. Rep. Chris Van Hollen, chair, DCCC, interview, November 30, 2010; Chris LaCivita, political director, NRSC, interview, November 17, 2010.

47. Mass media advertising is the one campaign activity in which Democratic and Republican House campaigns report receiving equal amounts of help from interest groups. These generalizations are drawn from questions VI.1 through VI.7 of the "2002 Congressional Campaign Study," Center for American Politics and Citizenship, University of Maryland.

48. The figure excludes contributions from politicians' leadership PACs.

49. All individual contributions referred to in this section were made in amounts of $200 or more.

50. "NRA-PVF Endorses Allen Boyd for U.S. House of Representatives in Florida's 2nd Congressional District," *South Florida Caribbean News,* October 18, 2010, www.sflcn.com/story .php?id=9282.

51. Quoted in David F. Damore, "Reid vs. Angle in Nevada's Senate Race," in Randall E. Adkins and David A. Dulio, eds., *Cases in Congressional Campaigns* (New York: Routledge, 2011), 32–54.

52. These figures, to some degree, underestimate total interest group efforts because they exclude interest group spending that is not reported to the FEC and individual contributions that are stimulated by interest group efforts, such as contributions made by interest group leaders and members.

6. THE CAMPAIGN FOR RESOURCES

1. Quoted in David Adamany and George E. Agree, *Political Money* (Baltimore: Johns Hopkins University Press, 1975), 8.

2. George Thayer, *Who Shakes the Money Tree?* (New York: Simon and Schuster, 1973), 25.

3. Unless otherwise noted, all campaign finance data were furnished by the Center for Responsive Politics and the Federal Election Commission.

4. The figures for House and Senate campaign contributions and coordinated expenditures include funds raised by all candidates involved in major-party contested general elections.

5. The denominator used to calculate the percentages is the candidates' total receipts plus any coordinated spending the parties made on the candidates' behalf. Coordinated expenditures are included because candidates have some control over the activities on which they are spent.

6. Peter L. Francia, John C. Green, Paul S. Herrnson, Lynda W. Powell, and Clyde Wilcox, *The Financiers of Congressional Elections* (New York: Columbia University Press, 2003); James G. Gimpel, Frances E. Lee, and Shanna Pearson-Merkowitz, "The Check Is in the Mail: Interdistrict Funding Flows in U.S. House Elections," *American Journal of Political Science* 52 (2008): 373–94.

7. Figures compiled from Paul S. Herrnson, *The Campaign Assessment and Candidate Outreach Project, 2000 Survey* (College Park: Center for American Politics and Citizenship, University of Maryland, 2000).

8. On direct-mail fundraising, see Kenneth R. Godwin, *One Billion Dollars of Influence* (Chatham, N.J.: Chatham House, 1988).

9. Figures are from question IV.2 of the "2002 Congressional Campaign Study," Center for American Politics and Citizenship, University of Maryland.

10. As noted in Chapter 1, individual contribution limits are $2,000 plus an adjustment for inflation.

11. Francia et al., *The Financiers of Congressional Elections,* esp. chap. 3; Sanford C. Gordon, Catherine Hafer, and Dimitri Landa, "Consumption or Investment? On Motivations for Political Giving," *Journal of Politics* 69 (2007): 1057–72.

12. Francia et al., *The Financiers of Congressional Elections,* chaps. 3 and 5.

13. The House members were Steny Hoyer, D-Md. (majority leader); John Boehner, R-Ohio (minority leader); Eric Cantor, R-Va. (minority whip); David Camp, R-Mich. (ranking member, Ways and Means Committee); James Clyburn, D-S.C. (majority whip); Earl Pomeroy, D-S.D. (chair, Subcommittee for Social Security of the Ways and Means Committee); Patrick Tiberi, R-Ohio (ranking member, Subcommittee on Select Revenue for the Ways and Means Committee); Nancy Pelosi, D-Calif. (House Speaker); Richard Neal, D-Mass. (chair, Subcommittee on Select Revenue for the Ways and Means Committee); and Allen Boyd, D-Fla. (member, Appropriations and Budget committees).

14. Figures exclude contributions from leadership PACs.

15. Figures exclude contributions from leadership PACs.

16. Some argue that preemptive fundraising by incumbents may discourage quality challengers from running. See Jonathan S. Krasno and Donald Philip Green, "Preempting Quality Challengers in House Elections," *Journal of Politics* 50 (1988): 920–36; Peverill Squire, "Preemptive Fundraising and Challenger Profile in Senate Elections," *Journal of Politics* 53 (1991): 1150–64.

17. Gary C. Jacobson, *Money in Congressional Elections* (New Haven: Yale University Press, 1980), 113–23; Jonathan S. Krasno, Donald Philip Green, and Jonathan A. Cowden, "The Dynamics of Fundraising in House Elections," *Journal of Politics* 56 (1994): 459–74.

18. On the impact of campaign contributions on political access see, for example, Laura Langbein, "Money and Access," *Journal of Politics* 48 (1986): 1052–62.

19. Forty-eight percent of all challengers spent one-fourth of their personal campaign schedule fundraising.

20. Robert Biersack, Paul S. Herrnson, and Clyde Wilcox, "Seeds for Success," *Legislative Studies Quarterly* 18 (1993): 535–53; Krasno et al., "The Dynamics of Fundraising in House Elections."

21. Paul S. Herrnson, "Campaign Professionalism and Fundraising in Congressional Elections," *Journal of Politics* 54 (1992): 859–70; Cherie D. Maestas and Cynthia R. Rugeley, "Assessing the 'Experience Bonus' through Examining Strategic Entry, Candidate Quality, and Campaign Receipts in U.S. House Elections," *American Journal of Political Science* 52 (2008): 520–35.

22. Robin Gerber, "Building to Win," in *After the Revolution,* ed. Robert Biersack, Paul S. Herrnson, and Clyde Wilcox (Boston: Allyn & Bacon, 1991), 77–93.

23. Herrnson, *The Campaign Assessment.*

24. Herrnson, "Campaign Professionalism and Fundraising in Congressional Elections."

25. This figure includes contributions from leadership PACs, which are included in party-connected contributions.

26. This figure includes contributions from leadership PACs, which are included in party-connected contributions.

27. The corresponding figure for all House candidates is 49 percent (see note 6 for this chapter). The figure for Senate candidates also draws from Paul S. Herrnson, *The Campaign Assessment and Candidate Outreach Project, 1998 Survey* (College Park, Md.: Center for American Politics and Citizenship, University of Maryland, 1998).

7. CAMPAIGN STRATEGY

1. Angus Campbell, Philip E. Converse, Warren E. Miller, and Donald E. Stokes, *The American Voter* (New York: John Wiley, 1960), 541–48; Michael X. Delli-Carpini and Scott Keeter, *What Americans Know about Politics and Why It Matters* (New Haven: Yale University Press, 1997); Michael S. Lewis-Beck, William G. Jacoby, Helmut Norpoth, and Herbert F. Weisberg, *The American Voter Revisited* (Ann Arbor: University of Michigan Press, 2008).

2. Figures compiled from Virginia Sapiro, Stephen J. Rosenstone, and National Election Studies, *American National Election Study, 1998: Post-Election Survey* (Ann Arbor: University of Michigan, 1999).

3. On Senate elections, see Alan I. Abramowitz and Jeffrey A. Segal, *Senate Elections* (Ann Arbor: University of Michigan Press, 1992), 39; Peverill Squire, "Challenger Quality and Voting Behavior," *Legislative Studies Quarterly* 17 (1992): 247–63.

4. Figures compiled from Nancy Burns, Donald R. Kinder, and National Election Studies, *American National Election Study, 2002: Post-Election Survey* (Ann Arbor: University of Michigan, Center for Political Studies, 2003).

5. Alan I. Abramowitz, "A Comparison of Voting for U.S. Senator and Representative in 1978," *American Political Science Review* 74 (1980): 633–40; Gerald C. Wright and Michael B. Berkman, "Candidates and Policy in United States Senate Elections," *American Political Science Review* 80 (1986): 567–88; Mark C. Westlye, *Senate Elections and Campaign Intensity* (Baltimore: Johns Hopkins University Press, 1992), 122–51.

6. Robert D. Brown and James A. Woods, "Toward a Model of Congressional Elections," *Journal of Politics* 53 (1991): 454–73; John R. Zaller, *The Nature and Origins of Mass Opinion* (Cambridge: Cambridge University Press, 1992), chap. 10.

7. Burns et al., *American National Election Study,* 2002.

8. Wright and Berkman, "Candidates and Policy in United States Senate Elections"; Westlye, *Senate Elections and Campaign Intensity,* chap. 6.

9. See, for example, Raymond E. Wolfinger and Steven J. Rosenstone, *Who Votes?* (New Haven: Yale University Press, 1980), 34–36, 58–60, 102–14.

10. Zaller, *The Nature and Origins of Mass Opinion,* chap. 10; Milton Lodge, Marco R. Steenbergen, and Shawn Brau, "The Responsive Voter," *American Political Science Review* 89 (1995): 309–26; Jon K. Dalager, "Voters, Issues, and Elections," *Journal of Politics* 58 (1996): 496–515; Robert Huckfeldt, Edward G. Carmines, Jeffrey J. Mondak, and Eric Zeemering, "Information, Activation, and Electoral Competition in the 2002 Congressional Elections," *Journal of Politics* 69 (2007): 798–812.

11. See Morris P. Fiorina, *Retrospective Voting in American National Elections* (New Haven: Yale University Press, 1981); James E. Campbell, "Explaining Presidential Losses in Midterm Congressional Elections," *Journal of Politics* 47 (1985): 1140–57; Samuel C. Popkin, *The Reasoning Voter* (Chicago: University of Chicago Press, 1991), esp. chaps. 3 and 4.

12. Alan I. Abramowitz, Albert D. Cover, and Helmut Norpoth, "The President's Party in Midterm Elections," *American Journal of Political Science* 30 (1986): 562–76; Henry W. Chappell Jr. and Motoshi Suzuki, "Aggregate Vote Functions for the U.S. Presidency, Senate, and House," *Journal of Politics* 55 (1993): 207–17. See also the studies cited in note 12; Ray C. Fair, "Presidential and Congressional Vote-Share Equations," *American Journal of Political Science* 53 (2009): 55–72.

13. David R. Jones and Monika L. McDermott, "The Responsible Party Government Model in House and Senate Elections," *American Journal of Political Science* 48 (2004): 1–12.

14. Morris P. Fiorina, *Divided Government* (Boston: Allyn & Bacon, 1996), 109–10; Stephen P. Nicholson and Gary M. Segura, "Midterm Elections and Divided Government," *Political Research Quarterly* 52 (1999): 609–29.

15. Rep. Chris Van Hollen, chair, DCCC, interview, November 30, 2010; Brian Walsh, political director, NRCC, interview, November 22, 2010; Chris LaCivita, political director, NRSC, interview, November 17, 2010.

16. Alan I. Abramowitz and Kyle L. Saunders, "Ideological Realignment in the U.S. Electorate," *Journal of Politics* 61 (1998): 634–52; Michael Tomz and Robert P. Van Houweling, "The Electoral Implications of Candidate Ambiguity," *American Political Science Review* 103 (2009): 83–98.

17. Raymond E. Wolfinger, "Candidates and Parties in Congressional Elections," *American Political Science Review* 74 (1980): 622–29; Gary C. Jacobson, *The Politics of Congressional Elections,* 4th ed. (New York: Longman, 1997), 106–108.

18. David R. Mayhew, *Congress: The Electoral Connection* (New Haven: Yale University Press, 1974); Stephen Ansolabehere, James M. Snyder Jr., and Charles Stewart III, "Old Voters, New Voters, and the Personal Vote," *American Journal of Political Science* 44 (2000): 17–34.

19. Richard F. Fenno Jr., *Home Style* (Boston: Little, Brown, 1978), esp. chaps. 3 and 4.

20. The discussion of the congressional election in Illinois' 10th district draws from Allyson Gasdaska, "Illinois' 10th District: Congressional Midterm Election 2010," unpublished paper, University of Pennsylvania, December 9, 2010, and the candidates' websites and advertisements.

21. Bryce Bassett, director of marketing support, Wirthlin Worldwide, presentation to the Taft Institute Honors Seminar in American Government, June 15, 1993.

22. See, for example, Robert Axelrod, "Where the Votes Come From," *American Political Science Review* 66 (1972): 11–20.

23. Manuel Perez-Rivas, "Opponent Tries to Make Party Label Stick to Morella," *Washington Post,* March 7, 1996.

24. These generalizations are drawn from responses to question III.3 of the "2002 Congressional Campaign Study," Center for American Politics and Citizenship, University of Maryland.

25. See, for example, Brian F. Schaffner, "Priming Gender," *American Journal of Political Science* 49 (2005): 803–17.

26. Axelrod, "Where the Votes Come From," 11–20; Henry C. Kenski and Lee Sigelman, "Where the Votes Come From in Senate Elections: Group Components of the 1988 Senate Vote," *Legislative Studies Quarterly* 18 (1993): 367–90.

27. This generalization is from question III.3 of the "2002 Congressional Campaign Study."

28. Paul S. Herrnson and James M. Curry, "Issue Voting and Partisan Defection in Congressional Elections," *Legislative Studies Quarterly* 36 (2011); 281–307.

29. See, for example, Patrick J. Sellers, "Strategy and Background in Congressional Campaigns," *American Journal of Political Science* 92 (1998): 159–71.

30. Joel C. Bradshaw, "Who Will Vote for You and Why," in *Campaigns and Elections American Style,* ed. James A. Thurber and Candice J. Nelson (Boulder, Colo.: Westview Press, 1995), 30–46.

31. The logic behind the battle for the middle ground is presented in Anthony Downs, *An Economic Theory of Democracy* (New York: Harper & Row, 1957), chap. 8.

32. J. Toscano, Greer, Margolis, Mitchell, and Burns, interview, July 1, 2007.

33. Ladonna Y. Lee, "Strategy," in *Ousting the Ins,* ed. Stuart Rothenberg (Washington, D.C.: Free Congress Research and Education Foundation, 1985), 18–19.

34. Kathleen Hall Jamieson, *Dirty Politics* (New York: Oxford University Press, 1992), esp. chap. 2.

35. Susan Kone for Congress, http://susankone.com/.

36. The quotation is from Southerland for Congress, www.southerlandforcongress.com/. The discussion of the congressional election in Florida's 2nd congressional district draws from Lauren M. Harding, "The Funeral Home Director Buries the Blue Dog," unpublished paper, University of Pennsylvania, December 9, 2010.

37. See Peter Clarke and Susan H. Evans, *Covering Campaigns* (Stanford: Stanford University Press, 1983), 38–45.

38. On the differences between valence issues and position issues, see Donald E. Stokes, "Spatial Models of Party Competition," in *Elections and the Political Order,* ed. Angus Campbell, Philip E. Converse, Warren E. Miller, and Donald E. Stokes (New York: John Wiley, 1966), 161–69.

39. See John R. Petrocik, "Issue Ownership in Presidential Elections, with a 1980 Case Study," *American Journal of Political Science* 40 (1996): 825–50; Owen G. Abbe, Jay Goodliffe, Paul S. Herrnson, and Kelly D. Patterson, "Agenda-Setting in Congressional Elections," *Political Research Quarterly* 56 (2003): 419–30; Constantine Spiliotes and Lynn Vavreck, "Campaign Advertising," *Journal of Politics* 64 (2007): 249–61. For a different perspective, see Noah Kaplan, David K. Park, and Travis N. Ridout, "Dialogue in American Campaigns?" *American Journal of Political Science* 50 (2006): 724–36.

40. Herrnson and Curry, "Issue Voting and Partisan Defections in Congressional Elections," 281–307.

41. Jacobson, *The Politics of Congressional Elections,* 112–16.

42. On the role of candidates' backgrounds in campaign strategy, see Sellers, "Strategy and Background in Congressional Campaigns."

43. David F. Damore, "Reid vs. Angle in Nevada's Senate Race," in *Cases in Congressional Campaigns,* ed. Randall E. Adkins and David A. Dulio (New York: Routledge, 2011), 32–54.

44. Richard F. Fenno Jr., "If, as Ralph Nader Says, Congress Is 'The Broken Branch,' How Come We Love Our Congressmen So Much?" in *Congress in Change,* ed. Norman J. Ornstein (New York: Praeger, 1975).

45. For a discussion of partisan divergence on the issues, see Spiliotes and Vavreck, "Campaign Advertising," 249–61.

46. See note 41 above.

47. Fred Hartwig, vice president, Peter Hart and Associates, presentation to the Taft Institute Honors Seminar in American Government, June 15, 1993.

48. Phil Duncan, ed., *Politics in America, 1992* (Washington, D.C.: Congressional Quarterly, 1991), 1133.

49. See, for example, James Innocenzi, "Political Advertising," in *Ousting the Ins,* 53–61; Barbara G. Salmore and Stephen A. Salmore, *Candidates, Parties, and Campaigns* (Washington, D.C.: CQ Press, 1989), 159.

50. See Richard R. Lau, Lee Sigelman, and Ivy Brown Rovner, "The Effects of Negative Political Campaigns," *American Journal of Political Science* 69 (2007): 1176–1209.

51. These generalizations are drawn from responses to question 11 of the "1998 Congressional Campaign Study" and question 28 of the "1992 Congressional Campaign Study." See also Ken Goldstein and Paul Freedman, "Lessons Learned: Campaign Advertising in the 2000 Elections," *Political Communication* 19 (2002): 5–28.

52. Richard R. Lau, "Two Explanations for Negativity Effects in Political Behavior," *American Journal of Political Science* 29 (1985): 110–38; Jamieson, *Dirty Politics,* 41.

53. On differences in the effects of negative campaigning on incumbents and challengers, see Richard R. Lau and Gerald M. Pomper, "Effectiveness of Negative Campaigning in U.S. Senate Elections," *American Journal of Political Science* 46 (2002): 47–66.

54. Lee, "Strategy," 22.

55. Amanda Paulson, "Rand Paul and the 'Aqua Buddha': Why Election 2010 Is Turning Nasty," *Christian Science Monitor,* October 18, 2010; Manu Raju, "'Aqua Buddha' Ad Backfires on Jack Conway," *Politico,* October 26, 2010, www.politico.com/.

56. J. Toscano, "Campaign Strategy and Communications," presentation at the University of Maryland, April 10, 2010.

8. CAMPAIGN COMMUNICATIONS

1. Matthew Katz, "Living without TV," *Washington Times,* September 17, 1998.

2. Pew Internet and Public Life Project, "Understanding the Participatory News Consumer," March 1, 2010, www.pewinternet.org.

3. Figures are compiled from Campaign Media Analysis Group data. They include ads broadcast in the 210 largest media markets and exclude ads disseminated on local cable stations. Courtesy of Michael Franz, associate professor, Department of Government and Legal Studies, Bowdin College.

4. Darrell M. West, *Air Wars* (Washington, D.C.: Congressional Quarterly, 1993), esp. chap. 6.

5. Quoted in Frank I. Luntz, *Candidates, Consultants, and Campaigns* (Oxford: Basil Blackwell, 1988), 77.

6. Darrell M. West, "Political Advertising and News Coverage in the 1992 California U.S. Senate Campaigns," *Journal of Politics* 56 (1994): 1053–75.

7. This generalization is drawn from responses to question IV.1 of the "2002 Congressional Campaign Study." For Senate campaigns, which are few in number in a given election year, additional information is drawn from the "1992 Congressional Campaign Study," Center for American Politics and Citizenship, University of Maryland, and Paul S. Herrnson, The Campaign Assessment and Candidate Outreach Project, 1999 and 2001, Center for American Politics and Citizenship, University of Maryland.

8. John R. Alford and Keith Henry, "TV Markets and Congressional Elections," *Legislative Studies Quarterly* 9 (1984): 665–75.

9. Luntz, *Candidates, Consultants, and Campaigns,* 76.

10. See, for example, Michael M. Franz, Erika Franklin Fowler, and Travis N. Ridout, "*Citizens United* and Campaign Advertising in 2010," paper presented at the Annual Conference of the Midwest Political Science Association, Chicago, April 1, 2011.

11. "In Susan's Words," YouTube video, 0:30, posted by "steve4congress," September 28, 2010, www.youtube.com.

12. As discussed in Chapter 7, whereas valence issues, such as a strong economy, have only one side and are universally viewed by voters in a favorable light, position issues, which would include either position in the abortion rights debate, divide voters because they have two or more sides.

13. "Steve for North Florida," YouTube video, 0:30, posted by "steve4congress," September 19, 2010, www.youtube.com.

14. Lauren M. Harding, "The Funeral Home Director Buries the Blue Dog," unpublished paper, University of Pennsylvania, December 9, 2010.

15. Kathleen Hall Jamieson, *Dirty Politics* (New York: Oxford University Press, 1992), 103.

16. "Seals for Dold," YouTube video, 0:43, posted by "DoldforCongress," October 26, 2010, www.youtube.com.

17. West, "Political Advertising."

18. Figure provided by J. Quin Monson, Department of Political Science, Brigham Young University, April 16, 2003.

19. Luntz, *Candidates, Consultants, and Campaigns,* 108.

20. Frank Luther Mott, *American Journalism* (New York: Macmillan, 1947), 411–30.

21. West, "Political Advertising."

22. Luntz, *Candidates, Consultants, and Campaigns,* 109–10.

23. West, "Political Advertising."

24. Lee Rainie, "There's a Robot on the Line for You," Pew Research Center, December 20, 2006, http://pewresearch.org/.

25. Kenneth R. Godwin, *One Billion Dollars of Influence* (Chatham, N.J.: Chatham House, 1988), chaps. 1–3.

26. Barbara G. Salmore and Stephen A. Salmore, *Candidates, Parties, and Campaigns* (Washington, D.C.: CQ Press, 1989), 86–87.

27. West, "Political Advertising."

28. Rainie, "There's a Robot on the Line."

29. Kristen Purcell, Lee Rainie, Amy Mitchell, Tom Rosenstiel, and Kenny Olmstead, "Understanding the Participatory News Consumer," Pew Charitable Trusts, March 1, 2010, www.pewinternet.org/.

30. Kristen Purcell, "The State of Online Video," Pew Charitable Trusts, June 3, 2010, www.pewinternet.org/.

31. See, for example, Emiliene Ireland and Phil Tajitsu Nash, *Winning Campaigns Online* (Bethesda, Md.: Science Writers Press, 2001), 3–48.

32. Kirsten Foot and Steven M. Schneider, *Web Campaigning* (Cambridge: MIT Press, 2006), 69–96; Philip N. Howerd, "Deep Democracy, Thin Citizenship: Digital Media and the Production of Political Culture," *Annals of the American Academy of Political & Social Science* 597 (2005): 153–70.

33. Peter Clarke and Susan Evans, *Covering Campaigns* (Stanford: Stanford University Press, 1983), chap. 6.

34. Xandra Kayden, *Campaign Organization* (Lexington, Mass.: D. C. Heath, 1978), 125.

35. Clarke and Evans, *Covering Campaigns,* 60–62; Doris A. Graber, *Mass Media and American Politics,* 4th ed. (Washington, D.C.: CQ Press, 1993), 262, 268–70.

36. Markus Prior, "The Incumbent in the Living Room: The Rise of Television and the Incumbency Advantage in U.S. House Elections," *Journal of Politics* 68 (2006): 657–73.

37. Kim Fridkin Kahn and Patrick J. Kenney, "The Slant of the News," *American Political Science Review* 96 (2002): 381–94.

38. Kayden, *Campaign Organization,* 126; Brian F. Shaffner, "Local News Coverage and the Incumbency Advantage in the U.S. House," *Legislative Studies Quarterly* 31 (2006): 491–511.

39. Clarke and Evans, *Covering Campaigns,* 60–62; Edie N. Goldenberg and Michael W. Traugott, *Campaigning for Congress* (Washington, D.C.: CQ Press, 1984), 127.

40. Anita Dunn, "The Best Campaign Wins," in *Campaigns and Elections American Style,* ed. James A. Thurber and Candice J. Nelson (Boulder, Colo.: Westview Press, 1995), 115.

41. These generalizations are drawn from the following four sources, which together demonstrate that political experience, campaign professionalism, and campaign receipts are positively related to the free media coverage that campaigns receive: (1) candidates' campaign receipts, (2) the political experience measure developed in Chapter 2, (3) the measure of campaign professionalism developed in Chapter 3 (total number of campaign activities performed by paid staff or consultants), and (4) responses to question I.6 of the "2002 Congressional Campaign Study" and to question 25 of the "1992 Congressional Campaign Study."

42. See Ronald A. Faucheux, ed., *The Debate Book* (Washington, D.C.: *Campaigns & Elections,* 2003).

43. West, "Political Advertising."

44. See also Clarke and Evans, *Covering Campaigns,* chap. 4.

45. This generalization is drawn from responses to question I.8 of the "2002 Congressional Campaign Study." See also Kahn and Kenney, "The Slant of the News."

46. On media bias, see Herbert J. Gans, "Are U.S. Journalists Dangerously Liberal?" *Columbia Journalism Review* 24 (1985): 29–33. On politicians and the press, see also Lance W. Bennett, *News: The Politics of Illusion* (New York: Longman, 1983), 76–78.

47. R. Michael Alvarez, Asa Hopkins, and Betsy Sinclair, "Mobilizing Pasadena Democrats: Measuring the Effects of Partisan Campaign Contacts," *Journal of Politics* 72 (2010): 31–44.

48. Alan S. Gerber and Donald P. Green, "The Effects of Canvassing, Telephone Calls, and Direct Mail on Voter Turnout," *American Political Science Review* 94 (2000): 653–64; Melissa R. Michelson, Lisa García Bedolla, and Margaret A. McConnell, "Heeding the Call: The Effect of Targeted Two-Round Phone Banks on Voter Turnout," *Journal of Politics* 71 (2009): 1549–63.

49. Rainie, "There's a Robot on the Line."

50. Paul S. Herrnson, "National Party Organizations and the Postreform Congress," in *The Postreform Congress,* ed. Roger H. Davidson (New York: St. Martin's, 1992), 65–66.

51. These generalizations are drawn from responses to questions V.15 and V.16 of the "2002 Congressional Campaign Study."

52. On the effectiveness of personal campaigning, see Gerber and Green, "The Effects of Canvassing."

53. See Table 8-3 in the third edition of this book.

54. The figure for independent campaigns includes all party, PAC, interest group, and IE-only committee independent expenditures, interest group internal communications for or against candidates, and spending by other groups reported to the FEC. The figure for grassroots campaigns is for national party transfers to state and local party committees. Unless otherwise noted, all campaign finance data were furnished by the Center for Responsive Politics (www.opensecrets.org) or the Federal Election Commission (http://fec.gov/).

55. See Table 8-4 in the fourth edition of this book.

56. Using a narrower victory margin to measure competitiveness did not substantively alter the findings.

9. CANDIDATES, CAMPAIGNS, AND ELECTORAL SUCCESS

1. Larry M. Bartels, "Partisanship and Voting Behavior, 1952–1996," *American Journal of Political Science* 44 (2000): 42–43.

2. Morris P. Fiorina, *Congress* (New Haven: Yale University Press, 1978); John A. Ferejohn, "On the Decline of Competition in Congressional Elections," *American Political Science Review* 71 (1997): 166–77.

3. The public opinion information is from AHFF Geoff, "Gallup: GOP Dominating Voter Enthusiasm for 2010 Elections," CentristNet, March 9, 2010, http://centristnetblog.com.

4. See Michael Krashinsky and William J. Milne, "Incumbency in U.S. Congressional Elections, 1950–1988," *Legislative Studies Quarterly* 18 (1993): 321–44; also see the sources cited in Chapter 1, notes 35–37.

5. On the effect of candidate gender on voting behavior, see Monika L. McDermott, "Voting Cues in Low-Information Elections," *American Journal of Political Science* 41 (1997): 270–83; Paul S. Herrnson, Celeste Lay, and Atiya Stokes, "Women Running 'as Women,' " *Journal of Politics* 65 (2003): 244–55.

6. The figures for candidate spending on campaign communications equal the sum of candidate expenditures on direct mail, television, radio, campaign literature, newspapers, mass telephone calls, the Internet, voter registration and get-out-the-vote drives, and other campaign communications. These funds exclude money spent on overhead and research and on contributions made to other candidates, party committees, and other political groups, which sometimes constitute considerable sums.

7. Tables 9-1, 9-2, and 9-3 were created using ordinary least squares regressions to analyze data from major-party contested House general elections conducted in 2002. The original regression for Table 9-1 is as follows: Percentage of vote = 57.28 − 1.96/(1.32) district is completely different or completely new + .15/(.03) partisan bias + .92/(.67) ideological strength − 3.71/(2.62) incumbent implicated in scandal − .84/(.21) opponent spending on campaign communications (per $100,000) + .13/(.20) incumbent spending on campaign communications (per $100,000) + 5.22/(2.31) incumbent received most media endorsements from local media + 2.02/(1.25) national partisan tide; F = 12.18, $p < .0001$, Adj. R-square = .48, N = 97. For ease of interpretation, the spending figures were transformed into 2010 constant dollars. One-tailed tests and a .10 significance level were used because the hypotheses were directional and the sample sizes small. The final models were selected for reasons of statistical fit, robustness, parsimony, and ease of interpretation. They replicated, to the extent possible, similar analyses for the 1992, 1994, 1996, 1998, and 2002 elections and verify that the basic relationships hold across elections. More information about the equations and an overview of the survey and statistical methods are available at this website: http://college.cqpress.com/sites/partiesandelectionsir/.

8. Gary C. Jacobson, "Barack Obama, the Tea Party, and the 2010 Midterm Elections," paper presented at the Annual Meeting of the Midwest Political Science Association, Palmer House, Chicago, March 31–April 3, 2010.

9. Partisan bias was measured using the respondents' answers to question III.2 of the "2002 Congressional Campaign Study," Center for American Politics and Citizenship, University of Maryland.

10. John H. Aldrich and David W. Rohde, "The Logic of Conditional Party Government," in *Congress Reconsidered,* 7th ed., ed. Lawrence C. Dodd and Bruce I. Oppenheimer (Washington, D.C.:

CQ Press, 2001), 269–92; Steven S. Smith and Gerald Gamm, "The Dynamics of Party Government in Congress," in *Congress Reconsidered,* 7th ed., ed. Dodd and Oppenheimer, 245–68.

11. The discussion of the congressional election in Florida's 2nd district draws from Lauren M. Harding, "The Funeral Home Director Buries the Blue Dog," unpublished paper, University of Pennsylvania, December 9, 2010.

12. A moderate incumbent would win 0 percent extra votes (0 multiplied by 0.92), and an extremely liberal or conservative incumbent would win 2.76 percent extra votes (3 multiplied by 0.92).

13. Most studies overstate the amount candidates spend on actual campaigning because they consist of all candidate disbursements reported to the FEC, including contributions to other candidates and other political organizations.

14. See, for example, Christopher Kenney and Michael McBurdett, "A Dynamic Model of Congressional Spending on Vote Choice," *American Journal of Political Science* 36 (1992): 923–37.

15. Figures include party coordinated expenditures because they are under the control of both the party and the candidate and exclude contributions to other candidates, party committees, and other groups.

16. Gary C. Jacobson, *Money in Congressional Elections* (New Haven: Yale University Press, 1980).

17. Local media endorsements are measured using respondents' answers to question I.8 of the "2002 Congressional Campaign Study."

18. Among those sharing this point of view are Rep. Chris Van Hollen, chair, DCCC, interview, November 30, 2010; Brian Walsh, political director, NRCC, interview, November 22, 2010; Ken Spain, communications director, NRCC, interview, November 17, 2010; Jacobson, "Barack Obama, the Tea Party, and the 2010 Midterm Elections."

19. These figures were compiled from FEC data.

20. The original regression equation for incumbents in races in which parties and groups sought to set the campaign agenda is as follows: Percentage of vote = 59.89 − 4.95/(2.29) district is completely different or completely new + .10/(.05) partisan bias + 1.93/(1.27) ideological strength − 9.03/(4.88) incumbent implicated in scandal − 1.02/(.33) opponent spending on campaign communications (per $100,000) + .13/(.26) incumbent spending on campaign communications (per $100,000) + 4.38/(3.33) incumbent received most endorsements from local media + 1.43/(2.25) national partisan tide; F = 6.82, p < .0001, Adj. R-square = .54, N = 41. The spending figures were transformed into 2010 constant dollars. See note 7 for details.

21. See Michael M. Franz, Erika Franklin Fowler, and Travis N. Ridout, "*Citizens United* and Campaign Advertising in 2010," paper presented at the Annual Conference of the Midwest Political Science Association, Chicago, March 31–April 3, 2011.

22. Van Hollen, interview, November 30, 2010; Walsh, interview, November 22, 2010; Spain, interview, November 17, 2010.

23. The original regression equation for Table 9-2 is as follows: Percentage of vote = 25.29 + .13/(.03) partisan bias + 2.46/(1.03) contested primary + 2.50/(1.05) targeted own party members, independents, or both + 1.84/(1.09) advertising focused on challenger's or incumbent's issue positions + .31/(.15) challenger spending on campaign communications (per $100,000) + .56/(.18) opponent spending on campaign communications (per $100,000) + 5.50/(2.12) challenger received most endorsements from local media + 2.50/(1.17) national partisan tide; F = 19.94, p < .0001, Adj. R-square = .52, N = 138. The spending figures were transformed into 2010 constant dollars. See note 7 for details.

24. See, for example, Richard F. Fenno Jr., *Senators on the Campaign Trail* (Norman: University of Oklahoma Press, 1996), 100.

25. Seth E. Masket and Steven Greene, "When One Vote Matters: The Electoral Impact of Roll-Call Votes in the 2010 Congressional Elections," paper presented at the Annual Meeting of the Midwest Political Science Association, Chicago, March 30–April 2, 2011.

26. The original regression equation for challengers in races in which parties and groups sought to set the campaign agenda is as follows: Percentage of vote = 29.71 + .24/(.05) partisan bias + 2.54/(1.51) contested primary + .47/(1.94) targeted own party members, independents, or both + 1.75/(1.72) advertising focused on challenger's or incumbent's issue positions + .50(.001) challenger spending on campaign communications (per \$100,000) + .20/(.001) opponent spending on campaign communications (per \$100,000) + 6.62/(2.84) challenger received most endorsements from local media + 2.22/(1.53) national partisan tide; F = 13.86, p < .0001, Adj. R-square = .61, N = 66. The spending figures were transformed into 2010 constant dollars. See note 7 for details. See also Franz et al., "Citizens United and Campaign Advertising in 2010."

27. The original regression equation for Table 9-3 is as follows: Percentage of vote = 24.15 + .17/(.06) partisan bias + 4.68/(3.15) targeted own party members, independents, or both + 7.42/(3.84) Republican ran on Republican issues + 4.18/(3.48) Democrat ran on Democratic issues + 3.81/(.83) natural log of open-seat candidate spending on campaign communications – 3.06/(.69) natural log of opponent spending on campaign communications + 6.70/(2.23) candidate received most endorsements from local media + 8.52/(3.46) national partisan tide; F = 14.69, p < .0001, Adj. R-square = .69, N = 50. The spending figures were transformed into 2010 constant dollars. See note 7 for details.

28. Allyson Gasdaska, "Illinois' 10th District: Congressional Midterm Election 2010," unpublished paper, University of Pennsylvania, December 9, 2010; candidates' websites and advertisements.

29. Spending figures are from the Center for Responsive Politics (www.opensecrets.org) and the Federal Election Commission (http://fec.gov/) data.

30. The Pearson correlations between the candidates' percentage of the vote and the communications techniques are as follows: campaign literature, r = .27 (p < .01); direct mail, r = .26 (p < .01); television = .05 (p = .31); radio, r = .29 (p < .01); campaign literature, r = .27 (p < .01); direct mail, r = .26 (p < .01); television, r = .05 (p = .31).

31. The original regression equation for open-seat candidates in races in which parties and groups sought to set the campaign agenda is as follows: Percentage of vote = 21.15 + .18/(.08) partisan bias + 7.39/(4.48) targeted own party members, independents, or both + 11.21/(5.80) Republican ran on Republican issues + 1.81/(3.88) Democrat ran on Democratic issues + 4.35/(1.10) natural log of open-seat candidate spending on campaign communications – 3.40/(1.02) natural log of opponent spending on campaign communications + 3.65/(2.97) candidate received most endorsements from local media + 6.39/(4.21) national partisan tide; F = 9.60, p < .0001, Adj. R-square = .67, N = 35. The spending figures were transformed into 2010 constant dollars. See note 7 for details.

32. Jonathan S. Krasno, *Challengers, Competition, and Reelection* (New Haven: Yale University Press, 1994), esp. chaps. 4–7; Peverill Squire and Eric R. A. N. Smith, "A Further Examination of Challenger Quality in Senate Elections," *Legislative Studies Quarterly* 21 (1996): 231–48.

33. Alan I. Abramowitz and Jeffrey A. Segal, *Senate Elections* (Ann Arbor: University of Michigan Press, 1992), 109–14; Kim Fridkin Kahn and Patrick J. Kenney, *The Spectacle of U.S. Senate Campaigns* (Princeton: Princeton University Press, 1999), 216–23; Ken Goldstein and Paul Freedman, "New Evidence for New Arguments," *Journal of Politics* 62 (2000): 1087–108.

34. Kahn and Kenney, *The Spectacle of U.S. Senate Campaigns,* 12.

35. See Mark C. Westlye, *Senate Elections and Campaign Intensity* (Baltimore: Johns Hopkins University Press, 1992), chaps. 7 and 8; Abramowitz and Segal, *Senate Elections,* 109–15.

36. The discussion of the Nevada Senate race draws from David F. Damore, "Reid vs. Angle in Nevada's Senate Race," in *Cases in Congressional Campaigns,* ed. Randall E. Adkins and David A. Dulio (New York: Routledge, 2010), 32–54.

37. The first four items in Table 9-4, and items seven, eight, nine, and sixteen are from the "2002 Congressional Campaign Study" (*N* for winners = 137; *N* for losers = 171); the rest are from the "1998 Congressional Campaign Study" (*N* for winners = 154; *N* for losers = 159).

38. The figures also include a small number of independent expenditures by individuals and other groups. They exclude issue advocacy ads used in parallel campaigns and the voter mobilization activities comprising coordinated campaigns.

39. See John W. Kingdon, *Candidates for Office: Beliefs and Strategies* (New York: Random House, 1968), chap. 2.

40. See the sources listed in notes 30–36 of Chapter 1.

41. See Kingdon, *Candidates for Office,* chap. 2.

42. Susan Kone, Republican candidate for Congress, interview, March 28, 2011.

43. See the sources listed in notes 30–35 of Chapter 1.

10. ELECTIONS AND GOVERNANCE

1. First-term House member, interview, November 1992.

2. See Roger H. Davidson, Walter J. Oleszek, and Frances M. Lee, *Congress and Its Members,* 12th ed. (Washington, D.C.: CQ Press, 2008), esp. chap. 1.

3. Richard F. Fenno Jr., *Home Style* (Boston: Little, Brown, 1978), 54–61.

4. Ibid., 153.

5. David R. Mayhew, *Congress: The Electoral Connection* (New Haven: Yale University Press, 1974), 49–68.

6. The distance of the member's district from Washington, the cost of local office space, and a few other factors also influence the funds members of the House and Senate receive. Ida A. Brudnick, "Congressional Salaries and Allowances," *CRS Report for Congress,* Congressional Research Service, Washington, D.C., January 4, 2011.

7. Congressional Management Foundation, *Setting Course* (Washington, D.C.: Congressional Management Foundation, 2006), chap. 3.

8. Timothy E. Cook, *Making Laws and Making News* (Washington, D.C.: Brookings Institution Press, 1989), 71.

9. Scott Adler, Chariti F. Gent, and Cary B. Overmeyer, "The Home Style Homepage," *Legislative Studies Quarterly* 23 (1998): 585–96; Colleen J. Shogun, "Blackberries, Tweets, and YouTube: Technology and the Future of Communicating with Congress," *PS: Political Science and Politics* 43 (2010): 231–33.

10. Laura Langbein, "Money and Access," *Journal of Politics* 48 (1986): 1052–62; John Wright, "Contributions, Lobbying, and Committee Voting in the U.S. House of Representatives," *American Political Science Review* 84 (1990): 417–38.

11. Richard F. Fenno Jr., *Congressmen in Committees* (Boston: Little, Brown, 1973), 13.

12. Harrison W. Fox and Susan Webb Hammond, *Congressional Staffs* (New York: Free Press, 1977), 121–24.

13. Fenno, *Congressmen in Committees,* 1–14.

14. Scott A. Frish and Sean Q. Kelly, *Committee Assignment Politics in the U.S. House of Representatives* (Norman: Oklahoma University Press, 2006), 77.

15. Susan Webb Hammond, *Congressional Caucuses in National Policy Making* (Baltimore: John Hopkins University Press, 2001); Jennifer N. Victor and Nils Ringe, "The Social Utility of Informal Institutions: Caucuses as Networks in the 110th U.S. House of Representatives," *American Politics Review* 37 (2009): 742–66.

16. Center for Responsive Politics, www.opensecrets.org.

17. For an excellent analysis of interest groups and policy making, see Frank R. Baumgartner, Jeffrey M. Berry, Marie Hojnacki, David C. Kimball, and Beth L. Leech, *Lobbying and Policy Change* (Chicago: University of Chicago Press, 2009), esp. 149–65.

18. Richard L. Hall and Alan V. Deardorff, "Lobbying as Legislative Subsidy," *American Political Science Review* 100 (2006): 69–84.

19. See, for example, Kristina C. Miler, "The View From the Hill," *Legislative Studies Quarterly* 32 (2007): 597–628.

20. See Gordon Adams, *The Iron Triangle* (New York: Council on Economic Priorities, 1981), 175–80; Hugh Heclo, "Issue Networks and the Executive Establishment," in *The New American Political System,* ed. Anthony King (Washington, D.C.: American Enterprise Institute, 1978), 87–124.

21. U.S. Chamber of Commerce, www.uschamber.com.

22. Center for Responsive Politics, www.opensecrets.org.

23. See, for example, Sarah A. Binder, *Stalemate* (Washington, D.C.: Brookings Institution Press, 2003), chap. 4.

24. David E. Mayhew, *Divided We Govern* (New Haven: Yale University Press, 1991).

25. David Rohde, *Parties and Leaders in the Postreform House* (Chicago: University of Chicago Press, 1991), 3–11.

26. Paul S. Herrnson and Kelly D. Patterson, "Toward a More Programmatic Democratic Party?" *Polity* 27 (1995): 607–28; Paul S. Herrnson and David M. Cantor, "Party Campaign Activity and Party Unity in the U.S. House of Representatives," *Legislative Studies Quarterly* 22 (1997): 393–415.

27. Kelly D. Patterson, *Political Parties and the Maintenance of Liberal Democracy* (New York: Columbia University Press, 1996), chap. 4.

28. See Leon D. Epstein, *Political Parties in Western Democracies* (New York: Praeger, 1967), 340–48.

29. Frances E. Lee, *Beyond Ideology: Politics, Principles, and Partisanship in the U.S. Senate* (Chicago: University of Chicago Press, 2009); Davidson, Oleszek, and Lee, *Congress and Its Members,* 282–90.

30. Rohde, *Parties and Leaders*; Steven S. Smith and Gerald Gamm, "The Dynamics of Party Government in Congress," in *Congress Reconsidered,* 7th ed., ed. Lawrence C. Dodd and Bruce I. Oppenheimer (Washington, D.C.: CQ Press, 2001), 245–68.

31. John H. Aldrich and David W. Rohde, "The Logic of Conditional Party Government," in Dodd and Oppenheimer, *Congress Reconsidered,* 7th ed., 269–92.

32. David E. Price, "Reflections on Congressional Government at 120 and Congress at 216," *PS: Political Science and Politics* 39 (2006): 231–35; Donald R. Wolfensberger, "Can Party Governance Endure in the U.S. House of Representatives?" paper presented at the Conference on Woodrow Wilson's Congressional Government, Woodrow Wilson International Center for Scholars, Washington, D.C., November 14, 2005.

33. Quoted in Luiza Ch. Savage, "Boehner's New House Rules," *Macleans,* January 5, 2011, http://www2.macleans.ca.

34. Hannah Pitkin, *The Concept of Representation* (Berkeley: University of California Press, 1967).

35. Bruce Cain, John Ferejohn, and Morris Fiorina, *The Personal Vote* (Cambridge: Harvard University Press, 1987).

36. For a useful summary, see Theo Emery, "2010 Legislative Summary: Immigration Policy Overhaul," *CQ Weekly* (December 27, 2010): 2928.

37. See, for example, Frances E. Lee, "Geographic Politics in the U.S. House of Representatives," *American Journal of Political Science* 47 (2003): 714–28.

38. Davidson, Oleszek, and Lee, *Congress and Its Members,* 295–96.

39. John Ferejohn, "Logrolling in an Institutional Context," in *Congress and Policy and Change,* ed. Gerald C. Wright Jr., Leroy N. Rieselbach, and Lawrence C. Dodd (New York: Agathon Press, 1986), 223–53.

40. In recent Congresses, legislation was supposed to stay within a set of overall budgetary limits in order to limit growth of the federal deficit. This zero-sum process has frequently required legislators to cut spending in some areas if they wish to increase it in others.

41. Paul Kane, "Value of Congressional Earmarks Increased in Fiscal 2010," *Washington Post,* February 18, 2010.

42. Herrnson and Patterson, "Toward a More Programmatic Democratic Party?"; Herrnson and Cantor, "Party Campaign Activity and Party Unity."

43. Paul S. Herrnson, Kelly D. Patterson, and John J. Pitney Jr., "From Ward Heelers to Public Relations Experts," in *Broken Contract?* ed. Stephen C. Craig (Boulder, Colo.: Westview Press, 1996), 251–67.

44. Baumgartner et al., *Lobbying and Policy Change,* 20–24.

45. V. O. Key Jr., "A Theory of Critical Elections," *Journal of Politics* 17 (1955): 3–18; Everett Carl Ladd Jr., with Charles D. Hadley, *Transformations of the American Party System* (New York: Norton, 1978).

46. Committee on Political Parties, American Political Science Association, "Toward a More Responsible Two-Party System," *American Political Science Association Review* 44, no. 3, part 2 (1950): 21; Leon D. Epstein, *Political Parties in the American Mold* (Madison: University of Wisconsin Press, 1986), 30–38.

11. CAMPAIGN REFORM

1. See, for example, John R. Hibbing and Elizabeth Theiss-Morse, *Congress as Public Enemy* (Cambridge: Cambridge University Press, 1995), 63–71.

2. These generalizations are drawn from responses to questions V.1 and V.2 of the "2002 Congressional Campaign Study," Center for American Politics and Citizenship, University of Maryland.

3. The winners were somewhat more likely to state that campaign issues were occasionally important and somewhat less likely to state that they were never important. These generalizations are drawn from responses to question V.3 of the "2002 Congressional Campaign Study."

4. Peter L. Francia, John C. Green, Paul S. Herrnson, Lynda W. Powell, and Clyde Wilcox, *The Financiers of Congressional Elections* (New York: Columbia University Press, 2003), 291–92; Campaign Assessment and Candidate Outreach Project, Center for American Politics and Citizenship, University of Maryland, 2000 Survey.

5. These generalizations are drawn from responses to question VIII.3 of the "2002 Congressional Campaign Study."

6. For a more detailed review of the BCRA, see Anthony Corrado, Thomas E. Mann, Daniel R. Ortiz, and Trevor Potter, *The New Campaign Finance Sourcebook* (Washington, D.C.: Brookings Institution Press, 2005).

7. 558 U.S. 08-205 (2010).

8. R. Sam Garrett, "Campaign Finance Policy after *Citizens United v. Federal Election Commission,*" CRS Report for Congress, Congressional Research Service, Washington, D.C., May 17, 2010.

9. On the passage of the BCRA in the House, see Diana Dwyre and Victoria A. Farrar-Myers, *Legislative Labyrinth* (Washington, D.C.: CQ Press, 2001); on unorthodox lawmaking, see Barbara Sinclair, *Unorthodox Lawmaking* (Washington, D.C.: CQ Press, 1997).

10. Adam Clymer, "Foes of Campaign Finance Bill Plot Legal Attack," *New York Times,* February 17, 2002.

11. Helen Dewar, "Lawsuits Challenge New Campaign Law," *Washington Post,* May 8, 2003.

12. Amy Keller, "Debate Rocks FEC," *Roll Call,* March 4, 2002; Helen Dewar, "FEC Rules on 'Soft Money' Challenged," *Washington Post,* October 9, 2002.

13. 540 U.S. 93 (2003).

14. 127 S. Ct. 2652 (2007).

15. 127 S. Ct. 2618 (2007).

16. Tomoeh Murakami Tse, "After Victory, Conservatives Mount New Challenges to Campaign Finance Limits," *Washington Post,* March 26, 2010; Adam Liptak, "Free Speech through the Foggy Lens of Election Law," *New York Times,* May 3, 2010.

17. Campaign Finance Institute, "Election-Related Spending by Political Committees and Non-Profits Up 40% in 2010," media release, October 18, 2010.

18. The parties of the golden age, especially the political machines, also had shortcomings, including corruption, secrecy, and formal and informal barriers to the participation of women and various racial, ethnic, and religious groups. For some lively accounts, see William Riordan, *Plunkitt of Tammany Hall* (New York: E. P. Dutton, 1905); Mike Royko, *Boss: Richard J. Daley* (New York: E. P. Dutton, 1971).

19. See Hibbing and Theiss-Morse, *Congress as Public Enemy,* esp. chap. 5.

20. As noted in Chapter 1, prior to the Apportionment Act of 1842 some House members were elected in multimember districts.

21. L. Sandy Maisel, "Competition in Congressional Elections," in *Rethinking Political Reform,* ed. Ruy A. Teixeira, L. Sandy Maisel, and John J. Pitney Jr. (Washington, D.C.: Progressive Foundation, 1994), 29.

22. Doris A. Graber, *Mass Media and American Politics,* 4th ed. (Washington, D.C.: CQ Press, 1993), 53–55.

23. Larry J. Sabato, *Paying for Elections* (New York: Twentieth Century Fund, 1989), 31.

24. See Ruth S. Jones and Warren E. Miller, "Financing Campaigns," *Western Political Quarterly* 38 (1985): 190, 192.

25. For countries and American states that offer citizens the opportunity to obtain tax credits for political contributions, see the case studies in Arthur B. Gunlicks, ed., *Campaign and Party Finance in North America and Western Europe* (Boulder, Colo.: Westview Press, 1993).

26. Francia et al., *The Financiers of Congressional Elections,* esp. chaps. 4 and 5.

27. Matthew Mosk, "Resignation of Lawyers at FEC Raises Concern," *Washington Post,* January 18, 2007.

28. Michael McDonald, *General Election Turnout Rates,* January 28, 2011, http://elections.gmu.edu.

29. Raymond E. Wolfinger and Stephen J. Rosenstone, *Who Votes?* (New Haven: Yale University Press, 1980), 61–88.

30. This reform was met with overwhelming satisfaction by its users. See Paul S. Herrnson and Michael J. Hanmer, *Report on Survey Results among Users of the Electronic Absentee Ballot Delivery System* (memorandum), Center for American Politics and Citizenship, University of Maryland, February 15, 2011, www.capc.umd.edu/rpts/2010/EABDS_Survey_Results.pdf; Paul S. Herrnson and Michael J. Hanmer, *Report on Survey Results among UM Students* (memorandum), Center for American Politics and Citizenship, University of Maryland, March 31, 2011, www.capc.umd.edu/rpts/2010/UMSurveyResults.pdf.

31. J. Eric Oliver, "The Effects of Eligibility Restrictions and Party Activity on Absentee Voting and Voter Turnout," *American Journal of Political Science* 40 (1996): 498–513; Peter L. Francia and Paul S. Herrnson, "The Effects of Campaign Effort and Election Reform on Voter Participation in State Legislative Elections," *State Politics and Policy Quarterly* 4 (2004): 74–93; Michael J. Hanmer, *Discount Voting* (Cambridge: Cambridge University Press, 2009), 106–82.

32. CalTech/MIT Voting Technology Report, "What Is; What Could Be," July 2002, 8–9, 21, 32, www.vote.caltech.edu.

33. Paul S. Herrnson, "Improving Election Technology and Administration," *Stanford Law and Policy Review* 13 (2002): 147–59.

34. Paul S. Herrnson, Richard G. Niemi, Michael J. Hanmer, Benjamin B. Bederson, Frederick G. Conrad, and Michael W. Traugott, *Voting Technology: The Not-So-Simple Act of Casting a Ballot* (Washington, D.C.: Brookings Institution Press, 2007).

35. On the impact of poll worker performance, see Ryan L. Claassen, David B. Magleby, J. Quin Monson, and Kelly D. Patterson, "At Your Service: Voter Evaluations of Poll Worker Performance," *American Politics Research* 36 (2008): 612–34.

Index

Notes Name Index